Practical Journalism

Practical Journalism

How to Write News

Helen Sissons

SAGE Publications
Los Angeles • London • New Delhi • Singapore

First published 2006

Reprinted twice in 2008

SAGE Publications Ltd
1 Oliver's Yard
55 City Road
London EC1Y 1SP

SAGE Publications Inc.
2455 Teller Road
Thousand Oaks, California 91320

SAGE Publications India Pvt Ltd
B 1/I 1 Mohan Cooperative Industrial Area
Mathura Road, New Delhi 110 044
India

SAGE Publications Asia-Pacific Pte Ltd
33 Pekin Street #02-01
Far East Square
Singapore 048763

British Library Cataloguing in Publication data

A catalogue record for this book is available
from the British Library

ISBN 978-0-7619-4926-8
ISBN 978-0-7619-4927-5

Library of Congress Control Number: 2005938005

Typeset by C&M Digitals (P) Ltd., Chennai, India
Printed on paper from sustainable resources
Printed and bound in Great Britain by TJ International Ltd, Padstow, Cornwall

CONTENTS

ACKNOWLEDGEMENTS

I have been amazed at how positively colleagues in the media have responded to this project. My thanks to all the journalists who have given their time and the benefit of their experience. They have, without exception, talked candidly and honestly about their work – its pressures, its high points and its low points. Their wisdom appears throughout the book explaining examples, recounting anecdotes or giving advice. Without them this book could not have been written, as it was a project born out of the belief that only those at the coalface can teach others how to mine.

Many of the journalists quoted are friends and former colleagues. Others responded to a phone call or email from a complete stranger asking if they would mind being stalked while they went about their duties and asked dozens of obvious or impertinent questions.

Among the latter the staff at 2BR radio station in Burnley, those at Ananova online newsroom in Leeds and the *Craven Herald* newspaper in Skipton stand out as being particularly helpful. But thanks to all the staff at the newspapers, radio stations, online organisations and television stations who tolerated my visits and endless questions or willingly passed on information, graphics and other material.

Of my friends and former colleagues there are some who need special mention. At the BBC Jo-Anne Pugh's encouragement, inspiration and sound advice were invaluable and Cathy Killick's patient reading of the text and her sensible suggestions were much appreciated. Gillian Hargreaves, Geeta Guru-murthy, Tom Symonds, Peter Sissons, Denise Wallace, Sophie Raworth, Jon Williams and John McIntyre helped with extended interviews, advice and insights as well as reading and commenting on chapters.

Thanks too to others who frankly shared their thoughts and to the BBC management who allowed me to spend days hanging round newsrooms in London and the north.

I owe a huge debt of gratitude to Shelley Bradley, a solicitor with the BBC who responded to a phone call out of the blue and agreed to read the law chapters (without pay). Her detailed suggestions and corrections were gratefully received. Any remaining mistakes are mine.

Elsewhere, thanks to Mike McCarthy of Sky for the time I spent in the Northern Bureau. To one of my first editors, Bob Bounds of the *Kentish Gazette*, who answered pages of questions patiently and with the kind of sagacity only one who has nurtured many young reporters would be able to provide.

Warm thanks to my former colleagues at the University of Leeds who helped me make the transition from hack to reflective practitioner and teacher. Among them Judith Stamper, Dr Graham Roberts, Dr David Gauntlett and Prof. Philip Taylor stand out.

I thank also my former students who gave me six rewarding years and highlighted the common challenges faced by young journalists. It is with them in mind that this book was written.

Credit goes to John Sissons for his perseverance in reading and re-reading the proofs, catching errors and repetitions and saving me from much embarrassment.

To Paul Denny for his help with Chapter 6 on online journalism and for rescuing early copies of the script from the computer when I carelessly fed it several cups of tea.

I am grateful to my editors at Sage – Julia Hall and Jamilah Ahmed – for asking me to take on the project in the first place and then encouraging me all the way. I've enjoyed the journey immensely.

Finally my thanks are due to the many newspapers, internet sites, radio and television bulletins from which I have quoted. Every attempt has been made to obtain permission to reproduce copyright material. If any proper acknowledgement has not been made, we would invite copyright holders to inform us of the oversight.

INTRODUCTION

Journalists are like horses. You can define what a horse is, but when asked what's their task, you're trying to define everything from a Shetland pony to a racehorse. (Jo-Anne Pugh, home news desk editor, BBC News, London)

The working journalist is not a homogeneous beast. There are myriad hybrids to the breed. You have the monthly women's magazine writers penning their lifestyle features and listing the ten best lipsticks/handbags/places to have sex. There are the monthly men's magazine writers with their lifestyle features and ten best gadgets/ties/places to have sex. There are the newspaper columnists taking their 'sideways' look at life/politics/latest fad diet. The travel reporters describing the horrors of flying with four kids or wandering down yet another impossibly narrow alley in yet another Mediterranean town; the motoring correspondents; real estate writers and so on.

Then there are the news journalists. They are what this book is primarily concerned with. Even here there are different varieties. You have the crime reporter of the metropolitan daily. The stories they cover will be a world away from those tapped into the screen of the staff writer at trade magazine *Builder's Week* or those of the online journalist for an activist website. You have the badly paid junior on a local weekly paper covering their first parish council meeting after a day of writing articles from golden weddings to the hiring of a new lollipop lady to the closure of the sub post office. Their life is very different from the senior correspondent on a regional television station who covers one or two stories a day and may have a researcher working alongside.

Yet a journalist who starts on a local newspaper can move to a specialist trade publication, or to a monthly glossy, or into broadcasting. Perhaps they stay as a print journalist but must file, in addition to copy, pictures or audio or any combination of these to the online site of their paper. Good journalists need to be able to move easily between different media and be comfortable reporting and presenting their stories to whatever channel is required.

Practical Journalism: How to Write News introduces the beginner to the skills needed to become a journalist. There are chapters covering interviewing and research techniques and news writing. Further chapters cover working in broadcasting and online. Throughout the book we hear from practising journalists. They share their thoughts on the profession and we watch them work – selecting stories, carrying out interviews and writing scripts.

Learning to interview effectively, report accurately and then to write in a manner that is not only truthful but is also attractive to read or listen to is difficult. It would still be a challenge if journalists were paid handsomely, worked in plush offices and had acres of time to complete their tasks. But they don't. They work to tight deadlines, in cramped offices, often for poor pay.

They can also be physically or verbally threatened by governments and other powerful interests wishing to prevent publication of embarrassing or damaging stories.[1]

Despite the challenges, young people still want to join the ranks of the more than 70,000 journalists practising in the UK.[2] Why? Some think it's glamorous (it's not); others enjoy writing. The best join because they want to know what's going on and to tell people about it, and because they realise news is not an optional extra for society. It is only with reliable information that people can keep abreast of events and monitor those in power.

It also has to be said that on the whole journalists love what they do. I was told many times during interviews for the book that it is 'one of the best jobs around', and it's hugely enjoyable having 'a front seat at the making of history' and what a privilege it is to write the 'first draft'. Clichéd, but the message is clear. Studies too have found most journalists to be satisfied with their choice of profession.[3]

We may be happy being reporters, but is anyone interested in reading or listening to what we do? Yes, they are. In Britain, people spend more time consuming the media than doing anything else except work.[4] News fulfils a fundamental human need to keep up with the latest gossip and important events. And good journalists have always been in demand. Since the earliest times people have shared news and desired that its tellers be accurate and entertaining.[5]

Today, news is being shared as never before, with new technology ensuring that breaking stories can travel around the world in seconds. Reporters from Britain could be covering a story in Pakistan for a news outlet in New Zealand. It is more than ever a time when the people need to be able to rely on the supply of information as reliable, accurate and independent.

Most journalists believe they work honestly and ethically, but few can explain how they come to their decisions and others admit to coming under pressure early in their careers to behave in ways they found unacceptable. This book looks at how journalists can work more ethically and provides a guide for those starting out.

I have approached the writing of the book as one that will be relevant to news journalists no matter what medium or media they aspire to work in. It is meant to be easy to read and to understand. The chapters are self-contained and able to be read on their own, so readers can dip in where they wish. Chapter 5, which covers broadcasting, is very long. For this reason it is divided into three parts that can be read separately: an introductory section, a section on radio reporting and a section on reporting for television. Each chapter concludes with activities for students and trainees and a list of further reading and useful websites for each topic. There is also a glossary of terms at the end of the book.

The book draws on interviews with dozens of working journalists; these are found throughout the text in the form of numerous unattributed quotes. Many are my former colleagues who have generously given their time and from whom I have brazenly stolen their best lines and ideas. To them my wholehearted thanks.

FURTHER READING

Keeble, R., *Ethics for Journalists*, London: Routledge, 2001.
Kovach, B., and Rosenstiel, T., *The Elements of Journalism*, London: Atlantic Books, 2003.
Lloyd, J., *What the Media Are Doing to Our Politics*, London: Constable, 2004.

Notes

1 Reporters without Borders, 'The deadliest year for a decade': 53 journalists killed. See www.rsf.org.
2 There were around 70,000 practising journalists in the UK in 2002 and the number was expected to rise. *Press Gazette*, 12 July 2002.
3 *Ibid.*
4 John Lloyd, *What the Media are Doing to Our Politics*, London: Constable, 2004, p. 9.
5 B. Kovach and T. Rosenstiel, *The Elements of Journalism*, London: Atlantic Books, 2003, p. 9.

THE JOURNALIST

Good journalists enjoy finding things out and then telling people what they have discovered. At work the journalist will

- ask the questions to which the public want answers
- persevere to find the truth of events
- be accurate and balanced when constructing the story
- present it in the clearest and most powerful way
- have an extensive network of sources.

Journalism is full of lying, cheating, drunken, cocaine-sniffing, unethical people. It's a wonderful profession. (Piers Morgan, then editor of the *Daily Mirror*, quoted in *GQ*, April 2002)

When journalists of my generation first entered newspapers in Britain in the 1980s, there was still a suspicion of graduates among news editors. Graduates were considered soft, lacking in life experience and practical common sense and, worse still, they were seen as expecting special treatment. On my first local paper there were journalists without degrees, some with no A-levels. Journalism was seen as a craft, which was more about natural instinct and talent than it was about education. A journalist, or 'hack', was a hard-bitten operator who could smell a story at 200 paces and was not averse to the odd questionable practice to sniff it out.

There are still editors around who adhere to this view, but when I joined the BBC a few years later, all the recent entrants were graduates. Many things were changing. No longer were newsrooms full of the clatter of typewriters and there were no hunching, chain-smoking, hacks stinking of booze (although this was always a stereotype beloved of Hollywood and Broadway). The journalists I work with are more likely to go running than drinking at lunchtime and the classic view of the journalist as grubby, hard-drinking and lacking in any of the social graces is incorrect, at least most of the time.

Some of the changes no doubt can be put down to new and faster technologies and we will be talking more about these later in the chapter. It is now possible to transmit a report from the most remote parts of the globe and have it on air minutes later. This is exciting, but it is also a challenge to the journalist who has little time to assess the significance of an incident or situation before they have to explain it to the general public. In addition, the online news organisations and 24-hour broadcast news channels press for constant updates, presenting huge demands (and opportunities) for the journalist.

Being a journalist

Journalism is about telling real-life stories and explaining the world beyond a person's direct experience. Good journalists shine lights where the public cannot see, they bring knowledge where there was ignorance and, if they are very good, empathy where there was antipathy and action where there was inertia.

The journalist gathers facts about the story; decides which of those to include and which to omit; how to structure the story and which words to use to tell it. But it is all a waste of time if they fail to communicate what they have found to the audience. If nobody is reading or listening or watching, then the journalist cannot inform, educate or enthuse. Therefore we have to find stories that people will be interested in and tell them in the most exciting but truthful way possible.

In essence the journalist is a pedlar of information. It has to be packaged attractively to be inviting to the reader, listener or viewer and it has to be accurate and fair to be a quality product. And journalists share many of the same characteristics whether they are weekly newspaper reporters covering council meetings, journalists on regional evening papers writing about important court cases, national radio reporters covering Parliament, or writers on a broadsheet or compact reporting a natural disaster on the other side of the world.

That is not to say that all working journalists are conscientious or moral. There are those who are sloppy and as lazy as, for example, the one who admitted to colleagues that when he worked on a national tabloid newspaper he would sometimes make up quotes rather than go out and collect them. He could predict, he said, what people would say. There are those who also take the credit for other people's work and those who abuse the trust of interviewees by lying about their true intentions, even stealing photos of loved ones once they have conned their way inside the house. I wish I could say these people do not prosper in the profession, but many do. So let's not be starry-eyed.

If journalism is to remain a profession that people can rely upon to help them make decisions about their lives, then journalists must resist the temptation to create content or alter the tone of an article. The latter can be particularly hard to resist.

Journalists can come under pressure from editors to 'jazz up' their accounts. And there are owners and advertisers who want to influence what is written (see Chapter 2). Many journalists work on under-resourced newspapers, internet sites and radio stations, and have little time to check out stories. Some rarely get out of the office and must conduct nearly all their interviews over the telephone.

But good journalists are badly needed. Public confidence in journalists and their journalism is at rock bottom. The exposure of Jayson Blair, the *New York Times* reporter found to be fabricating stories, and the fallout from the Hutton Inquiry into a BBC journalist's report that the Government made false claims in its dossier on the threat from the then Iraqi President Saddam Hussein's supposed weapons of mass destruction (WMD) have only added to public suspicion of the media. (See Chapters 5 and 12 for more about these cases.)

An ICM poll for the National Council of Voluntary Organisations in July 2002 found that half of the 1,000 people questioned believed journalists would not be honest when interviewed.[1] Moreover, research by the University of Leeds shows that while people rely heavily on the media for information, most of them distrust the media's motives and operational methods. They feel the news organisations are 'just looking for a story' and are driven primarily by circulation and audience figures. The scepticism affected all media, but mostly the press, and the tabloid press in particular.[2] The media ethics organisation, PressWise, reports that around 10,000 complaints a year in Britain are being made to regulatory bodies by people unhappy about what is reported about them.[3]

Yet journalists need the public to trust them, otherwise the very reason for their existence – to inform – is negated. Fortunately, despite poor pay, long hours and often difficult working conditions, there are excellent journalists doing sterling work. Most would not want to do any other job, because for anyone who wants to be where the action is, it is the best work going.

What makes a good journalist?

So what qualities does a good journalist need? It has to be noted that in talking to journalists while researching this book, many found it quite a challenge to explain how they do their job and what it is that makes them effective. For most practitioners, journalism and the skills needed to recognise and report news become over the years instinctive. However, when pushed they came up with the following qualities: being a people person, a questioner, a verifier, accurate, persevering, courageous, a good judge of news, curious, an able writer, creative, competitive, ethical, fair, balanced, objective, cultivating of contacts, well informed.

A people person

Journalism often involves dabbling in the stuff of other people's lives.[4] Good journalists do so responsibly and ethically.

Journalists have a fascination with the affairs of men – they are people-watchers and many love nothing better than sitting alone in a café or on a bus listening to other people's conversations. As well as being good listeners, journalists should be good communicators, able to deal with a wide variety of people and situations, from cabinet ministers to homeless people. They should be sensitive to people's feelings and able to win their confidence while recognising the news angle and pursuing it.

A questioner

The journalist wants and needs to know everything they can about the events on which they report or the issues that catch their interest. They must be full of questions and intent on establishing as many facts as possible. Sometimes that means asking a string of questions until the crux of the matter is clear, as only by understanding can they pass on the story to the general public.

Never be afraid to ask the obvious question, even if it makes you look stupid, says Mike McCarthy, bureau chief at Sky News in Manchester, who spent time covering the war in Afghanistan in 2001:

> When I arrived in Kabul, I had to go to a military briefing in a hotel. I got there a bit late and missed the introductions so I didn't know the name of the man leading the briefing who was also the military commander. I absolutely had to know his name, because it was a very important fact. For one thing, I didn't want to get caught out on air speaking live to a presenter and not know who had given out the information I was referring to. So I asked his name, I did feel stupid but not as stupid as I would have looked had I not known on air.

There are two lessons here – one is having the courage to ask and the other is being punctual. As Mike himself points out, if you arrive late to the event, as a journalist you are likely to miss the main story.

Accurate/a verifier

Asking questions is often to do with verifying the facts, not only questioning the people but questioning what they tell you. Always be sceptical of what people say and be willing to ask yourself why they are saying it. Never just accept what you are being told, especially by governments – even more so if those governments are at war.

Journalists have a duty to do all they can to present as accurate a picture as possible to the public. Every journalist I spoke to considered accuracy to be crucial. Ian Lockwood, editor of the *Craven Herald* in Skipton, says that journalists are often unfairly accused of making mistakes:

> People have to have some confidence that what they're reading is correct. There are some who believe there are lots of mistakes, but actually there are very few. For example, last week we wrote about a local boy who had a part in a television programme. We said he'd got the part because he could play the piano and he had curly blonde

hair. His grandmother rang up and said we'd got it all wrong. Yet when we went through it line by line there was actually nothing wrong. The problem for the grandmother was that she believed we'd implied he'd only got the part because of his piano playing and blonde hair, not because he could act.

In the era of instant news, getting it right all the time is becoming harder to achieve. Derek Crawshaw, who spent several years as a BBC 5-Live reporter in Belfast, explains that working for a station that prides itself on its 'live' nature gives the reporter special problems:

You have got to be there, be first and be live. But there are times when it's difficult to get as much information as you'd like. You have got to be secure and confident in knowing that what you're saying is correct and you've got to be confident enough to say 'I don't know enough yet'. You come under great pressure as a live reporter to go on air. You've got to be first and be accurate. It's an easy thing to say, but it's a hard thing to do.

Being able to say to a news editor that you're not ready to go on air or to hand in a story is an important part of the job of a reporter. Never publish facts you are not certain of but find out as much as possible in the time available.

By striving to uncover what you can, the journalist discharges their duty towards the people who cannot be there themselves, says Cathy Killick, a television reporter with BBC *Look North* in Leeds:

There was a bad crash on the A1. Hundreds of vehicles were involved. I knew nobody would know exactly how many, so with the help of a reporter from the *Yorkshire Post* newspaper I counted them. We found it was 600 vehicles spread over three-quarters of a mile of motorway. You could see the chaos from the pictures, but I wanted to verify the facts. I had the time; often you don't in this sort of situation. I think this is what my job is about. I am the eyes and ears of the public and I want to get it right. To do this you have to apply yourself.

Persevering

Without perseverance, a news journalist will never uncover anything but the most run-of-the-mill stories.

You have got to have your quarry in view and to keep going and get it or as close to it as you can. So you don't fall at the first hurdle, you don't knock on someone's door and if they don't answer think that person isn't in and give up. You leave a note, you try someone else who may be able to help you, you go back later. (Cathy Killick, BBC *Look North*)

However, never mistake persistence for harassment. A journalist should not try to obtain information through intimidation.

For some journalists it was determination that secured them a job in the first place. I was told by one foreign editor that as a young journalist he sat on the steps of the newspaper's building and accosted the editor every day until he agreed to take him on and give him a chance.

Persistence by the editor of a local paper resulted in freedom for a man wrongly convicted of murder. It took *Matlock Mercury* editor Don Hale nearly eight years of campaigning and investigating until he won an appeal hearing for Stephen Downing. The Court of Appeal quashed the conviction and Downing was freed after serving 27 years in jail for the murder of a Derbyshire woman, Wendy Sewell.

The miscarriage of justice that put Stephen Downing, then only 17 years old, behind bars came to light only because Don Hale decided to go against the advice of his superiors and investigate. By then Downing had been in jail 20 years and the case was largely forgotten. Hale's investigations found that although Downing had admitted the murder, he had a mental age of 11 and had told his father that he only admitted it so he could go home. Hale also discovered new witnesses who said they'd seen another bloodstained man leave the graveyard on the night of the murder.

When Don Hale started publishing stories about his findings, he suffered threats and intimidation and he was nearly killed by a speeding sports car, but he didn't give up. He said the intimidation only strengthened his belief that he was on the right track.

> I can think of nothing more frightening than to be locked away for life for a crime you haven't committed. Who can you turn to? Who is prepared to listen to a convicted killer? I was continually told that it was not my job to take on this sort of challenge. So whose job was it? Who else was prepared to endure years of persecution?[5]

Courageous

Journalists need courage in many situations. Sometimes it is the courage to go where you are not welcome and face very real dangers; at other times it might be the courage to ask the right questions.

Reporters Without Borders' (www.rsf.org) Annual Report, published in 2005, highlighted some of the dangers facing journalists worldwide during the previous year. Fifty-three journalists and 15 media assistants (fixers, drivers, translators, technicians, security staff and others) were killed worldwide in 2004 while doing their job or for the stories they wrote. This was up from the 40 journalists and 2 media assistants that were killed in 2003. Things were not looking much better for 2005, as in the first four months 19 journalists lost their lives. Many others are imprisoned or threatened every year. In 2004 at least 1,140 journalists were attacked or received threats and more than 900 were imprisoned.[6]

Despite the dangers, journalists continue to work to bring accurate information to the people. Marie Colvin, a *Sunday Times* reporter who lost an eye while reporting in 2001 in Sri Lanka, says journalism has become more dangerous and at the same time more important. In a speech to World Press Freedom Day in May 2002, she said that while in Israel the only way she could prove the Israeli Government was lying about Jenin Refugee camp on the West

Bank was to get out there and see. That was a dangerous undertaking. Israeli forces had invaded the camp in April and dozens of people were killed in the ensuing fighting.[7]

If it takes a lot of guts for international reporters to uphold the right to report freely and honestly, it possibly takes even more courage and fortitude when you are the local media and you do not have a plane ticket out of the situation. Speaking at World Press Freedom Day in 2001 was Mark Chavunduka, a journalist from Zimbabwe. He and another reporter were jailed and tortured by President Robert Mugabe's regime for reporting that an alleged plot to overthrow the Government had been foiled. They were charged with publishing information likely to cause alarm and despondency.

> What happened to us was a barbaric assault, which was worsened by the fact that the state never disproved the article that led to our arrest. What prolonged our incarceration was that we refused to reveal our sources. The military emphasised throughout that the reason we were being held was because we refused to reveal our sources in the military and I'm very proud to say that two years later that is still the case.[8]

Both men were released on bail because of the huge international outcry. They challenged the law under which they were arrested in the Supreme Court of Zimbabwe, and were successful. The Government has since been introducing new laws to restrict the media.

Refusing to name sources in a democratic country where you are not likely to face torture is less obviously courageous, but it takes a brave man to uphold a principle and face imprisonment. Individual journalists confront this dilemma every year. A *Manchester Evening News* journalist, Steve Panter, faced a possible jail sentence for contempt of court (see Chapter 10 for more on contempt of court) when he repeatedly refused to disclose the identity of the source of a story about the IRA. The article named the prime suspect of the IRA's bombing of a shopping centre in Manchester in 1996 which injured 200 people. The attorney general decided in July 2002 not to bring contempt proceedings, saying it was not in the public interest to prosecute.

Manchester Evening News editor, Paul Horrocks, said about the case:

> It took great personal strength [by Steve Panter] not to reveal his source when ordered to do so by a judge. He was standing by our basic code of journalism and we are proud of him.
> The public must be able to trust us not to reveal confidential sources, unless there are exceptional circumstances. There is a worrying trend in this country of courts wanting to know media sources. This must be resisted.[9]

Journalists need mettle to refuse to answer questions, and on occasion also when they have to ask questions that people do not want to answer. The journalist should be able to walk into a meeting full of high-powered politicians and be capable of dealing with them as equals. They should also be able to telephone or knock on the door of someone who doesn't want to speak and ask them awkward questions.

Often young or inexperienced journalists are afraid of asking questions that they think they should already know the answer to. A good rule of thumb is that if you don't know or understand something, there will be others who don't.

A good judge of news

A journalist who does not recognise a story when faced with one is no good to their editor or news organisation.

When I was on work experience I was told about a young reporter on a broadsheet newspaper who returned after a lunch break to find the office in a state of high excitement. She was told that a bank had been robbed very close by and they were making calls to try to find out more about it. The trainee said that she knew about the robbery as she had been in the bank when it happened. When asked why she hadn't told the newsdesk straight away, she said she hadn't realised it was important. Unsurprisingly she was fired then and there.

Her mistake was to think that because her field was business and finance, other sorts of news stories, such as crime, were of no consequence. When the World Trade Center was attacked on September 11, 2001 and around 3,000 people lost their lives, many news organisations had to rely on reporters who just happened to be in New York. Some were on other assignments, others on holiday. Everyone was expected to be up to the challenge.

The *Daily Telegraph*'s deputy editor, Sarah Sands, was there for New York fashion week. She was walking towards the World Trade Center when the attack started and was able to file a very detailed eyewitness piece for the paper.[10]

The *Sun*'s new New York correspondent, Brian Flynn, was flat hunting in the city and was on the phone to his London office when he saw the first plane hit the towers:[11] Similarly, *Shropshire Star* deputy chief reporter Tracey O'Sullivan was in New York for a family wedding when the attack happened.[12] Both were able to provide personal accounts.

In its analysis of the reporting of the attacks on America a few days after they happened, the *Press Gazette*, a trade paper for journalists, points out that it was perhaps the first time that the same story appeared on the front pages of the world's newspapers. It also led the world's television and radio bulletins.[13] It was a day when all journalists knew without a doubt which story, among all the other events that day, was the most important. In fact many editors even used the identical photograph to illustrate the attacks, taken by Spencer Platt, a photographer with Getty Images.

As a journalist you are almost never off duty. If you are on holiday and happen to witness or be part of a newsworthy event, then you should take out your notebook and start work. We will be looking at the question 'What is news?' in Chapter 2, but throughout your career you will be developing your news sense, learning which stories are the important ones, which angles the most interesting, which details should be highlighted and which ignored.

Curious

Much that has already been said is about being curious: curious about people and curious about events. Journalists are *what? how? when? where? who?* and *why?* people. In the last instance curiosity is the motivation for everything the journalist does.

Nosiness is what made a young BBC regional reporter, Clarence Mitchell, wonder why a fleet of police cars was speeding down the M1 motorway late one Friday night while behind them the motorway was being closed. Mitchell, who was then a reporter in Hull, increased his speed and followed the police cars until they reached the scene of a plane crash near the Leicestershire village of Kegworth. A British Midland passenger jet en route from Heathrow to Northern Ireland had crashed a few hundred yards from the runway at East Midlands airport. It had ploughed into an embankment of the M1 motorway, killing 47 people.

Clarence was the only reporter to reach the wreckage before a security cordon was put up. He was able to ring the BBC newsdesk in London and describe what he could see for listeners and viewers until a camera crew arrived to get shots to go with his reports. His resourcefulness led to a job with the national reporter pool in London.

An able writer

It's pretty obvious that words are the journalist's tools. No matter what medium the journalist works in, be it television, radio, print or online, they need to be able to express ideas and information in writing. So a clear, grammatically correct writing style is a basic requirement. And while a journalistic style can be taught, good spelling and punctuation are a prerequisite. Any mistakes in an application form will result in it going straight in the bin.

Gillian Hargreaves, a reporter with BBC Radio 4's *World at One* and *PM*, says the journalist has to love language: 'Your writing skills have to be lyrical. You don't need to use big words but you need to be able to explain the complicated simply and to convey the story whether it is the drama or the enormity.'

Creative

Being creative can mean using language in an original manner or thinking of new ways of manipulating pictures and sound. It can also mean finding creative ways of covering stories.

Output editor of the BBC's *Six O'Clock News*, Jon Williams, believes that looking at things in an original way is a key skill:

> Don't be formulaic – we want imaginative and creative reporters. I will never get angry with someone who tries to do something different and it doesn't work. If someone tries to be original, that's good. We covered the story of the GCSE results. The standard story is that girls do better than boys. Yet yesterday 30,000 people left with no GCSEs at all. That was our angle.

ITN's *5 News* were able to secure an unusual exclusive when they used a satellite videophone during the foot-and-mouth crisis of 2001. This allowed a farmer who was unable to leave his farm during the outbreak to file a regular diary for the programme. The farmer in Cumbria was in isolation for several weeks, but after neighbours delivered the videophone he could be interviewed regularly on the six o'clock news programme. It meant the programme could talk to the people living through the crisis as it unfolded. For example, the farmer was interviewed the day he received a letter saying his animals were included in a pre-emptive cull.

Competitive

Most journalists are competitive by nature and delight in beating other news organisations to an exclusive. Being first and fastest is a large part of the job.

Take John Simpson, the BBC's world affairs editor, who walked into Kabul, Afghanistan's capital, on 13 November 2001 after the Taliban fighters had retreated and before the Northern Alliance troops arrived. He gleefully told a Radio 4 audience that he and his team were the first into the city: 'It was BBC people who liberated the city – we got in ahead of the Northern Alliance. We passed through and walked in, and the scenes of rejoicing and delight were extraordinary.'[14]

Ethical and fair

What constitutes 'ethical' is one of the most vexed questions in journalism. Do the ends justify the means? Is it ever fair to trick someone into giving you a story? If the person will tell you their story only if you pay them, is that right?

Journalists talk little about ethics, but most face ethical decisions of one kind or another every day. Should they knock on the door of the family who have just lost two children in a car crash to ask for an interview and a photo, or telephone first or leave a note? Should they use the rash quote by the headteacher that most of her pupils are impossible to teach or the more reasonable quote, which more accurately reflects what she thinks, in which she says it is a challenge? The second is truer but less colourful. It is also less hurtful to the children.

Bureau chief of Sky News in Manchester, Mike McCarthy, says:

> You are the audience's representative, you're there to represent them. You are in a privileged position and you've got to do what the vast majority of people would find acceptable in the circumstances. In this way you are being ethical.

As John Herbert writes in *Journalism in the Digital Age*, ethics infuses all news gathering, reporting and communicating. If you ask a journalist whether they are ethical, the vast majority will say they are, but few can explain in any detail how. Most take each situation as it comes and have a personal set of ethical rules that works for them. Jon Williams agrees:

> Being ethical is the bottom line of anything. Some ethical beliefs are personal and there are some that are shared. But I'd be lying if I said I had a plastic card on which they are all written. But then if everyone is just following a corporate rule book, then

ethics would mean nothing. You have to ask yourself if you can sleep at night, then they mean everything.

Some organisations give guidelines to reporters. The *Guardian* in its editorial guidelines explains that journalists should be sensitive to any outside interests they have which may come into conflict with the integrity of the paper's journalism. Staff are warned they must not use their position for private benefit and that no payment, gift or other advantage should undermine accuracy, fairness or independence. Any 'freebies' can only be accepted on the understanding that the journalist will report the assignment as he or she sees fit.[15]

Most journalists will make ethical mistakes at one time or another during their career. Many do things as a young reporter that they later wish they hadn't.

Mike McCarthy has a typical story. In 1989, while working for a BBC local television news station, he covered the Hillsborough disaster, in which 96 football fans were crushed to death in Sheffield. In the evening BBC Network News in London asked him to film the bereaved families being counselled in a nearby church hall.

> I didn't want to do it, but I was relatively new to television journalism and too green to say no. I didn't feel confident to question their judgment. So I went along. It was disastrous. Even though the vicar agreed for us to go inside, some of the friends and relatives were very upset. We intruded into their grief. Now, in a similar situation, I would say no. I'm not saying you can't film people in grief but you have to be very sensitive to their experience and how they are likely to react.

Covering grief is one of the hardest parts of the job of a journalist, especially if it comes in the form of a 'death-knock', where you are asked to go to the house of someone involved in a tragedy. Some journalists never feel comfortable with this aspect of the job. Yet if you can get it right, interviews gained this way can lead to moving, emotionally raw news stories. Some people in this situation want to talk about their loved ones and tell others what a wonderful person they were.

If you borrow a photograph, make sure it is returned. A colleague once lost the only photograph of a dead husband. Think about how hard that would be to explain. It is a mistake they have always regretted and can never put right. Be aware that a photograph such as the annual school photo may have been taken by a professional photographer and will be copyrighted.

There are other forms of 'doorstepping', as it is called, and they too can cause ethical problems. Doorstepping is when a reporter approaches or confronts someone without prior arrangement. This can happen in public, say on the street, or when the reporter knocks on the door of their house. It is used in cases where it is felt this is the only way this person may speak to the reporter. Perhaps they are someone involved in a crime or anti-social behaviour and have repeatedly refused an interview on unreasonable grounds or they are a public figure involved in a scandal. They can also be, as is mentioned above, ordinary people involved in a tragedy.

But doorstepping is not the same as harassment and intimidation. If there are 15 or 20 people camped outside a house, looking through windows or prowling around the garden, they are bound to make those inside feel intimidated. The Editors' Code of Practice, which sets professional standards by which members of the press are expected to abide, includes sections on harassment and states: 'Journalists and photographers must neither obtain nor seek to obtain information or pictures through intimidation, harassment or persistent pursuit.' (See Chapter 12 for a discussion of the Editors' Code of Practice, which is set out in full in the Appendix.)

Balanced/objective

There is controversy in the world of reporting over whether the professional requirement to try to be impartial or objective is possible or even desirable. Many such as Jason Burke, the *Observer*'s chief reporter, accept that they cannot be objective no matter how hard they try to write the full story:

> The journalist lays out the situation for the readers to make up their own mind, but a journalist's own reactions will inevitably colour how they will report. Good impassioned reporting, with genuine sympathy and a good knowledge of the context, should be enough. No one can be entirely objective. The editing process starts when you choose who to interview.[16]

Andrew Sullivan in the *Sunday Times* agrees:

> Bias is inevitable in any grown-up journalist's work. You can try to be balanced (and you're a better journalist for it) but in your choice of topics, selection of guests, presentation of facts, you inevitably show your hand.
>   This isn't to say that journalism should degenerate into simple propaganda or outright advocacy, at least not in the presentation of news rather than opinion.
>   Trying to present many sides of an issue is the mark of an honest journalist; maintaining a distinction between news and opinion is the mark of an honest editor.[17]

On the extreme of this argument is Geraldo Rivera, a former television presenter and chat-show host who donned a flak jacket and became Fox News's chief war correspondent in Afghanistan. He brought with him a new style of war reporting that was anything but impartial. He said during a broadcast in November 2001: 'I've got a New York City fire department hat that I want to put on the head of [Osama Bin Laden's] corpse. We want Osama Bin Laden to end up either behind bars or six feet under or maybe just one foot under.[18]

For Reuters' Kabul correspondent, Sayed Salahuddin, however, impartiality is one of the most treasured tenets of journalism:

> I have this belief in Reuters' accuracy and impartiality – I am very proud of that. We should continue to follow that line and not be bullied by lies and propaganda of people

in the world. If we can follow that pattern, we will be able to remain impartial and people will trust in what we do.[19]

All journalists can make sure they balance their stories by explaining as many of the arguments involved as possible. And if you are accusing someone of something, they should be allowed to respond.

Cultivating contacts

One of the first things any journalist should do is set up a contacts book. This should be indexed so you can file names alphabetically and if it is loose-leafed it is easier to keep relevant, as you can add pages or replace those that are out of date. It is sensible to keep a copy of your contacts book, either on paper or on a computer. If you can afford it, think about investing in a personal digital assistant (PDA). These make excellent and very portable contacts books.

The journalist should enter in their contacts book anyone they speak to whom they may wish to speak to again. They should include as many details about them as possible: the name in full and correctly spelled, their address, a work and a home phone number, their mobile number, an email address and perhaps fax number. It is wise to include a brief note about their interests or expertise.

A contacts book is likely to include:

- doctors, surgeons and scientists
- academics
- emergency services, victim support units, the detective leading a murder investigation
- local courts, hospitals, health authorities and their press officers
- victims or their families who could speak out in future for changes in the law or comment on similar cases (e.g. a family whose child was killed during a school trip or was run down by a drink driver)
- pressure groups, campaign groups and charities. They are always useful for comments and you will find there are groups covering many of the issues on which you will report. You need to know those that are run nationally and have spokesmen and women in your area, and who they are, and those specific to your area
- schools, their headteachers and parents' representatives
- churches and their leaders. Make sure you know their correct titles: is it Reverend, Right Reverend, Father?
- Politicians, including MPs, local councillors and potential candidates
- those who know. These include shopkeepers, especially those working in the local post offices; postmen and women; milkmen and women; publicans; the neighbourhood watch; people who have lived somewhere for a long time
- representatives of any big companies or industries in the area and their unions.

There are many more, and we will be looking at sources for news in Chapter 8.

You should carry your contacts book at all times – you never know when you might need it. It is also not wise to share too many of your contacts with your colleagues, especially those who are not regular interviewees.

One of my best contacts when I worked on a local paper, and one of the most unusual, was a magician I met while doing a feature about children's parties. He was a member of the Magic Circle and gave me several exclusives that were picked up by national newspapers and television news programmes. He made it clear that he did not want it known where the stories were coming from or he could be thrown out of the Circle. I was careful to keep his confidence.

Keeping the anonymity of a source who speaks to you only on the understanding that their identity will be kept confidential is vital for journalists if they wish people to trust them. They may be risking the loss of their jobs or in some cases their lives. So if you promise not to reveal the identity of an interviewee, then you must keep that promise. In broadcasting this can mean obscuring the face of an interviewee and using an actor's voice. Anonymity is only really appropriate in a few cases and you should think hard before agreeing not to name someone. It may be warranted:

- for reasons of safety – a person may be risking their life by talking to you, for example, if they are a former member of a terrorist organisation
- if they may lose their job – for example, a whistle-blower in a big company
- to avoid undue embarrassment – this could mean someone with a medical complaint
- for legal reasons, although interviewing a criminal or someone trying to evade the law is not usually ethical
- because you will not be able to tell the story otherwise. You must think carefully whether the story is worth the promise.

Once a promise is given it must be kept, and that can mean the journalist coming under pressure from the police or the courts to show their notes or hand over pictures or names. It can lead to journalists facing a fine or jail for contempt of court. (See Chapter 10 for a full discussion of these issues.)

Well informed

Ben Bradlee, the legendary editor of the *Washington Post*, told a colleague of mine in an interview that the best thing a journalist can have is a good head.

Throughout their working life, the journalist will be scrutinising and interpreting the incidents on which they report. The reporting process involves the journalist deciding which people to interview and which facts are salient to telling the story. The general public relies upon the journalist to bring them a true interpretation of events.

To discharge the role well, the journalist needs to be able to make judgments about what is significant and what is not. They cannot do this well without a good general knowledge and familiarity with current events.

Aspiring young journalists sometimes lack the necessary broader perspective, possibly because they are the products of an age of niche marketing and personalised information. They take all they can get on their favourite subject but leave the rest. As a result, they may know little about nine-tenths of what is going on around them. What hope has a teenager of reaching a person aged 40 if he or she knows every scrap of minutiae about a film star or sports personality, but thinks the NASDAQ is a rock band from Seattle?[20]

A general awareness of how government and society works will help the journalist to establish quickly where to go for information. If you have a story about asylum seekers, you will be a lot quicker at collecting the information if you know the places to contact, such as the Home Office, British Refugee Council, Human Rights Watch and MigrationWatch UK.

Journalists should also know what stories their own newspaper, radio or television station is following. This means keeping up with the organisation's output and being aware of ongoing campaigns. There is little more irritating to an editor than having to explain a story that should be familiar to a reporter before they can set them to work.

Being aware of the news agenda of your organisation will also help you to pitch ideas at the morning meeting and the planning meeting if there is one.

The digital newsroom

New technology has transformed the way news is gathered and relayed to the public. An event across the globe can be on air as it happens or within minutes. This demands of the journalist an ability to respond to and sum up a situation more quickly than ever before.

On occasion you will still have to send a story through the post or fax it, but nowadays copy, even pictures and sound, can be phoned in or sent by computer from anywhere in the world, including the most lonely or inhospitable places. All you need is a satellite phone or a laptop attached to a phone line, mobile or satellite phone to transmit your story.

During the war in Afghanistan in the winter of 2001, lightweight and portable satellite videophones were vital for getting reports out for television. We saw regular live reports by satellite phone from Nic Robertson of CNN and others. He used a videophone to transmit pictures from inside the Afghan capital, Kabul.

The BBC's Emma Simpson filed a broadcast quality television report via the internet from Antigua in January 2003 about a 15-year-old schoolboy who had become the youngest person ever to sail the Atlantic Ocean single-handed. She also supplied a written report for the BBC's online news service.

Multi-skilling

This is the way the profession is moving; reporters are increasingly expected to file stories quickly from wherever they are and to be able to work across any medium. Whereas in the past you were a newspaper reporter, a radio reporter or a television reporter, now you are expected to be flexible and multi-skilled.

New digital technology is thus also affecting the way journalists gather and present information. If you work for a newspaper and are sent out to report an event, you could be asked to take still photos as well as to write a story for the paper. You may also be asked to supply a version of your story for the paper's internet site, including perhaps recorded interviews and moving pictures. You could, in addition, be expected to serve text services such as Ceefax and mobile phone news services.

As a broadcast journalist, you may need to supply a report for both television and radio and be expected to film and edit your own television pieces. Ian Myatt, a senior producer in new media for BBC English Regions, believes this is a positive move:

> Multi-skilling gives you more creative input into how you present ideas. A journalist will set up a story, go out and film it, conduct the interviews and collect some soundbites, come back and write it up. So you've got audio, video, still images and text. The journalist puts all that into a database and the computer will display the information on whatever platform the user wishes, PC, Wap phone, TV.

He acknowledges that currently some working journalists don't see the need for multi-skilling: 'People have got to take the blinkers off in newsrooms that say I work for TV or radio. There has got to be cultural change in all news organisations.'

With our round-the-clock news operations, some journalists complain they are pulled in all directions and are unable properly to gather the information because they are fielding demands from too many outlets. Online news organisations and 24-hour broadcast news allow news to be accessible when people want it, not when news organisations and journalists wish to present it. These outlets are voracious, insatiable beasts that constantly need to be updated, imposing huge demands on the journalist.

Much of what journalists do is what they've always done, only faster. For example, using the internet allows the journalist to locate information fast. But they still need to select only the relevant information and verify it. Knowing how to search for information on the web and turn it into news is an important skill for the journalist in the digital age.

Is journalism for you?

Journalism is not a nine-to-five occupation. You've just logged out of your computer and are packing your bag when a call comes in to say there's a fire or a siege or a riot and you are on your way. You are not home for dinner; you may not be home all night. The unpredictability of the work and the shift systems operated in many organisations can put a strain on personal relationships.

Many people want to go into journalism because they are good at English and like writing. That's fine, but it is not enough. You need to have a love of current events. If you have never read a newspaper or would prefer to watch Desparate Housewives rather than the evening news, then this is not the right job.

Sophie Raworth, presenter of BBC's *Six O'Clock News*, insists it's also not a job for those chasing fame and glamour:

> You have to have a passion for news and current affairs and for getting information together. You can't be in a newsroom and be obsessed with getting your face on screen or people will think that's all you want. You've got to have a good grounding in journalism and reporting.
>
> I never intended to present, I fell into it. I was working as a radio reporter and then as a producer in Brussels and I planned to be a producer. Then by accident I met a man who was a regional head of centre and he said I should go and work for him as a reporter. Through that I got on-screen experience and then I started presenting. To be honest I found it a very difficult transition to make but you have to be determined and never give up.
>
> It's an exciting job and a great business to be in. It's given me access to places, events and people I'd never have had. It's permanently interesting.

Editors look for people who do not need spoon-feeding, according to Ian Lockwood, editor of the *Craven Herald:*

> I look for an enquiring mind and someone who can come up with ideas. They have to be interested in what's going on and have the ability to supply us with stories.
>
> We give interviewees a simple test to see if they can recognise a story. We present them with some facts and see if they choose the correct angle.
>
> The worst kind of applicants are the ones that sit there and say they like writing. They might be able to write a beautiful 2,500 word essay on *The Tempest* but can they write four paragraphs on a charity race?

Zenobia Tilley graduated in 2001 having done a politics degree and has worked as a freelance journalist since then:

> What university doesn't teach you is how to survive 12-hour days and it doesn't show you how to think on your feet. I never realised what a constant battle it would be to get a story. When you're a student, people go out of their way to help you, and they're less suspicious. I've just spent a whole morning trying to reach people on the phone who don't want to talk to me.
>
> But even though it's badly paid I can't imagine doing any other job. I enjoy the buzz of the newsroom. I enjoy meeting people; I feel a part of society. It's a duty to fight for truth.

If you still wish to be a journalist, think long and hard about which area of journalism you wish to enter. If you wish to be a broadcast journalist, make an honest assessment of yourself – are you comfortable in front of a microphone and/or a camera and is your voice clear?

My career as a journalist by John McIntyre

The story of freelance reporter John McIntyre's career progression is a classic tale of someone determined to succeed and is worth repeating in full. When John decided to leave his
job teaching physics, he didn't slip quietly away. Instead he shouted his decision in the
loudest possible way – through a cartoon which he handed in on April 1. When it was
reproduced in the *News of the World*, his landlord didn't see the funny side and asked him
to leave. He set off with nowhere to go and no money. So when his car broke down
in Liphook he found himself homeless, jobless and penniless. He was taken in by a local
philanthropist and slept on the couch. The next day he saw an advert for a village
correspondent in the local paper paying 4.5p a line – must be able to type.

I told them I could write and that I had a phone and a typewriter. They were so impressed
with my enthusiasm they offered me 5p a line. Of course I had no experience, no phone
and no typewriter.

My first job was to report on Liphook carnival queen. I wasn't quite sure what to do
so I went and got some back copies of the newspaper and found the paragraphs that
matched the stories and just changed the names and a few facts. My first intro read
'Sweet 16 and following in her sister's footsteps, Beverley … is Liphook carnival queen.'

For weeks I worked in a local phone box putting money in to pay for calls. I didn't eat
so I could pay for the calls, except when I'd steal milk from doorsteps and have pan-
cakes. I stayed sleeping on the person's couch for about six months and used a child's
typewriter I'd bought as I couldn't afford a real one.

During this time I rigorously read what the sub-editors did with my copy and learned.
And I filed copy by the mountain. I went everywhere with my notebook. I went to all the
parish council meetings and banged on doors talking to everyone. If somebody farted
in Liphook, I reported it and the local paper printed it all. I then took on more villages
until I had five in all.

Visiting the police and reporting on parish council meetings, you soon learn how
important accuracy is. If you got anything wrong, they would slag you off in the next
meeting so you become a stickler for accuracy. If I couldn't remember a quote, I'd ring
the person and check. You need people to trust you will get it right. Soon people began
to ring me before the police.

I then went to the *Portsmouth News* but the contacts I made on the local paper were
crucial. The most important thing if you need a story quickly is to know who to ring.

I remember ringing the head of the NUT [National Union of Teachers] as he lived in
Liphook and saying I need a story now. I know there has been a ballot on strike action
and the results aren't in yet – it won't be from you but if there is going to be a teacher's
strike put the phone down. He did. I was able to write 'Schools throughout Britain are
bracing themselves for an all out strike.'

Another time there was a story in which a footballer had been arrested but we didn't
know who, so I rang the police and said I'd read out the numbers of the players and

when I get to the right number give me a hint. When I got to number 7 he said 'I've got nothing more to say' so I knew which player it was.

From the *Portsmouth News* I went into local radio. An independent radio station was just opening up and I went to the launch party and managed to persuade the Friday afternoon presenter that he needed a 'What the Papers Say'. I turned up the first time and I didn't know what to say. I was dreadful but he didn't tell me to go away, he helped me to improve.

When he moved to the Breakfast Show, he rang me up and asked if I wanted a job in radio. I became a journalist at Ocean Sound. I started broadcasting on my thirtieth birthday in 1988.

Within three weeks I was reading the news and learning all I could. I would listen to what other people were doing. I'd read copy, check how it was written. I always read out loud what I was writing for other people to check how it sounded.

Soon I was going out with a Uher [a tape recorder]. I made all the mistakes such as mike rattle but I was coming back with material the BBC didn't get near. My contacts were coming in handy. If a big story broke involving the police, I'd ring up and I'd be cheeky and not take 'no' from them. With perseverance I'd get the story.

I then got headhunted by another independent radio station, Southern Sound in Brighton. They increased my salary. I loved local radio; it was friendly and intimate. But I was itching to get into television. I'd had a hankering since working in the media resources centre as a student at university where we'd launched a television programme.

However, I thought to myself: who the hell would take an untrained journalist who was an ex-physics teacher? I rang a mate who was a cameraman and said I needed a showreel, so I got some students from Basingstoke Technical College and we went into Winchester and did some mock news stories. They weren't serious at all, although I reported them straight. One was a court case of a teacher who was arrested for trying to raise standards of education in schools. The second was about crop circles which turned out not to be caused by men from Mars but by a break-away group of Morris Dancers. We interviewed one.

I sent it to ITV and the BBC and I was given work experience at BBC South Today in Southampton. They told me: 'You look a bit suspect but we'll give you a go.'

On the first day the programme editor gave me a story to look into on traffic and travel. There was a dispute at Sealink but we didn't know much. I rang a few contacts and I started hearing rumours of Sealink being involved in a take-over. I rang a few more contacts and found out Sealink was indeed about to be taken over in a £100 million deal.

I ended up writing the lead story for BBC South. I brought in plenty of other stories. I'd phone up my contacts and get them to spill the beans. So when a job came up as a regional journalist, I got it and they agreed to match my newspaper wage.

But I was desperate to get on air. Every day the planner would put up the stories on a white board and the newsroom secretary would assign them to reporters and so I'd wipe off the name that was up there and put mine against it. I didn't choose the big stories, just the medium ones. Then when a reporter was off, I'd get to act up as a reporter in their place. I loved working with pictures and I think it was instinctive on my part.

I spent three or four years as a reporter at BBC South and would pester the national programmes to take my stories. I always believed they'd take me on and I developed a rapport with the programme editors.

In Southampton I'd now got a situation where I could, within reason, choose the stories I'd cover and I'd choose on the basis of which would sell to the national programmes. These were either the quirky stories or ones with children, the *Six [O'clock News]* liked these. So I'd go out on the story and ring the *Six* and sell it to them and then ring Southampton and say, oh the *Six* have been on to me and I'd do the report.

Then a job came up for two or three news correspondents nationally. I applied and worked my butt off for the board [interview]. I researched everything to do with current affairs. I talked to everyone and found out what the BBC believed in and who was on the board. I researched them as individuals, their hobbies. I felt fully prepared for the interview and had the courage of my convictions. In the board I stuck to my guns even though they tried to trip me up.

They called me that night and I was given the job. It was the culmination of everything: news correspondent on national news. I was soon trotting around the planet. My first foreign trip was Tahiti to cover rioting where I was tear-gassed during a live broadcast.

The biggest stories I've covered include the Dunblane massacre with Kate Adie [shooting in a school] and the Kosovo crisis. [We will look in more detail at John's coverage of these in a later chapter.]

One of the most fun things I've done was reporting from inside a shark tank, full of sharks, when the London Aquarium opened. I did ten minutes live for Breakfast News then for Radio 4 – without the pictures – and even BBC World. I used a 'Sea Trek' bubble hat to be able to transmit sound to viewers and listeners. I even had an interviewee.

My ethics were a bit dodgy to start with. But with experience they come. I was a comprehensive school kid and you weren't allowed to have dreams. Yet here I was broadcasting on the biggest programmes in the country. I was aware of the responsibility and I'd fought hard to get where I was and I wasn't about to lose it.

I recently decided to leave the BBC and make diving my career. I've now set up my own company, Bigfish Television and am making television about the sea, the marine life, the people, the wrecks.

Summing up

Journalists spend their lives trying to make sense of a complex and chaotic world. Using skill, tact and intellect, they cut through the official language of press releases and statements, obfuscation and disorder to bring understanding to the public.

We've seen in this chapter that the journalist needs to be knowledgeable, determined and diligent to carry out their role. They have also to strive to tell as close to the truth as possible – although a cursory glance at the *Guardian's* corrections column shows that even the best journalists make mistakes.

The remainder of this book aims to show the mechanics of being a journalist. How do you recognise a news story, research it and write it and what are the legal pitfalls to watch out for?

REVIEW QUESTIONS

1 What are the most important skills required of a journalist?
2 What do editors look for in a new recruit?
3 How important is fairness/balance in covering a story?

EXERCISES

1 List all the characteristics that you believe you have that a journalist should have.
2 Your editor asks you to cover a story about a 5-year-old girl who was killed when she fell into a canal while playing with friends. The canal bordered the playground and was not fenced off. Think whom you would want to interview and how you would approach the family. If you decide to visit the house, what would you say when they open the door?
3 How good is your general knowledge? Read one broadsheet, one tabloid and one local newspaper; listen to a radio news bulletin and watch a television news bulletin. Note how many of the stories you are already familiar with.

FURTHER READING AND RESOURCES

Randall, D., *The Universal Journalist*, London: Pluto Press, 1996.
Bell, M., *In Harm's Way*, London: Penguin, 1995.
Guardian's Editorial Code, *Guardian*, 2002, www.theguardian.co.uk.
www.NCTJ.com gives details and advice on how to enter journalism. The site is run by the National Council for the Training of Journalists. It points out that more than 60 per cent of new entrants to the profession are now graduates.
Herbert, J., *Journalism in the Digital Age*, Oxford: Focal Press, 2000.

Notes

1 See www.icmresearch.co.uk. The question asked was, 'When you watch a news report on TV, how honest do you think a journalist is likely to be when interviewed?' 8% said very likely, 38% quite likely, 32% quite unlikely, 16% said very unlikely, 5% said don't know.

2 *The Public Interest and Media Privacy*, by Prof. David Morrison and Michael Svennevig (2002), commissioned by the BBC, the Independent Television Commission, the Radio Authority, the Broadcasting Standards Commission, the Independent Committee for the Supervision of Standards of Telephone Information Services and the Institute for Public Policy Research, pp. 1–4 and 55–6.

3 www.presswise.org.uk, 'What can you do when a journalist gets things wrong?'

4 This is a corruption of a statement by Lord McGregor of Durris, founding chairman of the Press Complaints Commission from 1991 to 1995. The statement, released on the day Andrew Morton's book on Princess Diana began its serialisation in *The Times*, read: 'The most intrusive and specula-tive treatment by sections of the press (and, indeed, by broadcasters) of the marriage of the Prince and Princess of Wales is an odious exhibition of journalists dabbling their fingers in the stuff of other people's souls in a manner which adds nothing to legitimate public interest in the situation of the heir to the throne.'

5 Don Hale, *The Journalist*, May 2002.

6 See www.ref.org.

7 Marie Colvin, 'Jenin: the bloody truth', *Sunday Times*, 21 April 2002.

8 Mark Chavunduka, World Press Freedom Day, 3 May 2001, taken from The Freedom Forum at www.freedomforum.org.

9 Paul Horrocks quoted from www.mediaguardian.co.uk on 17 July 2002, Ciar Byrne.

10 Sarah Sands, deputy editor in Manhattan, 'Look. Oh my God, they are jumping', *Daily Telegraph*, 12 September 2001.

11 Jean Morgan, *Press Gazette*, 14 September 2001.

12 *Press Gazette*, 21 September 2001.

13 Morgan, *op. cit.*

14 Oliver Burkeman, 'Simpson of Kabul', *Guardian* G2, 14 November 2001.

15 The guidelines are set out on the *Guardian*'s website www.theguardian.co.uk. See also the BBC's *Producers' Guidelines* on www.bbc.co.uk.

16 Quoted in 'Give peace a chance' by Mary Stevens, *Press Gazette*, 8 February 2002.

17 Andrew Sullivan, 'Let's hear it for prejudiced television news', *Sunday Times*, 17 November 2002.

18 Oliver Burkeman, 'The chat show host who went to war', *Guardian*, 29 July 2002.

19 Mary Stevens, 'Truth amid the terror', *Press Gazette*, 29 March 2002.

20 Mike Ward, *Journalism Online*, Oxford: Focal Press, 2002, p. 43.

2

WHAT IS NEWS?

Good journalists have a nose for news. They work hard to 'sniff out' original stories and to find the facts of the events they are assigned to cover. They strive to

- know their audience
- understand what makes a strong news story
- recognise the best angle
- avoid repeating press releases verbatim.

In the last chapter we looked at the qualities needed to be a journalist; one of the most important is having a good sense of what is news. The first thing to note is that *news is created*. What we see, hear and read is just a version of events which has been crafted and shaped by the people assembling the newspaper, radio or television bulletin. It may be an honest and accurate interpretation, but it is still only a snapshot, an impression of some occurrences.

This chapter looks at why certain things that happen are turned into news while others are not considered newsworthy; why certain things cause the journalist's pulse to race with excitement and others see their eyes glaze over.

Some thoughts

> News is what is extraordinary, interesting and not known. (Gillian Hargreaves, BBC reporter with Radio 4's *World at One* and *PM*)

As Gillian Hargreaves rightly says, news is fresh information, what is not known. It can be about events, people or ideas, but for the information to be published it has to come into the category of 'newsworthy' – that is, interesting and extraordinary in news terms. What does that mean? How does a reporter know what is newsworthy? Which stories will make it to the page, airwaves or screen and which ones will end up on the 'spike' or in the recycle bin? How does a reporter sifting through council agendas, court lists and press releases identify those items that should be followed up and those of no interest? Similarly, if a member of the public phones the newsroom with some information, how does the reporter recognise when they are being given a story meriting their attention? What's more, once they have sniffed out the story, how do they judge how much prominence and space to give it? What is worth a short piece on page 5 or halfway down the bulletin, and what is worthy of the front page or top of the news bulletin on radio or television?

The short answer is that they just know. It's a gut reaction that comes from being around news – lots of it for a long time. After a while the reporter knows how to recognise a news story and to judge its 'news value' (although they're unlikely to use the term).

> Young writers can have a problem in that their news sense is not so acutely developed as that of their more experienced colleagues – and this is very difficult to teach. This means they sometimes miss the strong angle of a story.
>
> One of my trainees once wrote a story about a train breakdown, which caused delays for commuters. Not a bad story yet nothing to get too excited about until you get to the bit where the station staff had to wipe the rails with toilet roll to clean the track and get the train going again.
>
> Now the reporter got the facts but was unable to see the glaring news angle. This comes with experience and getting advice from news editors and subs, seeing how stories may be rewritten or restructured and having an insatiable and non-defensive appetite for feedback on their work. They should read their own paper and others all the time to get the feel for 'news copy'. See how the best stories allow the facts to speak for themselves and are not laced with unnecessary adjectives and clichés. (Bob Bounds, editor, *Kentish Gazette*)

News values

News can be divided into hard and soft news. Hard news is new information about significant events or ideas. It concentrates on the factual details of what has happened or what has been said. Soft news is lighter, more colourful, and is often more about entertaining the audience than informing them.

All events can be given a news value, although in newsrooms across the land precisely what news value a story merits can lead to some pretty heated arguments. That is because placing an item is not a precise science, and the audience the news is intended for as well as what other stories are around on the day must also be taken into account.

On a slow news day, a piece that would normally be worthy of only a few paragraphs on page three may be promoted to the front page, or a mid-bulletin story could become the lead. What you will never see, hear or read is: 'Today nothing newsworthy happened, so we aren't going to bother boring you with the irrelevant and unimportant.' Then again, on a day when an event of huge significance or interest happens, many other items that would normally be considered important may not appear because they get pushed aside in favour of more information on the main story.

This happened on 11 September 2001, when the World Trade Center in New York and the Pentagon in Washington were attacked and around 3,000 people were killed.

In the *Daily Telegraph*'s first section, pages one to nine were given over to the attacks. It was not until page ten that other news appeared, including a story about the ban on the movement of sheep to prevent the spread of foot-and-mouth disease and fears this could lead to hundreds of animals starving to death. It was a similar story in the other broadsheet papers, with the *Guardian* giving over the first 17 pages and *The Times* its first six pages to the attacks. All had more reports in pull-out or second sections.

The tabloid newspapers also had extensive coverage, with the *Daily Mail* filling its first 27 pages with the events in America, the *Mirror* its first 25 pages, and the *Sun* did away with its page-three girl and devoted the first 29 pages to the attacks.

By anyone's estimation, the attacks on the Twin Towers and the Pentagon were of huge significance. But events such as this or the outbreak of war in the former Yugoslavia or the arrest of Saddam Hussein, which would be without question the main story in all newspapers and broadcast bulletins, are rare.

On most days news editors have to choose between several potential main stories. In deciding what to make the lead story or 'splash', editors have to weigh up their relative strengths and weaknesses. What elements has the reporter gathered – interviews, facts, pictures? Is there anything to make you go 'wow' or 'ah' or 'ugh'? In television, how strong the pictures are – what footage they have – is very important (we will look at that in more detail in Chapter 5). News editors must also consider their audience and what they would wish covered, although there is a danger here. A journalist who panders too much to the audience will end up leaving out stories that would inform and challenge and using only those that reinforce the audience's world-view. The best journalism always works just out-side the comfort zone.

However, all news organisations take their audience into account to some extent. This goes some way to explaining why, on the same day, three national newspapers can have such different lead stories you could be forgiven for thinking they had been produced in different countries. Consider these examples from the *Guardian*, the *Daily Mail* and the *Sun* on the same day in April 2002. While the *Guardian* has as its main story the Israeli occupation of the city of Nablus in the West Bank, the *Daily Mail* leads on rising house prices and the *Sun* splashes on the ankle injury suffered by then Manchester United foot-baller David Beckham during the European Cup.[1] (see Figure 2.1)

Differences in audience can also lead to divergent angles on the same story. Take these two versions of a story about teachers voting to threaten strike action over six issues, including pay, national tests and training outside school hours:

Figure 2.1 The *Sun* decides to splash the story that David Beckham has suffered an ankle injury during the European Cup of 2002. Other papers lead with rising house prices and the Israeli occupation of Nablus.

NUT members defy leaders by strike threat

The National Union of Teachers conference delivered another snub to its leadership yesterday by voting to threaten industrial action on a sixth front.

Delegates in Bournemouth voted for 'rolling industrial action up to and including strike action' if demands for an immediate pay rise of 10% or at least £2,000 for all teachers and a £3,000 rise in the London allowance were not met. (*Guardian*, 3 April 2002)

Classroom chaos fear as union calls for a 10pc rise

Militant teachers yesterday moved closer to mass industrial action as they threatened national strikes or work-to-rules on six fronts.

They have stepped up their war with the Government over the national curriculum, pay, conditions and workload in a move which looks set to cause major classroom disruption. (*Daily Mail*, 3 April 2002)

Both the stories make judgments in the opening paragraph or intro, but they strike different notes. The *Guardian*, which has a large number of teachers among its readers, has presented the story in a fairly straight way, choosing as its angle the teachers' disagreement with union bosses. The *Daily Mail* on the other hand, whose readers are less likely to have sympathy for industrial action, stresses the effect on the children of a strike. It describes the teachers as 'militant', which is an emotive term conjuring up pictures of picket lines, placards and ranting.

A good idea is to try to picture your audience. One radio station that had decided their typical listener was a 33-year-old female had a photo of such a woman in the studio and instructed all presenters to talk to her while they were on air.

Despite the differences mentioned, most news professionals have a similar way of looking at events. If you were to give a set of journalists a list of potential stories and ask them to rank them in order from the strongest to the weakest, they would most probably produce lists showing only minor discrepancies.

Media researchers have tried to explain this by identifying news values. Their explanations are worth considering as a way of understanding how journalists think, because, if you accept that it would be impossible to include in a newspaper or news bulletin everything that goes on in the world, then you have to accept that news is selected. This means a judgment is made on what to include and what to leave out.

Academics Johan Galtung and Mari Ruge carried out what is probably the best-known study nearly three decades ago.[2] They identified the following factors as important to newsgatherers when deciding what is news:

- **Frequency or time span** of the event, i.e. when it happened in relation to when the newspaper is published or the radio or television news bulletin is broadcast. News becomes stale quickly and news organisations thrive on being able to bring fresh information to the public first – 'news just in' or 'breaking news' are favourite terms of the broadcasters. 'Exclusive' is one beloved by the press, meaning 'we have it first and you can only read it here'. (The exclusive tag has been devalued by the tabloids' insistence on using it unjustifiably – on any day several are likely to claim the same story as an exclusive.)
- **Meaning.** Putting out a story as the information comes in isn't such a problem with 24-hour news and the internet. But how long the event takes for its meaning to be understood is very important. The quicker its meaning can be arrived at, the more likely it is to be reported. So murders and disasters are very quickly understood and easily translated into news. On the other hand, news has a problem with stories that take a long time to unfold, such as economic, social or cultural trends. These need what's known as a 'news peg', a device such as statistics or an annual report on which a story can be hung – 'New figures suggest the number of teenagers becoming pregnant is rising' or 'The British now drink more coffee than tea, according to a survey published today.'
- **Significance.** How big the story is. How much of an effect will it have on the audience? This depends of course on the news organisation. A local paper may accept a smaller story, a flood of perhaps 10 or 15 houses. It would take several dozen to make it to the regional paper or local radio and perhaps several hundred to make the national press or evening television news. A large tsunami, though, will make a story of international significance.
- **Clarity.** The clearer the meaning of the event, the more likely it is to become news. This means the range of meanings must be limited, otherwise a subject will be difficult to explain within the time and space constraints of news. This again makes social and

cultural trends difficult to tackle. The European Union can be a challenge except when they pass some bizarre law on the shape of bananas.

- **Closeness to home.** News should relate to the culture of the society in which it is reported. It also helps if it is convenient to report. So the United States will be reported but we don't hear much from South America. However, if Britain or British people are involved, even small, far-off places will be reported. How many people had heard of the Falklands Islands before the war with Argentina in 1982? And we have become very familiar with Iraq since the wars of 1990/91 and 2003. Much news does not travel. A local councillor who gets married may get a photo and a couple of paragraphs in the local paper but it would not be considered as news in the next county or nationally.

- **Consonance or predictability.** The more predicted or anticipated the better. At first this might seem odd but when you think about it, it isn't at all. Events such as a general election, the death of the Queen Mother, or the divorce of a celebrity couple are not a surprise but are still considered important news by all or some sections of the media. The build-up to the war in Iraq in 2003 produced round-the-clock coverage. For several months beforehand it became more and more obvious that the United States wanted Saddam Hussein removed from the leadership of the country. By the time President George W. Bush delivered his ultimatum on 17 March that Saddam should leave Iraq within 48 hours or the Coalition forces would invade, the media were already on a war footing.

- **The unexpected or rare.** Again war comes into this category as being comparatively rare, as does murder, especially serial killings such as those carried out by Dr Harold Shipman. Shipman was a GP in Hyde, Manchester, who was found to be killing his patients with morphine. It was important news for several reasons, including the number of victims, which was more than 200 and more than any other serial killer in recent British history. That he got away with it for so long was also important, as was his position as a trusted family doctor.

- **Continuity.** Once a story has made it onto the news agenda it will stay there. For example, if a dog attacks a child in a horrific way, leaving him or her scarred for life, every dog attack for the next weeks or months will be reported, no matter how minor. Calls will be made for dogs to be muzzled in public or banned from parks – all angles of the story will be explored. This particular example is likely to result in what media researchers term 'moral panic'.

- **Composition.** Journalists like to run a variety of stories in order to get around their region or to interest all parts of their audience. If there are too many court stories, they will drop a couple, not because they are not newsworthy but to get a balance of stories.

- **Concentration on elite nations and individuals.** Actions by certain states will be reported more than the actions of non-elite nations. When France threatened to use its veto in the United Nations Security Council to show its misgivings about the war against Iraq led by the United States, it was given a lot more coverage than was the opposition of other nations such as Brazil. This is understandable when the actions of elite nations and persons have more significance. In the above case, France has the use of a veto, so it can affect a vote on a resolution profoundly; Brazil does not. This sort of bias means that reporting from non-elite nations, such as those in Africa or South America, concentrates on famines or floods and we are given a very limited view of life there.

As with elite nations, it is assumed that the actions of elite persons or celebrities are more consequential than the actions of unknown people. Before her death, Princess Diana's bulimia spawned acres of news print about eating disorders. When pop singer Kylie Minogue was diagnosed with breast cancer in May 2005 there were discussions in the media about how widespread the disease is, its diagnosis, treatments and how likely a person is to survive it. In this way a celebrity's actions can be used as a news peg for the reporting of health and cultural trends.

- **Person-centred.** This is related to the above. Individuals are easier for the audience to identify with, and so the media use them to personify an issue. This means the Government is the prime minister, Osama Bin Laden is the face of terrorism, the war in Iraq is Saddam Hussein.

  Another way this is done is to concentrate on individuals involved in a story. In a war the victims are highlighted: the refugees, the maimed, the children. The former BBC war correspondent, Martin Bell, tells of the difficulty of conveying the nature of the war in Bosnia in 1993, especially through television, except by talking to the victims:

  > This was not as intrusive as it sounds, for the victims were usually willing enough to talk, and they had surely earned the right to be listened to. It also somehow personalised the conflict, so that people elsewhere could relate to it more easily, as if it were their homes and families being targeted and not some foreign conflict of no consequence.[3]

Unfortunately this can mean the complex issues and politics behind the conflicts are downplayed. But it is more interesting to try to tell stories through the people concerned and all stories should be relevant in some way to the audience.

If a new drug is released by a pharmaceutical company, which it is claimed will ease the symptoms of multiple sclerosis, then journalists will go to someone with MS and see how their life will be changed. Can they get the new drug? Is it much more expensive? How much of a difference will it make? If there is a mistake in the marking of A-level examinations, the media tell the story through a young person who now has to wait while the papers are re-marked.

- **Negativity.** 'If it bleeds it leads.' Generally these sorts of stories are unexpected and they are unambiguous. Some people criticise the news for being too interested in the negative, but a study into news coverage of doctors showed journalists were merely doing their job properly. The study published in the *British Medical Journal* looked at coverage of stories involving doctors in three national newspapers. The researchers found that while there were twice as many negative stories as positive ones, it also found that the newspapers were responding to incidents rather than deliberately campaigning against doctors.[4]

  Any flick through a local or regional paper will show there are plenty of good news stories: golden weddings, have-a-go heroes, successful charity events and village galas.

It is just that bad news is more alarming, it is more out of the ordinary and it can be given more prominence. The village gala happens every year, but the foot-and-mouth crisis doesn't, or we hope to goodness it won't. Murders and abductions are also relatively rare, and that is why they are news.

Crime is negative, and violent crime is also relatively rare and so it gets a lot of coverage. There is a good argument for journalists to make the rarity of crime clearer when reporting it so that people do not feel more unsafe than they need to. Stories such as the abduction and murder of a child always make front-page headlines and this can give the impression that children generally are unsafe. Photos of an elderly person beaten up by a mugger can make the old fear they are more likely to be attacked than is the case.

Other influences

Besides those listed there are other influences that affect the selection of news and how it is presented. These are generally agreed among researchers to be: the law of the land; the way journalists work in order to meet tight deadlines; and financial influences – pressure from those who own the newspaper and its advertisers.

The law

We will look at the law in depth in Chapters 10 and 11, so I'm not going to discuss here its influence on what journalists can report, except to say you cannot attack an individual in a news report without proof to back up what you are saying. Even if you think you know someone is a liar or a cheat, you cannot report it unless you could prove it in a court of law. That is because the law of libel exists to protect the reputation of the individual from unjustified attack.

Because of the law of contempt of court, you cannot report anything that could prevent someone accused of a crime having a fair trial. You cannot say anything that might make people think someone is guilty before a court has come to such a verdict, although you can report evidence given during the trial. (There are exceptions discussed in Chapter 10.) In other words, you cannot say or write anything calculated to interfere with the administration of justice and to prejudice the outcome of a trial.

Work routines

Possibly the most important influences on the selection of stories for publication or broadcast are the work routines journalists set up for themselves to be able to meet deadlines and fill the time or space available. These routines to produce and present material may make it easier for the journalists, but they can also create habits in which things are done in a certain way because it is quick and efficient. For example, much news comes from established sources, including the emergency services, the local council, businesses, pressure groups and news agencies such as the Press Association (PA) and Reuters. This can result in news covering certain predictable topics: crime, accidents, disasters, fires, demonstrations and campaigns by pressure groups and large charities.

The need to meet deadlines can also lead to the formulaic presentation of stories. A piece about a court case on television will often begin with those involved – the accused, witnesses and lawyers – arriving at court. It will move to the evidence given, often over sketches of the courtroom (cameras aren't allowed) and pictures of the scene where the crime occurred before going to a 'piece to camera' from the journalist, perhaps quoting the judge. The piece is likely to finish with the accused leaving the court either on foot or in a prison vehicle. By structuring the item this way, the journalist can quickly and easily tell the story in a succinct way, but it is not very original. If you watch enough news you will see a pattern emerge in the way stories are told, pictures used and people interviewed. The same is true of radio and newspaper reporting.

The time or space given to a story can distort it. Complicated stories that are given only a short time can become one-sided or oversimplified. This is particularly true in broadcasting, where the story has to be told in a minute or two. Many complicated or potentially boring stories or those, in the case of television, that are difficult to illustrate are avoided altogether.[5]

Financial control

Ownership and financial control are also considered an important influence on what appears in the media and what does not.

According to some commentators, Rupert Murdoch, who owns the *News of the World*, the *Sun*, *The Times* and the *Sunday Times*, influenced the coverage of the war on Iraq in 2003. Besides his British papers, he owns more than 175 newspaper titles worldwide, and all were notably pro-war; not one argued against. It is known that Murdoch himself supported the war. Roy Greenslade, then a columnist with the *Guardian*, concluded:

> What a guy! You have got to admit that Rupert Murdoch is one canny press tycoon because he has an unerring ability to choose editors across the world who think just like him.
>
> How else can we explain the extraordinary unity of thought in his newspaper empire about the need to make war on Iraq? After an exhaustive survey of the highest-selling and most influential papers across the world owned by Murdoch's News Corporation, it is clear that all are singing from the same hymn sheet.[6]

Researchers in America asked journalists about the influence of owners. About three in ten believed that stories are ignored because they might conflict with the financial interests of their news organisations or advertisers.

Even more damaging was the admission by more than 30 per cent of the local journalists questioned and 15 per cent of the national journalists that they had softened the tone of a news story in deference to the interests of their news organisation.[7]

Among those interests are advertisers. Fear of upsetting advertisers can be a problem for small radio stations, as Stuart Clarkson, a young reporter with 2BR in Lancashire, confirms:

> The main angle of a commercial radio station is the selling of air-time. This shouldn't affect the journalism but if a client has an event on, even if it is very small, it will be passed on to us and we are expected to cover it, which I am not always happy about. If there is a genuine story behind it that is fine but not if it is a blatant plug. I feel it devalues the station, as the news might not be trusted. That is what makes us different from the BBC – it's because of the sales people selling air-time that we have a job.

News is relative

We have established that news must be new or at least not known. This means that a good story that has remained a secret can make headlines even if it's old. When former Prime Minister John Major's four-year affair with Conservative MP Edwina Currie came to light it was important news for the British media because, although it had happened in the 1980s, it only became known in September 2002 when Mrs Currie revealed the affair in her autobiography.

We have also discovered that news must be important and interesting to the audience at whom it is aimed. Thus tabloid newspapers have a different news agenda to broadsheet or compact newspapers and local newspapers a different agenda to national papers. Even the profile of the area covered means local papers can have very different agendas. This story in the *Isle of Man Courier*, headlined 'Unwanted scratch for parked car' read 'A Daihatsu Charade was scratched down one side while it was parked in Derby Road, Ramsey, on Saturday night' (20 March 2003). In an area that is relatively free from crime and serious accidents, this is a story, albeit a small one. In a metropolitan area with a higher crime rate this incident would not register on the news agenda.

Besides local and national audiences, there are specialist audiences such as those who read the *Lancet*, namely the medical profession, *Balance*, the magazine for people with diabetes, *Practical Parenting* and so on. Obviously articles for specialist magazines need to be more detailed than those intended for a general audience.

Sometimes countries can interpret events differently. In an article in the *Washington Post*, historian and columnist David Greenberg outlined some events that were given a very different spin by American newspapers to that of British and other newspapers around the world. The first was a report that the United States Army was investigating the deaths of two Afghan detainees and whether American soldiers had killed them. A military pathologist had officially characterised the deaths as homicides. American newspapers reported the facts and noted human rights groups' concerns. Newspapers abroad, in contrast, responded with indignation. While the US papers implied this behaviour was unusual, foreign papers disagreed: 'US prisoners beaten to death,' read a headline in Melbourne. The *Independent* in London claimed that the deaths were 'reviving concerns that the US is resorting to torture in its treatment of Taliban fighters and suspected [al Qaeda] operatives'.

David Greenberg tried to understand the differences. He rejected the idea that publishers, editors and reporters distort the news deliberately for ideological or economic reasons. Instead he argued that most American journalists take an essentially benign view of their leaders, refusing to believe that the beating to death of prisoners represented the norm, but rather that it was out of the ordinary. Britain and much of the rest of the world, however, are quite prepared to believe the worst of the US.[8]

News can also change with *The Times*. In the days of capital punishment, a murder trial would receive substantial coverage as the defendant's life was at stake. In the *Daily Telegraph* of the mid-1800s, an important court case 'could easily rate eight columns, or 15,000 words'.[9] There was also more agricultural news, as more people farmed the land. Furthermore, until relatively recently, married women were often referred to as housewives, because … well, many of them were.

Nowadays because more people travel there is more in the media about travel and holidays and even about the health problems associated with travel such as thrombosis and germs carried in the air conditioning of aeroplanes. Britain is more multi-ethnic and the news to some extent reflects this change, but in many people's eyes it does not reflect it in a positive manner.

In fact, it was found that British Muslims were very suspicious of television coverage of the September 11 attacks and the war in Afghanistan. Of 300 people questioned, many complained there was little debate or analysis and too much sensationalist reporting. They also felt there was an anti-Arab and anti-Muslim bias to the coverage and that reporting of the Middle East as a whole and Palestine in particular was biased towards Israel. Their dissatisfaction with the news service led to a significant increase in the use of the internet for information.[10]

Objectivity

As we can see, there are many influences and pressures that can affect the selection and presentation of news that make it impossible for it ever to be objective (undistorted by emotion or personal bias – *Collins Dictionary*). And as we discussed in Chapter 1, there is controversy in the profession over whether objectivity, even if it were attainable, is desirable.

Yet objectivity is still an important principle. Many journalists believe they are the eyes and ears of the public and strive to tell stories truthfully and neutrally. But it is unlikely they see and hear events in the same way as the people they represent. Even if they did, it would be hard to check, as the news journalist may offer a judgment, but rarely offers an opinion about an incident or an issue on which they report. In fact they try very hard to stay aloof.

Journalists use interviewees and sources to tell their stories and put across a range of views. However, as the journalist has to choose whom to interview to represent the arguments, some views and facts will be left out. Of those chosen, how much prominence in the story each view is given will also lead to bias. Even without overtly expressing their opinions (though nowadays some are more willing to give their analysis of a situation), journalists are putting their personal stamp on a story through selection.

News sources

So far we have looked at the various influences which affect news stories. Now we will consider some of the more important sources of news. These are studied in more depth in Chapter 8.

News releases

Many journalists will argue that the contents of a news release can rarely constitute real news. But like them or not, they are an important source of stories for the media. Each day in the post, and increasingly by fax or email, dozens of publicity handouts arrive in the newsroom from the many organisations trying to garner publicity for themselves and what they do or make. Campaign groups, political parties, government departments, private businesses, charities, police press offices, public relations firms – all use these news or press releases to canvass the journalist.

And they work. While many news releases do end up in the real or electronic rubbish bin, those that survive (along with material from the emergency services and the courts) are the most common source of stories for the local media. And in a news sense many of these releases carry important information about what is going on in the community. They may announce new plans by the council to run sports camps during the summer; a dog show to be held next month; a new police superintendent being appointed; disabled access being built onto the town library.

Journalists, however, have become increasingly and some would say excessively reliant on news releases as staff numbers have been reduced on local and regional papers. Organisations wanting publicity have seen the opportunities and moved in. Some employ teams of press officers producing material written in a news style and often including interesting quotes from people relevant to the news release and photographs – sometimes even videotape. It is not unusual for these press officers to claim that their releases are published in the media almost or totally unchanged.

Reproducing a news release almost verbatim may not matter when it is from a local arts group about a forthcoming exhibition. All that may be required is a quick rewrite in the style of the news organisation and a note in the diary. However, while news releases are a useful source of information about, for instance, organisations, businesses or local and national government, it is important to keep in mind that these handouts are essentially propaganda. They never, or almost never, contain bad news or negative information, and to get the most out of them, the journalist has to learn to interpret what is written, pick out the facts that are interesting or controversial, and be prepared to question the sender.

If we were to take the definition of news given by the media magnate, William Randolph Hearst, that 'news is something somebody does not want publishing ... all the rest is advertising', then we would never use a press release as the basis for a story. But most journalists believe they do have a place as long as they are handled with a degree of scepticism. (See Chapter 8 for more on dealing with news or press releases.)

Diary stories

As we've said, news releases often carry information about future events that the media will want to cover, such as royal visits, sports events, important anniversaries, council meetings, agricultural shows, village galas, festivals, court cases and inquests. All these should be entered into the newsroom diary along with any other event of interest that the journalist comes across. If a church is raising money for a new roof, the journalist needs to note down any fund-raising events and when the work on the roof will begin. The newsdesk is then able to assign a reporter when the time comes.

That news can be planned this way, that it is not all unexpected crises and disasters, may surprise some, but the fact is that most news is pre-planned and reporters are assigned in advance. For the journalist this affords some opportunity for preparation (if they are not too busy with other stories). If an important person is visiting the area, they could find some biographical information or look up when they last visited. If they are covering a council meeting, they could research any controversial items. Even if the journalist is very pushed for time, they can usually find a few minutes to consult the cuttings files.

Many, but not all, news organisations have a library of cuttings. These are files of material from newspapers cut out and stored in a library by subject. Large organisations file material from all newspapers; local or regional papers may just keep articles published in their own papers and these could be stored in a filing cabinet. Increasingly, cuttings libraries are being stored electronically and of course you can use the internet to search media organisations for past news items on almost any issue. This does not help if the story is very localised. If there are no cuttings files, it is a good idea, as soon as you start work, to begin one of your own of all the stories you cover and any 'running' (on-going) stories which you may be asked to work on.

News conferences

News or press conferences are an important source of on-diary news. They can be called by all sorts of organisations for all sorts of reasons. The police might call a news conference to give details of a murder and ask for the media and the public's help to catch the killer. A charity such as Age Concern might call one to release new statistics or a report on how many elderly people live below the poverty line. A company may organise a news conference to launch a new product. Some news conferences are regular briefings such as 10 Downing

Street's daily briefings of the news media, in which a spokesperson for the Government will answer questions from the assembled reporters and attempt to influence the political news agenda of the day. And that is the danger of news conferences: they are a useful means for the organisation calling them to try to gain publicity or put across its point of view.

All news conferences should be treated cautiously. We will discuss how to report on news conferences in Chapter 7, but the journalist should remember they are staged in order to gain news coverage – they are not news events in themselves, such as a flood or a murder or a royal visit. The organisation calling the news conference has a message to sell. It is imperative that the journalist does not end up becoming just another public relations officer for them – they are not paying you, the news organisation is, and it is paying you to think sceptically. What is the news value of this event? It is up to the newsdesk to decide whether or not this message is worth reporting. They may decide it isn't, but that there is something else newsworthy which is not the main message of the news conference, so it's worth going along to the conference in order to pitch a question.

Pseudo events

News conferences can come under the definition of 'pseudo events', defined by the social historian Daniel J. Boorstin. He has argued that increasingly what we see, hear and read as news is actually made up of pseudo events.

> [A pseudo event] is not spontaneous, but comes about because someone has planned, planted or incited it ... it is planted primarily (but not always exclusively) for the immediate purpose of being reported or reproduced. Therefore, its occurrence is arranged for the convenience of the reporting or reproducing media.[11]

For example, if a football club calls a press conference to announce they have just signed a new player then they are orchestrating the news.

The need for the media to have dramatic pictures has led to staged events that resemble spontaneous events. A demonstration called purely to gain publicity about something the demonstrators oppose is more picture-friendly and therefore more likely to get coverage than a few angry residents sitting around a kitchen table. Politicians too use photo opportunities to manipulate the news agenda: Tony Blair at a high school fielding questions from the pupils, President George W. Bush kissing a baby in Northern Ireland.

Off-diary stories

These stories are not handed to the reporter on a plate and they are also more highly regarded than the diary story. It is in the uncovering of off-diary stories that a young reporter can make their name; it is also where the prized exclusive tag is won. In the search for good off-diary stories a network of well-placed contacts, as mentioned in Chapter 1, is invaluable. Off-diary stories also require much more work to uncover and, at times, more creativity. The reporter must rely on their own observation, news sense and powers of persuasion. By being observant, the journalist spots the handwritten notice on a telegraph pole by a playground appealing to dog walkers not to toilet their dogs in the playground. A keen news sense helps them realise that knocking on a few doors and interviewing users of the playground as well as dog walkers could lead to a good story. Their powers of persuasion will convince a reluctant interviewee to tell them how insensitive dog walkers have made it impossible for her children to play there.

The news agenda at BBC Radio 4's *World at One*   Case Study

John Rigby, assistant editor at *World at One*, explains how the news is selected:

We have a very heavy domestic political agenda. That is our meat and drink. If we are not doing domestic politics then we are not doing our job.

It is about power, about the way that power is used by the people who have it. My role and that of the people here should be about finding out what's being done in our name. There are people doing things on our behalf and some may prove to be good and some prove not to be so good and it is our job to find out.

We are on air for 30 minutes, so we can only really do two or three stories. So we need to decide what the listeners really need to know. They can catch up with the other news in the bulletins. We also have a responsibility to veer away from trivia – which is particularly important in the domestic political arena and we are very careful about the selection of stories.

To a degree, foreign news can get in. Usually it will be either something of very great significance or an event of such magnitude that we could not *not* cover it. So today the Sri Lankan peace process, while it is very good that it is going on, does not have a hope of getting on to WATO. It isn't new and the other thing it doesn't have is a British Government angle. The foreign stories we cover are to do with the way the British Government conducts its foreign affairs.

So in this Blair administration the crucial ground is the public services – health, crime and education.

In dealing with spin we are fortunate in that the editor and the presenter [Nick Clarke] are both well versed in the operation of political parties, either from having worked within them or from dealing with them for many years. So they are well attuned to when the Government is trying to pull the wool over their eyes. We deal with it in one of two ways: expose the spin or ignore the story.

Selection is hard on days like this when there is not much news around. In a way it is easier when you come in and there are reams of paper to read and we have to fight our way through it. My [story] list today is of average length but there was really only one story – asylum seekers from Afghanistan being paid to go home.

We try not to lower our standards and to cast the net slightly wider, we work a bit harder and keep the standards high. The other thing we can do if our commissioning department is working well is to get hold of prepared material.[12]

Summing up

One of the most important skills a journalist can have is solid news judgment. Newsrooms rely on their journalists to bring in original well-sourced stories. They also trust them to be able to identify good stories among the dross in council agendas and find fresh or novel angles on stories given to them. However, in the search for news, the journalist should never depend too much on news releases and public relations departments. There should be a definite divide in the journalist's mind between news and advertising.

Editors also expect their journalists to know for whom they are writing. All journalists should have a clear idea of their audience, as it is only by knowing your readers, listeners and viewers that you can deliver what they want or need to know in a voice they wish to listen to and can come to trust.

REVIEW QUESTIONS

1 What factors did Galtung and Ruge discover as important to newsgatherers when deciding what is news?

2 What does the journalist covering a news conference need to bear in mind?

3 List the characteristics of a pseudo event.

EXERCISES

1 Take a recent story and check it against Galtung and Ruge's list of news tests. How many does it pass?

2 Think of some ideas for news stories that are suitable for your local newspaper or radio station. Test your ideas against the news test list.

3 Compare the news agendas of one broadsheet and one tabloid newspaper. How many stories were the same and how differently did they treat them?

4 Here is a list of stories. Try and rank them in importance for national media and local media around Manchester. See note 13 for an answer.

   i   A search is continuing for two 14-year-old girls who disappeared three days ago on their way home from school in Oldham.

   ii Health officials have closed a swimming pool in central Manchester because it is considered a health hazard.

   iii The bank interest rate is remaining unchanged this month for the third month running.

iv   The owner of a Robin Reliant has been fined and banned from driving after police caught him on the M4 motorway doing 104 mph.

v   A 35-year-old, married headteacher has resigned after admitting having a sexual relationship with a 17-year-old student in Sheffield. The two claim to be in love.

vi   The Government says it is planning to introduce a £10 charge to all adults to visit their GP.[13]

FURTHER READING

Engel, M., *Tickle the Public*, London: Indigo, 1996.
Harris, G. and Spark, D., *Practical Newspaper Reporting*, 3rd edn, Oxford: Focal Press, 1997.
Hartley, J., *Understanding News*, London: Routledge, 1995.
Hetherington, A., *News, Newspapers and Television*, London: Macmillan, 1985.
McNair, B., *News and Journalism in the UK*, London: Routledge, 1999.
Negrine, R., *Politics and the Mass Media in Britain*, London: Routledge, 1994.

Notes

1. Guy Patrick, 'England's World Cup rests on this foot', *Sun*, 4 April 2002; Steve Doughty, 'House prices to leap again', *Daily Mail*, 4 April 2002; Suzanne Goldenberg, 'Israel tightens its iron grip on 1m Palestinians in West Bank', 4 April 2002.
2. Johan Galtung and Mari Ruge, 'The structure of foreign news', *Journal of Peace Research* 2 (1), 1965: 64–9. Quoted in, among others: Ralf Negrine, *Politics and the Mass Media in Britain*, London: Routledge, 1996, pp. 120–21; Richard Rudin and Trevor Ibbotson, *An Introduction to Journalism*, Oxford: Focal Press, 2000, p. 6; Hetherington, A. *News, Newspapers and Television*, London: Macmillan, 1985, p. 6.
3. Martin Bell, *In Harm's Way*, London: Penguin, 1995, p. 99.
4. Nazia Y. Ali, Thoebe Y.S. Lo, Victoria L. Auvache, Peter D. White, 'Bad press for doctors: 21 year survey of three national newspapers', *British Medical Journal*, 6 October 2001. See www.bmj.com.
5. Andrew Kohut, 'Self-censorship: counting the ways', *Columbia Journalism Review*, May/June 2000. see www.cjr.org.
6. *Guardian*, 17 February 2003.
7. Pew Research Center and *Columbia Journalism Review*, quoted in Kohut, *op. cit.*
8. David Greenberg, 'We don't even agree on what's newsworthy', *Washington Post*, 16 March 2003.
9. M. Engel, *Tickle the Public*, London: Indigo, 1996, p. 34.
10. 'After September 11: TV News and Transnational Audiences', Milena Michalski, Alison Preston and Richard Paterson of the British Film Institute and Marie Gillespie and Tom Cheesman of the

Open University. The research was funded by the Broadcasting Standards Commission, the Independent Television Commission, the British Film Institute, the Open University, National Everyday Cultures Programme and the Economic and Social Research Council. The research was presented to an International Symposium at the Stanhope Centre for Communications Policy Research, London, 9–11 September 2002. See www,bfi.org.uk.

11. Daniel J. Boorstin, *The Image: A Guide to Pseudo-Events in America*, New York: Atheneum, 1961 as quoted in M. Mencher, *News Reporting and Writing*, New York: McGraw Hill, 2000, p. 170.

12. Personal Communication, 21 August 2002.

13. Nationally the top story is obviously the £10 charge to adults who visit the doctor, because this will affect everyone and may stop some people visiting the doctor when they need to. This is a story of enormous importance. Other stories of interest nationally will be the search for the 14-year-old girls. After three days, police will begin to wonder why they have not been in touch and whether some harm has come to them. The Robin Reliant story is an amazing tale that should have the tabloids in a state of excitement, as should the 35-year-old teacher and her 17-year-old lover. The bank interest rate, because it is not changing, will probably only merit a paragraph or two in the broadsheet papers and a short mention in the business news on radio and television. The closing of the swimming pool would only be of interest outside the area if someone had become ill or died as a result of its unclean state. If not, then it is a precautionary measure of significant interest to the people of Oldham but nowhere else – unless it is indicative of the state of swimming pools through-out Britain and then it could be used as a news peg. For the local editors the top story is likely to be the missing girls, although some will run with the £10 GP charge if they cover national news, as some local radio stations and large regional papers do. The closure of the swimming pool, as already mentioned, is an important story as it will affect a large number of people in the area. The speed-ing Robin Reliant will receive extensive coverage, not because it will affect anyone but because it is so extraordinary. But the teacher and student story will not be of interest unless either party comes from the Manchester area.

3

TELLING THE STORY
GRAMMAR AND STYLE

Good writers make it easy for their readers by using

- everyday words
- short, simply structured sentences
- active verbs
- anecdotes and quotes.

Good journalism requires good writing. If stories are badly written, readers desert the paper, listeners and viewers switch over, and the journalist has failed to pass on important news to the audience. Good journalism also requires accurate writing. Carelessly written stories can mislead the audience.

Good writing makes it easy for the reader, listener or viewer. It speaks directly to them in language they understand and explains clearly what has happened and how it affects them. Paragraphs are short so as not to overwhelm the reader and arranged to encourage them to stay with the story. And what distinguishes the great writer is the ability to call upon just the right word or phrase to sum up the mood and describe the scene. As John K. Hutchens, the American journalist and book critic, put it: 'A writer and nothing else; a man alone in a room with the English language, trying to get human feelings right.'

This chapter introduces the principles of news writing. It concentrates on print journalism; writing for broadcast is covered in Chapter 5. Many of the fundamentals apply to all journalists, as all journalism is about telling stories (real-life ones) skilfully, no matter what medium you work in.

What follows is aimed at helping you achieve an effective approach to writing – but it is just a start. You have to spend time developing your own style through reading many other writers and by writing as much as you can. English is a rich and flexible language – all the so-called rules can be broken by experienced writers. But there are some basic pointers.

Putting the message across

In order to write clearly you have to think clearly; you have to know what the story is and then tell it in the most direct and succinct manner. Ernest Hemingway summed up the writer's art when he wrote: 'My aim is to put down on paper what I see and what I feel in the best and simplest way.'

The language the writer uses must be appropriate for the audience. There is no point in using big words or specialist jargon that your audience will not understand. Good writing is not about talking down to people. It is about taking a complicated idea or issue and explaining it simply, and to do that requires understanding and intelligence. Even on the most erudite broadsheet, it is important for the journalist to tell serious and complex stories in a clear and engaging way. A reader should never have to go back over a passage because it is unclear.

The best reporters can, despite their own intimate understanding of a story, explain simply and powerfully what it means and why it matters. They use interesting quotes and anecdotes to bring life and colour to their work. And all good journalists use as few words as possible. Readers are busy people with better things to do than plough through paragraphs of turgid prose.

Good writing – some rules

- Be clear about what you want to say.
- Say it with everyday words.
- Use simple sentences.
- Use short paragraphs.
- Use verbs in the active voice (i.e. verbs with a personal subject performing the action).
- Report the details, draw a picture with words.
- Use a style that is natural to you.
- Keep adjectives to a minimum.
- Use strong quotes close to the beginning of the story.
- Avoid clichés as far as possible.

The do's

Be clear and say it simply

Before sitting down to write any news piece you have to know what you want to say. What is the message you want to get across? If you are unclear, get advice from your editor or spend more time thinking it through. If you are not sure, your readers will also be unsure why they should be reading or listening to your article. The writer in the extract below does not give a clear message:

Two Craven College students were working in a hotel in France at the centre of a gastric flu crisis.

The schoolchildren, from East Yorkshire and Devon, had been enjoying a skiing holiday when they caught a virulent strain of gastric flu and were rushed back to the UK. (*Craven Herald and Pioneer*, 22 February 2002)

The reader is left wondering whether the students were on holiday or working and why schoolchildren would be attending Craven College. It eventually becomes clear much later on in the piece that the college students and the schoolchildren are not one and the same. The college students were working at the hotel where the schoolchildren were staying when they became ill.

The hotel staff had to work flat out, as did the Craven College students, who were working abroad for the first time.

They had to clear up vomit, and make sure everything was disinfected and that the sick children had everything they needed.

The writer had not established the story in their own mind when they sat down to write. The first two paragraphs could begin two separate stories. They need to be combined in order to give the reader the full picture. The story could have started this way:

Two Craven College students on work experience at a hotel in France found themselves nursing a group of British schoolchildren who had fallen ill with gastric flu.

A reader should always be told early on why a story is of importance to them. Bear that in mind as you read this from the front page of a free weekly newspaper.

Far North Holdings Limited is acquiring SJ Ashby Boatbuilder Ltd of Opua.

The Ashby boatyard comprises more than 2 acres of land and an additional 2 acres of seabed for floating maintenance facilities including a new consent area of 4,531 square metres to be used for additional floating facilities.

The purchase of the boatyard is seen by Far North Holdings Limited as a major step towards the realisation of the Opua Development Plan, the primary focus of the company's development programme.

When we read the first paragraph our immediate reaction is, so what? The intro should answer that question. It doesn't, neither does the next paragraph. The reader needs to know how the deal will affect them. What the journalist does say is that Far North Holdings Ltd sees it as a step towards the realisation of the Opua Development Plan. So we know what the press release says, but what do other players think, important residents and local politicians? Later on we hear there are 'some concerns locally' but no specifics.

And use of the words 'acquiring' and 'comprises' alienates us even further. They are signs that this story was taken straight off a press release. Ordinary people do not use such words. If you ever said to a friend, 'I am acquiring a car', the first thing your friend would ask is, 'What do you mean? Are you being given it or are you paying hard cash?' They'd also want to know (though you may not wish to tell them) how much you are paying. Interestingly (evidence of the story coming from a press release with little re-writing) we are not told how much Far North Holdings paid for SJ Ashby Boatbuilder Ltd. Some writers believe that by using long words they will sound learned, but it often has the opposite effect, making them appear pompous or ignorant.

This article lacks important details, but we are left with numerous questions. What is the Opua Development Plan, does it mean spanking new pontoons, housing, an extension to the marina – what? What are 'floating maintenance facilities'? Don't use words like facilities, say what they are: pontoons, platforms, floating toilets, what? And where are they – which two acres of land are we talking about? What will this deal mean for the people of Opua? New jobs? What on earth is a new consent area? Good writing answers rather than throws up questions.

Sir Harold Evans, former editor of the *Sunday Times* and *The Times*, says all news writing should relate to human beings (as mentioned in Chapter 2). We should know how a story affects the readers. And we should know through words that give us specifics: 'Abstract words should be chased out in favour of specific, concrete words. Sentences should be full of bricks, beds, houses, cars, cows, men and women. Detail should drive out generality'.[1]

Here is an example of how to call up a picture with words. It is an article written during the foot-and-mouth crisis in Britain of 2001:

> The three slaughtermen are young, cheerful and clear-eyed. Killing is their business and they have never known trade like this. In the spring morning light, they were on a farm near Wigton, Cumbria, shooting more than 100 cows and 500 sheep. Now the Ministry of Agriculture has told them to go to Jim Hutcheson's Scale End farm near Penrith.
>
> Our mobile death-squad rattles through the lowlands south of Carlisle. We carry, in the back of a 16-year-old white van, cartridges, stun guns, decontamination suits, blue overalls, rubber gloves, sprays, wellington boots, forms and all the paraphernalia of modern slaughter.
>
> The landscape is flat and desolate. Most farms here have been condemned and there are no animals in the field. The white smoke of incineration pyres drifts into the van. We pass decomposing sheep carcasses piled high in the corner of fields where they have been waiting days to be picked up. The sickly stench of death hangs over some farms, while in others the cattle and sheep lie sweetly together, their limbs spread-eagled, bellies swelling, tongues rigid and out.

Scale End was condemned on Sunday, but in the watery sunlight it seems normal. At the end of a long closed road is a tangle of ancient and modern buildings. Seven lambs play in a small paddock behind the farm. A bull stalks the yard. The cattle low quietly in the barns and the sheep are penned in a field beyond. This is spring. There are daffodils on the roadside, birds in the hedges, and the Hutcheson family is waiting expectantly, as if for a relative. (*Guardian*, 31 March 2001)

The piece is not sentimental but the descriptions are powerful and full of observations. The reader is transported to that white van, and travels through the countryside looking out of the window seeing what foot-and-mouth has done to Cumbria and its farms.

Use the active voice

As we've said, short sentences are the ideal, but how they are constructed is also important. It is usually better to use the active voice or the Subject – Verb – Object model than the passive voice. The person or thing doing the action (subject) is followed by what they are doing (the verb) and to what (object). For example, 'A roof tile (S) killed (V) a woman (O) when it fell from an office block.' If we put this in the passive voice (O-V-S) it would read 'A woman (O) was killed (V) by a roof tile (O) when it fell from an office block.' This is not so effective. And, incidentally, many sentences could begin with the words 'A woman'.

Notice that in the article from the *Guardian* above the active voice is used throughout and it is the more potent for it.

Most broadcast sentences follow the Subject – Verb – Object model. For example, 'A large hurricane (S) is approaching (V) Miami (O) this morning'. In the passive voice (O-V-S) it would read like this, 'Miami is being approached by a large hurricane this morning'. The sentence loses some of the power and much of the surprise.

We must also avoid using too many subordinate clauses.

A hurricane, given the name Lizzie and with winds of 120 miles per hour, which has already devastated several Caribbean islands killing three people and leaving hundreds more homeless, is approaching Miami where it's expected to hit around lunchtime today.

This sentence is too long and too convoluted. While newspaper readers could look at it again until they understood it, most probably they would give up and go to another story. Radio and television audiences would have an even harder time, being given only the one chance to hear and understand. It needs to be broken up into several easily digestible sentences.

A hurricane, which has already devastated several Caribbean islands, is expected to reach Miami at lunchtime today. Hurricane Lizzie, with winds of over 100 miles an hour, has killed three people and left hundreds more homeless.

Use anecdotes

These can bring stories to life and take the reader right into a situation or to the scene of an incident.

> At a recent editorial meeting, Martin Newland, editor of the *Daily Telegraph*, stopped in mid-discussion to launch into a long, speculative disquisition about the nature of the relationship between Brad Pitt and Angelina Jolie. 'From the way they look at each other in these photographs', the editor concluded, 'they haven't shagged.' (*Guardian*, 5 September 2005)

The anecdote tells more about the move in the news agenda of the *Telegraph* towards popular culture under the then editor Martin Newland than several columns of analysis could.

The don'ts

Don't repeat words

In journalism we try not to repeat a word too many times, but some young journalists take this rule a little too far. Among students of journalism a common mistake is to go to absurd lengths to avoid repeating the word 'said'. Instead they use 'stated', 'added', 'explained', 'insisted', 'laughed', 'alleged', 'blurted out', 'commented' (very popular) and 'observed'. I've even had students write, 'proceeded to tell me', 'informed me' and 'addressed his views on'.

Don't bury your quotes

Good quotes add colour and energy to an article and should never be wasted by burying them too far down.

> Visibly shaken, the Queen Mother's loyal aide Billy Tallon paid tribute yesterday to the woman he served for more than half a century.
> 'She was the most remarkable person who ever lived,' said the head of her household. 'She was absolutely wonderful; there is no other word to describe her. It is just too heartbreaking for words.'
> 'I hope I was a good retainer to her. I worked for her for 51 years.' (*Daily Mail*, 2 April 2003)

Through Billy Tallon's words we can feel his loss. At the same time we are given a glimpse, by someone who knew her well, of the Queen Mother and the loyalty she inspired.

A potentially dry story is here spiced up with some pithy words from the foreign secretary, Jack Straw:

> The European Union faced crisis last night as make-or-break talks to agree a new constitution ground into deadlock.
>
> A gloomy Foreign Secretary Jack Straw warned Europe's leaders at the Brussels summit they needed the hand of God to get over the problems.
>
> He said: 'It is a matter with the Almighty. I do like placing a bet but I am not placing any money with any bookie on whether this is going to finish.' (*Daily Mirror*, 13 December 2003)

Don't be clichéd

Inexperienced reporters can be forgiven for believing that by employing clichés as often as possible they are buying into the language of journalism – that this is the way to write news copy. So they will write: 'Residents are up in arms at a council bid to axe the local bobby-on-the-beat.' And: 'Feathers flew when angry schoolchildren found their friendly seagull, Jack, was to be pushed off his perch on the canteen roof.'

While all journalists reach for clichés in a crisis, good writers try to describe what happened in an original way.

When it comes to clichés, sports journalists come top of the league. As one admitted in an interview for a trade journal, it is partly because the nature of their work affords them a restricted vocabulary. Whatever the reason, it seems these days in football journalism 'scored a goal' just isn't exciting enough. Instead players 'find the back of the net', 'slot one in' or waste 'gilt-edged opportunities' by 'striking wood' in their efforts to 'make the net bulge'.

Clichés cannot and should not be done away with altogether. Used sparingly they can add interest, but, overused, readers begin to disregard them. In some cases they sound hysterical, in almost all cases they sound stale.

Writers must avoid saying: 'A policeman was gunned down in broad daylight during a foiled bank heist'. It is better to write: 'A policeman was shot dead when he interrupted a bank robbery this morning.' It is more precise.

Writers who overuse clichés usually also have a penchant for adjectives. They will stick in, almost without thinking, certain adjectives when writing about certain subjects. For example, why are child victims always little or tiny? Why are even remotely attractive women described as pretty, striking or even stunning? The same applies to verbs, nouns and other parts of speech. Fires always rage with firemen wearing breathing apparatus struggling for hours to bring the blaze under control. Ambulances rush victims to hospital. Why is any unfortunate incident, no matter how trivial, always referred to as a tragedy?

The problem is that after a while overused words are cheapened in the reader's mind. Nothing can now be 'big'; it has to be 'mega' or 'gigantic'. And if a couple missing out on a holiday because of a strike by air traffic controllers is a 'tragedy', how do you describe the September 11 attack on the World Trade Center? Maybe this explains why the *Daily Star* headline on 12 September read: 'Is this the end of the world?' Clearly it wasn't, but there were few words left to reflect fully the horror of the incident. Adjectives need to be deployed sparingly or the reader stumbles through the swollen lines. Take this example from a local paper:

> What was once a safe river where children used to play in their favourite swimming hole, lined with willows that shielded historic 150-year-old homesteads from the main road and providing a haven for native birdlife, is now an ugly exposed scar marring the usually picturesque view.

Not only is this sentence far too long, at 48 words, there are so many adjectives we lose the main point of the sentence – that a previously safe river for children is now an ugly scar. Getting in the way is a 21-word description of the river. The sentence needs some brutal editing:

> It was once a safe river for children to play in – willows lined its banks, shielding 150-year-old homesteads from the road and providing a haven for birdlife. Now it is an ugly scar.

Breaking the sentence into two helps the reader to follow the argument. Several unnecessary adjectives have been cut: 150-year-old is historic – you do not need both – and the description of the river tells us it is picturesque. I have cut the passage from 48 to 36 words and, I would argue, lost none of the meaning.

Other unnecessary adjectives include:

> The *enormous amount* of £200m – the figure tells you it is an enormous amount.
> *Brutal* murder – there are few times when murder is kind and that is a story in itself.
> *Innocent* bystander – bystander implies they are not involved.
> *Totally* exhausted – exhausted.
> *Completely* gutted – gutted. Arguably 'completely gutted' is acceptable in some circumstances perhaps to distinguish from cases when part of a building is destroyed but the rest is left standing. Mostly it is unnecessary.
> *Vast majority* – most.

Verbiage of any kind wastes the reader's time, so be careful not to pad your piece with non-essential words. If you ever find yourself using words like 'really', 'basically' or 'there is no doubt that', which mean nothing, cut them out.

Here is another writer trying too hard – this time to convey emotion:

Furious students have been forced to take an AS-level exam again – after a college blunder meant an entire class was entered for the wrong exam.

Fuming parents and students have slammed the disgraced college officials and were tonight angry that a whole year of studying has been wasted. (INS News Group Ltd in Reading, 21 August 2002)

The writer didn't need to use 'furious' and 'fuming'; one adjective would have been enough, although I would argue neither was needed as the facts indicate the students would have been upset. By using both, the writer is cheapening the emotion. In fact the later use of 'angry' seems incongruous – are they fuming or merely angry? Either way we know he is adding topspin, and we disregard it. 'Slammed' and 'disgraced' are also unnecessary and 'slammed' is an ugly cliché. Other clichés used further on in the article include 'cock-up,' 'probe', 'stormed' and 'howler'.

Don't use 'officialese'

Journalists are interpreters between specialist sources and the general public, translators of scientific jargon into plain English, scourges of obfuscation, mystification, misinformation. Or they should be.[2]

It is very easy for journalists to pick up words that are constantly being used around them. The words and phrases become so familiar and ordinary that it is tempting to reproduce them in copy.

The danger of officialese is that it is used either to sanitise the reality such as military jargon during a war (surgical strikes) or government cuts (reviewing, reorganising) or firms laying off workers (downsizing, rationalising, restructuring), or to make the very straightforward look more complicated. It is also difficult for the public to understand, and so it is up to the journalist to translate it into ordinary English. Medical jargon can be particularly abstruse – pyrexia, for example, just means a high temperature.

During the Iraq War in 2003, the military unleashed a battery of jargon on journalists. While some news organisations made it clear to the reporters on the ground that they did not want them using military language, others willingly employed it. The audience was suddenly hearing terms such as 'embeds', short for embedded journalists, which meant journalists who were assigned to a particular military unit. Those who were not assigned to a military unit were called unilaterals. How many members of the public were confused by these terms?

It's not just the military that uses officialese. Local journalists will find plenty weighing down press releases, agendas and reports from local and regional councils, health authorities and the police. This press release from Lincolnshire County Council is typical of the releases sent out by local authorities:

> LINCOLNSHIRE Social Services is working on plans to provide support services for families of disabled children in partnership with the voluntary sector. The new scheme will address issues raised in a 2001 Best Value Review and help move forward a subsequent Improvement Implementation Plan.
>
> It aims to realign spending to provide support for more families, expand the range of services available, and work in partnership to modernise the service and make it more responsive. There are a number of specific benefits because voluntary organisations:
>
> - are generally seen as less stigmatising and threatening than statutory services, leading to better partnership working with children and families
> - offer flexible, responsive services and respond flexibly to need – local government systems are slower to change. (Lincolnshire County Council, 20 June 2003)

There is plenty of jargon to be avoided here. For example, what is the 'Improvement Implementation Plan'? What is meant by 'realign spending'? What is 'better partnership working with children and families'?

The rule is, if you don't understand the terminology then the audience certainly won't. That means you have to ask: 'What do you mean by that in plain English?' It is common for politicians, experts, etc. to try to bamboozle journalists with long words or complicated phrases. It can make what they are saying sound more acceptable. Never be afraid to ask for clarification. See Chapter 8, 'Handling a news release', for more on this.

Common grammatical errors

Despite few people nowadays knowing their subjunctives from their past participles, and fewer having the rules of English grammar exhaustively taught to them in school, journalists have to know the basics of English grammar because bad grammar distracts the reader and at its worst it can give the wrong message.

This is not a book on grammar, and there are some excellent texts out there already (see the end of the chapter for some suggestions for further reading), and so I am going to highlight only the most common errors that students and young journalists make.

Punctuation

In news writing, we use relatively short sentences usually containing only one main idea, therefore we do not employ a lot of punctuation marks. But if we have to punctuate a sentence it is important to get it right. Otherwise we may say something we didn't mean to.

'The two inch-long sprats covered a garden shed and several lawns in the area.'[3] Now that would be a miracle. There needs to be a hyphen between 'two' and 'inch' and not between 'inch' and 'long'.

The purpose of punctuation is to produce clarity and assist ease of reading, and the better it is done the less obtrusive it will be.[4]

Make sure you know the correct use of commas, full stops, colons, semicolons, dashes and exclamation marks. Student and trainee journalists often abuse the last. They should be used after genuine exclamations, such as 'Oh! Help!' or 'Get me out of here!' Not after statements such as 'It was the biggest vegetable I'd ever seen.' Or 'You'd never guess they were only six years old.'

The apostrophe

In my experience as a teacher of journalism, the most common error students commit is to misplace the apostrophe. It is put where it is not needed and left out when it is. The error is one some journalists never grow out of. The apostrophe is correctly used in two cases only: to indicate possession and when there are one or more letters missing, as in can't and wouldn't.

With the possessive in the singular, as in Karen's house and Charles's car, the possessive apostrophe comes before the 's'. When it is a plural, the apostrophe comes after the possessive 's', as in the horses' tails and parents' wishes. Plurals not ending in 's' (children, sheep, deer) follow the singular rule, i.e. the children's toys.

The possessives of hers, its, theirs, yours and ours do not carry an apostrophe. These are already considered possessive so we do not need to add the possessive apostrophe. However:

> Syed Mohammed Ali Bukhari, to use his full title, is a 26-year-old left-arm pace bowler who's career in his native Pakistan has yielded 170 first class wickets. (*Independent*, 25 April 2002)

This should read 'whose' not 'who's', which would be 'who is' or 'who has'.

We do not use an apostrophe with simple plurals such as several governments, schools, bananas, MPs and the 1980s. Sometimes we get an example of misuse of both the simple plural and the possessive apostrophe in the same paragraph:

> US website www.realtor.com. will give you details of Frank Sinatra's £12.5 million Beverly Hill's estate and recent celebrity house sales. Meg Ryan got £6m for her's but Kelsey Grammar bagged a mere £720,000. (*Observer*, 24 March 2003)

Two mistakes here: Beverly Hills is a plural, so we don't need an apostrophe. 'Hers', as we have seen, does not carry a possessive apostrophe. The use of the apostrophe in 'Sinatra's' is correct.

A mistake very often made by students and some working journalists is to write 'it's' when they mean 'its'. *It's* means it is whereas *its* is the possessive: 'It's a dinosaur which often ate its own young.'

Is it singular or plural?

If the subject is plural then so should the verb be. A subject and its verb must agree in number (singular, plural) and in person (first, second, third). Verbs tell us what a subject is doing or what state it is in.

> Threats of chemical and biological attack are terrifying enough but revelations that Al Qaeda has also developed a radioactive dirty bomb underlines the fact that these terrorists will stop at nothing to cause death and destruction. (*Daily Express*, 1 February 2003)

The subject is 'revelations' – not Al Qaeda – therefore the verb 'underlines' should be plural, 'underline'.

> Jerry Hall, cellulite, and what a difference two years makes. (*Daily Mail*, 8 July 2003)

The subject is 'two years', so it should read,

> Jerry Hall, cellulite and what a difference two years make.

Hanging or dangling participles

> Walking through Mayfair around midnight, three cars stopped within five minutes – one after the other, all driven by young women – and I was asked by their drivers if I'd like to spend some quality time with them. (*Daily Mail*, 22 March 2002)

Perhaps it is coyness that is behind the failure of the writer to mention himself until 22 words into the sentence. Whatever the reason, the writer's mistake is to suggest that what are walking through Mayfair around midnight are the three cars – which of course is impossible. This is known as a hanging or dangling participle and it occurs when the word the participle, in this case 'walking', is intended to describe is not there. When you have a clause like this at the beginning of the sentence, the subject should come next.
Better to say:

> Walking through Mayfair around midnight, I had three cars stop beside me within five minutes.

It is worth noting that in journalism such phrases are used sparingly. Also note that modifiers such as only, even, almost, nearly, should always be placed immediately before the word they describe. 'He only fell ill a month ago.' 'He fell ill only a month ago.' 'The president even decided to ignore his own advisers.' 'The president decided to ignore even his own advisers.'

Tautology

Even the best writers can fall into the trap of overstating their case – or saying the same thing twice just to make sure we have the message. An article about an Everest mountaineer said: 'He has spent the past week acclimatising and getting used to the cold weather' (*Isle of Man Courier,* 17 April 2003).

We get the message. Neither do we miss it in the next two examples.

> Police chiefs today said alcohol was to blame for dozens of drink-related incidents in Exeter. (*Exeter Express & Echo*, 27 December 2001)
>
> Potentially, Mr Pashley's find could have important applications in medicine and the chemical industry. (*Independent*, 20 February 2003)

'Potentially' is 'could have'. This sentence should read 'potentially . . . has.' Other examples include:

> 'In her/his own home' – at home. Either they are at home or not.
> 'Absolute perfection' – perfection.
> 'The building was completely destroyed' – the building was destroyed. Something can't be a little bit destroyed. Either it is destroyed or it isn't.
> 'Rise to a crescendo' – rise to a climax.

Neither, nor/either, or

Do not mix the two. If you start with neither, follow with nor; if you start with either, follow with or.

> Detectives suspect the Ingrams abandoned the pager idea that evening. Neither Pollock, of Cowbridge, Vale of Glamorgan, and Powell of Bristol, Avon was in court. (*Daily Express*, 8 April 2003)

It should read neither, nor. But the verb 'was' is correct in the singular.

As likely . . . as

This is often mistakenly used as, 'as likely . . . than':

> It blames much of the problem on new recruits, with drivers said to be twice as likely to drive through a signal at red during their first year than when they have acquired more experience on the job. (*London Evening Standard*, 13 May 2003)
>
> During the 1990s Germany had more than twice as many doctors per 1,000 population than the UK; and the French were only just behind. (*New Statesman,* 19 May 2003)

Note: Writers need to take care when using prepositions; for example, it is bored with or by but NOT bored of.

Poor spelling

Poor spelling is not acceptable. Journalists should always be checking their copy for spelling errors. Make sure your spell checker is set to UK English. There are many differences between US and UK spelling. For example, words that end in ise or isation or yse in the UK, such as recognise, realise and analyse, are spelt with a z in the US – recognize, realize and analyze. There are numerous other variations in spelling, some of the most common being:

US	UK
anemia	anaemia
archeology	archaeology
behavior	behaviour
catalog	catalogue
center	centre
defense	defence
fulfill	fulfil
gray	grey
imbedded	embedded
installment	instalment
license	licence [noun – in the UK license is the verb]
maneuver	manoeuvre
marvelous	marvellous
mold	mould
neighbor	neighbour
practice	practise [verb – in the UK practice is the noun]
program	programme
theater	theatre
tire	tyre
traveler	traveller

Homophones (words that sound the same but are spelt differently and have different meanings) are difficult to spot with a spell checker but many mistakes can be picked up this way. Homophones that commonly cause problems are listed below.

- **Complement/compliment**. To complement means that something is fitting (e.g. 'the curtains complemented the decor'). To compliment means to voice appreciation (e.g. 'he complimented the hostess on the meal').

- **Effect/affect**. To effect means to bring something about (e.g. change). To affect means to influence (e.g. 'He was very affected by the accident').
- **Elicit/illicit**. Elicit means to draw forth whereas illicit means forbidden.
- **Lead/led**. Lead as a noun is a metal ('The toy was made of lead'), whereas led is the past tense of the verb 'to lead' (e.g. 'He led them out of the building').
- **Peddle/pedal**. 'A steroid-pedalling East German spy' (*Guardian*, 12 June 2003) conjures up a wonderful cycling image. It should have read: 'A steroid-peddling East German spy'.
- **Phased/fazed**. Phased, means by stages, whereas fazed means perturbed or unsettled.
- **Piece/peace**. Piece is a portion of something, whereas peace is the absence of war or disturbance.
- **Pore/pour**. Pore means to study closely (e.g. 'He pored over the report'), whereas pour means to flow freely, rain heavily.
- **Principle/principal**. Principal means chief, something that is first in importance, whereas principle is a moral or physical law or rule.
- **Stationery/stationary**. Stationery means goods available from a stationer (e.g. writing paper), whereas stationary means not moving (e.g. 'The car was stationary')
- **Waste/waist**. Waste (as a noun) means something superfluous, whereas waist is a part of the human anatomy.

Summing up

While style cannot be taught, certain principles should be borne in mind when writing. Use short sentences and paragraphs, although not all the same length, as this makes for dull prose. Keep your language plain and free from jargon, clichés and puns. Choose your words carefully and write in specifics (bed, chair and table, not furniture; trees, plants, rivers, not landscape), use the active voice not the passive ('thieves stole a laptop and two cameras', not 'a laptop and two cameras were stolen'. 'Neighbours organised a demonstration outside the school', not 'a demonstration was organised outside the school by neighbours').

There are many students of journalism who do not believe grammar is important. I hope this chapter has illustrated the problems that can arise when it is not taken seriously. It is no good shoving a comma in wherever you think a pause should be, or believing the spell checker will pick up every spelling error. You have to be constantly on the look-out for mistakes and read and re-read your copy.

REVIEW QUESTIONS

1 What is a hanging participle?
2 Why do good writers avoid using clichés?
3 List the most important rules of good writing.

1 Rewrite the following passage from a tabloid in plain English free from clichés and hysterical adjectives:

Vile racist Ian Gaskell was caged for life yesterday after he refused to show any remorse for a merciless knife attack on a taxi driver.

The homeless dosser plunged an eight-inch kitchen blade into father-of-two Zafar Iqbal's eye when he asked for his £1.10 fare. (*Daily Star*, 20 October 1999)

2 Have a look through a local paper and see how many references you can find to the following:

(i)   Close-knit communities
(ii) Tragic or tragedy
(iii) Communities 'coming to terms with' something.

How many other clichés can you find?

3 Spot the homophones in the following sentences:

(i)   Waist not want not.
(ii) If we are low on notebooks you need to make sure we have more ordered on the stationary list before June 1. After that a new system of ordering is being fazed in.
(iii) If you tell him you are an admirer of his, you are more likely to illicit a positive response. He is easily flattered and it effects his judgment.

FURTHER READING

Bagnall, N., *Newspaper Language*, Oxford: Focal Press, 1993.

Evans, H., *Essential English for Journalists, Editors and Writers*, London: Pimlico, 2000.

Gooden, P., *Who's Whose? A No-nonsense Guide to Easily Confused Words*, London: Bloomsbury, 2004.

Hicks, W. with Adams, S. and Gilbert, H., *Writing for Journalists*, London: Routledge, 1999.

The New Fowler's Modern English Usage. ed. R.W. Burchfield, Oxford: Clarendon, 1998.

Strunk, W. and White E.B., *The Elements of Style*, New York: Macmillan, 1979.

Truss, L., *Eats, Shoots and Leaves*, London: Profile Books, 2003.

Waterhouse, K., *On Newspaper Style*, London: Penguin, 1993.

Notes

1 Harold Evans, *Essential English for Journalists, Editors and Writers*, London: Pimlico, 2000, pp. 32–33.

2 Wynford Hicks, et al., *Writing for Journalists*, London: Routledge, 1999, p. 9.

3 *Collins Dictionary of English Usage*, London, 1970, p. 236.

4 *Guardian*, 7 August 2000.

4

■ STRUCTURING THE STORY

Good writers structure their stories clearly and logically, enticing the reader in and encouraging them to keep reading. They

- focus on the strongest angle
- write an intro that attracts the reader
- set out the facts faithfully and lucidly
- structure the story to encourage reading
- use the most compelling quotes early on.

There is a feeling among some editors that in this fast-moving society where people lead busy lives and there is so much demand on their time and attention, we need to tell the story in the first three paragraphs for the 'scanners'. That is a particular writing skill.

However, it is dangerous to think that the reader cannot be drawn into the story beyond the third par. The job of the writer is to structure the story thus, but, depending on the subject matter, extend the attention span of the reader. He does this by good writing. That is clear, unambiguous, clean setting out of facts. (Bob Bounds, editor, *Kentish Express*)

The intro/cue

The first paragraph – intro in newspapers in Britain, lead in America, cue in broadcasting – of any news story is the most important. It is the shop window of the story and you want a reader skimming the paper or listener/viewer only half tuning in to sit up and take notice. 'Hey, commuter – this is important for you' or 'You parents stop cooking tea and listen – this could affect your kids' or 'The strangest thing happened – just look at this.'

A motorist who killed a grandmother while using his hands-free mobile phone was jailed for four years yesterday. (*Daily Mirror,* 13 December 2003)

House prices are continuing to soar, jumping almost 9 per cent in the past five months alone and defying earlier forecasts of a slowdown in 2002, according to new figures yesterday. (*Guardian,* 4 April 2002)

A disabled boy of six who was kept out of his school's Christmas Nativity play and school photographs was unlawfully discriminated against and deserves an apology, a tribunal has ruled. (*Daily Telegraph,* weekly edition, 24 December 2003)

Giving cod-liver oil to babies reduces the risk of getting diabetes later in life, researchers have found. (*Daily Mail,* 15 December 2003)

A gran aged 60 has dumped her hubby to wed a 22-year-old Moroccan she met on the internet. (*Sun,* 21 August 2003)

Notice that the first paragraph must explain to the reader, ideally in no more than 30 words, why they should read on. It has to have something particular to say. It usually mentions who is involved in the story – either as a source of information (a tribunal, researchers) or of action (a disabled cyclist, a gran) – something of what happened and where it happened. Notice too that it is important to point out how fresh the information is; putting a time to it such as 'tonight' or 'yesterday' can do this.

Identifying the intro

The intro writer has to give the gist of the story – enough to arouse the curiosity of the casual reader or listener without getting bogged down with too many facts. It is for this reason that it can be the hardest paragraph to write. This attempt failed:

The latest campaign, launched at the beginning of this month, focuses on the ever-present fire risk from cigarettes.

Fires started by cigarettes kill more people than any other kind of fire, accounting for one third of all fatal fires within the UK.

More worryingly, the number of deaths due to cigarette fires within the UK have [sic] increased by 11 per cent. (*Isle of Man Courier,* 14 March 2002)[1]

All intros should tell the reader something new and interesting – this story admits that it is just the latest campaign and moreover that it was launched two weeks earlier, a bit whiskery in anyone's estimation. Moreover we are not told whose campaign this is (the source) and so we don't know how authoritative it is.

However, the story gets much more interesting in the second and third paragraphs with the strongest news angle or 'peg' buried at the end of the third paragraph – the number of deaths caused by cigarette fires going up by 11 per cent. This is what makes it fresh and relevant to the reader. But how many readers would have been attracted enough by the opening paragraph to read far enough to discover this important new information?

The intro and succeeding paragraphs could have been written like this:

> [The] number of people dying in fires caused by cigarettes has risen sharply – in fact more people are killed in these fires than any other kind.
>
> New research shows the number of people who die in fires started by cigarettes has gone up by 11 per cent. They now account for one third of all fatal fires in the UK.
>
> A campaign was launched this month to highlight the danger of fire from cigarettes.

Identifying the nub or main point of the story is one of the most challenging parts of the journalist's job and is illustrated very well in a scene from the film of Annie Proulx's book, *The Shipping News*. A new recruit on a local newspaper has written some copy about an accident in which a person was killed. It begins: 'The policeman ate breakfast at the Cod Cape diner before he arrived at the accident scene.'

This is a common mistake among trainees, to start at the beginning and write chronologically. But people are not interested in the contents of the policeman's stomach – they want to know about the accident. Did they know the person who was killed, or did it happen at an accident black spot?

A more experienced reporter takes the new recruit under his wing and tries to explain the job.

Old hack:	'Your spelling is fine and I've seen plenty worse grammar. But finding the centre of your story – the beating heart of it – that's what makes a reporter. You'll have to start by making up some headlines. Short, plucky, dramatic headlines. Now have a look. What do you see? Tell me the headline?'
New recruit:	'Horizon fills with dark clouds.'
Old hack:	'Imminent storm threatens village.'
New recruit:	'But what if no storm comes?'
Old hack:	'Village spared from deadly storm.'

The seasoned reporter tries to isolate the effect of the storm and answers the 'so what?' thoughts that a reader may have with the 'horizon fills with dark clouds' intro. That intro, like the first one the new recruit wrote, 'the policeman ate breakfast . . .' is chronological. It takes too long to get to the best bit. And it is not how you would tell the story to a friend. If you witnessed an accident on your way to class or to work you would not relate it to a friend by beginning: 'I woke up this morning and, as it was a bit cold, I put on my warmest jacket before setting off. On the way, as I came round the corner, you'll never guess what I saw. There were bodies everywhere.' No – you'd rush up to them, grab them by the arm and say:

> A car ran into three students just on the corner outside the college. I saw it all, it looked like a war zone – all three were on the ground. Two doctors from the hospital

across the road came out and were treating the worst injured, a young woman, before the ambulance came. The police had the car driver and were asking him questions – he looked really shaken up.

And that, pretty much, is the intro and the next couple of paragraphs. A little trimming and polishing perhaps but it could read something like this:

A student was seriously injured and two others knocked to the ground when a car ran into them as they crossed University Road this morning.

Doctors from City Hospital treated the most seriously injured, a young woman, at the roadside before she was transferred by ambulance to the intensive care unit. Her condition is serious but stable. The other two students are being treated for cuts, bruises and shock.

Police are still questioning the driver and say they don't yet know how the accident happened.

Intros need to answer the questions – 'who' is involved and/or 'what' happened. Essentially every story is either about a person who has said or done something interesting or important or an event that is of significance or interest to the audience. The reporter must decide which is the more important.

When I started a tutor said to me, if you've just come through Indian lines and have been shot through the heart and have a few seconds to live what would you tell General Custer?

There are 400 Indians out there. (Ian Lockwood, editor, *Craven Herald and Pioneer*)

When it's a 'who' intro

When the person is more important than the event, the reporter has to highlight that person and describe what it is they have said or done. If the person is instantly recognisable, then it is appropriate to exploit that in the intro by naming them. People will read the story just to know the latest on this person.

David Beckham had to rush his frantic wife Victoria to hospital in a scare over their unborn baby. (*Sun*, 21 August 2002)

A broken-hearted Sir Paul McCartney yesterday bade farewell to his friend and 'baby brother' George Harrison. (*Daily Express*, 1 December 2001)

Gordon Brown clashed with MPs last week over claims that his Budget plans will force thousands of teachers and nurses to pay higher tax. (*Daily Telegraph*, weekly edition, 24 December 2003)

If the person is less well known but the story is still centred on them, either what they have said or what has happened to them, then some form of introduction is needed.

The rail regulator, Tom Winsor, last night risked controversy when he decided that there were no grounds for him to rule that Virgin rail was charging excessive fares on the west coast main line between London and Glasgow. (*Guardian*, 1 December 2001)

Here the label is the person's job title whereas this next intro uses a description of parts the person has played in films – of course, they could also have said 'former footballer':

Movie hardman Vinnie Jones avoided jail yesterday – after he threatened to have airline staff murdered during a boozy rampage on a jet. (*Sun*, 13 December 2003)

It can sometimes be difficult to know when to give a label to someone; another newspaper decided it didn't need to introduce Jones. The rule must be when in doubt, tag them.

Vinnie Jones attacked a TV boss on an airliner and threatened to have the crew murdered, a court heard yesterday. (*Daily Mirror*, 13 December 2003)

Sometimes the person is totally unknown and it is necessary to identify them to the reader by a label or a description. If their job is of interest, use that as the label, otherwise fall back on 'a man' or 'a woman' etc. It is not usual to name them in the intro.

A grandmother in a wheelchair has admitted being the mastermind of a network of pickpockets who stole hundreds of dollars over two years, in shops from Miami to Atlanta. (*The Times*, 3 April 2002)

A shopkeeper stabbed in the eye by teenage thieves told yesterday how he had been robbed more than 100 times in four years. (*Daily Mail*, 3 April 2002)

But look at this:

Eighteen-year-old maths student, Tony Printer, was last night approached by seven youngsters while he was waiting at a Hyde Park bus stop.

The gang started throwing fireworks at him and two fellow students from across the street in the early hours of yesterday.

We are immediately expecting to recognise, at least by name, Tony Printer, or to be told an absorbing tale in a longer news feature. Of course we don't know him and neither is this intro the start of a news feature; the story needs reworking. The intro is not who the student is or the approach of the youngsters (the reporter has written the story chronologically and using the passive voice 'was approached by'), it is the attack.

A gang of youngsters threw lighted fireworks at an 18-year-old maths student as he waited at a Hyde Park bus stop.

Tony Printer and two fellow students were lucky to escape uninjured from the attack early yesterday.

The rewritten version goes straight to the action and uses the active voice 'youngsters threw lighted fireworks at a student' (see Chapter 2 for more on the active voice). It labels Tony Printer in the first paragraph and names him in the second.

When it's a 'what happened' intro

If it is an event that is important or unusual, the reporter must highlight what is of significance or importance. The reporter uses the intro to describe what happened as briefly and dramatically as possible.

> The Scottish salmon industry is facing a major threat today from an invasion of foreign jellyfish capable of devastating its stocks. (*Evening Standard*, 21 August 2002)
> At least 11 people were killed and 20 injured in clashes between Hindus and Muslims in India's western Gujarat state, police said yesterday. (*Guardian*, 1 April 2002)
> The Bank of England yesterday began reissuing the new £5 notes, almost three months after their release was suspended when it was discovered that some serial numbers could be rubbed off. (*Daily Mail*, 22 August 2002)

Writing the intro

Having isolated the main news point and identified if it's a 'who' or a 'what' story, the reporter should ask themselves if there is a dramatic word or phrase which would add colour to the intro. In the examples above, plenty of powerful and emotive words have been deployed: threat, invasion, devastating, killed, clashes, suspended.

> A bear snatched a sleeping baby from her pushchair and mauled her to death. (*Sun*, 21 August 2002)

Here the words 'snatched a sleeping baby' convey the violence and unexpected nature of the bear's attack much more vividly than 'took a baby'.
It is important in the intro to highlight whatever makes the story out of the ordinary:

> It is worth concentrating on the opening word of an intro and visualising how that will look in print. I would not suggest that you 'sex-up' the opening sentence, but understand that 'A lone gunman held up a security van outside a bank this morning' is preferable to 'Police are hunting a man who held up a security van this morning' – simply because virtually every crime story can begin with the latter. (Bob Bounds, editor, *Kentish Express*, Canterbury)

If it's a complicated story don't try to explain everything in the intro.

> A transatlantic trade war threatened to reignite this week after the United States rejected a final ruling from the World Trade Organisation that its protectionist tariffs

on foreign steel are illegal and the steel industry accused it of planning fresh measures. (*Guardian Weekly*, 13 November 2003)

The intro is too long at 41 words and tries to cram too much in. It should really stop after 'illegal'. The accusations by the steel industry can be explained later on.

Sometimes a writer will take a straightforward intro and try to spice it up. This, from a regional daily, has been given a little too much flavour:

> A high-flying curry conman is leaving airline operators with a nasty taste by fleecing them for expensive flights in publicity stunts where he claims to be flying Indian meals to the rich and famous around the world.

So far we have concentrated on the hard news intro. In most newspaper journalism this is the preferred option for news stories. Hard news writing is the straightforward telling of the facts of an incident or an event yet to happen, starting with the most interesting or new. What happened, when and to whom? And, if known, how did it happen and why? However, there is another approach to writing news intros.

The delayed or drop intro

This can work well in background news pieces and features where a delay in delivering the punchline can be very effective. These pieces are usually longer than a hard news story and can afford to hold back the main angle, either until the end of the intro or until several paragraphs in. It's what Keith Waterhouse called the intro which starts to 'sell' a news story, as opposed to the hard news intro which starts to 'tell' a news story.[2] But delayed or drop intros have to be handled with care. If the writer fails to arouse the interest of the reader, they will not read far enough to get to the main point of the story. Which of the following do you believe is the more effective?

Straight news intro

> A mum faces 15 years in jail after allowing three of her four children to become severely sunburned. (*Daily Mirror*, 22 August 2002)

Delayed intro

> She had taken her children for a fun day out at the county fair. But when police saw three of Eve Hibbit's youngsters in their pushchairs, she was arrested – because they were sunburned. (*Daily Mail*, 22 August 2002)

Here the delayed intro is very effective:

> While the sacred waters of the Ganges are said to cleanse the soul and ease the path to heaven, no such claim has been made for the River Aire in West Yorkshire. Until now. (*Daily Telegraph*, 21 August 2002)

We are engaged right away – why is the River Aire now being thought sacred? We want to read on and find out. In the next paragraph we are told what would have been given to us straightaway in a hard news intro.

> Hindus and Sikhs want to scatter the ashes of relatives in the Aire and have asked the council for permission on behalf of many British Asians who cannot afford to travel to India.

The narrative intro

Keith Waterhouse also mentions another type of intro: one that starts to tell a 'story' (as opposed to one that starts to tell a 'news story'). This narrative style is often used if the story is best told in a chronological way.

> Farmer Ted Jewell arrived at the slaughterhouse in Eastleigh, Hants, yesterday to find that the back of the lorry was completely empty. The eleven-stone pig he had loaded at the start of the journey had completely vanished.[3]

What reader wouldn't want to know what happened next? The narrative style can also be deployed on background pieces to the day's main news story – for example, an important court case. Here is the start of an article about rescue workers in New York following the terrorist attacks:

> Out of the iron grey cloud tinged with pink came the rescue workers yesterday, their faces smeared with grime, their tread heavy, like miners at the end of a shift. Most had been working since Tuesday without rest.

Stories that start this way have to enthral the readers. This one succeeds. It continues:

> Jonathan Sanchez, a construction worker, swaying with sleeplessness, was going home for a couple of hours before returning.
> 'I could not stop,' he said. 'I could hear people in there, screaming for help, but I couldn't get to them. I heard someone shouting, 'get me out', but you cannot get through all the rubble. It's going to take another three days to get under that rubble.'
> (*Daily Telegraph*, 14 September 2001)

Breaking stories and breaking the rules

As we've said, for breaking stories or big events, the hard news intro works best. In these cases it is about getting information across as quickly, clearly, memorably and accurately as possible in few words. These intros went on the news wires on 31 August 1997, the night Diana, Princess of Wales died. Clearly they are meant for journalists to use as the basis for the stories they will write but they are worth looking at for how concisely they tell the news.

00:54 PA
Diana, Princess of Wales, was badly injured in a car crash in which another person is reported to have died in Paris shortly after midnight, according to French news agency reports.

00:58 Reuters
PRINCESS DIANA SERIOUSLY INJURED IN A PARIS CAR ACCIDENT – POLICE

01:15 Reuters
Harrods heir Dodi Al Fayed was killed in an accident, which occurred shortly after midnight police added.
A police spokesman said the accident happened while the princess's car was being pursued by press photographers on a motorcycle.

04:41 PA
Diana, Princess of Wales has died, according to British sources, the Press Association learned this morning.

04:50 Reuters
PARIS – PRINCESS DIANA DEAD – FRENCH MINISTER

There are always times when rules can be ignored. A truly momentous event happens, but one that was witnessed by most people on television. How should the writer approach telling the readers? On the morning of 12 September 2001, after terrorists had attacked New York and Washington, the writers of the lead stories took several different approaches. One used a narrative style, one wrote an eyewitness piece, others tried to make the intro as up to date as possible, others still wrote only the bare facts.

> Dozens of people – one man said that he had seen at least 40 go 'bam, bam, bam' – met their wretched end in a freefall. (*The Times*, 12 September 2001)

This is the start of the eye-witness report on the front of *The Times*. On the inside was a straight news story:

> Terrorists laid waste to the citadels of American capitalism and defence yesterday with co-ordinated attacks that destroyed the World Trade Centre [*sic*] in New York and struck the Pentagon in Washington, killing thousands and spreading fear and chaos across America. (*The Times*, 12 September 2001)

The intro is 39 words long but the facts set out are so powerful that the reader is carried along. The *Daily Mail* kept it shorter:

> In the most devastating and murderous terrorist attack in history, Middle East fanatics struck at the very heart of America yesterday. (*Daily Mail*, 12 September 2001)

Other papers started with the latest information.

> The US military is on a near war footing this morning following terrorist attacks on New York and Washington DC that left thousands dead and plunged the country into crisis. (*Financial Times*, 12 September 2001)
>
> President George Bush placed all United States forces on worldwide alert last night after a shell-shocked nation sustained its worst attack since Pearl Harbor at the hands of suicidal terrorists. (*Guardian*, 12 September 2001)
>
> The world was waiting with bated breath last night after terrorists launched the biggest attack on America since Pearl Harbor. (*Sun*, 12 September 2001)
>
> Shattered America last night vowed 'total war' against the monsters behind the worst terror attack in history which may have killed more than 10,000 people. (*Mirror*, 12 September 2001)
>
> It was the day America's luck ran out. The day you suspected might one day come but could not comprehend when it did – neither the dimension of the tragedy nor the motives [of] those who did it. And above all, perhaps, how they did it. (*Independent*, 12 September 2001)

The *Independent* chose a narrative style that concentrated on the effect on America of the attacks and delayed retelling until the fifth paragraph what, to be frank, almost everyone already knew.

What to avoid

As we've said, rules can be broken, but normally, when writing news intros, there are certain things you should avoid because they slow down the flow or hinder clarity.

Questions

Questions are rarely used in hard news intros. They are for setting out the facts of fast-moving events or breaking stories, not for leaving the reader guessing. But sometimes this approach works.

> A tiny British spacecraft was last night on the verge of solving one of the great mysteries: Is there life on Mars? (*Sun*, 15 December 2003)
>
> It is a problem faced by multinational companies: how do they tap into the concerns of local consumers to make their advertising more relevant? (*Guardian*, 21 August 2002)

Questions can be useful in features, especially the lighter ones. This was the intro to a health feature on the problems of excess wind:

> What do Zoe Ball and Kate Winslet have in common? Apart from tricky marriages, they're among a host of celebrities pretending to break wind on a Comic Relief commercial promoting baked-bean crisps. (*Daily Mirror*, 11 February 2003)

It's all about engaging the reader.

Quotes

As with questions, these should be used sparingly in hard news intros and often as only a few significant words rather than the whole paragraph being taken up with a quote. The stronger the quote, the better it works.

> Tony Blair predicted yesterday it would be 'very, very difficult' for EU leaders to strike a deal on a new treaty for Europe at their marathon summit talks this weekend. (*Daily Express*, 13 December 2003)
>
> The capture of Saddam Hussein was confirmed yesterday with the historic words: 'Ladies and gentlemen, we got him.' (*Sun*, 15 December 2003)

Starting with the date

Students writing their first intros often fall into the trap of answering the 'when' question instead of the 'what happened' and 'to whom'. Only occasionally is the date more important than the event.

> On Tuesday, 6th November, The Bassment was the venue for the resurrection of a monthly club night, 'Confused?' which had formerly been at the Hi-Fi Club.
>
> 400 people packed into Bassment, to witness Doctor Octopus and DJs 'Trademark' and Will Law electrify the ambience with hard beats and harmonies.

> On the morning of 14 November, Leeds Magistrates court found a young man guilty of shoplifting.

In these examples it is plain the date is not important. Starting with it slows the story down and can, if it's a few days old, make it old-hat. Neither of these intros tells the reader anything. In the first story the interesting information is in the second paragraph. In the second story we want to know the man's punishment and the details of the theft. What makes this theft different to others? Many court stories could start with this intro, so the writer needs to find the facts that make it interesting.

Promises in the intro which the story does not deliver

Do not jazz up the intro to a level where it is no longer accurate. If you claim villagers are seething over plans to allow a historic barn to be turned into offices, the story had better illustrate their fury and not show that they are just a little frustrated.

The ideal intro

In summary, good intros come from the reporter knowing what the main point of the story is. So the questions you must ask yourself are:

1 Does your intro highlight the most important or interesting point of the story?
2 Do the first six or seven words present a fact that will attract the reader?
3 Can it be read aloud without stumbling or gasping for breath?
4 Is your sentence structure simple enough for a reader to grasp the meaning at first reading?
5 Have you used the active voice?
6 Is it the preferable length – between 18 and 30 words?

Structuring the story

Good stories flow like honey. Bad stories stick in the craw. What is a bad story? It is a story that cannot be absorbed on the first time of reading. It is a story that leaves questions unanswered. It is a story that has to be read two or three times before it can be comprehended. And a good story can be turned into a bad story by just one obscure sentence.[4]

Once you've identified the intro, the rest comes more easily. But the process of structuring a story should begin as soon as a reporter is given an assignment. For example, when you are sent to cover a fire some some basic questions should spring to mind: Are any people injured? Anyone evacuated? How did it start? Is it an important landmark that has been damaged? How many firemen tackled it? With the answers to these questions comes a structure. Remember to use any strong quotes towards the top of the article (see Chapter 3 for more on using quotes).

Case Study: A reporter's thoughts on structuring a story

Let's meet a reporter and see how she goes about structuring a story. Viv Mason is a senior reporter at the weekly *Craven Herald and Pioneer* in Skipton, North Yorkshire. She has just received a phone call from a young man whose company is making a feature film, a romantic comedy, set in Skipton. She is interested but what makes the story even better is that the film company is run by four friends who all went to school in the town.

When I thought about the story I thought this is a nice human interest story. The important facts are 'what' (the film) 'where' (Skipton and Aireville School) and 'who' (these four young local men). I thought if I could highlight these facts it would be enough to make people interested.

So Viv has isolated the main points of interest and she starts writing.

I spend more time on the first couple of paragraphs than I do on the rest of the story, as the intro is really important for encouraging people to read on. It might be a page three lead so it needs to be about 300 words long. It also might go into *Target*, our free paper.

Her first draft is begun:

Four Aireville School old boys have reunited in the town to fulfil a mission.

After leaving school six years ago all the students went their separate ways in their working careers, yet each was linked in one way or another to the big screen.

Now the men have got together to make a feature film set in Skipton. The 185-minute romantic comedy 'Sleeping Genie' has been made possible through a Prince's Trust grant, and when finished will hopefully be taken to the Cannes Film Festival next year.

But Viv is not entirely happy:

Intros are so important and this one is a bit boring. I need to jazz it up. The fact that the four lads went to school and went their separate ways but in similar areas before coming together again is really interesting and I need to get that into the first couple of paragraphs. But it's not right yet.

I'll put the names further down as people will be interested and scan down to check the names so it will encourage them to read down the story. I can explain more about who the boys are then.

She starts again and, when finished, the piece is longer than she had planned and is placed in a prominent spot on page 5 of the paper. Her intro is more colourful, the main point is delayed to paragraph three and should draw the reader in to the story. Viv has been able to retain a local angle as well as explain how the boys' interests remained the same despite their years apart.

A life of scripts, clipper boards, out-takes and cuts beckons four former pupils of Aireville School who have picked Skipton to get their feet on the ladder to stardom.

After leaving the Skipton school six years ago, the four went their separate ways in further education – yet each was linked to TV, filming, programme production and the performing arts.

Now the men, three of whom still live locally, are about to begin the filming of a feature-length comedy, *Sleeping Genie*. All four have their part to play from directing through to acting.

The 185-minute script has been penned by Mark Thorrington, who is also supervising producer. In charge of the camera is Richard Allison while the film is being directed by Richard Jones. Taking a lead acting role is David Barclay. Since leaving school, both Mark, a chef, and David, an in-between-work actor, have worked extensively in theatre. Mark appeared in *Les Misérables* in the West End, while David created the 'Funnies' workshop, helping comic performers discover characters through improvisation.

'Both Richards have worked together, writing for Pathé and Meg productions. Their short film *Bugged* has had much critical acclaim at film festivals around the world,' explained Mark.

The men's latest venture has created interest across the country. 'There is a cast of around 20 people altogether, and for the leading parts we advertised in the Stage Magazine. We got more than 3,000 applications,' explained Richard Jones, who hails from Keighley and at the moment is carrying out bar work.

In the end they picked professional actors whose faces have yet to become familiar.

Sleeping Genie will be Reality Pictures' first feature film. It follows two best friends on two very different nights out, and will be filmed predominantly in and around Skipton, with other scenes shot in Keighley and Leeds.

The news triangle

News stories should flow logically from the first paragraph. They should have pace and no unnecessary elements should slow the story down. And even though readers won't see a structure, there is one. For hard news there is quite a strict structure. One way of looking at it is through the news triangle or inverted pyramid. Generations of journalists have been brought up on this (see Figure 4.1).

As you can see from the diagram, this formula for writing news shows that stories are very top-heavy with the most important information at the start and secondary information following on.

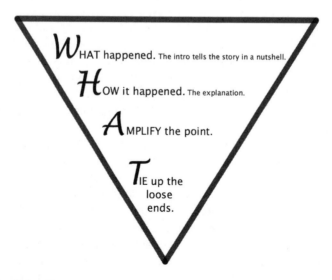

Figure 4.1   The News Triangle

1 The first paragraph of a story should give the reader the most dramatic or important information. There should be enough to tell them what the story is about, but still interest them enough to ensure they read on.

2 Next there should be some further explanation. How it happened or what happened next. The strongest quotes can go here.

3 Then amplification of the points already made. Perhaps telling the story again in further detail and more chronologically.

4 Finally, any loose ends should be tied up or further, less important information given.

The news triangle works well for the many news stories that have to be written quickly. And if they need to be cut to fit their allocated space on the page, they can be cut from the bottom, where the least important information is. The formula also helps the reader, who often wants to know what has happened but doesn't want to work too hard. The best writing has the material arranged in an order that is easy to understand and keeps the reader interested to the end. However, if the reader moves on after a couple of paragraphs they will have enough information to understand the main points. This way of thinking has, however, been challenged as restricting, especially if there is more than one element or theme to the story.[5]

Another way of thinking about organising stories is in units or thematic sections. This way the news writer can move from one theme to another. Take this two-theme story:

A group of disabled kids has been banned from advertising their Christmas production of *Grease* – by bosses of the star-studded version.

Theatre chiefs insisted the children from Oldham could only put on the musical if they did not promote it while the professional show was in nearby Manchester.

So despite practising for four months, the kids have been banned from putting up posters.

One angry parent said: 'It's disgusting – the kids worked so hard.'

About 110 children from four schools are in the show. More than 70 of them come from three special schools.

The professional *Grease* runs at the Palace Theatre from Wednesday until late January.

The cast, including Robbie Williams' pal Jonathan Wilkes and Pop Idol's Hayley Everetts, have sent a letter to pupils wishing them luck. (*Sun*, 15 December 2003)

Theme 1. A group of disabled children have been banned from promoting their musical *Grease*.

Theme 2. That it is people involved with a professional version of the same musical playing in nearby Manchester who have banned them.

• The intro outlines both theme 1 and theme 2.
• Paragraph 2 tells us more about theme 2.
• Paragraphs 3, 4 and 5 move back to theme 1 by describing the ban and reaction to it and telling us about the children.
• Paragraphs 5 and 6 explain more about the professional production and who is involved.

What is always important to bear in mind is, whichever approach you take, always keep information on one theme together. Don't jump about too much between themes or you will confuse the reader.

With a story that is written with a delayed intro or in more of a feature style, it is still necessary for the reporter to identify the main theme or themes. The delayed intro must then fit carefully into that theme, and supporting material, quotes etc. must still be arranged in a logical way.

> A year ago Rhys Evans's world was the interior of a sterile plastic bubble.
>
> The baby boy had no immune system and his parents feared that every day may be his last.
>
> But yesterday Rhys was free of his germ-like bubble and out playing in the park like any other 18-month old after a pioneering gene therapy was declared a complete success.
>
> After almost a year of hospital therapy, he can now go outdoors, get himself dirty and go home to his own bed.
>
> He was sealed off from the outside world after doctors diagnosed a rare congenital disorder. Even the most ordinary infection could have killed him.
>
> He was denied even a cuddle from his mother and father – and doctors told Mark and Marie Evans that Rhys might not live to see his fourth birthday.
>
> But the miracle for which they had prayed arrived in the form of a treatment never before used in this country.
>
> 'Now we live at home like a normal family,' said Mrs Evans, 31. 'He can walk and run around like any toddler.' (*Daily Mail*, 4 April 2002)

If we look at the start to this news feature in the *Daily Mail* we can see that the first couple of paragraphs introduce us to the 'who' of the story – Rhys – and set the scene. We are inside Rhys's world, but we are also advised that this was a year ago. So already a theme is being hinted at and worked towards. In the third paragraph the theme is revealed – pioneering gene therapy – and from that point on (18 more paragraphs) the story progresses in much the same way as a news story with a hard news intro. We hear how the therapy has altered Rhys's world and then we are taken back to the beginning of his treatment and talked through it chronologically with quotes from the delighted parents and the doctor in charge of the gene therapy team.

If we compare the structure of the above story to the way the same story was structured in the *Guardian*, it is possible to see how both feature-style stories and those written in a straight news style are built in thematic sections.

> An 18-month-old boy has successfully undergone pioneering gene therapy to correct a potentially fatal bone marrow condition that left his frail body incapable of fighting infection.
>
> Rhys Evans, a toddler unaware of his place in British medical history, is the first recipient in this country of a treatment that scientists hope will pave the way for conquering a host of other diseases, from haemophilia to cancers and cystic fibrosis.

But he and his parents are, for now, more interested in catching up on the time they lost from four months into his life, when repeated chest infections then pneumonia turned him into skin and bone, a mere 12lb (5.44kg) in weight, little more than a healthy newborn baby. (*Guardian*, 4 April 2002)

The reporter has chosen to handle the story as a straight news story and for this reason has spelled out the consequences of Rhys's treatment in the first paragraph and broadened it out in the second. It is in the third paragraph that he really shows us how desperate Rhys's situation was before the therapy. So the themes are the same but the order is reversed in the second example. The *Guardian* in the following 17 paragraphs, like the *Daily Mail*, reverts to a chronological telling of the story.

News questions

A report that is well structured and written should, whenever possible, answer the six news questions – who, what, when, where, how and why. When tackling any assignment, a reporter should keep them in mind and check, before handing the story in, that all the questions have been answered as far as is possible.

Eduard Shevardnadze's 30-year domination of Georgia ended in ignominy last Sunday after he stepped down as president, following weeks of street protests, in what his opponents hailed as a velvet revolution. (*Guardian Weekly*, 27 November to 3 December 2003)

Who	Eduard Shevardnadze
Where	Georgia
How	After he stepped down as president
What	30-year domination ended in ignominy
When	Last Sunday
Why	Following weeks of street protests in what his opponents hailed as a velvet revolution.

This intro is stuffed with facts. In 32 emotionally charged words (domination, ignominy, protests, revolution) it answers all six questions, but it is a bit overloaded. It is not necessary for all the news questions to be answered in the intro, as long as the writer ensures they are included somewhere in the story.

Transitional words

To cram all this information into the sentence above the writer has to use the linking words 'after' and 'following'. Linking or transitional words and phrases are a useful way of moving smoothly from one part of a story to another, but sometimes they are relied upon too much.

It seems our writer wished to add drama to the intro and describe the manner in which Shevardnadze had ruled and how that rule ended before spelling out that he had stepped down as president. To do this it was necessary to go back a step and say his domination ended in ignominy 'after' he stepped down. But the writer also had to explain a little of why he stepped down, so was forced to use yet another transitional word, 'following'. The result is a little clumsy. The writer could have kept it simple:

> Eduard Shevardnadze stepped down as president of Georgia last Sunday following weeks of street protests, in what his opponents hailed as a velvet revolution.

Other useful transitional words and phrases are:

Although	Moreover
And	Nevertheless
And so	Next
As	Nonetheless
Before	Now
But	On the other hand
Despite	Then
Even so	Whereas
Furthermore	While
However	With that
In addition to	Yet
Later	

Paragraphing

This chapter has talked a lot about structuring news pieces, but the humble paragraph is perhaps the most important component. Many young journalists do not see the need to organise their writing into easily digestible paragraphs. They present the reader with great blocks of text and when they do start a new paragraph it is not because they have started a new thought but because they think it is time to hit the return key. Such writers forget the paragraph is a wonderful device, designed to aid the writer to structure their work and the reader to enjoy it. The advantage of good paragraphing is that it coaxes the reader to tackle what you've written. They can see there are plenty of spaces in which to pause and no unreasonably long tracts of text to overcome.

> The purpose of the paragraph is to give the reader a rest. The writer is saying to him: 'Have you got that? If so, I'll go on to the next point.'[6]

Ask yourself if you'd want to read this story written by a young journalist on a first assignment:

> Vandals were seen fleeing the Camfield Hotel last night after attempting to flood the building's cellar, in Sims Lane. Eye-witness Karen Porter, the hotel's manager, managed to scare the gang away: 'I saw a group of young lads running away after they heard me opening the back door,' she said. 'They were using the outside hose to try and flood the cellar.' Mrs Porter and husband Graham have experienced many problems from local gangs since moving to the hotel. 'They tend to be aged between eight and sixteen years old. They have verbally and attempted to physically abuse customers and local residents,' said Graham. The police have been called to the areas regarding these offences. No action has been taken due to difficulties pinpointing the perpetrators.
>
> Over four hundred calls were made to police during the summer by residents reporting vandalism by youngsters . . .

There are 136 words in this 'intro'. Tackling it as a reader is the mental equivalent of taking a long hike in hilly terrain. Yet the young journalist has isolated the news point, collected lots of interesting facts and the sentences are clearly written. It is off-putting because of its size and the number of elements included in a single paragraph.

Avoiding overly long paragraphs does not mean that we always write uniformly short ones. Paragraphs have to be thought out with each one working towards the smooth progression of a story. Writers should ensure that a paragraph deals with only one topic and each new paragraph (perhaps using transitional words) either gives additional material on that subject or takes us to a new subject.

> POSH sausages have helped to boost sales of British bangers to record levels.
>
> More than £500 million worth of sausages were sold last year as the traditional dish enjoyed a resurgence in popularity.
>
> One of the reasons was demand for 'upmarket' sausages, according to the study by analyst Mintel.
>
> Recipes ranging from pork and leek to red Thai and lemongrass have proved a hit with shoppers looking for a dish with quality ingredients.
>
> Sales of premium sausages have grown from £137 million in 2002 to £166 million last year. (*Daily Express* (international), 20 September 2005)

The paragraphs in this story work hard to guide the reader. The intro tells us what is being claimed, that sausages are selling in record numbers because of 'posh' ingredients. This is substantiated in the second paragraph, which gives us some figures. In the third paragraph the writer sets out a reason for the record sales and we learn who the author of the study is. The fourth paragraph gives us more detail about the ingredients of the premium sausages and shows how sales of these have increased. The reader is always clear where they are being taken as the paragraphs lead them smoothly through the story.

Everything in a news story that is not common knowledge or obvious fact should be attributed. Unless a reporter has witnessed the event, then they should be looking to tell the reader where information or opinion stated in the story has come from. Letting the audience know the source of material makes them trust the report. It also allows them to judge for themselves how reliable the information is, based on their opinion of the credibility of the source.

> As many as 3,000 anaesthetic machines, nearly a third of those in NHS hospitals, do not have a device that could save lives in the event of an accident, contrary to European standards, doctors say today. (*Daily Telegraph*, 14 September 2001)

When we read that it is doctors who are the source of the story, we are likely to take the claims seriously. How would we feel if it were a claim by opposition politicians? Later in the story we learn the names of the doctors and that they have published their concerns in the *British Medical Journal*.

Who is the source of this next story?

> The young girl crouches low in the long, unkempt grass, eyeing the camera warily. With her deep-set eyes, prominent cheekbones and bobbed brown hair, she could almost be a fashion model in an artful pose.
>
> Then, suddenly, she lunges forward, barking fiercely, rearing up and throwing her hands towards the lens. For a moment she seems to be playing a silly game – a young girl showing off for the camera.
>
> But the bark is so horribly realistic, so deep and raw and bestial that no normal person could create such a sound. Her teeth are bared and her eyes are blazing with such ferocity that it is clear that this young woman is deeply, terrifyingly disturbed.
>
> This was the creature that confronted horrified police near the city of Kiev, in the Ukraine, when they were sent to investigate the case of a neglected child. (*Daily Mail*, 15 December 2003)

For the first three paragraphs, we are led to believe the reporter is there watching the child, only in the fourth paragraph does the reporter come clean and tell us it is the police in the Ukraine who are the source of the information. The writer has only seen moving or still pictures of the girl. This kind of news writing is very effective, but it is important the writer tells the reader they are writing a second- or third-hand account.

A reporter should attribute every statement of opinion or comment and every accusation. However, attributing statements does not constitute a defence against libel. Just because you quote someone else saying the local MP is a fraud does not protect you from a lawsuit as it is your news organisation that has published the statement. (For more on libel see Chapter 11.) So which statements of opinion and which accusations you publish

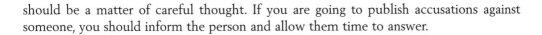

should be a matter of careful thought. If you are going to publish accusations against someone, you should inform the person and allow them time to answer.

Balance

Making every attempt to be fair to people you write about is not only about avoiding complaints, although it helps, it is also an ethical issue.

> Michael Jackson claims he was mistreated by police while in custody on child abuse charges and has photos to prove it, his brother Jermaine said yesterday.
> Jermaine, a former member of the Jackson Five, said: 'I won't go into detail. He will come out with the proof very, very soon.'
> When asked if it was physical mistreatment, he replied: 'Yes. You will see. The pictures will show you everything.' Police are said to have filmed Jackson's every move inside the police station.
> Santa Barbara Sheriff's Department said: 'At no time was he mishandled or subjected to any form of mistreatment.' (*Daily Express*, 13 December 2003)

These are serious charges made by a very well-known individual and as yet no proof has been given. It is right that the denial by the police is placed immediately after the accusations. If someone is being criticised or accused of something, then they have a right to give their side of the story. And they should be given the time to respond.

> In a controversial story a denial should be no lower than the fourth paragraph. 'Judges in libel hearings like that', a legal adviser told me recently. (Bob Bounds, editor, *Kentish Gazette*)

Showing both sides of an argument or, if there are more sides than that, making an effort to represent all views, allows the audience to have a more accurate picture of the issues.

It is particularly important to balance coverage of candidates in elections, although that does not mean giving each candidate an equal number of lines or minutes in every story published.

Laying out copy

Traditionally all copy had to be presented in a certain way to conform to the rules of the newsroom. Nowadays, as journalists key their copy straight into a computer and send it electronically, many of these rules no longer apply.

However, a journalist will still use a by-line (your name) and the story will still need a catch-line (the name of the story). It is important to use a catch-line that identifies the story. 'Fire' is not enough as it does not differentiate the story from other fires, whereas calling it 'restaurant fire' would. The same goes for accidents or burglaries. (The rules of laying out radio and television pieces are discussed in Chapter 5.)

Summing up

Don't throw away a good story because of sloppy structure. A news story can be well researched, accurate, scrupulously fair and balanced, well attributed, it can even be written in excellent news English, but if the intro is weak and the information is badly organised the reader or listener will not be interested.

Take special care with the intro. This is the most important paragraph and the most difficult to write. When organising the rest of the story, think of the inverted pyramid – the news point and the most important information at the top, supporting information in the middle and less important material at the bottom. Use strong quotes as high up as you can to give colour. And make sure you attribute information fully. From the moment you are given the story, be thinking about how you will approach answering the news questions.

Once your article is written, read it aloud to make sure it flows easily and logically to its conclusion. Once you have double-checked it for mistakes, you can hand it in or file the copy.

REVIEW QUESTIONS

1 What are the six news questions?
2 When should you attribute statements and why is attribution important?
3 Explain the rules of the news triangle.

EXERCISES

1 Using the rules of the news triangle, arrange these mixed-up paragraphs into the most logical order. (Answer is at the end of the chapter under Note 7.)

(i) The masks, selling for 99p, carry the importers' brand name Left Moon inside. Anyone who has one should return it to the shop.

(ii) It is believed hundreds of the masks have been bought and there is concern that they may be worn by children carrying pumpkins or lanterns that have lit candles inside.

(iii) Warnings have been issued about Halloween facemasks that could prove dangerous.

(iv) The masks have been on sale in a number of outlets including large chain stores and supermarkets.

(v) The masks have failed flammability tests and trading standards officers fear children could be badly burned if fake green hair attached to the masks is exposed to flame.

2 Look through several national newspapers and examine the intros they have chosen for the same stories. Answer the following:

(a)   How many of the news questions do the intros answer?
(b)   Do the popular papers take a different approach to the 'heavies'?
(c)   Which of the intros do you find the most effective and why?

3 Study your local paper and compare their intros to the ones you saw in the national papers. What differences do you find?

4 The following report has been sent in by one of the village correspondents to your paper. She is a part-time untrained reporter who keeps the paper aware of what is going on in her village and writes a regular round-up of events. Re-write her report as a three-paragraph news story:

This morning, while on her daily shopping trip to Oldton, 90-year-old Violet Robinson was knocked to the ground in Fast Road by a mugger, who also stole her handbag. She was taken to hospital, where she was found to have a broken arm and badly bruised leg as well as shock. She will remain in hospital overnight. The attack happened just outside the newsagents, Watson's. The manager, Sue Liddle, saw it all: 'He was a big lad, about 14 and wearing a hooded jacket. He just ran straight into her. She went flying. He grabbed her bag and was off. It happened so fast.'

Inspector Allan Green of Oldton station said his officer will interview Mrs Robinson, who's a widow, and Mrs Liddle this afternoon.

FURTHER READING

Pocket Fowler's Modern English Usage, edited by R. Allen, Oxford: Oxford University Press, 1999.

Evans, H., *Essential English for Journalists, Editors and Writers*, London: Pimlico, 2000.

Fowler's Modern English Usage, revised by Sir Emest Gowers, Oxford: Oxford University Press, 1965.

Hicks, W. with Adams, S. and Gilbert, H., *Writing for Journalists*, London: Routledge, 1999.

Keeble, R., *The Newspapers Handbook*, London: Routledge, 1998.

Mencher, M., *News Reporting and Writing*, Boston: McGraw-Hill, 2000.

The New Fowler's Modern English Usage, edited by R.W. Burchfield, Oxford: Clarendon, 1998.

Randall, D., *The Universal Journalist*, London: Pluto Press, 1996.

Strunk, W. and White, E.B., *The Elements of Style*, New York: Macmillan, 1979.

Waterhouse, K., *On Newspaper Style*, London: Penguin, 1993.

Notes

1 The writer uses the construct: 'the number of deaths have increased'. This is wrong – it should read: 'the number has'.

2 Keith Waterhouse, *On Newspaper Style*, London: Penguin, 1993, p. 132.

3 Damon, C. and Wilson R., *Weird News Stories*, London: Paragon, 1996.

4 Arthur Christiansen, editor at the *Daily Express*, 1933 to 1957. The quote is taken from www.northflow.fsnet.co.uk/Christiansen.

5 By journalists and academics including Keeble (1998, p. 123) and Mencher (2000, p. 131).

6 *Fowler's Modern English Usage*, Oxford: Oxford University Press, 1965, p. 434.

7 The order of the paragraphs should be: iii, v, ii, i, iv.

5

WRITING FOR BROADCAST

Broadcast stories are written to be read out loud. Radio and television journalists should be able to:

- write as they speak
- use the present tense
- include only one idea per sentence
- explain a story live from the scene
- use sound and pictures effectively.

INTRODUCTION

The purpose of broadcast news

> Just because your voice reaches halfway around the world doesn't mean you are wiser than when it reached only to the end of the bar. (Edward Murrow, US broadcast journalist, 1908–65)

News on radio and television is expected to deliver the latest and most important news to the viewers and listeners. Think of it as edited highlights of real events: the stories are short and analysis and opinion are kept to a minimum. And while newspapers can target their readership according to education, political leanings etc., broadcast news, especially on television, tends to be for a general audience. This means the bulletins must attract a large cross-section of people and be understood by everyone.

Another important difference is that, unlike newspapers, broadcast news is viewed and heard, not read. As a result, broadcast journalists work to a different set of rules to print journalists.

This chapter will first discuss the language of broadcast journalism and some general rules of writing for broadcast, and then look separately at working in radio and television. At the end of the chapter we join a television reporter on the road covering a typical story for a regional bulletin.

The language of broadcast news

> It is our job to communicate clearly and effectively, to be understood without difficulty, and to offer viewers and listeners an intelligent use of language which they can enjoy. Good writing is not a luxury; it is an obligation.[1]

Broadcast journalists write for the ears rather than the eyes. Their scripts should sound natural when spoken and avoid complicated sentences and unfamiliar words. It's an informal, conversational style, less hidebound by the rules of grammar than newspaper writing. However, this is no excuse for careless, clumsy or ungrammatical English. Good, clear and precise language is just as important, perhaps more so, in broadcast journalism as the audience has no second chance at understanding. If they miss the point at the first listening, they must wait until the next bulletin.

> Think. Don't write yet. Just think. Think about what you want to say and how best to say it: clearly, concisely, conversationally.
>
> Write the way you talk. But remember: in writing, spelling counts, punctuation counts, English counts. Avoid big words, odd words, weasel words, wasted words, fancy words, foreign words. Shun clichés. Don't distort, exaggerate or misrepresent. Can the cant.[2]

Broadcast copy demands to be written in good spoken English. When we talk to each other we use short sentences with a clear structure. And most of us use words that are easy to say and easy to understand. Here are some examples of copy-only stories from radio bulletins.

> The space shuttle, Atlantis, has landed safely in California – forty-eight hours after it was due to return to earth. Its planned arrival at the Kennedy Space Center in Florida had to be cancelled because of bad weather.
>
> A Halifax theatre group is to perform a play deemed so controversial it was removed from cinemas by its own director. The Red Brick Theatre company is putting on Anthony Burgess's *A Clockwork Orange* – about a brutal gang of futuristic thugs. The play's being staged next month.
>
> The World Food Programme has issued an urgent appeal for more supplies for hundreds of thousands of survivors of the two devastating earthquakes to hit El Salvador. It says international aid has run out – and the situation could soon become very serious.

A study of one thousand Gulf War veterans has concluded that there's no such thing as Gulf War Syndrome. A report in the *British Medical Journal* says there's no doubt that the service men and women are ill – but there's no single cause.

Keep stories brief

Broadcast stories, like those shown above, are short and to the point. Broadcast journalists must learn to tell their stories in far fewer words than print journalists, so every word must earn its place. If you counted up the words, you'd probably find the number contained in a half-hour bulletin on television would fit onto one page of a typical broadsheet newspaper and a two-minute radio bulletin would amount to one average-length story.

Keep it simple

As we have said, viewers and listeners get one opportunity to understand the story; therefore the writer should not overload their copy with informational clutter and even the most complex stories must be distilled to their very essence. By being told simply, the meaning is clearer.

> You must strike a balance between giving the viewer the benefit of your expertise and that same viewer clearly and completely understanding what you're trying to get across. Unfortunately, when in doubt, less experienced correspondents err on the side of including that extra fact or sequence which makes the story more difficult to understand.[3]

The most effective scripts are those written sparsely, using short sentences and containing as much natural sound as possible. Here is the start of a television package by the BBC's Middle Eastern correspondent, Orla Guerin. It's about a young Palestinian boy whom Israeli soldiers have caught wearing a suicide bomber's belt of explosives. It starts on pictures of the boy standing on his own. Soldiers sheltering behind army vehicles surround him at a distance.

> Poised between life and death, apparently wired up to kill.

> Soldiers taking cover, they've been waiting for an attack since Monday's assassination of Sheikh Ahmed Yassin.

> The troops shouting instructions. He tries to get free as Palestinians are held back. The army says by now the boy was terrified and didn't want to die.

> [An explosion]

> This, the controlled explosion after he'd got rid of the vest.[4]

This piece has plenty of breathing spaces, where the viewer can take in the pictures and listen to the natural sound. Each set of pictures (or sequence) has very little script and what script there is explains what the pictures mean but lets the story unfold naturally through them.

If what you've written doesn't sound right, it isn't. Would you ever say to your friends, 'He's a self-described pacifist' (CNN, 14 February 2004)? No. So it should not be used in broadcast journalism. Instead use a construction such as 'says he's a pacifist' or 'calls himself a pacifist'. What about 'lightweight footpath furniture' used in a story about tables and chairs being blown over in a storm (Sky News, 30 January 2004)? Again, you wouldn't talk like this. You would say they are tables and chairs from pavement cafés.

Attribution

In Chapter 4 we talked about the importance of attribution, i.e. telling the audience the source of your information. This way they can judge for themselves how reliable the information is by what they think of the source. In newspapers the source is usually at the end of the sentence:

> At least fifty people have been killed in the annual pilgrimage by Muslims to Mecca, according to police in Saudi Arabia.

Broadcasters should almost always identify the source of information or opinion before spelling it out:

> Police in Saudi Arabia say at least fifty people have been killed in the annual pilgrimage by Muslims to Mecca.

This is pretty much how we would relate the story in a conversation and it helps the listener or viewer immediately to gauge the value of the information. It is of course possible to delay the attribution to the second sentence if the facts are not in doubt and the information is powerful.

> At least fifty people have been killed in the annual pilgrimage by Muslims to Mecca. Saudi Arabian police say the deaths happened when the crowd surged forward at the stoning of the devil.

Contractions

You will have noticed that, like spoken English, broadcast writing contains many contractions. Words like 'shouldn't', 'should've', 'can't', 'didn't', 'wasn't,' 'they'll', and 'we're' are part of everyone's normal speech. They are, therefore, used by broadcast journalists.

Abbreviations

The rule of thumb with abbreviations is to spell everything out to make sure that there is no confusion. So Church St is Church Street and Col Mustard is Colonel Mustard. It is the same with the initials of organisations; these should be explained before referring to them by their acronym. The UNHCR should be introduced as the United Nations High Commissioner for Refugees and the AUT as the Association of University Teachers. If the full title is cumbersome, instead of spelling out every letter of the acronym, explain what it does. So a reporter could say 'Members of the shop workers' union USDAW' instead of using its full name of Union of Shop, Distributive and Allied Workers. There are, of course, some organisations so well known they need no introductions: the BBC, NATO, CIA.

Numbers

Numbers should also be spelled out and used sparingly. When reading out copy it is very easy to confuse 2600 with 26000. Listeners too need numbers explained. If possible, make the numbers mean something, such as 'The Chancellor has raised VAT by six per cent, that's the equivalent of a holiday to Spain this year for every family in Britain.' But remember that a story with too many figures is difficult for listeners and viewers to take in, as in the following example:

> The first outbreak of foot-and-mouth disease for twenty years has been discovered in an abattoir in Essex. A five-mile animal exclusion zone was set up when a routine inspection found twenty-seven contaminated pigs. (BBC, General News Service (GNS) 21 February 2001)

This turned out to be a huge story, but how many radio listeners grasped the significance of the story among all these figures? Another version, the cue to a voice piece, is clearer.

> Experts have identified the first case of foot-and-mouth disease in the UK for 20 years. The disease – which can affect sheep, cattle, pigs and goats – was identified in pigs at an abattoir south of Brentwood in Essex. A five-mile exclusion zone is now in place. (BBC, GNS, 21 February 2001)

Actually, there are a couple of reasons why the second example is better, not just that it contains fewer figures:

- The significant phrase 'first case of foot-and-mouth' comes several words into the cue, giving listeners a chance to tune into the story before hitting them with the killer facts.
- It uses active not passive verbs, making it more dramatic. So, whereas in the first cue foot-and-mouth 'has been identified' (passive), in the second 'experts have identified' (active). Attributing the discovery to experts also gives the story authority. Also in the first cue – a five-mile exclusion zone 'was set up' (passive and in the past tense). In the second 'a five-mile exclusion zone is now in place' (active and in the present tense). See Chapter 3 for more on active and passive verbs.
- However, the second cue does not spell out the number 20. It is always better to write out numbers for broadcast so that they are crystal clear.

Present tense

As we saw in the examples above, using the present tense gives the story more impact. Broadcast news is all about bringing information to the audience as quickly as possible, and telling the stories in the present tense gives the listeners and viewers the sense of events being covered as they happen. You'll often hear claims from stations saying they bring you 'the news as it breaks' or 'the very latest news' or 'the news this hour'.

Writing the cue

As a broadcast journalist, you'll find yourself writing a lot of cues or intros, often to other people's stories. There are several points to bear in mind.

Keep it short

Broadcast cues should be as short as possible. They should explain the basics of the story as it stands at the time of the broadcast and be compelling enough to hold the listener or viewer. If a story is running for several consecutive bulletins it should be rewritten to incorporate the latest developments or, if there are no developments, refreshed to keep the audience's interest.

The latest developments

Even the smallest developments should be exploited fully by being written into the first line or top line of the story. Here is how BBC Radio Sheffield covered the same story over several bulletins. See how the story develops during a morning and how each bulletin makes the most of any new information or rewrites the old to make it sound fresh, even if there is nothing new.

1. A man has died at a steel company in Sheffield after being crushed by huge steel bars. The body of the man, who has not yet been named, was found at the Special Steel Company on Bessemer Road this morning. Health and safety inspectors have been called to investigate.
2. Health and safety inspectors investigating the death of a man who was killed by falling steel at work in Sheffield say he was alone when the accident happened. The man, who was found dead at the Special Steel Company on Bessemer Road this morning, has not yet been named.
3. Police say they're still trying to formally identify a man in his early sixties who was killed this morning at the Special Steel Company in Sheffield. The man died after becoming trapped under a pile of steel. Health and safety inspectors are still at the site.

4. The police have named a man who was killed by falling steel while at work in Sheffield. The body of Sami Yehia, who was in his early sixties, of Birdwell Road in Sheffield, was found at the Special Steel Company on Bessemer Road early this morning. The Health and Safety Executive are investigating the cause of Mr Yehia's death.

Notice how number 3 is essentially a refreshed version of number 2 as there is nothing new to add, except the man's age. The cue has been turned around to highlight a different angle – the police's efforts to find out who the dead man is.

Cue and story should match up

The cue is part of the story and it should sound as if it is. Therefore before writing the cue to a story you have not covered, you should either talk to the reporter or read/listen to their script. There are real pitfalls if you try to improvise and write the cue from a press release or your own knowledge of the story. For example, the first sentence of the cue could repeat what is said in the first sentence of the main body of the piece.

> **CUE:** A family from Ipswich claims they're being victimised by malicious vandals who have smashed virtually every window in their home. The authorities insist they're monitoring the situation, but the Coopers say they're becoming increasingly distressed by the attacks.
>
> Sally Rapier reports . . .
>
> **RAPIER:** The Cooper family say they're becoming increasingly distressed by the attacks on their home. They believe they're being victimised by malicious vandals but they have no idea why.

Or the cue could promise something that the piece does not deliver. For example, a cue saying scientists have developed a cure for arthritis which is followed by a piece that actually says scientists believe they are close to a cure but that the clinical trials are in their very early stages.

Introducing the reporter

Do not end every cue with 'Sally Rapier reports' – it becomes very monotonous. There are plenty of alternatives, 'Here's Sally Rapier', 'Sally Rapier has been following developments', 'Sally Rapier was in court/at the scene/at the home/among the crowd' etc.

Read your copy aloud ▇▇▇▇▇▇▇▇▇▇▇▇▇▇▇▇▇

In any broadcast newsroom on any day at any time you will hear a background murmuring. Look closer at the reporters and you'll see their lips moving. This is not the start of an old joke – there is a very good reason for it. Words on paper may look good, but when spoken aloud those words can sound awful or be impossible to say without stumbling.

> In order to fish efficiently, shoals of salmon and shellfish thriving in the shallows have to be traced by the latest technology.

It is not just difficult words but rhythm that can be a problem. The example often given to young reporters is:

> There were scenes of delight in Port Talbot tonight, as news of the settlement spread.

Written down the sentence looks fine. It's only when it's spoken that its sing-song nature becomes apparent. No one wants to go on air with a sentence like that. So if you find you've written 'six Swedish fishing smacks', rewrite it as 'half a dozen Scandinavian trawlers'.

Make sure you read what you have written and enunciate clearly. It's not fair on your listeners if you mumble. And remember pronouncing a word incorrectly or getting someone's name or the name of a town wrong is the quickest way to lose credibility.

Going live

New satellite and digital technologies mean journalists can file a story from almost anywhere on the planet and viewers can see live pictures of the most inhospitable or remote spots. This makes for amazing real-time coverage of stories but places demands on broadcast journalists never encountered by their counterparts in the past. They have to judge the strength and angle of a story almost instantly, prepare reports more quickly, and be ready to broadcast live within minutes of arriving at a scene.

The key to successful live reporting is to relax and stick only to what you know, says Tom Symonds, the BBC's transport correspondent. He was one of the first reporters called on to comment after the first aircraft hit the World Trade Center on 11 September 2001. He was asked to explain to viewers what they were seeing on their television screens and what it might mean.

> When I arrived, we thought it was either a helicopter or a small plane. It was only as I was going into the studio that we found out it was a passenger jet.
>
> As I sat down I thought, what should I say? In that sort of situation you mustn't speculate, but you can say what the likely options are. You can say that air crashes are very rare and that terrorist hijackings are even rarer. As a specialist I could also say there are four airports in that area, say how close an aircraft can fly to the buildings and talk about the shut down of air traffic.
>
> The most important thing is to watch everything that comes in [agency copy, pictures, official statements, stories from reporters on the ground] so you have something to say. (Tom Symonds, BBC transport correspondent)

Live 2-ways (interview between reporter and presenter) can also tempt reporters into dangerous speculation. One of the most notable examples involved the BBC Radio 4 *Today* programme and its defence and diplomatic correspondent, Andrew Gilligan. Gilligan held a live 2-way with presenter John Humphrys on 29 May 2003 about the Government's Iraq dossier, which outlined its reasons for going to war. It is worth looking at this example closely as it led to a serious breakdown in relations between the Government and the BBC and eventually to significant changes in the BBC's guidelines on live 2-ways as well as other areas of its journalism.

The 2-way between Gilligan and Humphrys was aired just after 6 a.m. and a script was not followed. In it Gilligan suggested that the Government had 'sexed-up' the dossier and inserted the claim that Iraq could launch a chemical or biological attack within 45 minutes, even though they probably knew the claim was wrong.

In a further scripted report just after 7.30 a.m., Gilligan was more careful in his use of words, describing the 45-minute claim as 'questionable'. But an article, written by Gilligan in the *Mail on Sunday* on 3 June 2003, compounded the original allegation and mentioned the prime minister's communications director, Alastair Campbell, as being responsible for the 45-minute claim. These two charges put the BBC dangerously at odds with the Government.

The Government and particularly Alastair Campbell were furious at the assertion they knew the 45-minute claim was wrong as it was central to their justification for going to war and they wanted to know who Gilligan's source was (more on sources and their protection in Chapter 8). Gilligan refused to name the source: the Government put him and the BBC under huge pressure.

Eventually, Government weapons expert David Kelly admitted he had spoken to Gilligan. His death, by apparent suicide, led to an inquiry under Lord Hutton, a senior law lord, into the circumstances surrounding the death and the role played by Government officials and the BBC.

His report, published on 28 January 2004, was devastating for the BBC. Hutton concluded that Gilligan's story made very grave allegations that were unfounded. He condemned the BBC's editorial controls as 'defective' because they allowed Gilligan to go on air and report that the Government had deliberately exaggerated the threat posed by Iraq's alleged weapons of mass destruction without having a prepared script.[5]

In the light of such a critical report, both the BBC's chairman and its director-general resigned, as did Andrew Gilligan. The BBC's governors apologised 'unreservedly' for the errors and tightened up its editorial controls, including appointing a deputy director-general to oversee complaints and banning BBC journalists from writing for newspapers and magazines.

The BBC also conducted its own inquiry into the editorial lessons for the organisation arising from the Hutton Inquiry. One of its recommendations, which was incorporated into the BBC's *Producers' Guidelines*, was that it should not normally be appropriate to use live 2-ways to break stories that contain serious or potentially defamatory allegations. And when breaking any story in a 2-way, precise language is essential.

Despite the pitfalls and thanks to the voracious appetite of 24-hour news on radio and television, journalists do many more live 2-ways than in the past. Mike McCarthy, bureau

Figure 5.1   Mike McCarthy reporting live from a rooftop in Kabul, Afghanistan

chief of Sky News in Manchester, says lives are part of the staple diet at the station because Sky prides itself on its presence at important events.

> Lives are about capturing the drama of what is going on, on the spot. You are close enough to be able to transmit some of the drama of it. It is also putting a human face on something and putting the Sky stamp on it. We are there. (Mike McCarthy, bureau chief, Sky News in Manchester)

It is important to keep your answers reasonably short. Rambling in lives soon loses the audience. Three or four shorter answers keep the pace up and are more memorable than one or two long answers.

Another good use of lives is to use them after a reporter's package. They can either add another perspective, or flesh out some of the points made in the package or they can give the latest developments on a breaking story.

For television reporters who do on-camera reports or 2-ways, it is not easy to refer to notes, therefore the ability to organise a story quickly and retain information accurately is essential. One way of helping your memory is to make a brief outline of what you want to say – do not write out every word or you will sound as if you are reciting rather than explaining.

Mike McCarthy uses bullet points:

> What I tend to do is in the time available, which is never very much, I gather as much information as I can about the story, to be confident about the facts. The presenter can ask anything. You can try and guess what the questions will be but it's hard, so I cram my head with as many facts as I can.
>
> I then put down bullet points of four to five points and underline important figures. I hold the pad when I'm giving the live as there is no reason why a reporter shouldn't refer to their pad. If I'm outside court and I'm quoting a legally sensitive case, it is advisable to refer to notes. It gives me confidence and confidence is very important. The knowledge is important, being confident is important and trying to get the story across with some authority is important.

Remember the style of English used is even more conversational than that used for packaged broadcast pieces. But always be careful how you phrase things or you can end up talking nonsense. For example, 'Anglo-French relations have never been so bad in a long time' (BBC World, 21 March 2003).

On the other side of the 2-way is the presenter. Presenters asking questions of reporters must be sensitive to the pressures on them, says Geeta Guru-Murthy, a presenter for BBC World.

> You've got to know as a presenter what the person on the ground knows, otherwise in a 2-way you can ask the wrong questions.
>
> With technology we can cover more for less money but there isn't always the back-up for the reporters and correspondents. We had a story about a siege in Berlin and were ringing the correspondent to find out what was going on. That correspondent was also being rung by News 24, Bush House, Radios 4 and 5 and was under huge pressure. You know they have copy from the wire service and not much else unless you give them time to make some calls to the police etc.

PART ONE: RADIO

Using sound

While all broadcast journalists approach reporting in broadly the same way (many aspects of the job are the same), there are some things in radio journalism which differ from television – most obviously, radio journalists work with sound and not pictures. This section of the chapter will concentrate on the areas of radio journalism that are specific to the medium.

Radio is the oldest of the broadcast media and in many parts of the world it is the only form of broadcasting available and relied on by tens of millions for accurate and up-to-date news.

Radio has the potential to be immediate. Done well, a station can have breaking news on air almost instantly. We've talked a lot about deadlines, and journalists live by deadlines. But in print the deadline is more distant and you work towards it, whereas in radio it is almost always now. Because of this, radio journalists have to work speedily.

> There is an argument to say that you have to work more quickly in radio newsrooms, with more and tighter deadlines. Therefore a 'good ear' is needed for the story – instantly knowing what is the clip to use, and how to write the cue powerfully in a short space of time. (Tim White, media consultant and former head of news and sport for Radio Aire, independent local radio station in Leeds)

Radio also enjoys a more intimate relationship with its audience than do television and newspapers. Listeners come to regard their favourite radio station as a friend and companion, often having it on as they go about their daily tasks. It benefits from being a medium you can be listening to while doing other things – driving, cleaning, working, gardening. This intimacy with listeners is something radio journalists must be aware of when broadcasting.

> Radio is more personal than television. Something I try to get into most stories I do is the word 'you'. If someone from television says 'you', they mean you plural. When I say 'you', I'm talking to the one person in my head that I'm telling the story to. If someone goes on radio and says 'Hello to all you people out there', they have got it wrong.
>
> There are presenters who have a photo in front of them and I know one who has one of his two children and he broadcasts to them. You should always know who you are talking to. (Stuart Clarkson, broadcast journalist with 2BR, independent local radio station in East Lancashire)

Radio audiences

There are many specialist or local radio stations with specific audiences and each requires suitable news stories and an appropriate approach to news. For example, the audience of a rock music station will want different stories and a more informal style to those listening to a classical music station and both will expect less news than will the audience of an all-speech station. And the audience of Radio City in Liverpool will want stories local to them and different from those given to the audience of Radio Cornwall. This 'localness' is one of the great strengths of radio, says Tim White.

> Although regional TV is offering more and more opt-outs, it can still get nowhere near the 'localness' of local BBC or ILR stations. The future may bring more and more local cable TV stations, but this is likely to be countered by more, smaller community radio stations, maintaining radio's advantage.

Types of programmes

Radio news programmes come in many forms, from the two-minute headline summary to the three-hour, agenda-setting morning news programme. As a radio journalist you will be contributing pieces to these programmes; as a producer you will also have to select the stories that make up the programmes.

- **News headlines/summary**. A short roundup of the main news events, each story is summed up in one or two sentences.
- **News bulletin**. Usually on the hour, this is a synopsis of the main news stories. It will consist of about half a dozen stories, some containing audio (clips, voicers etc.).
- **News programme**. This is longer than a news bulletin, usually 15 or 30 minutes or an hour and broadcast at breakfast, lunchtime or early evening. It includes extended reports, packages and interviews.

Radio news report

These are the main types of report that make up a bulletin. All except copy-only reports are introduced by a cue read by the presenter.

- **Copy**. A news story with no audio in it. It is read by the presenter and is usually no more than three or four sentences or 20 seconds long.
- **Voice pieces/voicer/voice report**. A scripted piece of audio read and written by the reporter and usually pre-recorded in the studio or on location. It can also be read live. Voice pieces are used to put across more information than a copy-only story or to allow a journalist who has been at the scene to tell the story in more detail. It is usually no longer than 40 seconds.
- **Clips/cuts/inserts**. Audio which has been pre-recorded from an interview and one answer or part of an answer has been edited to form a news clip or 'sound bite'. A clip is used to convey opinion or emotion. It is usually 15 to 20 seconds long.
- **Wrap**. A voice report that contains clips.
- **Package/feature**. This is a longer report and includes a reporter's script interspersed with clips, actuality (wild track/real sound recorded on location) and music.
- **Vox pops** (voice of the people). A series of short, tightly edited comments from the public on a current issue. Unlike clips, their names are not given.

Other types of radio news journalism

These are used in longer bulletins or news programmes

- **2-way or Q&A (Questions and Answers)**. A presenter interviews a reporter on air about a story he or she is covering.

- **Interview**. Here the presenter interviews someone involved with a news story. This can be a politician, an expert, a celebrity or a member of the public.
- **Round table discussion/DISCO**. This includes several participants with contrasting views on a subject and is chaired by a journalist.

Building a news bulletin

We've talked about what makes news in Chapter 2 and it is still relevant here. However, rather than placing an item on a page – page 1 for the most important and so on – the radio journalist places their stories in a running order from most to least important. They often finish on a light or amusing story. When building a bulletin, the bulletin producer must bear in mind the following.

- The first story or lead is usually given more time and will contain audio, unless it has just become known (breaking news).
- The stories should vary in length. If you find you have two voice pieces, try to separate them with a copy-only story or an interview clip.
- If you work for a local radio station, try and have stories from all the different areas covered by the station. This keeps your listeners, and your news editor, happy.
- Another trick is to link separate but related stories. For example, if you have the release of a report that claims students at university expect to graduate with more debt than ever before and you have a story that employers claim universities are not preparing students for the workplace, linking the two helps the bulletin flow logically. A sentence such as, 'Despite getting into debt for their education, students coming out of university are often ill equipped for their future careers, says a survey of top employers' moves you from one story to the next smoothly.

Case Study

Building a local news bulletin

Alex Worsick of 2BR, a small commercial station in East Lancashire, is preparing her news bulletin. She has in front of her a selection of stories. Like many commercial stations, 2BR gets a news feed from Independent Radio News (IRN). IRN sends city news, business, entertainment packages and interviews. Alex puts the stories in which she's interested into a bulletin builder file on her computer. This helps her to organise and time bulletins.

She also checks press releases which have been sent to the station. Many now come in by e-mail or fax on the computer. She or another reporter will also make check calls to the emergency services. Once she has all the material in front of her, Alex can start to choose and rank the stories. When a story is written and saved in the builder she moves on to the next one. All voice pieces written by her must be voiced by another reporter as she will be the bulletin's presenter. When everything is written and the timings checked, she prints it all out.

Ideally a local story will go at the top but it depends on the strength of the story. If there isn't a good local story then we shouldn't be afraid to use a national one. We choose on merit.

This bulletin is mostly local news, which is good. I have a new story about the arrest of 31 people during a crackdown on drugs gangs. We try to use real people so you can hear from them; I have a couple in the bulletin. And I try to get a different 'and finally' for each bulletin as if you hear a quirky story twice it is not so funny.

Here is how the bulletin looks. With weather and headlines, it comes to 3 minutes. Seconds are usually abbreviated thus:". Minutes are usually abbreviated thus:".

1 News intro, headlines
2 Lead story, local – Police appeal. Cue + voice report. Total 35"
3 National story – Missing 10-year-olds. Cue + clip. Total 32"
4 Local story – Drugs arrests. Copy only. Total 19"
5 National story – Legionnaires scare. Cue + clip. Total 25"
6 Local story – Sex assault. Cue + voice report. Total 22"
7 National story with local angle – Unemployment figures. Copy only. Total 17".
8 And finally – Ferris wheel. Copy only. Total 17".

This bulletin leads with a voice report of an appeal by police for information about a 14-year-old girl who is missing after a night out in Burnley. The second story is a related national story, the continuing search for two 10-year-old girls in Soham, Cambridgeshire. It is a cue and clip with one of the detectives involved in the search. The third story is copy-only about the drugs initiative in Nelson. A short story here gives variety of length and pace. Then there is a national cue and clip on the closing of a swimming pool because of fears of Legionnaire's disease. Following this is another local story, a voice report, on a sexual assault on two teenagers in Burnley. Then the national unemployment figures are localised in a copy-only report and finally, an international story about a ferris wheel on which you can take your car.

Figure 5.2 Alex Worsick presenting the bulletin she has just prepared for 2BR in East Lancashire

Because radio reporters do not have pictures to help them illustrate their stories, they must use language to conjure up images in listeners' minds. Gillian Hargreaves, a reporter with BBC Radio 4, says she is very aware of the need to take her listeners to where the story is. Sometimes she does this by using a play on words:

> I was doing a piece about carbon emissions around the world and so I talked about filthy rich nations. Recently I was covering the low level of attritional violence in Northern Ireland and I ended with, 'some people get no peace under this ceasefire'. It was a little bit of playing with words.

In another example, she brought a story to life by going to where the story was set and recording at the scene. She was asked to report on the scale of the chancellor of the exchequer Gordon Brown's influence over other Government departments. She began by drawing a picture for the listener:

> If Gordon Brown gazes out of the Treasury window he can see where his money goes. Across the street is the Department of Health, which spends forty-nine billion pounds. Next door, the hugely expensive work and pensions ministry swallows one hundred billion. Half a mile away is transport, which spends six billion pounds.

When assigned the story, Gillian thought this was potentially a very dry piece. First she decided who to interview – who knows about it and is an entertaining talker. She chose two people who would bring a bit of spice to the story: 'In the end journalism is showbiz and what's the point of our job if everyone turns off?'

She did not know where the Treasury was, but she believed it wasn't far from other Government departments. The germ of an idea was beginning to form. She confirmed her hunch by phone and went down there and was able to record those opening lines. Getting out and doing live links – recording the words at the scene of the story – gives atmosphere and shows you are there, even if the sound is rougher than it would be in the studio.

Later in the report she talks of Government ministers 'trooping down Treasury corridors with their departmental begging bowls requesting their slice of the three-year comprehensive spending review'. It's a vivid picture of just how powerful the Treasury is.

Radio's strengths are best exploited through atmospheric recording, lively, knowledgeable interviewees and vivid language.

Writing radio news

Gillian Hargreaves now talks us through a piece she did for Radio 4's *World at One*. The brief was to explore race relations in Stoke-on-Trent in the Midlands and the rise of the far right British National Party (BNP). She explains how the story came about:

> The idea was to go to the north to see how things were getting on, three months after they had elected BNP councillors in Burnley.
>
> I phoned around and found the BNP were putting up candidates for mayoral elections in Stoke in October, so I realised I had a story.
>
> Then I met someone at a barbecue who advises the Home Office on racial issues. I asked what they were doing for the white working classes in these areas as this has something to do with the rise of the BNP. She told me about the Community Cohesion money. I then went to my editor and arranged to go up north. I had the BNP story and the money angle.

As soon as Gillian arrived in Stoke, she put her ideas for a cue on paper while still sitting in her car in the car park. She believes it helps to focus the mind on the message of the story. If the story changes or you find new information, the cue can always be altered. In this case, when the final version was written, it had changed little. This is how the finished cue and script details looked.

> Thirteen months after racial disturbances across the north of England, the far right British National Party has confirmed to this programme that it will stand candidates in the elections for Mayor in Stoke-on-Trent and also in Mansfield in Nottinghamshire. This, despite a government decision to spend millions of pounds promoting what it calls 'Community Cohesion' this summer. The new Home Office phrase arises out of an official report into the race riots in Burnley, Bradford and Oldham last year. That report revealed that there was very little mingling of the white and Asian communities in some towns and cities, which in turn led to the riots. But as we've discovered, discontent over Government policy continues, and far right groups like the BNP which actively campaign on issues of race are busy on the ground. Gillian Hargreaves has been to Stoke-on-Trent.
>
> [GOTO AUDIO
>
> NAME: BNP/Stoke]
>
> IN WORDS: 'are you enjoying yourselves'
>
> OUT WORDS: 'make a multicultural society work'
>
> TO: 3'48"
>
> DURATION: 3'48"

Gillian's full script follows. The script is on the left: her thoughts as she was writing are on the right.

In a park, in one of the poorest cities in Britain, the Home Office is on a mission to build inter-racial friendships

The piece starts at a cricket match between white and Asian children so before the script starts, I have sound of the cricket match and someone asking them if they are enjoying themselves and more sounds of the cricket match. This sets the scene of what the Government is trying to do.

The first link is about capturing the audience. Once you've got them, then you can take them through the arguments. When it starts they don't know what the story is, yet the children's enthusiasm in the cricket match should interest them. And I then explain in the link what it's about.

Thirteen months ago this city had its first racial disturbances and the Government is fearful that Stoke could become as racially tense as Burnley, Bradford and Oldham. This summer the Government is spending six million pounds to try to rebuild communities and make lives better … but a year on white and Asian residents, like Stephen Austen and his neighbours, can't see much difference.

It is important to give the main message early on. Only certain stories allow for much of a delay. This was complicated enough that I needed to make sure I got the message across that millions of pounds are being given for racial cohesion and that the BNP is active in the area and has a mayoral candidate.

In this link I wanted to build up to knock down. I say the Government has put all this money in and it still doesn't work. I also repeat what is said in the cue about the Government spending money and then added some information.

[GOTO AUDIO
NAME: fx of kids shouting]
[GOTO AUDIO
Name: white and Asian vox pops]

Sound effects here of children let the piece breathe. Then we hear the opinions of the local people.

According to the Racial Equality Council, racist crime in Stoke has risen by seven hundred and fifty per cent in one year. But, even more worrying for the Government, Stoke-on-Trent is ripe for political extremism. Two out of every five houses are unfit for human habitation, there is a chronic low wage economy, the local education authority scores badly in the league tables, cancer survival rates are some of the lowest in the country. And in October

In this link I introduce a list which works because it shows what a grim place Stoke is. I varied the numbers as if you have too many percentages it gets boring plus, for accuracy's sake. Two out of every five is the correct statistic, almost half is an exaggeration but two-fifths is not as emphatic. When I wrote this list I wanted to cry as it made me realise how awful it is. And this is my city, where I am from. I was going to use the phrase 'Government indicators', which is what these are, but you don't talk like that, so people here will get the chance to vote for a new city mayor. The far right British National Party is putting up a candidate.

I cut it out. Everybody understands the list; using words like 'Government indicators,' dehumanises it.

I put the killer fact of the BNP putting up its candidate at the end of the link for impact; it builds to the climax. This is the key bit of the whole package.

[GOTO AUDIO] Name: BNP Clip]

The interviewee introduces himself to remind people again who he is and he says, 'We are fielding candidates and we think we have hope here.'

Despite Simon Darby's confidence, the BNP stands little chance of winning the mayoral contest, in this solidly Labour city ...
But critics say local councillors have been complacent about racial issues in the past and a visit to the Racial Equality Council in Stoke on Trent is a dismal experience. The decaying office stairwell stinks of urine, there is a sign urging drug pushers to keep out. But Mohammed Tufail and his staff are defiant, saying the BNP won't prosper here.

I made the point that the BNP can't win but that Labour was complacent. Then I thought, how do I illustrate this complacency? The trip up the stairwell to the Racial Equality Council was it. It was one of the grimmest experiences I've ever had. What shocked me first was the smell, then I looked at the wall and the 'drug pushers keep out' sign and that shocked me. You don't see those signs very often.
Powerful writing is about detail.

[GOTO AUDIO] Name: REC in Stoke clip

The challenge in radio is finding different ways of introducing people. What I hate is 'so-and-so from ... council said.' That's not radio. So here I don't use his title, there is no need as we know from the words 'his staff' that he is the boss.

Even though there are many costly problems in this city, the Home Office cohesion money is welcome. In the end it's people not governments who make a multicultural society work.

I recorded the last link outside, as I was talking about the city.

When writing, Gillian always tries to remember her audience.

There is no point in using big words that nobody understands. We have to take complicated ideas and make them simple. That's not talking down to people, it's clarifying and it takes intelligence to do that. In my earlier reports when I had less experience,

> I would put too much information in reports – overwrite and over-explain. What you have to do is to walk away and think 'What is the story?'. Have an imaginary conversation with an imaginary listener.

Script layout

No matter how good your script is, it has to be well laid out to be any use.

- You need to be able to read your scripts.
- If it is not you reading it, then the presenter has to be able to read the cue, see the timings and understand the instructions for playing-in the audio.
- If you are working with a technician or producer who will play-in audio for you, they need to be able to read the script.
- A producer or editor may want to check your script.

Newsrooms vary in the way they lay out scripts, but they are likely to include:

- a catchline or name of the story, and the name of the person who wrote the story
- the date, and sometimes the time
- whether there is any audio and, if so, the details of the person speaking (a reporter in a voice piece or an interviewee for a clip/cut)
- the in and out words of the audio. This helps the presenter to check they have the clip at the beginning before playing it, and then to know when to start speaking again once the clip has finished
- the duration or how long the piece is. This is vital information for a bulletin or programme producer when they are timing their bulletin
- some include the source, wires/newsline/press release.

Here is an example of the layout for a cue and voice piece:

Catchline/name of reporter	What it is	Date	How long it is
Hijack/Jones	VP	31 March 2004	Duration: 0'50"

Police say the hijackers holding more than one hundred and fifty passengers aboard a plane at Stansted Airport have not made any threats to harm them. They've also not made any specific political demands. So far eight passengers have been released – including two baby girls. From Stansted Airport, Daniel Jones:

[GOTO AUDIO]
NAME: Jones/Hijack
IN WORDS: The hijackers
OUT WORDS: Calm for now
DURATION: 0'34"

Notice how the duration at the top is different from at the bottom. The top duration is the overall duration, which is the cue added to the voice piece. Sometimes this comes at the bottom of the page. You calculate the time of the cue by taking every three words to be one second, as the average person reads copy at three words a second. There are 47 words. The cue is 16 seconds. Add this to the 34 seconds of the voice piece and it comes to 50 seconds. Most computer-based news systems will do this work for you.

Sounding the part

As a radio journalist, you will have to read or present news at some time. Even if not presenting programmes or bulletins, you will have to read reports that either you or someone else has written. Therefore, the ability to present copy well is necessary for a successful career and it takes a lot of practice.

What makes a good radio newsreader? First a good voice, one that is easy to listen to and to understand. Having a voice with severe impediments such as a stammer or a lisp may make it difficult to become a newsreader. Less serious impediments such as a voice that is too high or nasal can be improved with voice training.

Even the best voice can still present badly if it is not used properly. A good radio presenter will:

- **Speak clearly so that every word is understood**. This means opening your mouth properly to make sure words are said distinctly.
- **Breathe without destroying the flow**. This is often a problem and presenters can end up running out of breath before the end of the line and either tailing off or having to pause for breath in an unnatural place (try saying that sentence out loud). So when you are writing your script, say it aloud and make sure you have enough breath. Over time and with practice you can improve your breathing.
- **Read a few words ahead**. This is essential for a smooth delivery, otherwise you end up stumbling over words that you did not see coming and losing the sense of the script.
- **Use a full vocal range**. Speaking in a monotone puts the audience to sleep, so alter the tone of your voice to suit the sense of what you are saying. Modulating your voice helps comprehension. If you are reading a bulletin, you can indicate the end of the story by lowering the pitch of your voice and starting the next story at a higher level. If you want to sound happy, then smile. Frowning helps your voice sound more sombre.
- **Vary the speed of reading**. On average, newsreaders present at three words a second, but if every sentence were spoken at the same pace it would become monotonous. It is useful to begin a piece at a slower pace, so the listener can get used to your voice, then speed up after a few seconds. For important sentences slow down, pausing before a word you want to emphasise. You can speed up a little for those passages that are

less important. But don't gabble; some trainees race through a script as if their life depended on it.

- **Understand what they are reading.** This is possibly the most important requisite of a good presenter. If you don't know what you are saying, how can you expect the audience to? Always look through what you are about to read and check you understand. Then think about the best way of putting across the meaning. This requires you to know which words and phrases to emphasise. Some reporters get into a rhythm of stressing every third word because it feels right, not because they have thought about the meaning of what they are saying.
- **Mark up scripts as a guide.** It can be daunting facing a script or series of items, so marking up can help. Underline all words that you intend to stress. Slowing down can also emphasise a key word; a broken line is used here. A forward slash (/) indicates a pause, two slashes a longer pause.

Editing sound

Much radio journalism involves editing audio material. For example, choosing clips from an interview, cutting down a 2-way, taking out long pauses from an interview, putting together a package. This is now done using digital computer software. The audio is recorded onto the computer system and is then shown on the computer screen in a waveform. Editing is achieved by highlighting material, then deleting it, or copying and pasting it into a different section. So long as you take a copy of the material before you start editing, you can make as many mistakes as you like and you will always have a back-up. Whatever you do, try to make the edit sound natural; that means not cutting it too tightly, otherwise it sounds jerky.

Figure 5.3 Radio sound editing. The sound is shown on the computer in a wave form and the reporter highlights the part they wish to work with.

PART TWO: TELEVISION

Using pictures

The main difference between radio and television is pictures. This may sound obvious, but you would be surprised how many journalists who make the transition from radio to television forget this. They write their scripts with little regard for the pictures and, rather than moulding their story around the pictures, they use them as wallpaper. This is bad television.

In radio you have to paint pictures with words. In television you have the pictures and so you have to clarify what the viewer is seeing without telling them what they are seeing. They know they are seeing a field of cows, you need to say why the cows are important. This is harder than it sounds.

Team effort

Another difference is the number of people involved in covering one story for television. All broadcast news is a team effort, but radio reporters can record and compile reports on their own. In television working on your own is still the exception rather than the rule (see section on video-journalists). And because of its dependence on pictures, television is slower than radio. The point is made by former BBC foreign correspondent, Martin Bell, about reporting during the Bosnian War of 1992.

> The very minimum team is seven people: a newsgathering unit cameraman, interpreter and reporter, a producer or 'fixer' at the heart of the operation, and at the transmission end a videotape editor (sometimes doubling as sound recordist) and two engineers with the satellite dish. Later we reduced it to six by doubling the roles of producer and interpreter. The dish itself, and the ton of ancillary equipment that goes with it, needs the capacity of two and a half Land Rovers to move it, and the best part of a day to set it up.[6]

At home the team is smaller. A reporter will normally film with a cameraman and, once back in the newsroom, cut the piece with an editor – sometimes the editor and cameraman are one and the same person. The graphics department may be involved in producing a map or statement. On important stories a producer may work with the reporter to organise interviews, graphics etc. A researcher may also be involved making phone calls to gather information, setting up interviews or sorting out relevant library material.

The television audience

While radio can be a constant and easy-going companion, television demands attention from its audience. People have to sit and watch as well as listen. Consequently, television journalists keep their stories short, at about 1½ to 2 minutes, no matter how complex.

Radio stories vs. television stories

As we have seen, there are fundamental differences between radio and television and these can influence the stories each medium chooses to cover. At the BBC, the national radio and television news services cover many of the same stories but sometimes one sees news value where the other does not. For example, when a painting by the sixteenth-century Venetian artist, Titian, turned up seven years after it was stolen, television sent a reporter out and ran it as an end item. Cheryl Garnsey of BBC Newsgathering (radio) urged Radio 5 to cover it:

> They said it's a picture story, but I think the fact that it was found in a bag was a good story in itself. The difference is, TV do stories because there are pictures or a producer has thought of a fancy way of making a slight story into a good watch. Radio will say, but where's the story?

Colleague Jo-Anne Pugh puts it down to television's dependence on pictures:

> Radio is a purer intellectual medium – you can choose a story purely on its merit. You can do a 40-second straight voice piece and tell a listener all they need to know. However, in television you can have an important story that's impossible to illustrate either (i) logistically because it's broken too late and it's too far away, as in the Lockerbie plane crash or (ii) there are no pictures to be had, as in a complicated fraud case. Here you can do a 2-way with the reporter but the story may not make the running order because it is not so important to sacrifice pictures to tell the story. It's a trade-off between the importance of the story and the need for pictures.

This means it is less important to get a journalist to a breaking incident than to get a cameraman there and get the pictures back. She explains that as long as you have pictures, you can cover the story.

> If there is only one seat on a plane heading to an incident, you would get the cameraman there. He can tell you basically what's going on to write a script. The pressure to get pictures is enormous. You realise how utterly dependent you are on planning and technical resources.

Writing for television

Whether you like it or not, pictures are the most important element in a television story. They influence whether a story is covered and its place in the running order. As a television journalist, write to the pictures and you will get the best out of them but don't describe what people can see for themselves. It is a waste of the audience's time. The best television reporters use the pictures to tell the story and complement them with a script that explains what the viewer can't see.

Therefore you should never write a script before you have seen the pictures in the hope that the words will fit. Often you will be forced, by time constraints, to fashion a script before entering an editing suite, but this should not stop you looking at your pictures, choosing the best shots and then, once you know what pictures you have, scripting. It is also a good idea if you have time to write a list of the shots you have.

If you haven't the time to watch the pictures, but you were with the cameraman who shot them, you will know what material you have and can script with that knowledge. Be prepared, however, to alter your script if your editor has some better ideas for the pictures.

Types of report

These are the main types of television news material. All except copy-only involve pictures.

- **Copy-only story**. A news story with no pictures. It is read by the presenter and is usually no more than three or four sentences or 20 seconds long. These are visually less interesting than other types of report and they are almost the same as radio copy. However, they may lead a news programme if there is an important breaking story for which no pictures are yet available.
- **OOV (Out of Vision)**. Pictures over which the presenter reads a script but does not appear in vision. These are often read live. When writing these, it is important to make sure the words complement the pictures.
- **Clips/cuts/insert**. Audio which has been pre-recorded from an interview and one answer or part of an answer has been edited to form a news clip or 'sound bite'. A clip is used to convey opinion or emotion. It is usually 15 to 20 seconds long. Sometimes OOVs are followed by a clip.
- **As live**. This is a pre-recorded 2-way between a reporter and a presenter or reporter and guest/s or presenter and guest/s and set up as if it were live.
- **Graphics/captions**. Any still photographs, maps, charts, courtroom sketches, written statements etc. These can make a short report for a bulletin or form part of a package.
- **Package/feature**. This is a longer report and includes a reporter's script interspersed with clips, graphics, actuality (wild track/real sound recorded on location) and sometimes music.
- **Vox pops (voice of the people)**. A series of short, tightly edited comments from the public on a current issue. Unlike clips, their names are not given.

Presenting copy

Television scripts differ from radio scripts because they contain both the presenter/ newscaster's words and instructions to the director. This format is called the split page (see Figure 5.4). At the top of the page in bold are the instructions to the director giving the title, the fact that this example is second in the running order after the headlines, that the duration is 32 seconds and that it is a live read, i.e. not pre-recorded. The bottom words are the copy that will be read by the newsreader, in this case, Fiana Bruce. The newsreader will only be able to see this part of the script on the autocue/teleprompter.

2 FRANCE-INTRO   **Duration: 0'32''**

```
[Live Read:]
BRUCE:
Good evening. The French President has
called for unity tonight and said his country's
resounding no to the European constitution
wasn't a rejection of the European ideal -
rather a call for the government to listen and
to take action. Jacques Chirac sacked his
Prime Minister, and put a new man into the
job - Dominique de Villepin - and promised to
focus on the economy and create jobs. He
acknowledged France and Europe were
facing a period of difficulty and uncertainty.
More from our Paris correspondent Allan
Little.
```

Figure 5.4   A typical split-page script which includes instruction to the director

Story construction (packaging)

There are several elements that go into a good package. Sometimes one or other of these is missing because of lack of time or refusal by the people involved to be filmed or interviewed, but ideally when you sit down to compile your report you have the crucial elements.

1 **Pictures to tell the story**. We will talk more about working with a camera crew and planning what pictures you require later, but suffice to say without the shots it is very hard to script a story.
2 **Information and a good script**. You still need the facts even if you have the pictures. And the words covering any sequence of pictures must relate to or add to the pictures. Do not assume the viewer will understand the significance of what they are seeing. Then again do not tell the viewer what they can see for themselves. The more powerful the pictures, the less script is needed (see the Orla Guerin script in the introduction to this chapter). Viewers need time to absorb very powerful images. If you have important information to put across, use more general pictures.
3 **Interviewees**. It is important to try to include interviewees that are relevant to the story. Good clips bring a story to life and also back up what you are saying. Unlike radio,

interviewees do not need introducing in television. Set up the clip properly and then use a 'name super' or 'aston' to tell the viewer who they are. Check spellings and titles. In setting up the clip, do not repeat what the viewer is about to hear the interviewee say.

4 **Piece to camera**. The piece to camera or stand-up can help establish the reporter's authority and credibility but you have to have something to say. A piece to camera should add information for which you don't have pictures or make a point that increases the viewer's understanding of the story. Make sure the background to the piece to camera is pertinent and interesting.

5 **Graphics**. These involve still photos, maps, written statements and such like. See below for scripting to graphics, but if you do need a graphic make sure you talk to the graphics department early so they know what is needed and by what time.

Remember: make the words fit the pictures and not the other way around. And once you've written your script, re-read it, trimming it as you go, paring it down to the essentials. The best scripts are minimal.

Writing for television as a foreign correspondent | Case Study

Former BBC reporter and foreign correspondent, John McIntyre, explains his thoughts on a story he did for BBC News while covering events in Kosovo:

No matter how big the story is you have to apply the same principle: that is, to simplify it in the same way you would a small story. I was in Kosovo when I covered a story about a mass burial of 64 bodies. The smell was overpowering, you wanted to vomit, it was so gut-wrenchingly horrible.

There are only two occasions ever – the other being Dunblane [children shot in a primary school gym in the Scottish town of Dunblane] where I have said to myself, 'Oh my God, this is heavy duty'. You have got to take yourself away mentally and remain impartial.

I had to think what is the construction of this story? What pictures do I use, where? Everyone remembers the mass exodus of Kosovo and the tractors carrying people. Here we had a convoy of tractors again but this time using them to carry the bodies of the dead. My intro focused on that: 'The convoy that only a month ago carried thousands of people away from the tragedy of war now became a pitiful funeral cortege as they carried the dead.'

I knew I needed to get an interview with someone who had lost their family. I explained to the person that what you tell me will be seen by people all around the world. If you feel up to it, tell your story as you want to. I won't pressure you and I will make sure I respect the way you tell it.

The man I spoke to had lost 14 or 15 members of his family. They fell on him after being shot. He too was shot and almost suffocated.

I knew this was powerful. The more powerful it was for me, the more simply I had to write and ditch any sensationalism. I needed a simple script with lots of pauses. Overwriting destroys the emotion.

This is John's script:

This is the grim reality of dealing with death on a large scale. Men, women and children in black body bags, afforded what dignity was possible in the circumstances.

Figure 5.5 Body bags being loaded onto tractors

Sixty-four bodies were loaded onto lorries and tractors each carefully draped with the Albanian flag. It took well over an hour.

Once all the bodies had been officially returned by British police and forensic experts investigating the massacre, tractors used in the mass refugee exodus of Kosovo now provided a make-shift funeral cortege. First they headed for the village school.

Figure 5.6 Tractors carrying the dead

Everyone in the village of Bela Crkva gathered here to mourn their collective loss. This was the saddest of days.

Figure 5.7 Gathering at the village school

Photographs of the dead were held with pride along a sombre line of sons, daughters, parents and grandparents who'd lost their loved ones.

All the victims of a bloody massacre by Serb forces on March 25, the day after the NATO bombing started.

Figure 5.8 Photographs of the dead

This grieving woman said today was the first time she cried. She'd held it all back for 3 months.

Isuf Zhenigi survived and bears the scars of that dreadful day. He said at 9:15 in the morning, the Serbs rounded up the villagers in a field and separated the men from the women and children, then shot everyone, some at point blank range.

Figure 5.9 Victim Isuf Zhenigi

Then came the time, finally, to lay the dead to rest. The first Albanians to be buried after a full murder inquiry inquiry by Scotland Yard detectives investigating Kosovo war univers.

Interview Scotland Yard Detective:

Figure 5.10 Laying the dead to rest

'They were men, women and children and some of the children were as young as four. They'd all been shot, quite deliberately. They weren't in uniform, they were a little isolated group. There was absolutely no reason for them at all to have been hurt in any way whatsoever.'

Figure 5.11   War Crimes Investigator

This was the biggest organised funeral in Kosovo, more will inevitably follow.

Figure 5.12   The Graves of the Dead

PTC: Today is a painful but important part of the healing process. Now it's up to the International War Crimes Tribunal to try to complete that process, by bringing to justice those responsible for the killings.

Figure 5.13   John McIntyre's Piece to Camera

Finally a gun salute by KLA soldiers. Peace seems a long way off in Kosovo.

Figure 5.14 KLA soldiers give a gun salute

John McIntyre, BBC News, Bela Crkva.

The order John chose to run the pictures tells the story logically. He starts on action shots of the bodies being placed on the lorries and explains what is happening, then we get a long shot to show the scale of the tragedy. Next we meet the people and see and hear from eye-witnesses – lots of close-ups here to get the human response. We hear also from the 'expert', a Scotland Yard detective, who verifies what we have heard from the people, then a piece to camera puts the reporter on the spot and we finish with powerful shots of militiamen firing into the air.

Writing to graphics

This is a skill you will be expected to master early on in your newsroom career. It may be writing over a picture of the council leader about her decision to stand down at the upcoming local elections. It may be a map of a town showing a proposed by-pass. It may be a sketch of a wanted man. Whatever it is, there are several points to bear in mind.

First, the viewer needs to know what they are seeing as soon as it appears. A graphic should be explained straight away. If it is a photograph or a map, it should appear when the name or location is mentioned in the script.

It is also important when using photographs that they match the tone of the script. If you are talking about race riots across the country, it is appropriate to have a picture of the home secretary but probably not with him or her smiling.

When the graphic is a quote, the presenter or reporter's script must use the same words that appear on screen in the quote. There is nothing more annoying than hearing words that are at variance with what you are seeing. It is not a clever way of getting more information across – it is more likely to result in less or no information being communicated.

How long should a graphic stay on the screen? You need to give viewers enough time to absorb the information, but once they've done that, they soon get fed up. The minimum time is about four seconds and the maximum around six to eight seconds for a simple graphic such as a photograph. You can stretch this time if you have more complicated graphics. However, if a graphic is too complicated, you and the graphics department have wasted your time as the viewer will have given up and gone to make a cup of tea.

Note: It is often helpful to explain numbers using graphics.

Pieces to camera

The ability to deliver an effective piece to camera (PTC), also known as a stand-up or stand-upper, can be the difference between having an on-screen career and not. So if you want to be a reporter in the field, you need to know when and how to perform them.

Figure 5.15 Delivering effective pieces to camera is an important skill for a television reporter

Pieces to camera help to establish you in the audience's mind and show you are in the thick of the action. They are also useful if you are short on good pictures. Types of pieces to camera include the 'introduction' at the start of a piece to the 'summary' or 'comment' at the end. Other examples are the 'where the action is' piece, the 'bridge' or 'link' piece which moves the audience from one part of a story to another, and the 'demonstration' stand-up showing the audience how something works. But one role a piece to camera should not play is as a vanity appearance by a reporter. These have nothing of value to say and resort to bland statements such as, 'One thing is certain, if the two sides can't agree there'll be no solution.'

The setting of a piece to camera is crucial. While reporting for 5 News, Geeta Guru-Murthy was sent to the United States to cover the story of President Clinton and his affair with the White House intern, Monica Lewinsky. She headed for Champaign, Illinois, for Clinton's first speech since the story broke. The rest of the world's media were also there; how could she stand out from the others?

> It was in a huge hall like the Albert Hall with crowds waiting to see him snaking around the building. Most of the reporters were doing pieces to camera outside to show the crowds. They were getting shots inside but not doing pieces to camera as it was very noisy inside. I thought I would do something different, so I started the piece on shots of Clinton with actuality and pulled out to me. It was very short and very noisy but it was different. Now I see it done a lot at press conferences, but it doesn't always work. I had also done a straight piece to camera with the crowds in case the one inside didn't work.

Geeta's plan had the advantage of showing the action – Clinton during his speech. If it hadn't worked she had a back-up piece to camera which was less atmospheric but would, nevertheless, have illustrated the story.

When thinking about the location of a piece to camera, you need to be sensitive about the people you are talking about. In the rush to get everything filmed it can be easy to forget to convey the humanity of a story, but you can lose the empathy of your audience in the process. For example, if you are at a hospital doing a story on waiting lists, don't just stand in front of someone in bed and say, 'Old people like this need hip replacements.' Rather, draw in that person, '86-year-old Milly here is waiting for a hip replacement'.

It can be nerve-wracking delivering a piece to camera, but you need to look relaxed. It is painful for the audience to watch a reporter wide-eyed with fear, face tense. They end up feeling tense too. Natural movements of your body such as your head and hands help the appearance of being relaxed, but be careful not to look like a windmill. If you are standing still, don't stand square on to the camera but at a slight angle.

Your piece to camera is your chance to talk directly to the audience, so keep the script conversational and don't shout. No one likes being yelled at. It helps if you keep it short and simple, then you are not worrying that you will remember the words. Anxiety about being able to complete your piece without making a mistake shows in your face and can lead to you speeding up your delivery in a race to get to the end.

What you wear while doing a stand-up is also important. Wearing the appropriate clothes increases your authority and helps gain the trust of the viewer while unsuitable clothes have the reverse effect. Ask yourself how the audience would feel if you wore a pinstripe suit to cover the plight of a farmer who had lost his crops because of a flood or you went to interview the prime minister in jeans and a tee-shirt.

███████████████████████████ **Making the most of the pictures**

> The brilliant thing about tele is the visuals. You don't have to see things the way every-
> one else does. In fact you shouldn't fall into the trap of filming everything in a formu-
> laic way. Go for drama, originality and surprise. For example, in an economics story, can
> you use apples and pears? What you don't want are desks and computers. If jobs are
> going at a company, ask the company director if you can drive with him/her from home
> on the day the losses are to be announced and film them hearing the announcement
> on the car radio. You can also film them on a mobile phone. Think differently; take people
> to new locations or film at different times of the day. (Geeta Guru-Murthy, presenter BBC
> World and former Channel 5 reporter)

All television journalists, whether they work as video journalists or with a crew, have to
understand what makes good pictures. They must have an eye for which shots work best,
what lighting is needed and how to make the best of the natural sound.

In order to tell a story through pictures, you need sequences rather than a set of dis-
jointed pictures that do not relate to each other. A sequence is made up of several
pictures, which together portray something. So if you wanted to show someone buying a
packet of cereal in a shop, you wouldn't take one long shot of them walking into the shop,
searching the shelves, taking their cereal packet to the till, paying and walking out, as it
would take too long. The act needs to be broken up into parts which, when edited
together, make it appear as a continuous action.

What would also not work is a set of badly thought-out pictures. For example, you could
end up with a view of the shop, the man walking along an aisle and a shot of him leaving.
But no picture of him going into the shop, or choosing the cereal pack, or paying – no
close-ups either of the cereal packet, money changing hands, the man saying 'thank you'
or the shopkeeper. In this case you would get to the cutting room and find you don't have
enough pictures to show what happened or to script to.

Before you start filming, you should decide what shots you need and make sure that you
get those pictures. Before you stop filming, ensure you have enough shots to cut the story
and some natural sound to break up the script. Shots you are likely to need include a
general view of where the story is set (the shop), action shots of what's happening (picking
up the cereal packet, paying), close-ups of the action (hand on cereal packet, money) and
those involved (man and shopkeeper) and natural sound of the action (till and thank you).

The following are the standard camera shots in television. They refer to the distance the
thing you are shooting is away from the camera and how much of the frame is filled
by it.

- **The long shot (LS)**. Often used for establishing shots or general views (GVs) to show
  the location or all the action. Can also use a very long shot (VLS). A long shot of a
  demonstration outside a council chamber would show the whole group and much of
  the building. If filming a person it takes in the whole person from head to feet.

- **The medium long shot (MLS).** Brings the action closer or a smaller part of the action. When filming one person, it would show their head to just below the knees.
- **The medium shot or mid-shot (MS).** We are now getting more detail. At the council demonstration this shot would pick out small groups in the crowd, say a mother and her child. If filming one person, it shows the head to the hips.
- **The medium close-up (MCU).** These last three shots are detail shots. At our demonstration this shot would take in a couple of excited or angry faces or a placard. When filming one person, it shows head and shoulders.
- **Close-up (CU).** The camera person now starts picking out individual faces in the crowd, waving hands, placards, chanting. Close-ups give viewers a sense of involvement. When filming one person, it shows the head only.
- **Big close-up (BCU).** This shot is good to show intense emotion: an angry or shouting or singing face. It is a very close shot. When filming one person, the whole screen is filled with the features of the face.

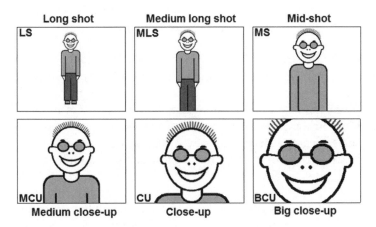

Figure 5.16 Standard camera shots

Any camera moves that you take must be held at the beginning of the shot for at least five seconds and also at the end of the shot. This gives the editor a chance to use a still if he doesn't want the move. There are a number of different camera moves:

- **The pan.** The camera moves from left to right or right to left in the horizontal plane. Must start and end on strong frames. A pan can follow a person, car or bird.
- **The tilt.** Camera movement up or down in the vertical plane. This can be from the face of a child to the jigsaw they are completing or from the front step of a house to the top window where someone is leaning out.

- **The zoom**. Varies the focus length of a shot, taking it in or pulling it out. Inexperienced camera operators tend to use too many zooms. Only zoom when necessary, otherwise your audience gets dizzy.
- **The tracking shot**. This is where the camera films while moving. Typical tracking shots are filming from a moving car, walking through a house, down an alleyway or moving through the woods.

When interviewing, you will need some or all of the following pictures:

- **The set-up**. Introduces the players and can show the geography of the location.
- **Interviewee** with relevant background.
- **Close-ups**, especially if it is an emotional interview.
- **Cut-aways**. (e.g. hands or pictures in the room) used as a bridge in editing. These add to the variety of material and give the editor a choice.
- **Reverse shots** also known as **noddies**. Shows interviewer listening to the interviewee, often nodding. Can help the editor piece together the interview.
- **Two-shots**. Shows back of interviewer's head and interviewee's face listening. This helps if one of the interviewer's questions is to be used.

In this section we have stressed the importance of getting enough of the right shots to illustrate a story and to give some flexibility in the edit suite. And remember when shooting, don't just vary the size of the shot – you should also vary the angle. Shoot high and low, back and front to make it more interesting. However, try not to take lots of unnecessary pictures as you want the minimum to look through when compiling your report. Overshooting or taking too many pictures is also something camera operators really dislike. It is a waste of their time and effort if most of their carefully framed pictures are never used.

> Skill in storytelling involves great attention to detail. And attention to detail is often what marks out the best camera operators from the rest. Small details make a big difference.
>
> Nervous hands; pictures on a mantelpiece; someone whispering into an ear; a hand clutching a toy; details of a life.[7]

Successfully working with a crew

Maintaining a good working relationship with a crew is important if you are to get the best out of them. Here are a few tips:

1 Communicate. Make sure your camera person knows where you are filming and at what time. If possible, arrange parking near where you are filming as cameras are heavy. Give the crew details of any unusual conditions which may need special equipment or extra time, such as if you are filming at a hot baths or at night or if they have

to carry their camera up six flights of stairs. Explain simply and briefly what the story is about and what you hope to achieve. Make it clear that you value their advice and listen to what they have to say – they may be far more experienced than you are.

2 Try to arrive at the location before the crew. It is not fair to leave the crew to introduce themselves or to have them waiting around. Make sure you know the name of the camera person and introduce them to those being filmed.

3 Remember that crews can work on several stories in a day and yours may not seem that interesting. Your enthusiasm for the story and ability to demonstrate this to the crew can make all the difference.

4 Once you start filming, talk with the crew about what pictures you want. If there are several different locations, do not overload them with all the details of every location but give them a broad outline. Then at each location talk in detail about what you want from here before the crew starts filming.

5 If there is no soundman (and it's unlikely there will be one), it is up to you to watch out for the crew when they are looking through the lens. Watch their back in a crowd or if they are filming beside a road.

Graham Hough, a cameraman with BBC North, highlights the importance of planning the picture and not overshooting:

> A journalist should know what shots they want and know when they have enough to cover the story and not have the cameraman getting lots of extra elements. But they should also be flexible if things don't go exactly the way they want.

Technology

There is a revolution going on in the technologies used to gather news. What could once take days to get to air can now be seen live thanks to satellite phones, mobile dishes and laptops, which allow live pictures to be sent from the most difficult or remote locations.

At the end of 2003 the BBC began kitting out some of its reporters with mobile videophones that enable them to shoot and then e-mail still and moving pictures with sound back to news headquarters. The phones use special software that allows the handsets to record up to 15 minutes of video. When finished, the reporter transmits the pictures to the newsroom. The idea is that the speed the phones offer in getting pictures back will help the BBC to break stories and become one more tool in the broadcaster's armoury.

The first report to be done using the phones was by reporter Richard Bilton, who filmed the arrival in Hartlepool of toxic 'ghost ships' from the US to be cleaned. Bilton and other reporters were on a tugboat travelling alongside the ships and he filed the report from the tugboat while other crews had to wait until they were back on shore to send from their satellite trucks.[8] Since then the phones have helped the BBC to other scoops, including a bus accident in Wales where a producer with one of the phones reached the scene earlier than camera crews.

The handsets differ from the grainy satellite phones used by Nic Robertson of CNN in Afghanistan in 2001 and by many reporters in Iraq in 2003. These are ordinary cell phones, using standard mobile networks, rather than having the images beamed via satellite.

The technology will only get better and more and more organisations and individuals will start using it. Phones with the ability to capture, print, edit, store and send still pictures and videos via the internet (and add special effects such as music or text) have been available to consumers since 2004. It's a far cry from the days of film.

> New technology has reduced the reporter's control. At one time the newsdesk couldn't contact you, it was down to you to contact them. Now, for example, during the riots in Burnley and Bradford in 2002, the minute I got there I could file live from the mobile phone doing eye-witness reports. That's even before the camera arrived.
>
> The technology enables you to do the same thing in Afghanistan as you'd do from a street corner in Bradford. In Afghanistan everybody congregated on the rooftop of the hotel in Kabul. There we were looking down on one of the poorest cities in the world with millions of pounds of hardware. We had a satellite dish on a truck, we had two satellite phones as there was no phone service. We sent our material from the sat truck. We had a laptop and one of the engineers linked it to the internet through the sat phone.
>
> We were in Kabul but things were happening in the north and the south of the country that we needed to be aware of, so we got information off the internet and by talking to the newsdesk in London. (Mike McCarthy, bureau chief of Sky News, Manchester)

Mike McCarthy highlights the most important effects of new technology on reporters: they are now expected to work a lot faster than in the past and there is almost nowhere on the planet where they cannot be contacted by the newsdesk.

Whether or not they are better served, technology has had a profound effect on the relationship between the viewer and the programmes they watch. News programmes now have permanent contact with their audiences through text messages, email and phone calls. These can be collated and sent to the in-boxes of presenters on air. It's a huge step forward for broadcasters who have spent years trying to find ways of interacting with the audience.

> I spend three hours on air being chatted to by viewers. I get anything from marriage proposals to comments on, or questions about, stories. And if they don't like your clothes, they'll tell you. We get a lot of reaction from the audience. When the actress Gwyneth Paltrow said British men don't ask her out so they're not romantic, we got a huge reaction. We ended up doing a vox pop about it. So through the technology you have a clearer idea of what a lot of people are interested in. (Sophie Raworth, presenter of the BBC's *Six O'Clock News* while she was still a *Breakfast News* presenter)

The launch of interactive services on digital television has also helped broadcasters communicate with their audience. For example, viewers can vote on an issue being covered on a news or talk show via their remote control, which allows the broadcaster to get instant feedback on where viewers stand on an issue. Moreover, viewers can choose which news stories they wish to watch and in what order.

24-hour news

Rolling news needs feeding constantly. It is an insatiable beast grinding on hour after relentless hour. When stories break, the station must cover them instantly and continue with them whether or not they have pictures. For example, the day of the release of the official report into the murders committed by Manchester GP Harold Shipman, Mike McCarthy of Sky News did 13 lives, the first at 7 a.m.

Some would argue that it's hard to follow a story if you are on air all the time. Take this description of a typical day for Peter Arnett of CNN during the Bosnian War of 1992:

> His day began – and for that matter continued and ended – on the roof of the TV station, whence CNN beams its reports to Atlanta and the world. The first thing he did was to produce a small bag from which he extracted a hand-mirror and powder puff. With these he prepared himself for his stint at the CNN coalface – fourteen live shots, one after the other, in which his task was to use news agency reports to brief his viewers on what was happening on the battlefronts. If he could see or hear anything from his rooftop perch, that was as close to eyewitness reporting as the rules of the game allowed. He pleaded with Atlanta to be let out to the front lines, in the traditional mode of war reporters, to find things out for himself. It was what he was good at and how he had made his name.
>
> 'Of course, Peter', they said. 'That's fine. Just be back in 40 minutes.'[9]

Technology has aided continuous news: it can have more lives, pictures arrive more quickly and from remote places, the newsdesk can keep in touch with reporters and move them from one story to another. But all this made covering the war in Iraq in 2003 quite arduous, says Marek Preszewicz, strand editor for BBC News 24.

> It feels like we've been covering the war forever, it's been all-consuming.
>
> Editing rolling coverage on one channel is hard enough – these days you're likely to be doing it on three simultaneously.
>
> It runs like this – roll war coverage on News 24, and at the same time opt-in BBC One – then keep it going on network [BBC One] for however long they require – while also opting in BBC World. Then opt BBC One back out smoothly, continue on two channels and opt BBC World back out – still rolling on and on with the war.
>
> Make sure the latest pictures are on as fast as possible. Embedded correspondents spring up – don't keep them waiting around in the middle of a war zone. Watch out for live Bush, Blair, Rumsfeld and Centrom [Central Command] briefings, and keep across all the wires. Running orders? Always a work in progress.[10]

There were instances when the appetite for the next new titbit meant 'facts' were being reported before they'd been confirmed, or pictures used without context. On the other hand, there were periods when nothing had happened but reporters and correspondents still had to fill the time. So in the first few days of the war, CNN showed pictures of smoke above Basra but the presenter had no idea what it meant or what was happening. A cartoon in the *Evening Standard* showed a presenter asking an interviewee, 'Not much has happened in the last 30 seconds – can you comment on that?'[11]

So what happens when stories aren't developing fast enough or perhaps they are difficult to illustrate because of a lack of pictures or access? Traditionally television would avoid these stories or keep them short, but rolling news needs them, hence it develops new devices to overcome the problems. These have included video walls, 3D virtual courtrooms, and a virtual battlefield with 3D models of planes and tanks during the Iraq War.

Video-journalism: Jack of All Trades?

Video-journalism is still in its infancy but already it is causing bunfights in newsrooms. Its supporters claim it is the future of television news, allowing journalists to become more adventurous: going places large cameras would never be accepted and getting closer to their subjects. Refuseniks say it's mediocre television on the cheap.

The guru of video-journalism is Michael Rosenblum, a former CBS producer, who has been trying to persuade news organisations of the efficacy of the video-journalist (VJ) since the late 1980s. To Rosenblum, if a newsroom has 120 members of staff, that should mean there are potentially 120 cameras rather than the half-dozen crews there would traditionally be.

In 2001, the BBC started listening. It signed up Rosenblum to train a percentage of its staff in the nations and regions (regional newsrooms and those in Scotland, Northern Ireland and Wales). These 'Rosenblumers' were given £2,000 Sony PD150 cameras, which provide broadcast-quality footage that can be edited using £400 Final Cut Pro software on a standard PC laptop.

Health correspondent Andy Joynson was among those first trainees:

> If you watch the news, in a usual piece you have a standard set of shots, say three shots, a walking shot, a clip, a piece to camera and finish. It's not hard, not taxing. It's very efficient but it's not adventurous. This new equipment is good at getting you into places you can't get with a conventional crew and you can stay with a subject much longer, all weekend if necessary getting more shots.
>
> In conventional news when any producer gives you a crew at 10 a.m they can be pulled at 12 p.m. And in conventional news you have a £40,000 camera, a cameraman, a journalist and an editor. Now you have perhaps £10,000 of equipment and only one man.

Jane Birch works as part of a team of VJs in the Hull newsroom of BBC North. In Hull there are only two reporters who still work in the traditional way and three one-person camera crews.

> It's a cliché but I have to say there is no such thing as a typical day. For instance, yesterday I worked with a camera crew and also had a craft editor for my story. Other

days I will be filming and editing a news story that has to be turned around for that night's programme. I also preshoot quite a lot of my own material as there is the opportunity to work on your own ideas 'off rota'. It's what the BBC likes to call a 'mixed economy' with a range of ways of working.

So what difference have these VJs made to the news operation? Jane says having more cameras available has increased the number of stories they are able to illustrate with pictures and allows them to respond very quickly to breaking news stories.

For instance, when a bus ploughed into holidaymakers at Skegness I was the first camera on the scene and network [the BBC's national news] were happy to use those pictures. Foreign shoots and off rota work are also easier to achieve. There's also a knock-on benefit that I think you get journalists who are more picture literate. It's no longer a case that the camera crew does the pictures and the reporter does the words. The fact that we also edit our own stories adds to that.

Rosenblum would be delighted with Jane's experience as he argues that training video-journalists is not primarily about cost-cutting, but about expanding the number of people who can bring in footage, not taking away crews but adding to them. Many are suspicious and those in the newsrooms say that on the whole the quality of the stories covered by VJs is not as good as those filmed and cut the traditional way. One producer gave the reason as a mixture of lack of experience, the cameras they are using and that a video-journalist has to think of several things at once. This last reason is mentioned as a problem even by VJs themselves. As Jane Birch asks, do they make sure they have the pictures, or secure the interviews first? And what about listening to answers while filming?

I really believe you can only truly concentrate on one thing at a time, so if you're worrying about the framing of an interview and whether the interviewee is going to move out of shot, then you can't be paying full attention to the content of what they're saying. I can't think of a specific example of where I've missed an important quote but it is always a worry!

I also sometimes feel that working as a VJ doesn't give you any time ahead of the interview to actually just chat with the guest, make them feel at ease or even find out information that might help with your questions. When I work with a crew I would normally do this as he/she were setting up the camera. As for picture-gathering, the camera I use has certain technical limitations and the more experienced you become as a VJ the more you are aware of this.

Many of those interviewed for this book believe that there are people, like Jane and Andy, who can make successful VJs – but it shouldn't be forced on everyone, not every television journalist will make a good camera operator or editor. They believe VJs should be part of a mixed economy and they accept there are benefits to training staff: when a story breaks and the nearest camera crew is too far away, they have people they can send.

Backpack journalists

If journalists picking up a video camera and cutting a few pictures are courting controversy – what about the 'backpack' or 'multimedia' journalist? They cover even more ground. Some loathe the concept.

> The Backpack Journalist – a multiple media multi-tasker capable of operating a video camera, performing a TV standup, telling a print story, writing a broadcast script, creating a Flash animation, compiling a photo gallery, grabbing an audio clip and muckraking masterfully – is like a Martha Stewart of the digital journalism age.
> What a promising, efficient concept – or is it?
> The problem is, whipping up a satisfying meal of professionally prepared multimedia journalism with a little video, audio, text, photo album, Flash, and with chat moderation à la mode, is a feast few journalists can serve up. While exceptions exist, the old adage applies: Inevitably, most backpack journalists are a 'Jack of all trades, and master of none.'[12]

Others, like Jane Stevens, who are practising backpack journalists, are thriving on the range and flexibility afforded them.

> I am a backpack journalist. I use a video camera as my reporter's notebook. I can put together multimedia stories that include video and audio clips, still photos grabbed from the video, as well as text. I can throw together graphics information for Web designers. I can throw together a simple Web page. I can't do Flash yet, or simple graphics but they're on my list because they're handy skills to learn. I can do a little muckraking, if needs be, as well as write a broadcast script and a print story. I'd rather be called Maxine Headroom than Martha Stewart.[13]

Not surprisingly Michael Rosenblum, who trained Jane Stevens, believes it is the only way forward.

> I was delighted to see Jane's piece and that she still practises the craft. We have come a long distance since VNI was founded in 1988, and the technology has improved a great deal – DV cameras, laptop edits. Much more progress has been made in Europe and in the US, and recently we entered into an agreement with the BBC to train more than 500 of their reporters to work in this way. In my opinion, within ten years all broadcast journalists will work in this way. Jane, and people like her, are simply on the cutting edge of what is going to happen … and soon.[14]

How impartial?

No matter how it is produced, broadcast news, unlike print journalism, has – by law – to be impartial. This means the BBC and commercial channels broadcast in the UK have a duty to produce news that is balanced, fair and accurate. The regulators charged with overseeing compliance with the rules are Ofcom for commercial channels and for the BBC, the BBC Trust and Executive Board. (For more on regulators see Chapter 12.)

The BBC's *Producers' Guidelines*, which echo Ofcom's draft code, are circulated to all editorial staff and state that within news programmes:

> Reporting should be dispassionate, wide-ranging and well-informed. In reporting matters of industrial or political controversy the main differing views should be given due weight in the period during which the controversy is active. News judgments will take account of events as well as arguments, and editorial discretion must determine whether it is appropriate for a range of views to be included within a single programme or item.
>
> News programmes should offer viewers and listeners an intelligent and informed account of issues that enables them to form their own views. A reporter may express a professional, journalistic judgment but not a personal opinion. Judgment must be recognised as perceptive and fair. Audiences should not be able to gauge from BBC programmes the personal views of presenters and reporters on controversial issues of public policy.[15]

But some critics have accused reporters, especially those in the BBC, of blurring fact and commentary. They claim there has been a growing reliance on commentary and analysis by specialist correspondents leading them away from their duty to be impartial in their reporting. The danger, the critics say, is that when correspondents resort to personal views and speculation they can end up misleading viewers.

> Recent editions of the *Ten O'Clock News* have provided plenty of cause for concern – with speculation, supposition, preaching and teaching by BBC journalists usurping quotes from established sources.
>
> The BBC's Washington correspondent, Stephen Sackur, was talking about US Defence Secretary Donald Rumsfeld's attitude to the Camp X-ray inmates when he threw in the imaginative passage: 'While he was much too polite and charming to say it to me, I can tell you his body language and his tone suggested he has not the merest jot of interest in what he might describe privately as the liberal bleatings of the human rights lobby.'
>
> This was an example of a reporter failing to get the quote he wanted out of a politician and resorting to speculation – bordering on mind-reading – to include it anyway.[16]

The BBC defended the trend. Deputy head of newsgathering, Vin Ray, said:

> There's no point in having people who really understand their subject for them not to make a professional judgment. What we don't want is people's personal opinions interfering and, of course, there's a fine line between the two.[17]

In the wake of the Hutton Report there has been a tightening up of the rules at the BBC in favour of impartiality. An internal investigation resulted in the Neil Report. This described impartial journalism as part of the DNA of the BBC and said that, in a world where impartiality is increasingly under pressure from partisan journalism, the BBC's continuing commitment to it is the reason why the Corporation remains one of the most trusted sources of information.

The Neil Report acknowledged impartiality is under pressure and anti-impartiality lobbyists now argue it should be done away with. They claim those who believe in impartiality are deceiving themselves and their audience. It would be more truthful, they say, to allow a wide range of openly biased news.

Supporters of impartiality say the danger of ditching the impartiality regulations and having British broadcasters offer a range of biased news such as that in newspapers is that only the loudest and richest will have their voice heard. (For a discussion of impartiality and objectivity, see Chapter 12.)

> Anyone advocating this course of action should first listen to 'shock jocks' such as Nick Ferrari on LBC, John Gaunt on BBC London, and almost anyone on talkSPORT. This is to enter a world in which, frankly, the impartiality regulations have already ceased to exist, and in which numerous complaints upheld by the various pre-Ofcom regulators appear to have been ignored. This is not a world in which a thousand ideological flowers bloom in a deregulated Eden, but one in which oafish, loud-mouthed, bullying presenters appear to have complete freedom daily to peddle views which make the *Sun* look positively liberal, and to shout down and belittle all those who have the temerity to disagree with them. Ofcom please note.[18]

Looking and sounding the part

If you have become 'on screen talent' either as a reporter or a presenter/anchor, then you will have several qualities that have helped you succeed. The most important will be the ability to appear relaxed and behave naturally in the most unnatural of circumstances – while staring into a camera lens. As one very experienced presenter explained when I was a junior, the key is to appear sincere.

Delivery

If you are relaxed and spontaneous in front of the camera, you are more likely to be able to deliver scripts effectively, putting in the appropriate stresses and emotions. In television, as in radio, a good voice and effective delivery is a must. It doesn't matter how good you look and how well you write, if you sound dull or affected your work will be weakened. See the passage on using your voice in the radio section for some useful tips. And remember that you are telling someone a story, not just reading a script.

Appearance

We've already talked about dress in the section on live reporting and everything said there is relevant here. The bottom line is that whatever you choose to wear, it should not be distracting. If you are presenting a bulletin or doing a 2-way on a big story, you do not want viewers talking among themselves about your outfit: 'That mauve shirt clashes dreadfully with the brown jacket; whatever possessed him to put those two together?' Or 'I do wish she'd tie up her hair. Whenever the wind blows, it always ends up in her mouth.'

Like it or not, how you appear to the viewers influences what they think of you as a journalist as much as, if not more than, what comes out of your mouth. If you are scruffy or inappropriately dressed it damages your credibility. Research from the United States backs this up. It shows how viewers receive messages.

- 55 per cent of the messages come from body language
- 38 per cent of the messages come from tone and attitude
- 7 per cent come from the words.[19]

Try to be smart, keeping your clothing and jewellery simple. It's a good idea to keep a spare set of clothes in your car or at the office in case you need them.

> No one said anything to me about appearance when I started presenting. But it's a visual medium and therefore if you watch television yourself, you'll notice who and what looks good. There are certain colours and shapes. For example a tailored jacket still conveys authority although reporters are increasingly unjacketed. Don't wear patterned jackets; simple, cleanly cut jackets are better. In the winter I had a red coat. I wore it for years, I realised it suited my colour and looked good – and it went over everything. I lived in a trouser suit - I had to wear something that could take me from a farmer's field to an inner city estate to an interview with a Government minister. (Geeta Guru-Murthy, presenter, BBC World and former Channel 5 reporter).

The television reporter at work

Case Study

Cathy Killick is a reporter at BBC North in Leeds. Here she takes us through a typical day, although every day presents its own challenges, as we shall see.

It's 8.30 a.m. and *Look North* producer Trudy Scanlon is briefing Cathy on the story she wants her to cover today. It's a development on a story that *Look North* first reported five years ago.

The AP (Associated Press) wire is saying that a man has been arrested in Brazil on suspicion of being a member of the militant Islamic organisation that was behind the killing of 58 tourists in the Egyptian city of Luxor five years ago. Among the dead were three generations of the same family from Ripponden near Halifax in West Yorkshire.

Cathy takes down some details: the victims were grandma Joan Turner, 53, her daughter Karina, 24, and granddaughter Shaunnah, 5; the man the Brazilians arrested is Mohammed Soliman; the terrorist group is the Islamic Group.

Trudy says *Look North* spoke to a nephew, Kenneth Robertshaw, at the time of the original shooting but his contact number was not put into the computer system. If it had been it would have saved a lot of time. Instead she's had to use Cameo, the electoral roll software, to look up the name. There are three listings in the Ripponden area but none has a telephone number listed. Cathy must go and knock on the doors to see if any of these Kenneth Robertshaws is the nephew. She takes down the three addresses.

Ripponden is an hour's journey from Leeds, so Cathy checks her map, briefs cameraman Graham Hough and sets off. At this point, she is already thinking about the structure of the piece and the pictures. She knows she has pictures from the original shooting but she hasn't seen them. She also knows she has photographs (stills) of the three victims.

I've got to get a family member to speak as the story won't really work without their reaction. Then I think we could go to Ripponden and ask the local people if they remember the family and what they think of this development.

Cathy starts thinking about what she will ask Kenneth Robertshaw if she tracks him down.

It's a straightforward, 'What's your reaction to this news?' interview. I want to probe for an emotional reaction, either it's raked up all the old emotions or more likely as he's a former police inspector he's glad to see the wheels of justice in motion. I'll also ask what ultimately is his hope now an arrest has been made?

At 10.00 a.m. Cathy arrives at the first address. She gets out of the car and puts on her smart coat: 'First impressions count,' she says, and walks up to the door. Cathy thinks this could be the home of a former police inspector. Inside the large glass porch is immaculate and on the wall is a poster from the military. But there is no answer. Cathy writes a note explaining who she is and what she wants. She leaves her contact number.

The cameraman Graham arrives; the office has just given him the name of someone who spoke to *Look North* at the time of the original story. They don't know what relationship she had to the Turners. Her name is Jackie Stark.

Leaning on the bonnet of her car, Cathy gets a number from Directory Enquiries. Jackie Stark is not at home, but the person who answers gives Cathy a mobile number. She also says Jackie Stark was Joan Turner's employer and a friend. She almost went on the holiday to Egypt. Jackie Stark is happy to speak but won't be back in Yorkshire early enough to be interviewed for tonight's programme.

Cathy and Graham head off to the two other addresses on their list. Neither is the home of the Robertshaw they are looking for.

At 11.20 a.m. they speak to the newsdesk, who have contacted the local MP, who knows the family. They are organising an interview with the MP that Cathy can use in her piece. Graham and Cathy set off for Ripponden to carry out some vox pops. When they arrive, Cathy speaks to two women who do not wish to appear on camera but they tell her the graves of the family are in the churchyard round the corner.

Cathy thinks the graves would make some powerful shots on which to end her piece. They are set out in a row: Karina on the left, Shaunnah in the middle and Joan on the right. There is a basket of flowers on Shaunnah's grave. Cathy finds a card, which says it is from her father on her birthday. She asks Graham to make sure he gets a shot of that.

Figure 5.17 Cathy and Graham interview a shopkeeper

These pictures are natural end shots. They bring home the result of the killings. I'd like some close-ups of the graves so you can see the names and the card from Shaunnah's father. I'd also like a wider shot showing the church and the lovely setting. All in all enough for a 15-second payoff.

They then make their way to the town centre, where Graham shoulders his camera and they go in search of people to question. Unfortunately, it is half-day closing, so they go to the vicarage. The vicar says the family has asked him not to speak to the media. Cathy feels it is a long time since he spoke to the family, but has to accept his refusal.

They are pointed to a shop that the family used to own. It is now a flower shop – the woman working there is willing to speak and they carry out a short interview.

Outside Cathy and Graham meet a man whose daughter went to school with Shaunnah and they were best friends. He agrees to talk.

Cathy now feels she has pursued all the angles she can, but she's worried that she doesn't have all the elements she needs.

The problem with this story is that the today angle is a one-line story. A man has been arrested in connection with the murder of three generations of a family from Ripponden. The rest happened five years ago. It's a way of revisiting and updating what was an important story. A lot of people were very affected by the story at the time and that is why we are covering it now. But I'm disappointed because I haven't got the family member. If I had time I would be knocking on more doors, trying to find Shaunnah's father.

It's 1:45 p.m. and time for a quick lunch. Cathy doesn't want to give up on the family member so after lunch she and Graham head back to the first address. This time an elderly woman answers the door. She is the mother-in-law of Kenneth Robertshaw and reluctantly admits he is the one they are looking for, but says he is out. Cathy explains why they are interested in contacting him and asks if he has a mobile phone. She promises that if he doesn't want to talk she won't pressure him.

It's 3 p.m. Sitting in the car outside the house she dials the mobile telephone number she has been given. Kenneth Robertshaw answers. He tells her he is willing to give a radio interview but does not want to appear on television. Cathy offers to send a cameraman to him wherever he is. He again insists he doesn't want his face to appear on television but he would give a telephone interview.

She speaks to the office; Trudy says she'll get someone to speak to him on the telephone. Cathy heads back to the office. She's thinking about how to put the piece together.

I can't start on today shots because I haven't any – except the grave shots and they wouldn't work as the first shots, I'd have to script to them and say something like: 'These are the graves of three people shot . . .' I think that is naff.

I'm looking for ways to use all the best material. We mustn't forget that news is partly entertainment – no-one will watch if it isn't entertaining.

Cathy arrives at the office at 4.30 p.m. She reports to Trudy. She reads the cue that Trudy has written (so she can see the angle taken and not start with the same words) and gathers the six tapes with the archive stories on them.

5 p.m.: Cathy is sent to edit in one of the five edit suites with *Look North* editor Ron Southern. She discusses the story with Ron and checks the library (archive) shots. Ron tells her they have 16 seconds of shots from the temple and of an Egyptian reading an Arabic newspaper. They need a graphic showing where the arrest took place and how far from Egypt it is. Cathy goes to talk to graphics. They suggest a map of the world that would turn from Egypt to Brazil; in this way they could show the distance between the countries. She also asks if they could do a phone graphic to put over Kenneth Robertshaw's clip.

Cathy goes back to the edit suite and begins telling her story. She first decides on the structure with Ron: Luxor archive/stills of victims/map graphic/clip of MP/funeral shots/clip Robertshaw/Ripponden shots/vox/payoff with pictures of graves.

She starts to write the script. As she writes, she speaks the words to hear how they sound. She first writes 'The temple in Luxor is still a magnet for tourists' but decides against this; there aren't enough pictures for anything but the bare facts. She starts again:

It was in November 1997 that fifty-eight tourists died on the steps of this Egyptian temple in Luxor. They were gunned down by Islamic militants wanting the freedom of their leader who was jailed in the United States.

Figure 5.18 *Look North* graphics department creating Cathy's map

Now come the still shots of the Turners.

> Among those who died were three generations of a family from Ripponden. Joan Turner, her daughter Karina and her granddaughter Shaunnah had been on holiday – in the wrong place at the wrong time.

At first Cathy thought 'in the wrong place at the wrong time' might be a bit tasteless, but the scale of the tragedy meant in this case it was appropriate.

Next it's the map graphic showing where the arrest happened. Cathy hasn't seen the graphic as it's not finished but she has a rough idea what it will look like. At first she writes: 'Last night requested by the Egyptian authorities, Brazilian police arrested – but it isn't ideal to write in the passive voice and the graphic will start on Egypt so she scratches that out and puts:

Figure 5.19   Cathy Killick and Ron Southern editing

> The Egyptian Government has been pursuing the suspected terrorists for nearly five years and had requested the extradition of one – Mohammed Soliman – from Brazil. Last night he was arrested by the Brazilian police and will remain in jail while the extradition request is considered.

After this it's the clip of the MP. So Cathy has her script down to the first clip and Ron asks her to go to the voice booth to lay her voice down so he can begin editing the pictures. He takes her voice level by asking her to read one sentence and then cues her for the recording.

The graphics arrive and Ron puts the pictures down and then lays the graphic in. They then watch the MP's interview. The first two answers cover ground Cathy has already scripted but then the MP starts to congratulate the Egyptian Government for its dogged pursuit of the terrorists – that's the clip.

Ron edits in the clip while Cathy writes the next link to go over shots of the funeral. She first writes, 'The arrest has brought back painful memories for the Turner family', but as the viewer is seeing pictures of the funeral here and not the arrest, the words won't fit the pictures. Better to write:

> The Turner family put their loved ones to rest years ago while the pursuit of justice continued – albeit slowly. Last night's arrest has brought back painful memories.

This takes her into the clip with Kenneth Robertshaw. He says:

> 'The fact that this man's been arrested is not going to bring our relations back. It's not going to reduce the heartache that we've all felt but at least if he's prosecuted and punished he's not going to be in a position to do it to anybody else.'

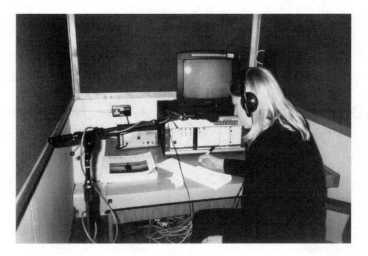

Figure 5.20 Cathy Killick in the voice booth

Looking at the time, the piece is already at 1' 18" (1 minute 18 seconds) long. She has enough time to put two of the vox pops in but not enough for a written link from the clip. She asks Ron to try putting the voxes straight off the back of the phone clip. It works because it's obvious that these are local people commenting on the arrest in Brazil.

Cathy then goes through to the voice booth to lay the last piece of voice track down. This is called the pay-off and it is over the pictures of the Turner family graves.

It's five years since the Turners died – five years that've seen an alarming increase in Islamic terrorism. It'll clearly take many more years to bring those responsible to justice and end the deaths of the innocent. Cathy Killick, BBC *Look North*, Ripponden.

As soon as she is back in the edit suite Cathy enters the details of the piece into the running order on the computer. She types in the length of her piece and the names of the interviewees and where they appear in the piece. These are important as they tell those responsible for timings in the programme – the producer, director, the news transmission assistant – the length of the piece and the times of the astons (names of interviewees).

Cathy can now review her day. It has been frustrating.

I'm generally a bit dissatisfied. I'd have liked to have a still of the man arrested. And because Mr Robertshaw wouldn't appear on camera, I had to put the MP clip before the family member, so I couldn't structure the piece in the way I wanted. There was also a lot of my voice before the first clip, which is not ideal, but I had no alternative. The end shots were the ones I wanted though.

Ron thought Cathy had done a good job with what she had. For an editor, putting together a piece like this is different from editing one where all the shots are taken on the day.

Figure 5.21 *Look North* meeting

This was basically a library piece with only a few new shots, so for me it's not taxing. With this sort of piece, a script can be ready as it's only library shots. You can edit the pictures to the script. But if you are doing a more feature-style piece, I think it's better if you can use the pictures and write the script after.

As in many newsrooms, there is a post-mortem after each night's programme where the items are discussed individually and any problems aired. The general view was that Cathy's piece lacked new material. As programme editor Ian Cundell said:

This is a classic case of Cathy having to make compromises all along. But that is the lot of a reporter and some days are easier than others. It was flawed at only having a phone clip with a member of the family and there were an awful lot of library shots.

Summing up

Broadcast news is written for the ear rather than the eye. It is written using simple words and a conversational style and is usually set in the present tense. The sentences are short using the S-V-O form.

- Numbers are spelled out.
- Attributions come first – who said it comes before what they said.
- Initials of organisations or agencies are not used unless they are widely known – NATO but not NATFHE without an explanation.

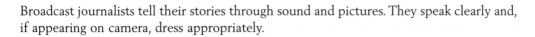

Broadcast journalists tell their stories through sound and pictures. They speak clearly and, if appearing on camera, dress appropriately.

1 Note down five rules for good broadcast writing. For example, use conversational English.
2 What do you have to bear in mind when writing to graphics?
3 How do you prepare for a live report or 2-way on television? What must you avoid when reporting live?
4 List some advantages and disadvantages of video-journalism.

1 Listen to several different newsreaders in both radio and television. Note who performs best in terms of (a) authority, (b) a good voice that is easy to listen to and (c) clarity of speech.
2 Record yourself reading five news stories from the Radio Newsroom on the internet. How do you compare with the newsreaders you listened to?
3 Keep a listening diary for a week. Listen to news bulletins on BBC and commercial national and local radio stations. Compare the style and content of the bulletins.

   (i)   Which do you prefer and why?
   (ii) Can you identify the stations' intended audience from listening for just a few hours?

4 Compare a bulletin on the same day (as close in time as possible) on BBC Radio 4 with a bulletin on BBC TV. Are pictures an advantage in telling a story? Which medium did you find the most effective?
5 Choose one important story, which is covered by all national television news services, and compare how each covered it and where they placed it in the running order. Decide which you prefer and why.

Allen, J., *The BBC News Styleguide*, see *www. bbctraining.com*/pdfs/newstylewide.pdf.
BBC, *Producers' Guidelines*, London: BBC. See also www.bbc.co.uk/guidelines.
Bell, M., *In Harm's Way*, London: Penguin, 1996.

Block, M., *Television Newswriting Workshop*. See www.mervinblock.com.

Boyd, A., *Broadcast Journalism: Techniques of Radio & TV News*, Oxford: Focal Press, 2001.

Halberstam, D., *The Powers That Be*, New York: Dell, 1980.

Harrison, J., *Terrestrial TV News in Britain*, Manchester: Manchester University Press, 2000.

Hetherington, A., *News, Newspapers and Television*, London: Macmillan, 1985.

Humphrys, J., *Devil's Advocate*, London: Hutchinson, 1999.

Online Journalism Review, Annenberg School for Communications at the University of Southern California. See www.ojr.org.

Ray, V., *The Reporter's Friend*, BBC News, 2002.

Ray, V., *The Television News Handbook*, London: Macmillan, 2003.

White, T., *Broadcast News, Writing, Reporting and Production*, Oxford: Focal Press, 2001.

Yorke, I., *Television News*, Oxford: Focal Press, 2000.

Notes

1 John Allen, *The BBC News Styleguide*, p. 7. See www.bbctraining.com.

2 Mervin Block, *Television Newswriting Workshop*. See www.mervinblock.com.

3 Vin Ray, *The Reporter's Friend*, 2002. p. 19. This is an internal publication for staff in the BBC's television news department.

4 Orla Guerin, BBC World, 24 March 2004.

5 Quoted in *The Neil Report*, 23 June 2004. See www.bbc.co.uk/info/policies.

6 Martin Bell, *In Harm's Way*, London: Penguin, 1996, pp. 113–114.

7 Vin Ray, *op. cit.*, p. 101.

8 *Broadcasting and Cable*, www.broadcastingcable.com, 12 December 2003.

9 Martin Bell, *op. cit.*, p. 209 writing about Peter Arnett whom he admired as a brave and brilliant reporter for Associated Press in Vietnam. He was now with CNN and had come to Sarajevo during the Bosnian War in 1992.

10 *Press Gazette*, 24 April 2003.

11 ITC survey carried out the week beginning 7 April 2003 about news coverage of the war in Iraq, particularly television news coverage.

12 Martha Stone writing in *Online Journalism Review*, a Web-based journal produced at the Annenberg School for Communications at the University of Southern California. See www.ojr.org 2 April 2002.

13 Jane Stevens, *Ibid*.

14 Michael Rosenblum writing in *Online Journalism Review*, www.ojr.org 9 April 2002.

15 BBC, *Producers' Guidelines*, p. 37.

16 Ollie Wilson, former TV editor of the *Daily Star* and CNN producer, now freelance. *Press Gazette*, 1 February 2002.

17 Vin Ray, cited in *Press Gazette*, 1 February 2002.

18 Julian Pefley, Professor of Film and Television Studies at Brunel University and joint chair of the Campaign for Press and Broadcasting Freedom, *British Journalism Review*, vol. 15, no. 1, 2001.

19 *Economist*, 17 June 2004.

6

ONLINE JOURNALISM

Online journalists need to work fast. On the internet deadlines are measured in seconds not hours. When a story breaks it should be published immediately. Online writers

- use simple language
- write very succinctly
- use links to guide their readers to other relevant information
- use audio and video as well as text to tell their stories
- interact with their audience routinely.

There are those who insist that the internet is just another method of distributing information to go alongside print, television and radio. This is clearly too narrow a view. News on the internet offers services never before available and hence has fundamentally altered the relationship between journalists and their audience. For journalists it requires a transformation of the way we think about the presentation of news and the way we treat our audience. The audience now expects news on demand, in greater depth and on the subjects they and not the news producers choose. They also expect to be able to register their views on a story through feedback mechanisms.

News on the internet

First let's consider what the net offers users who are interested in news.

- **Speed**. Internet users want their news fast and the online journalist can publish their stories the moment they are keyed in. A website can be updated very quickly, easily and relatively cheaply. Web users don't have to wait to hear or see the headlines at the top of the hour or read yesterday's news in the paper over breakfast.

135

- **Global reach**. National borders do not restrict internet users and they can visit sites all over the world. Bear in mind, though, that it is not a totally unrestricted environment. There are some controls placed by government agencies and your actions can be monitored.
- **A media-rich environment**. The internet can incorporate all other media. Text stories can be enhanced with moving pictures, audio, maps and other graphics. Television and radio packages can be streamed through the net. Stories with or without sound and pictures can be streamed onto PDAs (personal digital assistants), mobile phones, and in the future probably a selection of electronic devices in your house. The holy grail of future news dissemination and its collection and editing environment is what we could call the 'ubiquitous communications device' – this means the one device that will do it all. This could be PDA-like, but will be able to store and edit audio and video. It will be able to playback and record in high quality and be able to receive or send in real-time anywhere in the world. It could also have GPS and distress beacon facilities that could be very useful to lost or kidnapped hacks. You may be able to use it to pay for things. It will be secure when transmitting data and will identify you as the only person able to use it.
- **User control**. Unlike audiences of television and radio news, internet users are in control of what they watch, read or listen to. They can play news stories in any order, decide whether they wish the audio, text or video version and move on when they have heard or read enough.
- **'Personalised' news**. Many news websites allow you to personalise the content that you view on your login page and make available "news alerts" for the topics you choose, for example your home team's football score to your mobile phone. This personalisation may also be implicit: driven by the webserver monitoring your visits to the news website. It may add features tailored to you based on the personal information that you gave when signing up for a login account. My Yahoo is a good example.
- **RSS feeds**. These give you updates against chosen topics or areas of a website in summary form. A user can sign up with a news organisation, say the *New Scientist*, to be fed any stories to do with oral health; they can also sign up with the *Guardian* to be given education stories. A programme known as a feed reader or aggregator can check RSS-enabled web pages on behalf of a user and display any updated articles that it finds. RSS saves users from repeatedly having to visit favourite websites to check for new content or be notified of updates via email.
- **Links** (hyperlinks) embedded in the story allow the user to follow a theme or a subject thread, be it sound, text or film.
- **Sharing of stories**. Most news organisations allow feedback to themselves and easy forwarding to friends via email forms. The internet provides a very fast means of communication and virtual communities can be set up by people sharing the same interests.
- **Interactivity**. No longer does the journalist sit oracle-like, aloof from the audience telling them what's happened or is likely to happen. Now the journalist is just a click away and users can and do contact them with comments, updates or criticisms.

The ability for the user increasingly to interact with the news organisation has fundamentally altered the relationship between the journalist and their audience.

> Papers and TV are desperately searching for as much interactivity as their outdated formats will allow – with email addresses and phone-ins – begging the audience to give them their views. It's about connecting with your audience. We do that very well, and if you reach out to them they will come back. (Trevor Gibbons, online broadcast journalist, BBC Leeds)

It must be noted that digital television service providers have added a basic level of interactivity to some of their broadcasts. In news, for example, viewers have a choice of output from different regions, continuously updated news, sport with extra viewing and commentary options and weather. As the formats converge there will be fewer differences in what you can get through your television, phone and computer.

There is potentially a very large online audience. In Britain, a majority of homes are now online according to Ofcom, the industry's regulator (for more on Ofcom see Chapter 12) and accessing news is one of the most popular activities with online users.[1] Many people also access the internet at work.

British websites, however, are not restricted to a British audience. They can and do attract visitors from all over the globe and worldwide there are around 600 million people online. During the Iraq War in 2003 the BBC's website, which normally could expect 10 million hits a day, was getting 30 million hits a day, and many were from outside the UK. Mike Ward of bbc.co.uk put this down to regular visitors coming more often as well as new visitors coming to the site. He added that on the internet, websites can archive stories and information. This allows people using the BBC site to pick and choose what they see or read and what they follow up.[2]

It is now accepted by the industry that online journalism is distinct from other forms of journalism and has an important future. In 2001 for the first time the British Press Awards included the category of Online Journalist of the Year.

In this brave new world, what is the role of the journalist? There are some characteristics of the internet that should worry journalists. Potentially everyone is a reporter – in the United States 'bloggers' have used the internet to challenge mainstream journalism (see Chapter 12). Alternative news websites are also becoming more popular in Britain. Some commentators argue that as more people discover a journalistic approach or style that suits them on the internet, they could turn away from the traditional news suppliers in numbers sufficient to concern them.

Some of these suppliers recognise the challenges thrown up by the internet. Rupert Murdoch – the world's most powerful media mogul – has acknowledged that newspapers are out of touch with their readers and with what is expected by the next generation of news consumers.[3]

There are some who believe more people in the developed world will get news from the internet than from a daily paper.[4] In fact this may already have happened. A report by Freeserve (now Wanadoo) on people's daily internet habits claims it is now the third most popular medium after TV and radio. The study looked at 1,000 people over a two-week period. Further research showed that among 18- to 34-year-olds 44 per cent use the web once a day to find news, but only 19 per cent use a printed newspaper – and just 9 per cent described newspapers as trustworthy.[5] Because of this trend most papers now have a web presence. The *Daily Telegraph* and the *Financial Times* were among the first in the mid-1990s.

In addition, it is possible for everyone to access primary sources that would have been difficult to get hold of before. When a story breaks about a new cancer drug, the reader can go to the full report released online by the research organisation, drug company or specialist journal and bypass the main news organisations. Equally, when a football club signs a new player, the web user can go to the club's own site and read the announcement for themselves.

The popularity of 'personalised' news should also be considered – where the user orders a selection of the news he or she is interested in, receiving stories only relating to those categories. Where does that leave journalists as the people who decide which stories are important, and which are worth covering?

In fact, how relevant are the traditional stages of reporting: (1) identifying the story, (2) gathering information and (3) presenting the facts as effectively as possible? This chapter attempts to answer those questions by investigating how working online affects the journalist's approach to reporting and presenting news.

The online journalist

> People talk about online journalists as if we've got three heads. (Trevor Gibbons, online broadcast journalist, BBC Leeds)

Many online journalists still come from the traditional media, but when they join an online newsroom, they soon realise it's a very different way of working.

Speed

First, the online journalist has to work fast. The aim of online news is to get it on the website or 'live' as soon as possible. As quickly as the copy is written (and, in organisations such as the BBC, checked) it will be published on the site. While in most newspapers the information is at least eight hours old, on the web it can have been received by the newsroom just minutes before.[6]

> For us every second counts. With a big story we don't wait for the wire copy. We put the details on the site immediately. We are in the business of live breaking news rather than analysis. If the Prime Minister makes an announcement that Britain is going to join military action against Iraq, we will report that. We'll say it's happened rather than get involved in analysis of why. (Simon Glover, news editor, Ananova)

As and when the story develops, the journalists at Ananova write short follow-up pieces rather than waiting to do a round-up at the end of the day. Users can also view still pictures related to the stories.

Accuracy

Online journalists are expected to be accurate, despite working quickly. When employing staff, online news organisations tend to look for solid journalists who will maintain high journalistic standards rather than those who are purely technically skilled.

> It helps if the journalist has an interest in pioneering technologies but they've still got to be good journalists. There is no need to know HTML or other languages as if you go to other traditional news organisations they all have different software packages you have to learn. (Simon Glover, Ananova)

Multi-skilled

Increasingly, however, organisations expect you to be familiar with some of the packages in use. They also expect their employees to be willing and able to work with audio and video (see Chapter 5 for more about working with sound and video and on multi-skilling). Online journalists need to be able to write and sub-edit copy, design web pages, take photographs, in some cases operate a camera, edit the pictures and perhaps even present bulletins.

In fact video and audio are growing in importance as more news sites are now weaving increased amounts of both into their online reports. Even newspaper sites are realising the benefits. The *Liverpool Echo* increased its web traffic by more than 25 per cent in just 12 hours after broadcasting CCTV footage on the site of a man attacking an off-licence. The footage was given to the reporter while he was carrying out interviews on the story and the paper's online editor had it digitised into an Mpeg format and burned onto a DVD by a local video firm. The Mpeg was then placed online and a story in the paper pointed readers to the website. It was the first time the paper had used its website in this way and it proved so popular that since then reporters have been encouraged to treat video and audio footage as they would still pictures and to get permission to use them whenever possible.[7]

Therefore, while the journalistic standards of fairness, accuracy and writing to deadline may still be important, additional skills are needed and one core skill is being altered fundamentally.

Agenda setting

The traditional role of the journalist as agenda setter or selector of the news to be received by the audience is changed on the net. Increasingly the user decides what news they wish to receive. They do this in several ways:

- By communicating directly with the journalist or organisation.
- By using the personalised news options offered by news organisations and news based portals.
- By accessing only the stories they are interested in and in the order they wish.
- By going straight to the primary sources.

The audience

Arguably the biggest difference between journalists in traditional news organisations and their online colleagues is the relationship with the audience. Traditionally the news media kept the audience at arm's length and most journalists only had a vague idea of the make-up of their audience. Phone calls to newsrooms from members of the public, unless they brought an exclusive story, could be and in certain cases still are considered by some journalists to be a time-consuming annoyance. The audience should buy and read or watch and listen, but not be heard.

Online journalists cannot escape from their audience – and don't want to. Their audience has an active relationship with the news rather than passively receiving it. Ian Myatt, senior producer for BBC New Media in the English Regions, says online news breaks down the traditional barriers between journalist and audience. It's about communicating information both ways. Through email or form-based feedback the audience is only a click of the mouse away. There is no need to traipse to the post box with your letter or pick up the telephone and spend ten minutes trying to get through to the right person.

On the internet 'angry of Tunbridge Wells/Istanbul/Vancouver' can rant to his or her heart's content with very little effort. And they do. If the audience thinks something is important they will say so, even if the journalists would rather ignore it.

For example, users of the BBC Leeds site started to talk about the large number of *Big Issue* sellers in the city who were approaching people in an aggressive manner. It was such a popular topic that first the online site wrote it up as a news article and then BBC radio and television picked it up and also covered it.

It is relatively easy to follow up comments made by users because emails sent in have addresses attached. You can use the address to contact the sender and carry out a full interview. This gives the journalist access to a 'victim' or someone at the centre of a story. (Always keep in mind that it is possible to create a false email address, although you can protect yourself by using digital signatures and encryption.)

But if the journalists thought that, by covering the story once, it would satisfy users they were very much mistaken. News doesn't die online as in traditional media where a story is covered and then not looked at again for a long time. Users can keep it going. It makes journalists less precious about what is news.

> Users know what the news is and by Jove they're going to tell you. And if you get something wrong, they soon let you know. We have to be very responsive to our users and

what they are interested in. We've got to be able to follow up other people's ideas very quickly. (Trevor Gibbons, online broadcast journalist, BBC Leeds)

It was users of the Leeds bbc.co.uk message board (talkboard) who began and kept alive the topic of the *Big Issue* sellers. Message boards illustrate the potential of the web to encourage communities of users. News providers of all kinds on the web use them to enable readers to mobilise around specific issues or stories.

Many news organisations also offer personalised news. Online users want news that is relevant to them delivered as it happens and wherever they are. People also use portals such as Yahoo to set up a personalised desktop environment which is 'always on' – always linked to the internet. Users choose what categories of news they want to receive and will be sent ('news alerts') when a story breaks, perhaps to their mobile phone or PDA or to their desktop.

If you are going to get an alert, say an SMS message, the important thing is the quality of the information. Is it what you want? Is it important enough for you to want to be interrupted by this if you were going round Tesco's? (Simon Glover, Ananova)

Even if the user didn't tell news organisations what news they wanted to receive some news organisations would use 'clickstream' analysis to find out. Each time a user clicks on a site or a story, the action is recorded and the statistics fed back to the organisation. This tells them the 'stickiness' or popularity of certain pages or topics. For example, if someone remains on a particular internet page for an hour at about 12.30 p.m., the news organisation will know about it. The question they won't be able to answer is whether the person is really interested in that page or whether they have gone to lunch. They can guess, though, that if a hundred people spend a long time on the same page it is a popular topic.

Users of personalised news services can choose from several thousand different categories. They can have these stories emailed or they can receive short text messages on their mobile phones.

What used to be decided by the producers of news – the media bosses, the editors, the journalists – is now decided by the receivers – you. You ask us to contact you with the news that you're interested in and we'll get it to you as soon as it's available. (www.ananova.com)

So if users are setting their own news agenda and can ignore other news, where does this leave the journalist? Simon Glover believes to some extent the public has always sifted out unwanted news:

Even when people read newspapers, they select news and only read the stories they want to. To some extent we now try to do that for them and send them stories they will be interested in. As a newsroom we try to cover as much as we can so we probably fill about ten newspapers a day but we only send people the stories they want to read.

The online journalist may not have the power of journalists in other media to select the news, but the way they present the story still involves selecting what the reader will and won't see. Before we look at selection in more detail, I want to consider how we write online news. It differs from writing in the traditional media in several aspects.

Writing online

If you can't write the story in two screens then junk the idea. Users hate scrolling. (Trevor Gibbons, online journalist, BBC Leeds)

When people read online, they read differently from the way that they read newspapers. As we have already said, online users want information quickly. If a page is slow to load or they can't find what they want easily, they will go to another site. To keep them on your page, the writing must be even sharper than print and more like the spoken word.

Online writers should remember the following:

- Use everyday language.
- Get to the point quickly.
- Avoid long words, subordinate clauses or jargon.
- Make sentences and paragraphs short.

When writing on the web, always keep in mind that you are writing for people who won't give you much time to get to the point. Your copy should avoid puns and idioms as your readership could come from anywhere in the world and too many cultural references will put foreign readers off. That does not mean your writing cannot have personality, but the style and tone should reflect your intended readership. If you are writing for teenagers, then your style will not be the same as it would be if writing a retrospective or a page dedicated to tracing old friends. (See Chapters 2 and 3 for more on identifying audiences and developing style.)

Mike Ward refers to Crawford Kilian at www.contentious.com and Jakob Nielsen who between them give some sensible rules for presenting a story on the web.

- Use bullet points instead of blocks of text.
- Include questions as they make us seek the answer.
- Include unusual statements as readers love to be surprised.
- Include the promise of conflict – we love fights.
- Address the reader directly.
- Use links to split up long blocks of information into multiple pages.[8]

The last one in the list is very important. Online users wish to be able to follow threads (links) that interest them. What you must realise is that on the internet, stories are not read in a linear fashion, or from beginning to end; users want to jump in and out of a story. They may be following a link inserted into the story by the journalist or seeking additional sources using a search engine.

A link (hyperlink) is a highlighted piece of text or a graphic that takes the user to another part of the web. This could be a different place on the same web page, a different page on the same website or a page on a different website altogether. Links allow the user to follow different threads in the story. The writer inserts the link, by marking up the text or graphic, to allow the user to jump to relevant pages or sites. For example, if you are writing a story about the launch of a political party's election manifesto you could insert a link to the full audio interview with the party's spokesman and/or a link to the party's own website.

Good links explain or expand upon elements of the story forcing the reader to think about the text in a way that print or broadcast texts do not.[9] Objects that are marked up can take a range of forms – video, text, tables, audio or photographs.

Compared to old media, websites provide almost limitless areas for text, and so if a story is complicated, it should be split into parts or 'chunks' and written separately. A newspaper or broadcast journalist usually has to cover an event in one story even if there are 'hard' and 'soft' elements. In addition, they often have to choose between several possible angles. Covering the same story for the web, you can divide it into the different elements and use the appropriate style for writing each: the hard news style for the latest developments and a feature or soft style for the human interest angle.

For example, imagine you are a web journalist covering a story about so-called designer babies. A couple wants to have a baby who would be a donor of tissue or bone marrow that could save the life of another of their children. You start with the hard news story: the court's decision to grant a licence to allow doctors to carry out embryonic screening to ensure the baby would be a perfect match and the subsequent outcry from those opposed to the practice. You also write a feature-style story about the sick child and his daily struggle against the illness along with the family's thoughts about the ethics of 'breeding a cure'. There is another family in the same position and you write a feature about them. Finally you carry a story (which could be written in either a feature style or a news style) giving further information on fertility treatments.

Audio or video could be added to any of these elements: pictures of the sick child playing could complement the feature, clips with campaign groups or churches could go alongside the hard news piece. The stories could be fully packaged as audio or video stories as well as text. Finally, the online journalist must always be on the lookout for opportunities to engage the user. This story would be a good one. Most people have their opinion and so you could include user feedback.

Despite the differences, the internet remains fundamentally text-driven. The ability to write and structure a story clearly is tremendously important. Online journalists, like their old media colleagues, must still communicate their message as effectively as possible. Let's look at some examples.

Here are the opening paragraphs of two stories that appeared on different sites after the Queen Mother died in 2002. They both report Liberal Democrat MP Simon Hughes calling for the erection of her statue in Trafalgar Square.

Queen Mother Statue mooted for Trafalgar Square

There are calls for a statue of the Queen Mother to be erected in Trafalgar Square.

Liberal Democrat MP Simon Hughes says it should be placed on the empty fourth plinth in the Square.

An advisory committee to Mayor of London Ken Livingstone is currently considering what should be placed there.

'It seems to me that the Queen Mother, and a statue of the Queen Mother, fits many of the criteria people have argued for,' the Lib Dem home affairs spokesman told the BBC.

'They've said they didn't want another man, because all the other statues are men, they didn't want somebody in military uniform, who's a member of the armed services.'

'They did want somebody who was popular and would bring public affection and public attraction to one of the most public places in the country.' (Ananova)

Call for Queen Mother Statue

A statue of the Queen Mother should be erected on the empty fourth plinth in Trafalgar Square, an MP has said.

Liberal Democrat home affairs spokesman Simon Hughes said the square would be an ideal place for a memorial sculpture – and the Queen Mother in turn should be a suitable figure for the central London square.

'It seems to me that the Queen Mother fits many of the criteria people have argued for,' Mr Hughes told BBC Radio 4's *Today* programme.

'They've said they didn't want another man . . . they didn't want somebody in military uniform.'

'They did want somebody who was popular and would bring public affection and public attraction to one of the most public places in the country.' (www.bbc.co.uk)

Both stories follow the basic rules. They use simple language, get to the point quickly, use short sentences and there is also the promise of conflict. Both sites also offer links. The BBC has links to reports on the funeral, feature stories on her life and views from the public as well as the chance for users to give their views on a statue in Trafalgar Square.

The Ananova story is perhaps more tightly written. The full version of the story is nine paragraphs. The BBC's story runs to 22 paragraphs and includes four pictures. It gives a lot more detail, including some of the history of the fourth plinth in Trafalgar Square.

The story proved a popular talking point with users of both sites. The users of Ananova were on the whole against the proposal, while at the BBC there was support.

It's interesting to read the opening paragraphs of the original Press Association agency copy used as the basis for both stories. You can see how much or how little rewriting was done for the online versions.

Statue Mooted for Empty Fourth Plinth

By Jane Merrick, political correspondent, PA News

A statue of the Queen Mother should be erected in Trafalgar Square in Honour of the royal matriarch, an MP said today.

Liberal Democrat home affairs spokesman Simon Hughes said there had long been a debate about what should be erected on the fourth plinth in the Square, and a statue of the Queen Mother would be the most fitting.

An advisory committee to Mayor of London Ken Livingstone is currently considering what should be placed there, Mr Hughes said.

'It seems to me that the Queen Mother, and a statue of the Queen Mother, fits many of the criteria people have argued for,' he told BBC Radio 4's *Today* programme.

'They've said they didn't want another man, because all the other statues are men, they didn't want somebody in military uniform, who's a member of the armed services.

They did want somebody who was popular and would bring public affection and public attraction to one of the most public places in the country.

I can't think of anybody at the moment who would better fit that model than the Queen Mother, and although I'm not somebody who believes that the only way to commemorate somebody when they've died is a statue, there is bound to be a statue somewhere, so why not Trafalgar Square?'

The idea received a cautious response from Mr Livingstone, who said: 'The question of the empty fourth plinth in Trafalgar Square is one that is being considered by an advisory committee which will be reporting to me within the next few months.'

Blogging

Blogs are personal journal-style websites allowing updates to be easily made by the owner and allowing others to contribute comment. The popularity and power of news blogs as shown in the US has led some to say the internet has become a fifth estate as the fourth estate has lost confidence and trust. (see Chapter 12 for more on this argument.)

A new form of personal website is also becoming popular that encompasses all the rich media found on websites: video, audio, graphics, etc. This is being called the vlog or video blog.

Selecting the facts

Radio and TV are broadcasting to everyone at the same time and so they select news of general importance and interest. In a half-hour bulletin there is usually only time for about half-a-dozen stories and a few short OOV and copy items and it's the journalist's job to decide what news the viewer or listener should be given. In newspapers, although there is more space, a similar selection process goes on.

Online news is all on demand, and therefore you don't have to be as selective. It's also much cheaper to publish than traditional media are; hence a huge variety of news can be included in a site as long as you put a navigation system in place for people to find their way around. This will normally include a site map, news hierarchy, search engine and archive.

In this environment the user has control in choosing when and what stories to access. They are also able to go back to the primary sources – the Government press release, the scientific report, the academic paper, etc. Potentially, the journalist's traditional role of assessing information and sources for their credibility and checking for accuracy is less important. But it is not altogether redundant. Among the millions of documents, sites and sources the online user can get lost among the unreliable or the lunatic; and the latter are as available as the well researched and responsible. It is as a gatekeeper or guide that the journalist can prove very useful. They can provide links to trusted sources and other relevant sites when writing up the story and signpost sites of interest that perhaps have a viewpoint or are less reliable. The online journalist is still being selective, but the coverage is a lot fuller than in the traditional media.

Newsgathering and researching using the web

Before the online journalist can decide which facts are important for a story and write them up, they – like journalists in other media – must have researched the story. In Chapter 8 we will look in depth at researching a story and examine different sources of news. However, one thing must be recognised: the internet has vastly increased the number of potential news sources. In many cases it has also heralded the end of days spent in industrious library research and poring over hundreds of pages and pieces of paper because so many things are available at the click of a mouse.

Using the internet a journalist can find information on just about any topic, including documents, photographs and video. There are several billion web pages built by every kind of group or organisation from commercial companies, governments and news organisations to charities and pressure groups.

You'd be surprised just how much information companies, for example, will put on the internet. Many use it to serve themselves and their shareholders, and so as a journalist you can find reports, memos and sensitive statistics. Many websites now offer RSS, such as the BBC, government sites and others. These may provide a useful avenue to monitoring incoming news and updates.

The internet is also an effective way to find people, not just named people (pop stars, politicians, etc.) but people who feel strongly about things or people who have been involved in events. In fact it's hardly a disadvantage these days to work in an office without a cuttings file, or to work from home. The journalist with online access has unparalleled amounts of information at hand. The trick is knowing where to look.

Examples of the internet in newsgathering

The potential of the web as a disseminator of information – and so a rich research resource – has been shown in many events during the past decade. During the foot-and-mouth outbreak in 2001, resources on the internet included statements from DEFRA and lists of farms where foot-and-mouth had been found. This list became part of the story, with some television news stations shooting pictures of the website to show in a dramatic way the confirmed cases – they were highlighted in red. Also some farms that were cut off used webcams to communicate with the outside world.

In the same year, the internet demonstrated its popularity as a source of information with the public during the September 11 attacks. Mainstream news organisations were hit with huge volumes of traffic – *ITN New Media* had a 450 per cent increase in traffic in the hours following the attack on the World Trade Center.[10] People were logging on at work, and those who had access at home logged on for the very latest updates. Many of the sites went down under the strain. Even so, the interactive nature of the web came into its own, and its ability to pull in information as well as push it out proved very useful for news organisations. The BBC's website received 7,000 emails within 24 hours, the most moving of which they passed on to the *Today* programme and television news.[11]

But it was the non-mainstream sites that proved their worth immediately after the attacks. The online news agency Wired (www.wired.com) reported community websites, discussion groups and mailing lists as lighting up with vast amounts of information.[12] Sites such as *Slashdot, Scripting News* (see Figure 6.2) and many others published eye-witness accounts, amateur photos, video and audio of the attacks. They provided an alternative source at a crucial time.

Home
Weblog
2002
2001
2000
1999
1998
1997
1996
1995
1994
Who Reads
DaveNet?
Random
Top 50
Subscribe

Bulletin: Terrorist attack in NY

Tue, Sep 11, 2001; by Dave Winer.

Good morning ↵

Two planes crashed into New York's World Trade Center 45 minutes ago.

A hijacking, terrorism, rumors flying. Has the Pentagon been bombed too?

Most of the major news sites are inaccessible, but news and pictures are reaching us through email, webcams and the weblog community.

Tune into http://www.scripting.com/ for frequent updates through the day.

Dave Winer

Figure 6.1 Scripting News on the morning of 11 September 2001

The Hutton Inquiry in September 2003 into the circumstances surrounding the death of the government scientist Dr David Kelly showcased how quickly the internet can publish information and make it easily accessible. More than 1,000 documents, memos, reports, emails, faxes and notes were put onto the Hutton Inquiry's website by a team of eight people. Their aim was to publish the transcript of the hearing and relevant documents within three hours of receiving them. Hundreds of journalists and members of the public visited the site, making it the most popular political website in the country.[13]

Footage taken on a 3G mobile phone during the post-football riots in Croydon in June 2004 and used by ITV News gave the organisation an idea how the internet could help them. The pictures were clear enough when broadcast to lead it to place an appeal on its website asking viewers to send in up to 20 seconds' worth of 3G videophone footage on other news stories via email.[14] Since then news organisations have used material from readers and viewers regularly.

Online archives

A further excellent resource is the online archive. Many media organisations have them and allow users free access. A note of caution must be sounded here. Just as inaccuracies in paper cuttings files can, if journalists aren't careful, be repeated again and again, so it is with archives on the internet. It can be an even greater problem online, where material is easy to get hold of but perhaps difficult to check. Some organisations make a note if the material is the subject of litigation or has been found to be inaccurate, but not all. Sources must be handled with care. All online journalists should take the lesson from 'old' media, that information should be checked and corroborated.

Don't forget the telephone

In certain circumstances it can be helpful to talk to people. Online journalists must not become so reliant on data, documents, email and newsgroups that they are reluctant to pick up the phone. There are times when people who email you may have information on a story that you can get only by interviewing them. (Remember the story of the *Big Issue* sellers). All journalists, no matter in what media they work, should be skilful interviewers. (For a fuller discussion of interview techniques see Chapter 7.)

Check your information

The danger of not checking information picked up online is illustrated by the April Fool's joke which ended up as a serious news story on BBC Online and other news organisations. Here is the copy the BBC's website ran on Wednesday 3 April 2002:

Chesterfield Sign Paraguay Star

Chesterfield have pulled off their 'most amazing transfer deal ever' following an audacious swoop for Paraguayan international midfielder Paolo Rifkojels.

Pending the award of a work permit, Rifkojels will join the Spireites after the World Cup finals, where he is almost certain to be on international duty.

The 27-year old is married to a girl from Chesterfield, who he met when she was a student in Italy and he was playing for Vicenza.

Rifkojels, capped 47 times by his country and set to face England in a friendly at Anfield later this month, is currently with Argentinian champions Racing Club.

The source of the bbc.co.uk story was an article that ran on 1 April 2002 on Chesterfield Football Club's own site, Chesterfield-fc.co.uk. It was obvious from comparing the two stories that the BBC journalist took all the information in his story from the Chesterfield site. No other facts were added.

The next day, April 2, Chesterfield ran a follow-up:

Passport Issue With Rifkojels

Paraguayan star Paolo Rifkojels looks unlikely to sign for the Spireites, his
passport dropped out of his pocket and all the letters of his name reappeared
in a jumbled up way to spell APRIL FOOLS JOKE.

There are several very basic ways the journalists at the BBC (and they weren't the only
organisation to fall for this) could have checked the story:

1 They could have gone back to the site late Tuesday 2 April or early Wednesday 3 April
   to see if there were any developments.
2 They could have picked up the telephone and spoken to the club.
3 They could have checked the BBC's own archive for his name against the Paraguayan
   World Cup team.

Getting it wrong in this way makes the journalist and their news organisation look silly
and in certain circumstances can result in the public being seriously misled.

How to carry out a web search

Carrying out a search online can seem a daunting prospect. There are several billion pages
of information on the internet.[15] If you don't search properly then you are likely to
retrieve thousands of web pages. Few, if any, will be relevant.

As a general rule, the more specific your search the more likely you are to find what
you are looking for. So if you want to find out information about floods in Lincolnshire,
search for 'Lincolnshire floods' not 'floods'. Even better, search for exactly what you want,
'homes flooded in Lincolnshire in 1947'.

When I tried out the search on Google, 'floods' got back 994,000 matches, which was
far too many to look through; 'Lincolnshire floods' 2,180 matches and 'homes flooded
in Lincolnshire in 1947' got back just 27 matches, a more manageable number and the
results were much more relevant.

Search engines

Search engines such as Google are powerful pieces of software that will scan web pages
and highlight those that have your chosen keywords in them. www. google.com is considered to be one of the best search engines. Familiarise yourself with the advanced search
option to better hone your searches and avoid trawling through mounds of irrelevant
information. But be aware that no search engine has a reference to every item on the
internet. You should try to keep abreast of what search engines are available – Google isn't
the answer in every case.

While Google can be a good starting place for a search, it cannot replace good old-fashioned investigative journalism techniques. If one thread of your search fails follow another, be creative in your searches and think of different angles to come at it. You'll be amazed how much information is out there if you know where to look. With Google you can search newsgroups as well as websites. Websites in other languages should not be ignored as Google and others have translation facilities.

Email

It is estimated that there are more than a hundred million users of electronic mail and the numbers are growing.[16] Email can be used to make contact with individuals or groups. It has the advantage of being very quick and very flexible. You can also set up your email to request a read receipt, although that doesn't guarantee the receipt will be returned even if the mail is opened by the receiver.

Finding an email address

It is not always easy to guess an email address, even if you know where the person works and have the organisation's web address. Organisations use different styles of email address, but there is a recognised 'best practice'. A person called Susan Watson working at a firm called Glovers in Britain should have an email address of susan.watson@glovers.co.uk. But this is not necessarily the case.

If you know the style used for email addresses in the organisation, you could send the message and in it politely enquire that you hope you have the correct Susan Watson. If you haven't, with luck they may forward it to the Susan Watson you want to contact.

You could of course go to the website of the organisation that Susan Watson works for and see if her email address is listed there. The place to look is in the 'contacts' or 'staff' or 'about us' section. Don't spend hours trying to find an email address when you can pick up the phone and get in touch more quickly.

Always remember that email is not a secure form of communication and can be read and perhaps tampered with in transit. So be careful what you put in an email and be aware that a reply may not come from the source you intended.

News groups

By joining and monitoring news groups, you can tap into discussions and expertise on just about any subject you could dream up. They are especially useful for accessing specialist information. Through news groups (also available through Google) you can search around a billion postings covering an enormous range of subjects. Whatever you are researching, from railways to horses to classical music, you will find groups dedicated to the subject and within those groups experts in the field saying interesting things.

Mailing lists

Another avenue of information is the mailing list. Subscribing to a mailing list from a company or organisation covering an area you are researching can keep you up to date with useful developments and debates.

Chat rooms

You can find chat rooms on many niche subjects involving people as diverse as traders discussing a specific company, to academics talking about a recent conference, to fans evaluating a pop group's most recent performance. Listen in and you could find some interesting leads.

Summing up

Because people who get their news online expect to have the latest information 24 hours a day, online journalists must provide accurate news as it happens. That is a tall order for anyone. There is a temptation to bash out a story and publish it before you've had chance to check it out properly. But forgetting the maxim 'better right than first' has ruined many careers. Publish only what you know to be right.

At the beginning of this chapter the question was posed of how relevant are the traditional skills of reporting in online journalism. We've seen they are just as important as they ever were. If a potential news story comes to an online journalist, perhaps via a bulletin board or email, they must be able to identify it as a story, follow it up by gathering all the relevant facts, and then write it up in the most interesting way. All this has to be done quickly.

While in the traditional media reporters are taught their ABC – Accuracy of fact, Brevity in making their point, and Clarity so there is no doubt what happened – in online they could add one more – D for Deadline now.

It has to be noted that the 'A' for accuracy becomes more important as increasing numbers of people turn to news online for their information. If journalism of any kind is to be trusted and relied upon, it has to be understandable and correct.

REVIEW QUESTIONS

1 What makes online journalism different from journalism in other media? Try and think of at least three differences.
2 What are links? How are they used?
3 How is online feedback used? Can this be helpful to a journalist?
4 What are the advantages and disadvantages of personalised news (a) to the journalist and (b) to the user?
5 Is it more important to be accurate or to be first with the news?

EXERCISES

1 Join a news group. Choose a subject in which you are interested.

2 Pick a story that has been covered in the newspapers, online and by the broadcasters. Compare the way each has covered it:

(i) How much space or time has each given it?

(ii) How does the language differ?

(iii) How is it presented?

(iv) Taking the online version, how are the links used? Why do you think these particular links were used?

3 Next time you are going away for a few days, search on the internet for any information about where you are going. If you are flying, try to find the cheapest airline ticket.

FURTHER READING AND RESOURCES

Bibliography

Gauntlett, D., *Web Studies*, London: Arnold, 2000.

Hall, J., *Online Journalism – A Critical Primer*, London: Pluto Press, 2001.

Rudin, R. and Ibbotson, T., *An Introduction to Journalism. Essential Techniques and Background Knowledge*, Oxford: Focal Press, 2002.

Ward, M., *Journalism Online*, Oxford: Focal Press, 2002.

Websites

www.bbc.co.uk — The BBC's online site gives you access to the day's news, a huge archive, you can even find its *Producers' Guidelines* and style guides online.

www.cjr.org — Site of the online version of the *Columbia Journalism Review* produced by the School of Journalism at Columbia University in New York. It has produced some excellent articles about online journalism.

www.cyberjournalist.net — Visit their 'great work gallery'.

www.guardian.co.uk — *Guardian Unlimited*, the *Guardian*'s website, was named internet site of the year in 2002.

www.interactivenarratives.org — Carries some excellent examples of online storytelling.

www.j-lab.org — Site for the Institute for Interactive Journalism.

www.ojr.org — Site of the *Online Journalism Review*, a US site.

www.onlinenewspapers.com — Directory of online newspapers from around the world.

www.parliament.uk/hansard/hansard.cfm — Hansard: the edited verbatim report of proceedings in the Houses of Parliament.

www.statistics.gov.uk — Access to national statistics on anything from numbers of babies born to how many prisoners are being held in UK jails.

www.wired.com — Good example of a web start-up and highlights the differences in the journalism required by the internet. Note that editorial standards can be just as good.

Notes

1 Ofcom Internet and Broadband Update January 2004, at www.ofcom.org.uk. News popularity is according to Oftel (2002), www.oftel.gov.uk.

2 Mike Ward of *BBC Online* talking on BBC World, second day of Iraq War.

3 Rupert Murdoch speaking to the American Society of Newspaper Editors in Washington, *Press Gazette*, 22 April 2005.

4 Jim Hall, *Online Journalism*, London, 2001, p. 16.

5 'Cyberview', *Press Gazette*, 2 August 2002 and 'Journalists are out of touch with readers, says Murdoch', *Press Gazette*, 22 April 2005.

6 Hall, *op. cit.* p. 65.

7 *Press Gazette*, 15 April 2005.

8 Mike Ward, *Journalism Online*, 2002, pp. 128–30.

9 Hall, *op, cit*, p. 49.

10 Philippa Edward, commercial director, *ITN New Media*, quoted in the *Guardian*, 17 September 2001, p. 43.

11 Mike Smartt, new media editor-in-chief, BBC News, quoted in the *Guardian*, 17 September 2001, p. 42.

12 Leander Kahney, *Wired*, 12 September 2001, www. wired.com.

13 *Guardian*, 8 September 2003.

14 *Press Gazette*, 18 June 2004.

15 Mike Ward, *op. cit.*, p. 70.

16 *Ibid.*, p. 90.

7

■ EFFECTIVE INTERVIEWING ■

Good interviewers are easy to trust and can put people at their ease. When conducting an interview they

- have a clear idea of its purpose
- prepare carefully and consider lines of questioning
- interview rigorously but fairly
- remain well-mannered at all times.

How important?

Interviewing successfully is one of the great arts of reporting and a sure way to a good story. Why? Because a lot of what you write will be based on information given by people either in person or over the telephone. For the most part, these people will be giving the information in response to your questions. How effective your questions are and how good your interview technique is, are crucial.

You will also use quotes taken from your interviews to add colour and weight to stories. In fact, if you look at a newspaper, listen to a radio news bulletin or watch television news, most stories will contain at least one interview.

Moreover, in broadcast news the interview has become a form of packaged news in itself. Its question and answer (Q&A) style has the advantage of giving a journalist or presenter an opportunity to explore issues in greater depth and challenge a public figure on their position more rigorously. Because interviews are essentially unscripted, even if both sides have an agenda in mind, you can never be absolutely sure what will be said or how interviewee and interviewer will get along. This can make for lively listening and watching. Journalists who show skill at questioning and interrogating in this environment are pretty much guaranteed a bright career.

What exactly is an interview? It is a conversation with a source. But it is not the same as an informal chat, even if it can appear that way sometimes. The source has information important to you, so an interview is to get them to tell you. A journalist should always have a clear idea of the purpose of each interview – why you are talking to this person and what it is you want to know.

It's not as straightforward as it may seem. In fact, meeting and questioning people in this way requires good planning, plenty of tact and patience, a certain amount of psychology and – obvious as it may seem – courtesy.

> I once heard about a reporter on a local paper covering the Bradford football stadium disaster [56 fans were killed when a wooden stadium at Bradford City Football Club caught fire in 1985]. She was the only one out of about a dozen reporters that a bereaved family spoke to. Why? Because she shut the garden gate after her. (Bob Bounds, editor, *Kentish Express*)

Types of interview

Clearly, no two interviews are ever quite the same and you will have to employ a variety of questioning styles. To guide you, we can look at interviews as broadly falling into three categories according to what it is a reporter wants from them. First, we'll discuss the categories and then look at the different approaches needed.

The informational interview

In these interviews you are trying to get a description of what is happening or has happened. You will want to establish the facts of a situation and gather information about those involved. If the story centres on a person, you will want to encourage them to open up to you. This sort of interview can involve questioning a member of the public or the emergency services or an expert on a particular subject. Often these people are not used to being interviewed, so you must gently draw them out. With these interviews it is normally not appropriate to be too confrontational.

The expositional interview

This is where a politician or campaigner on an issue is putting forward their point of view or justifying themselves and they need to be challenged to allow balance. The big set-piece interviews on BBC 2's *Newsnight* or the *Today* programme on Radio 4 fall into this category. When conducting such challenging interviews beware of getting into arguments with interviewees. Sometimes a softly-softly approach works better; as Jon Snow explains: 'As long as you ask something reasonably charmingly, you can ask more or less anything' (Jon Snow, presenter, *Channel 4 News*).[1]

The interpretative interview

Here you want members of the public to give their opinion on something that affects them. These can be short vox pops carried out on the street or longer interviews. Although they are giving a point of view, it is not appropriate to give them too hard a time in the interview. Rather, as they are not seasoned interviewees, they should be encouraged to open up in the same way as in an informational interview.

Two famous examples

Let's look at a couple of well-known interviews and see what category we think each is in and why.

The first is an interview on the BBC2 *Newsnight* programme between presenter Jeremy Paxman and former home secretary, Michael Howard, in May 1997. It centres on the sacking of the head of the prison service, Derek Lewis.

Howard had claimed before the House of Commons that although he set policy in the prison service, he did not get involved in operational matters. This was contradicted by some of those involved and if they were right it would mean Howard had misled the House of Commons. Paxman uses the sacking of Lewis and the circumstances surrounding it to test whether Howard was, in fact, involving himself in operational matters.

Howard claims he dismissed Derek Lewis because of weaknesses in the management of the prison service. Lewis, on the other hand, claims he was dismissed because he wouldn't sack the governor of Parkhurst Prison on the Isle of Wight. Howard wanted the governor sacked after some prisoners escaped. Derek Lewis refused and claims Howard threatened to overrule him. If this were the case, Howard would be involving himself in operational matters.

We enter the interview as Jeremy Paxman (JP) is asking Michael Howard (MH) directly for the first time whether he threatened to overrule Derek Lewis.

> *JP*: Mr Lewis says: 'I (that is, Mr Lewis) told him what we had decided about Marriott [the governor of Parkhurst] and why. He (that is, you) exploded. Simply moving the governor was politically unpalatable. It sounded indecisive, it would be seen as a fudge. If I did not change my mind and suspend Marriott, he would have to consider overruling me.' You can't both be right.
>
> *MH*: Mr Marriott was not suspended. I was entitled to express my views; I was entitled to be consulted.
>
> *JP*: Did you threaten to overrule him?
>
> *MH*: I was not entitled to instruct Derek Lewis and I did not instruct him. And the truth ...
>
> *JP*: Did you threaten to overrule him?
>
> *MH*: The truth of the matter is that Mr Marriott was not suspended. I did not...

JP: Did you threaten to overrule him?

MH: I did not overrule Derek Lewis.

JP: Did you threaten to overrule him?

MH: I took advice on what I could or could not do...

JP: Did you threaten to overrule him, Mr Howard?

MH: . . . and I acted scrupulously in accordance with that advice, I did not overrule Derek Lewis.

JP: Did you threaten to overrule him?

MH: Mr Marriott was not suspended.

JP: Did you threaten to overrule him?

MH: I have accounted for my decision to dismiss Derek Lewis . . .

JP: Did you threaten to overrule him?

MH: . . . in great detail before the House of Commons.

JP: I note you are not answering the question of whether you threatened to overrule him.

MH: Well the important aspect of this, which is very clear to bear in mind . . .

JP: I'm sorry, I'm going to be frightfully rude, but – I'm sorry – it's a straight yes or no answer.

MH: You can put the question and I will give an answer.

JP: Did you threaten to overrule him?

MH: I discussed this matter with Derek Lewis, I gave him the benefit of my opinion. I gave him the benefit of my opinion in strong language, but I did not instruct him because I was not entitled to instruct him. I was entitled to express my opinion and that is what I did.

JP: With respect, that is not answering the question of whether you threatened to overrule him.

MH: It's dealing with the relevant point, which is what I was entitled to do and what I was not entitled to do and I have dealt with this in detail before the House of Commons and before the Select Committee.

JP: With respect, you haven't answered the question of whether you threatened to overrule him.

MH: Well you see the question is what was I entitled to do and what was I not entitled to do? I was not entitled to instruct him and I did not do that.

JP: We'll leave that aspect there.

If you had this interview down as falling into the expositional category, you'd be right. It involved a politician – former home secretary Michael Howard – justifying his dismissal of the head of the prison service and being challenged on the details by *Newsnight* presenter, Jeremy Paxman.

This is a very well-known and extreme example of a journalist pushing for the answer to a question and a politician doing all he can to avoid a direct answer. Paxman asked the same question 14 times and still did not receive an answer.

Notice how Paxman starts with a challenge to Howard to explain why his story contradicts Derek Lewis's. Then he begins to try to corner him by throwing a closed question, 'Did you threaten to overrule him?' which demands a yes or a no answer. He doesn't receive a direct answer, even when later on he points out that the question needs a simple yes or no response. His repetition of the question and Howard's continual avoidance of a direct answer is a wonderful example of the ping-pong style of political interviews. It also shows how politicians will rephrase a journalist's question to make one they *do* want to answer: 'Well you see the question is what was I entitled to do and what was I not entitled to do?' But rarely does a journalist expose so fully the reluctance of a politician to address the question.

The second interview is Martin Bashir's interview for the BBC's *Panorama* programme with the Princess of Wales not long before her divorce.[2] We will look at just a few minutes from the interview but it is a representative section where Bashir (MB) questions Diana (PW) about her bulimia. It starts with the princess explaining the illness.

PW:	You fill your stomach up four or five times a day (some do it more) and it gives you a feeling of comfort. It's like having a pair of arms around you, but it's temporary. Then you're disgusted at the bloatedness of your stomach and then you bring it all up again and it's a repetitive pattern, which is very destructive to yourself.
MB:	How often would you do that on a daily basis?
PW:	It depends on the pressures going on. If I had been on what I call an away-day or I'd been up part of the country all day, I'd come home feeling pretty empty because my engagements at that time would be to do with people dying, people very sick, people with marriage problems, and I'd come home and it would be very difficult to know how to comfort myself, having been a comfort to lots of other people. So it would be a regular pattern to jump into the fridge. It was a symptom of what was going on in my marriage. I was crying out for help but giving the wrong signals and people were using my bulimia as a coat on a hanger. They decided that was the problem – Diana was unstable.
MB:	Instead of looking behind the symptom at the cause?
PW:	[Nods]
MB:	What was the cause?
PW:	The cause was a situation where my husband and I had to keep everything together because we didn't want to disappoint the public, and yet obviously there was a lot of anxiety going on within our four walls.
MB:	You mean between the two of you?
PW:	[Nods]
MB:	And so you subjected yourself to this phase of bingeing and vomiting?
PW:	You could say the word subjected, but it was my escape mechanism and it worked for me at that time.
MB:	Did you seek help from any other members of the royal family?

PW: No. You have to know that when you have bulimia you're very ashamed of yourself and you hate yourself. And people think you're wasting food, so you don't discuss it with people. And the thing about bulimia is your weight always stays the same whereas with anorexia you visibly shrink. So you can pretend the whole way through, there's no proof.

MB: When you say people would think you're wasting food – did anyone suggest that to you?

PW: Oh yes, a number of times.

MB: What was said?

PW: Well it was just, I suppose you're going to waste that food later on. That was a pressure in itself. And of course I would, because it was my release valve.

MB: How long did this bulimia go on for?

PW: A long time, a long time. But I'm free of it now.

MB: Two years, three years?

PW: A little bit more than that.

This is an informational interview. There had been a lot of reports about the state of the Princess's health and her marriage to Prince Charles, but this is the first time she has talked publicly about it. Martin Bashir wants to give her the opportunity to explain her situation.

To encourage her, he uses lots of open questions: What was said? How long did this go on for? These questions demand an explanation, the opposite of closed questions, which need only a yes or no answer. But he also asks some closed questions when he wants a point clarifying: 'You mean between the two of you?'

Martin Bashir carefully takes the Princess step by step through her story, gently clarifying but moving on when he has got all he can. He does not press too hard for an answer when one is not forthcoming, for example on exactly how long she suffered from bulimia.

Preparation

In both interviews above, the interviewers were very well prepared. They knew the people they were interviewing and thoroughly understood the topics that were to be covered. From the start they were able to adopt the style they felt to be most appropriate and ask pertinent questions. They also knew when their questions were being answered and when they were being evaded. What about this next example?

A young journalist is despatched to interview an actor promoting the play he is starring in at the local theatre. The editor wants a story for that evening's paper. Although the reporter has heard of the actor, he doesn't know a lot about him and when they meet he mispronounces the actor's name. He is corrected and both men look uncomfortable. The reporter decides on an easy first question and asks if the actor likes the city. 'Yes, very much,' is the reply. Pleased, the reporter asks why. 'Well as you probably know, it's my hometown,' the actor says, looking at his watch.

The reporter did not expect this and realises he is losing his way with the interview. He struggles to think of the next question and finally asks if growing up in the town has shaped the actor's career in any way? The actor brightens. 'Of course it made me who I am and I have drawn on the characters I knew in my childhood for many parts I've played. In fact, the part I'm playing in this play is based on my old English teacher at the High School here.'

The reporter is worried, he is getting somewhere now and would like to pursue this line of questioning, but he does not know much about the play beyond its title and general theme. He wonders whether to try to bluff his way out and get the actor to describe how the character resembles the teacher and check more details when he gets back to the office, or to come clean.

He decides against bluffing, as it would limit the questions he can ask, and comes clean, asking the actor to explain the play in detail and the part his character plays in the story. While a little taken aback, the actor obliges and even hands over some promotional material. Relief for the reporter – he is now able to talk easily with the actor and the remaining ten minutes of the interview are very fruitful.

Luckily, in this instance the reporter recovered the interview, but the example highlights the importance of preparation before an interview. You should do as much research as you can on the person and the interview topic. This helps you establish the interviewee's confidence in you. It also means you can ask the right questions – questions the interviewee can answer. Good preparation also stops you being fooled or bamboozled by interviewees.

The problem, obviously, for our young reporter was that he didn't prepare adequately for the interview. He had no background information about the actor at all and so was singularly unprepared for the answers he got. Therefore, for the first few minutes he failed to establish any rapport with the actor and was in danger of losing the interview altogether. You should not be afraid to admit you don't know something – but there are some things you would know if you had done your homework. Before speaking to the actor, our reporter should have found out everything he could about him and his reason for being in the town.

How to prepare

As we've said, it's important to do your homework before an interview. This may include choosing an appropriate interviewee, in which case you have to make sure he or she is qualified to comment and is available to be interviewed.

When your research begins you may have time only for the most basic preparation, but in a few minutes you can gather some information and do a little planning. If you have more time, then try and work through the list below. It has been compiled after talking with working journalists and reading Fred Zimmerman's advice in Melvin Mencher's *News Reporting and Writing*.[3]

- First check the library clippings for any stories your news organisation has done before on the person and the topic. If your paper doesn't have clippings files, you can do a quick search on the internet (for more on using the internet, see Chapter 6).

- Think about what you want from the interview. What is the main point of the story? What are the arguments that you need fleshing out? It helps if you start to consider the structure of your story.
- You will need quotes, anecdotes and other evidence to support the arguments. Think of lines of questioning which may elicit these.
- Some people write out their questions beforehand, others just jot down notes. But if you do write out the questions, never slavishly follow your list as it stops you from listening to the answers you are being given and following up new leads.
- In preparing for interviews on sensitive subjects, theorise beforehand what the person's attitude is likely to be towards you and the subject you are covering. What is their role in the event? Whose side are they on? What kind of answers can you logically expect to your key questions? Based on this theorising, develop a plan of attack that you think might mesh with his or her probable attitude and penetrate his or her defences.

These are general guidelines, but you must adapt your technique to suit the specific situations, i.e., the person you are interviewing and the reason you are interviewing them. This last one is important – is it a purely informational interview or do some of the arguments need rigorous testing?

| **Case Study** | **The television interviewer** |

Geeta Guru-Murthy, presenter, BBC World:

Guests are either in the studio or down the line. When I know who I am interviewing, I prepare by getting background information. Sometimes I ring and talk to them about their position and angle on the story. Perhaps too I will ring other people to get the other side.

If talking to the Under-Secretary of State for African Affairs for Washington about a famine, I would look at the wires and I might find Unicef had said something. The producer might give me a press release for background and if you have time you might ring Unicef and ask for their view.

An interview will last around 2 minutes 30 seconds or 3 minutes 30 seconds if it's a big interview. It can be combative; we are not there to give them an easy ride.

You have to remember to ask the questions the audience need to know. The African viewer will know more about the area than you do, so will want more detail, but the Chinese viewer will know very little, so getting the level and tone right is hard.

But there are more people not from the area than are, and there are different levels of knowledge about stories. Most people know more about Bush than many other leaders.

It's hard to know exactly who the audience is. Research says it's obviously people with TV and in some countries this means a small number of ABC1s: decision makers, politicians and diplomats. So there is no point in making things too simplistic. And on big stories everybody still listens and watches the BBC and trusts us. A number of people have told me that everyone watches us in Kabul. It makes you realise it matters and people are following your interviews.

Figure 7.1   Geeta Guru-Murthy in the BBC World studio

The interview

> Building a rapport, even with the most obdurate of interviewees, is important. But accepted that many people will feel uncomfortable, suspicious or even hostile, the important factor is to remember to do the basic job right; gather the facts, check them and be polite at all times. And finally, after you have asked the dreaded question of their age, get a contact number (and tell them not to talk to the opposition paper!).
> (Bob Bounds, editor, *Kentish Express*)

Now it's time to look at what you do when you get to the interview.

First impressions

On meeting you, an interviewee is going to decide fairly quickly whether it is in their interests to talk to you. If you have put them at their ease and made them think you can be trusted, then you are more likely to get what you want. There are some cases, usually in expositional interviews, when you may want to be confrontational from the start in order to wrong-foot an interviewee, but these are special cases. Usually when you first get into an interview you will wish to project an image that is friendly, empathetic and competent.

Make sure you are wearing appropriate clothes and are well turned out. Scruffiness shows a lack of respect for the interviewee – you couldn't even be bothered to tidy yourself up before seeing them. It is also a sign of sloppiness, the opposite of the image you wish to project.

You should introduce yourself politely, give your name and the news organisation you work for, and explain why you want to talk to them. Many inexperienced reporters forget these preliminaries and launch straight into the questions. This is off-putting for the interviewee. Imagine talking to someone about a subject of importance and not knowing who they are or which organisation they represent. Introducing yourself properly is not only good manners, it also helps more experienced interviewees tailor their answers to suit your audience. If they know you are from the local weekly paper, they can give you more details – names of local people who are involved, where they work/live and so on – than would be needed for the regional evening paper.

The art of questioning

You have introduced yourself and you're about to ask the first questions. Thorough preparation for an interview will lead you to the topics that should be covered, but even if you've had little time to prepare, you should have a good idea of what information you want from an interviewee before you start questioning them. In this way the pertinent questions will become clear. Keeping the structure of your story in mind will also help you to ask the questions that will elicit the information needed to flesh it out.

Simple is not stupid

Before you get to the meaty questions, you may want to loosen up your interviewee. A good way to do this is to gather some basic information: check the names of those involved and their titles, ages and addresses. Make sure you have the correct spellings. If you are talking to someone well-known, you may ask about their latest activities. These sorts of questions help to relax an interviewee and get them used to talking to you. It can also give you a chance to double-check information gleaned from the files.

Checking names and titles and going over the basic information is something that young reporters can neglect. They forget – or perhaps think it is impertinent – to ask the headteacher Mrs Smith for her first name. Your editor will not be impressed if you come back with only half a name or an incomplete job title. These details give the reader confidence in the veracity of a story and, if there is more than one headteacher called Mrs Smith, it identifies which one you are talking about. This is particularly important in court cases.

Once the preliminaries are over you can get on with the substantive questions. What style of questioning you use will depend on the kind of interview it is. Many interviews will be part informational and part expositional or interpretative, and so your questioning style will change during the interview.

Questioning for an informational interview

A lot of interviewing is making sure you have answered the six news questions: Who? What? When? Where? How? Why? In stories about incidents such as accidents, fires, floods, crimes, it is vital you answer as many as you can and build up a clear picture of the sequence of events. In this case you need to use lots of open questions: What happened? What happened next? Where did they go? What did they do then? How did they react?

Figure 7.2   An informational interview for radio

Sometimes you will be interviewing eyewitnesses or victims who may find it difficult to gather their thoughts. It is a good idea to take them step by step through what happened, gathering as much material as you can.

> So when you get to the core action, slow them right down and get every detail that you can. Ask them what happened at every moment, what they saw, the colours, smells, noises. Ask them where they were standing, what people were wearing, what they shouted, what the weather was like.[4]

Use lots of open questions to draw out the information. These are questions to which you can't answer yes or no. They're the opposite of closed questions such as: Were you frightened? Do you think it was the right thing to do?

With people who are reluctant to talk, if you use the wrong technique you will get nowhere. John Sergeant, formerly BBC chief political correspondent and political editor with ITN, describes his experience as a cub reporter on the *Liverpool Daily Post and Echo*. He was despatched to find out the details of an accident at a factory, which killed a worker.

> I arrived with a determined air, and placed my notebook firmly on the desk. 'Well,' I asked, 'so how did the man die?' I had a clear belief in the right of the press to information and was somewhat taken aback by the reply.
>
> 'We are not saying anything,' the manager announced. 'The whole matter will be dealt with by head office.' My disappointment, which I did nothing to hide, failed to

move him. Nor did my protestations that the last edition of the *Liverpool Echo* was only minutes away.

Sergeant persisted but failed. Then the chief reporter, Don McKinley, arrived projecting a mood of unhurried calm.

'I suppose you're not saying anything.' He smiled sympathetically at the manager. 'I should think you'd want head office to deal with this one.' The manager nodded vigorously. 'Quite right, too,' Don continued. 'What an awful business.' He paused and looked out of the window at a pile of rubble in the centre of the plant, which I had failed to notice on the way in. 'Was that it; did the wall fall down?'
'Yes,' said the manager sadly.
'Oh dear,' said Don. 'It must have been 30 feet high?'
'No, no, 20 feet.'
'He couldn't have had a chance?'
The manager sighed. 'Not a chance.'
'Been with the firm a long time?' Don ventured.
'It was his first week in the job,' the manager sighed again.
The whole exchange lasted little more than a minute. We said our farewells and walked slowly across the plant. Immediately we were in the road outside Don made a run for a nearby telephone box; for a middle-aged man he had a surprising turn of speed. He dictated the story straight to a copy taker; at no point had he used a notebook. It made the lead in the last edition of the *Liverpool Echo*. I was beginning to realize what it was like to be a reporter.[5]

Being aggressive or pushy was the wrong course of action, as it usually is in these situations. The more experienced chief reporter used a mixture of gentle closed questions, comment and open questions. Often with reluctant interviewees you have to gently coax information out of them. Seeking confirmation rather than asking direct questions can work very well.

The less threatening you can be the better. Making statements can work here. For example, rather than a brusque, 'How do you spell your name?', a less threatening approach is, 'I'd just like to check how you spell your name.' You could perhaps delay taking out your notebook, or as in the example above, don't take it out at all (but only if you have a very good memory).

Questioning for an expositional interview

Exactly how you carry out this kind of interview will depend on whether you are doing a set-piece interview for radio or television or gathering some quotes for a print article. But whatever the purpose, it is important to be well prepared for an expositional interview. During your preparation, you should be asking yourself: Why is this person talking to me? What is their agenda? The answers you come up with could suggest a line of questioning or put you on your guard.

It is usually not a good idea to open your interview with a challenging question. At this stage you need the interviewee to trust you or at least feel comfortable enough to begin to open up a little bit. So start by asking open questions and get them chatting in an easy manner.

In the early stages you are collecting information: their attitude to the subject, their position, their objections. All the time you should be listening closely to what they say and gauging their tone. Watch the body language too – are they tense, aggressive or relaxed? Is this the way you thought it would be, is your background work correct?

Note down anything interesting to follow up that you hadn't thought of, and remember to fill in facts needed to write your story. At this stage if they are talking fluently and about things relevant to the story, you may not want to interrupt them to follow a new line, but remember to come back to it later. As they are talking, you can encourage them through your body language- nodding, smiling- and 'keep going' questions such as, Why did you do that?, What do you mean? and Could you tell me a bit more about that?

Your questions should be leading them logically through the arguments. Keep in mind the structure of your story. Have you got any interesting quotes or anecdotes? If you don't understand something, don't be afraid to ask. If you don't understand, you can be sure plenty of your readers, listeners or viewers won't either. Even someone who has prepared well, even specialist reporters, can't know everything about a subject.

This is all leading up to the tough question or questions that are the point of the interview. Don't ask these until you have enough to write your story anyway, as the interview may end abruptly once you start. Local newspaper reporter, Jacob Rezneck, in his first job since graduating, finds this technique helps him when he is interviewing.

> I use the 'I am not a threat' approach. You lead in with all the easy stuff and hit them with the tough questions at the end. That way at least you walk away with something.
>
> One of the greatest challenges is to keep one step ahead of the interviewee and have the right follow-up question on hand. I have to do a lot on the phone, and after I hang up I say, 'damn – I should have asked them this or that question.' That is why I conduct interviews in person whenever possible.

One of the hardest things to do is to keep control of the interview but also follow up any interesting points made by the interviewee. If you don't want to interrupt at a given point but they have hinted at something potentially interesting, make a note of it and follow it up later. 'You mentioned a few minutes ago that at one meeting things got a bit fraught between the foreign secretary and his French counterpart. How fraught?' Otherwise interrupt and ask for more information at once and return to your original questions later. This works if you judge that the flow of the interview won't be unduly affected.

When the time comes, don't be afraid to ask the difficult question. To make it less confrontational, you can couch it in a roundabout way, by saying, 'Your critics say that it was only because your brother-in-law was chairman of the council's planning committee that you got the job. What would you say to those critics?' This way other people are the baddies and you are offering a right of reply.

Always remain polite, but if it is a public servant – a politician, councillor, police chief, health official – then you have a right to press hard for an answer. Just because someone refuses to answer doesn't mean that you should give up. You can try and change their minds in a number of ways. You can show surprise or disbelief at their refusal, rephrase the question, remind them the public has a right to know what they are doing on their behalf, say you will have to write the story anyway and let them know how a 'no comment' will look in print.

Some reporters find it hard to ask the tough questions that may upset or offend. A young journalist once asked if it were possible to avoid these situations, 'because I don't think I can do it'. The answer given to that student and to all would-be journalists is there is no alternative. You have to ask the questions. It is your responsibility. If you really can't find it in you to put someone on the spot, you need to think of another job. But just because we have to do it, does not mean we relish the prospect. Many journalists don't like verbally roughing people up, but they realise that sometimes it is necessary to get to the truth.

The challenging first question

There are some occasions when you may wish to put aside the gentle warm-up questions. It may be that in a set-piece interview with an experienced politician or campaigner you do not want them to relax. Instead you may want to unsettle them, to try to cut through the armour-plated media coaching and demand straight answers to difficult questions. Then it is appropriate to wade in hard with the first question, closing down the options for the interviewee.

Tough set-piece interviews can offend. They can be especially abhorrent to those who have been their target. Over the years programmes such as BBC Radio 4's *Today* programme have been criticised for the way they interview politicians by (surprise, surprise) politicians of all sides.

In a particularly scathing attack, the Labour Party general secretary complained that he found it hard to think of an instance where the *Today* programme had dealt with a politician of any party as though they were not a consummate liar who was trying to line their own pockets.

> People in public life make mistakes like anybody, but, generally speaking, I have run into hardly anybody who did not have honest and honourable intentions. The idea it is all just corrupt is corrosive and there is now a very significant problem in getting people to want to engage in political life or political debate and we cannot afford that.
>
> The way in which people are interrogated seems to me now to have a great deal more to do with the ego of the interviewer than it has to do with any illumination of the facts.[6]

Rod Liddle, the then *Today* programme editor, defended their interviewing style:

All we want to do is find out the truth. As politics is more and more stringently managed, it becomes that much harder to get to the bottom of issues.

Interruptions are justified when presenters need to bring an interview back on track.

We do not see any need to change our approach. *Today* listeners expect to hear politicians challenged.[7]

Today presenter John Humphrys believes it's imperative that policies and ideas are tested rigorously on air because more and more people now get their political information from television and radio.

The vast majority of political interviews are conducted with reason and good humour on both sides and most are straightforward attempts to find out what a particular policy or political development is all about. Sometimes the minister does not want to say, and then the interviewer will persist or, at least, should persist. Sometimes the minister will mislead, or deny the blindingly obvious. Then the interviewer will argue and it may become a little heated. Sometimes the interviewer will stray into an area the politician would prefer not to discuss. When that happens the politician will invariably use some dismissive phrase such as 'tittle tattle'. You know the sort of thing.

'It really is a great shame, John, that all you people in the media seem interested in is the entirely unproven allegation that sixteen government ministers were involved in a wife swapping orgy on board Concorde when what really matters to the ordinary voter – to real people – is the disgraceful way the other party behaved when it was in power.'

'Well yes, minister, but there is the small matter of Concorde being chartered at the taxpayers' expense and ...'

'You see! There you go again. Tittle tattle! That's all you're interested in. Now let me tell you what this government has achieved since we came to power ...'[8]

Questioning for interpretative interviews

These interviews are similar to informational interviews in that your interviewees are unlikely to be experienced and therefore need gentle handling. You'll be talking to people about their views on something that is happening or has happened to them. Perhaps it is the closing of the local school, or the siting of a wind farm next to their village, or the threat of job losses in their factory.

You want to hear what they have to say, so ask them open questions and listen carefully to their replies. They may have very strong opinions that will need challenging, but the challenges should be gentle. Inexperienced interviewees do not deserve to be roughed up by interviewers, except in rare circumstances when they are peddling very extreme or unpalatable views.

Sometimes these interviews are vox pops and so there is little time for preliminaries. You may believe that carrying out a vox pop is easy – a quick question to a cross-section of people on a given topic – but it is not. The exact wording is crucial.

Take the example of a vox pop in a town where a wind farm is planned. An open question, 'What do you think about the council's plans to site a wind farm here?' could give long unfocused answers or you could get some angry, to-the-point replies, but it's a bit of a lottery. A closed question, 'Do you want a wind farm on your doorstep?' could get a plain no or yes. Then you have to follow-up with 'Why?' You could also try 'Are you in favour or against a windfarm?' Again you may get very short answers that don't tell you much. Sometimes asking two questions at once – 'Are you for or against the windfarm and why?' work, but more often than you'd think interviewees answer only one of the questions and forget the second one.

When you approach people for an interview, do not just stick a microphone under their nose. Instead, take a minute to introduce yourself and explain why you'd like to speak to them. Then you can ask your question.

Getting good quotes

Good quotes animate a story. When readers see the quotation marks, they expect to be shocked, amused or moved. It is the journalist's job to make sure that they are not disappointed by the mundane and the drab.

Quotes bring the human element to stories, so always quote an individual if you can rather than an organisation or institution. 'Fred Parks of Age Concern said' is preferable to 'Age Concern England said'.

Ensuring you get strong quotes takes dedication. The only way is to listen carefully to what an interviewee says, show you are interested in their story and follow up any promising leads. If you don't listen you will miss the quotes, and if you appear indifferent to a source they will not give of their best.

> All interviewees perform better with an appreciative audience – so let them know how interesting you find them. This often helps a lack-lustre performance rise to meet expectations.
> … What stops interviewees talking is a brisk efficiency in getting to the next question, a 'hurry-up-I'm-on-deadline' approach, reducing the interviewee to info-fodder.[9]

If you are listening attentively, you will not make the mistake of many trainees or inexperienced interviewers of slavishly following your list of questions, clinging on to them like a drowning man clinging to a floating log. If the interviewee says something fascinating but unexpected, let go of the questions, float away from them for a while. You can come back to them once you have explored this new line of questioning.

It is very easy to take refuge in your questions. Let's listen in on a trainee interviewing the manager of a chemist's shop after a fire. The trainee starts well, introducing herself and checking the name of the manager and how it is spelled. Her opening questions are also good.

> *Q*: Could you tell me what happened?
> *A*: Well yes, we had a fire in the stock room. It started around 1 a.m. A couple of passers-by spotted smoke coming from the shop and let the police know.

Q: Do the police know how it started?

A: We're not sure how it started but we think it might have something to do with animal rights activists.

Q: How much damage was caused?

After such a good start, it is disappointing to see the trainee go straight past the story. Instead of following up on the extraordinary statement that it is thought the fire may have been started deliberately by animal rights activists, she asks the next question on her list – how much damage was caused by the fire?

This was only a training exercise, but in the real world the trainee would have missed the most interesting angle: the information that sets this story apart from other shop fires. By not asking why the manager believes the fire was started by animal rights activists and what the staff feel about being targeted in this way, the trainee has forfeited the most worthwhile and probably the most emotive quotes. She had her list of questions and she was damn well going to get through them come what may.

What also won't have helped her performance was that she rarely looked up from her notebook. It is important to maintain eye contact with an interviewee. Obviously you have to look down to take notes, but look up often to encourage the interviewee to keep talking. Eye contact also tells the other person you are listening and are interested in what they are saying.

Once you have the quotes, sometimes you may find that the interviewee has made some grammatical errors. Should a print journalist correct them (it is obviously not an option for a broadcaster)? It's a moot point but I believe that it depends who they are. If it is the prime minister avoiding a question and sinking into gobbledegook, or a celebrity giving a nonsensical speech at an awards ceremony, then the lack of eloquence can be a news story in itself. But with ordinary people involved in a news story, perhaps people whose first language is not English, then you should be ready to correct some of their mistakes. You want to protect them from ridicule, but don't take away their character, the pattern of speaking that makes them who they are. And don't turn dialect into standard English, otherwise everyone will end up sounding the same.

General points about interviewing

- Always check the name of the person you are interviewing and how you spell it.
- Check their job title.
- Tailor questioning to them. Listen to the answers. Follow up any interesting leads.
- Always be polite. Don't laugh if it's not appropriate – you would be amazed how many young reporters laugh when they shouldn't, often out of nervousness.
- Make sure you have all, their contact details – their home phone number, office number, fax number, cell phone number, weekend email address, cottage address and phone number. There is nothing worse than needing some extra information and not being able to get hold of someone.

- Write up your interview as soon as you can, while everything is still fresh in your mind; that way impressions and observations will be incorporated.

Silence can be golden

Sometimes it isn't a good question that elicits the best answer, it's a well-placed silence. No one likes silence and many people will automatically fill gaps in a conversation. Wait for them to finish their answer and then pause before asking your next question. Leave it just a few seconds – sometimes the extra time helps the interviewee think of something else to add; at other times the silence makes them uncomfortable and they blurt out something far more interesting than anything said up to then.

Punctuating quotes/layout of quotes

In most newspapers quotes are laid out thus:

> Herbert Baker said: 'If the council doesn't listen to us, we will take to the streets. It'll be a cold day in hell before I'll let them build that monstrosity here.'

> Or: 'If the council doesn't listen to us, we will take to the streets,' Herbert Baker said. 'It'll be a cold day in hell before I'll let them build that monstrosity here.'

If a quote is too long and you need to shorten it, then make it clear you have done so:

> In a statement on Monday, the foreign minister said: 'In the immediate future the EU will … take appropriate measures, including sanctions, against the government of Sudan and all other parties … if no tangible progress is achieved in this respect.'

Obviously the ellipsis (…) indicates where part of the quote was cut. If you find yourself having to cut too much, you may decide to put the quote into indirect speech. That is, to use your own words. For example:

> In a statement on Monday the foreign minister said that, unless progress was made, the EU would take measures, including sanctions, against the government of Sudan and all other parties.

Sometimes partial quotes are used, but these should be reserved for extraordinary words and usually by or about famous people:

> A furious row has broken out over claims in a book by the BBC broadcaster James Naughtie that Colin Powell, the US secretary of state, described neo-conservatives in the Bush administration as 'fucking crazies' during the run-up to war in Iraq.

Or they can be used for expert opinion:

> Experts say that reducing the nation's salt intake would have 'significant public health benefits'.

Note: The punctuation falls outside the quotation marks (inverted commas) and the first words are not capitalised.

If you have quotes within quotes, then double quotation marks are used within singles (or vice versa) depending on house style.

> He said: 'High blood pressure really is the "silent killer", as those living with it are three times more likely to develop heart disease and stroke, and twice as likely to die from these diseases as those with normal levels.'

Choosing interviewees

As mentioned earlier, when choosing an interviewee you need to ensure they are qualified to talk about the subject and available. It's no good questioning a hospital porter about patient waiting lists unless all you want is a perspective from someone working in a hospital of what they see day to day. But such an interview wouldn't tell you why waiting lists happen, the effect they have on patients and the medical profession, or what is being done to alleviate the problem.

When choosing an interviewee you should always bear in mind what their angle is – why is it they are saying what they are saying and whether they have any axes to grind. Having said that, you want someone involved with the story. The closer to the story they are, the more compelling they will be. As a listener, viewer or reader, it grabs you far more and you are much more convinced by the piece if the person you are listening to is talking to someone who has been affected by the story.

Clearly, the more fluent and lively the speaker is, the more likely they are to provide good graphic quotes. This is particularly important in broadcasting where their words will be heard. Monotone or halting speakers sound terrible on radio or television.

> Choosing interviewees is very important in radio. You have to have good talkers. If they are dull, keep trying to find alternatives. You've got to have a person with the right credentials, with the right experience, and a fluent and expressive talker. (Gillian Hargreaves, BBC reporter with Radio 4's *World at One*)

However, if the interview has to be done quickly, the crucial thing is availability of the interviewee, so you may have to be less fussy.

Taking notes

It is a fundamental part of a journalist's job to keep an accurate record of what's said during an interview. One way is to take everything down verbatim, but that's not the ideal. Better is to recognise what is important and what isn't. Accomplished and confident reporters just take down the relevant facts, any interesting anecdotes and strong quotes to illustrate the main themes. Writing down everything someone says, even if it were possible, is a waste of time and effort. It just means you have pages of notes to go through, much of which will be irrelevant.

Editing on the hoof is a skill that gets easier with experience. Eventually journalists know when a good quote is about to come. And if you fail to get it down precisely, don't worry about asking someone to repeat a statement. Flatter them: 'That was interesting, could you say it again, I'd like to get it down properly.' If you are unable, for whatever reason, to ask a source to repeat what they've said, you can paraphrase a quote giving the meaning, if not the actual wording.

It is easier to keep up with what people are saying if you have shorthand. Many training courses for journalists provide classes in shorthand, and to gain some qualifications you need to be able to write it at 100 words per minute. Shorthand is also a requirement if you want a job on a lot of local and regional newspapers. For covering courts, Parliament and council meetings accurately, a good shorthand note is an advantage as no tape recordings are allowed.

Nevertheless, many national and broadcast journalists don't have shorthand and some provincial journalists, having struggled to 100 words a minute, don't keep it up and eventually lose the skill. Some people develop their own systems of speed-writing. Whatever you do, ensure you have a fast, accurate note in a well-ordered notebook.

How well you keep your notebook and whether you can decipher what is written could mean the difference between winning and losing a court case. Spiral notebooks are a good choice, the pages turn easily and they fit into a pocket. You can also tuck a pen or pencil inside the spirals. The date you started the book and finished it should be recorded on the cover and stored. Then if a complaint is made against one of your articles, you can find the relevant notebook and check the notes against the article. All notebooks should be kept for at least a year, as libel actions have to be started within 12 months of an article being published. Web journalists need to keep their notebooks for at least 12 months after the article has been removed from a website.

Each new day should be dated. It's also a good idea to give stories you are working on a catchline and write the name of interviewees clearly. Make sure you note the right quotes with the right people. If you are interviewing more than one person, this can be trickier than you think.

Tape-recording interviews can be very tempting, especially to young reporters not confident in their note-taking abilities. Tape recorders are useful if you are doing a one-to-one, in-depth interview or covering a complicated and controversial issue. If a source challenges you on a quote, you will have the perfect comeback if you can produce a tape. But there are drawbacks: batteries run down; you may forget to turn it on; background noise could ruin the recording and, the biggest drawback of all, you have to transcribe the interview or find the vital quotes. If you have a tight deadline, tape recordings are useless for all but checking quotes.

The importance of taking a trustworthy note is illustrated perfectly by the following three cases. The first returns us to the Hutton Inquiry.

Lord Hutton's inquiry into the death of the weapons expert, Dr David Kelly, saw the notes of three journalists displayed. At the inquiry the journalists were asked to match the notes in their notebooks made during interviews with Dr David Kelly with the stories they eventually wrote. Andrew Gilligan jotted his notes into a hand-held computer. He later typed up a fuller manuscript, fleshing out both the questions he had asked and Kelly's answers. Susan Watts, *Newsnight's* science editor, used a mix of shorthand and freehand. In a later conversation she used a dictaphone to record the conversation. Gavin Hewitt, the BBC's special correspondent, jotted notes including a diagram planning a piece to camera, phone numbers and references to other stories. Although Hewitt could not decipher everything in his notebook, what shocked many was that Gilligan did not have any handwritten notes.

> The use of a Psion organiser is unusual, possibly unprecedented. But I think this case shows that some journalists are more diligent than others. And if you are going to a briefing meeting, as Gilligan did with Kelly, it's a bit surprising if you don't take anything with you to write with. (Richard Shillito, partner, Farrer and Co.)
> One of the things to come out of this inquiry is how important a notebook could be. If you can't do shorthand and it's important, then use a tape recorder. I can't imagine how Gilligan managed to use one of those personal organisers. And if you are going to use £300 worth of kit, why not get yourself a tape recorder? (Bob Atkins, broadcasting tutor, Cardiff School of Journalism)[10]

The second case involved *The Times*. The newspaper lost a libel action brought by international businessman Dr Grigori Loutchansky in 1999, when the journalist involved was unable to produce notes. The stories made serious allegations that Loutchansky was involved in money laundering and smuggling. When the reporter was asked in court to produce notes he had made of the conversation he claimed to have had with his most important source, he said he thought he must have made the note on a scrap of paper that he had subsequently thrown away.[11]

The third case offers an interesting contrast. In 2000 the *Leeds Weekly News*, a free newspaper, was being sued for an article warning readers against the activities of a doorstep salesman. It succeeded in defending the libel action, thanks largely to the reporter keeping a good note. Even though the reporter had lost some of her notes, those she had were in transcribable shorthand, which the judge weighed in the paper's favour.[12]

Covering news conferences

These are called by organisations wanting to get a message across to the public. They generally involve several journalists questioning one or more people together. They can be called by the police trying to find witnesses to a crime, in which case a press release will be sent out inviting reporters to a news conference where details of the crime will be given. Sometimes victims or the family of a victim give a plea for information or a photofit of a suspect may be released.

A local authority may call a news conference if they are launching a new initiative or campaign. Charities trying to draw attention to their cause may call them at the start of a fundraising drive or the release of new statistics. Companies with a new product to sell will hold one to try to get the media on side. Governments at times of national crisis are also likely to hold a news conference to reassure the public.

In all these cases the reporter has to be aware that those calling the news conference have a message they want to be reported. However, as a reporter you are not a public relations officer. You can ultimately decide whether or not you go along with their message or decide on a different story or angle. We shall look at this in more depth in the next chapter.

When you arrive, it will normally be that the spokesperson for the organisers will give their speech and then take questions from the journalists. You may receive an information pack, perhaps even a copy of the speech or speeches (check them against what is said in case there are any changes). When covering these meetings, you must make sure to note down:

- why the news conference was called – the announcement of policy, statistics, product launch, opening or closing of premises
- the main points being made by the speaker or speakers
- the consequences of the news conference
- the names and job titles of the speakers
- the best quotes (strict accuracy is essential here)
- any good points to come out of the follow-up questions asked by reporters.

Among those reporters asking questions should be you. As a representative of your news organisation, you should make sure that you put your questions and try to get answers. This can be a fight if there are lots of other media there, but you should still try. If you work in broadcasting ensure you are recorded putting your question, it may be useful when putting together a package.

In many cases there are opportunities to carry out interviews afterwards. You can then clarify any complicated points, check quotes, names, etc and also use it to explore any angle that may provide an 'exclusive' that perhaps you didn't want to advertise to other journalists. Don't be afraid of putting questions that you know the organisers won't welcome – they called the news conference, so they should be prepared to face the media. If they are seasoned holders of news conferences they will know what to expect.

Doorstepping

Doorstepping is one of the hardest parts of the job. It involves going uninvited to someone's house or waiting outside a restaurant, cinema or court in the hope of getting a few comments from someone. Public figures involved in the news expect to be approached by the media, but ordinary people who have become caught up in a news story should be handled carefully.

> Nobody likes doorstepping – the families of crash victims are the worst. Our general approach is to ask would they be willing to speak, perhaps say it is an opportunity to talk about the person who has died. But you should beat a hasty retreat if you're not wanted. (Ian Lockwood, editor, *Craven Herald*, Skipton)

Sometimes you are doorstepping people who have refused requests to be interviewed and not given good reason or not responded to requests for an interview. Often these stories involve crimes or anti-social behaviour. Here you should be polite but persistent and insist on putting your questions. They should realise the only way to get rid of you is to agree to talk.

We have been talking until now about the face-to-face interview but a considerable number of interviews – the majority for many journalists – will be carried out where the interviewer and interviewee are not in the same room.

Telephone interviews

> Perhaps one of the most worrying and frustrating aspects of life on local newspapers is being so office-bound. Of all the impressions I had of the profession before getting my first job, relying so heavily on telephone interviews and the internet was not one of them. Journalism should involve developing relationships with contacts and getting to know your patch inside out.[13]

Telephone interviews are a very quick way of obtaining information but they have downsides: you cannot see your interviewee and have no opportunity to read body language. It is harder to establish a rapport when using only your voice and devices such as your facial expressions can't be used. If you have not the time or the opportunity to visit an interviewee, then at least you can obtain information or quotes this way. And, thanks to understaffing, more and more is now done on the phone.

Accepting that much of a journalist's work must be done on the phone, technique is essential. You have to work to make up for the rapport that you would naturally be able to build up in a face-to-face. People are much more suspicious and reticent when dealing with a voice on the end of the phone, especially when they don't recognise the person. So the tone of your voice has to make up for the lack of body language and facial expressions.

You are often interrupting busy people, and so you must be polite and explain straight-away who you are, which organisation you represent and why you are calling. You should also be clear about the questions you need to be answered because you are unlikely to be given an opportunity to indulge in chit-chat. The hurried nature of phone interviews can result in young reporters forgetting to gain basic facts and background information that would come out naturally in a face-to-face interview. That is why it is so important to know what you want before you pick up the phone.

When telephoning an organisation, try to ask for someone by name, otherwise you could be passed to a junior who cannot answer your questions. Even if the name you have is for a person in a different department, they will probably know who you should speak to in the relevant department. If you don't have a name and are just looking to speak to the person responsible for a particular area, then the switchboard operator can probably tell you who that is, but is unlikely to put you straight through. You will probably be passed to their assistant. If you want background information or the answer to a straightforward question then the assistant may be able to help, but if you need the top person, either for a quote or to put questions to, then insist you speak to them. Always thank people for their time before hanging up.

> It is one of the sad aspects of journalism that so much is done over the phone and there is no doubt that the quality of reporting suffers. I think news editors fall into the trap of thinking that having all the reporters in the newsroom improves copy flow. I am not convinced that this is necessarily true, yet clearly there are some stories which should be done over the phone rather than expending half a day to go out to.
>
> I get nervous when I see all my reporters in the office. I don't think they are connecting with people and getting close to the subject matter. The great element of attending an event is that in most cases everyone is there –you can usually come away with the story in your notebook, whereas you are impeded if you remain in the newsroom. (Bob Bounds, editor, *Kentish Express*)

Broadcast journalists will use telephone interviews when there is no alternative, but the sound can be bad and listeners don't like straining to hear.

Figure 7.3 Gillian Hargreaves carrying out a telephone interview

I always try to do it in quality [face-to-face]. Phone interviews are OK but you never get the sound effects. They should only be used as a last resort if you are too close to deadline to get out. In terms of questions I don't find any difference unless they're nervous or it's sensitive, then sometimes it's better face-to-face – but the telephone is so familiar that people are quite comfortable.

To me doing a telephone interview is only marginally better than television doing one without pictures. If you want a piece to sing you need quality. (Gillian Hargreaves, BBC reporter)

If you telephone someone and they are likely to be reluctant to talk, try not to agree to being called back. No matter what their office, wife or they say, they probably won't ring you. Instead say you will call them in 20 minutes or an hour or whatever, or you will stay on the line if they are on another call. If you have to agree to be called back, fix a time, and if they miss that time, call them back.

Email or submitted question interviews

Questions submitted in writing and answered in writing are now often done by email and are really useful if you want to interview someone abroad in a different time zone. You do not have to stay up all night to phone them. Email answers also have the advantage that you can cut and paste them into your story so there is no danger of misquoting what someone says.

When emailing, make it clear who you are and how you intend to use their answers. Include a full list of questions so that you are not going back and forth too much.

The problem with email is that you cannot ensure that you will receive an answer or even that someone will read your email. Some people don't check their inboxes for days. So you must always be prepared to resort to other means if you fail to get a response to your email.

Ethical issues

Journalists forget sometimes that for many people being interviewed by the media is a daunting experience. It may be the first and only time they come into contact with journalists. We owe it to people who talk to us to be fair and accurate and to respect their confidence.

People often want to give you information 'off the record'. Make sure you understand what they mean by this. Is it that they are giving information – background – that you must confirm with another source or is it that they can be quoted but not named?

Before you agree to speak to someone off the record you need to ask yourself a couple of questions: Will they speak to me if I don't agree to their request? Can I get the information any other way? Don't agree without trying to persuade them of the importance to the story of named sources. If you still cannot persuade them to go on the record, complete the interview and try to find a quote they are happy to have used. Remember that it is only off the record if both of you have agreed before the start of the interview.

What if an interviewee realises during an on-the-record interview that they have said too much and then insists the quote is off the record? What should you do? Like most things in journalism, it depends who is saying it. If it is one of your best contacts and it isn't that good a titbit, then it is probably better to go along with the request rather than risk losing the contact. But if the information is important and in the public interest, and if the person knew they were talking to a reporter, then they cannot expect you not to quote them.

Never allow a source to tell you how to use their quotes and it is usually not a good idea to show them completed stories before publication unless you wish to check you have written it up accurately. The *News of the World*'s cricket correspondent David Norrie regretted emailing copies of an interview with England cricket captain Michael Vaughan to the England and Wales Cricket Board before it was published. The Board promptly forwarded the email to two rival papers, the *Sunday Times* and the *Independent on Sunday*, which both printed excerpts.

Once you have promised to keep someone's name confidential, do not go back on your word. This can be risky and has led to some valiant stands by journalists threatened with jail terms for contempt of court. Sometimes it is the companies that have had confidential documents leaked who demand to know the source or it is an individual who has been embarrassed or harmed by leaked information who wants to know where it came from. Sometimes a tribunal looking at an issue will wish to know the source of a journalist's information. Whoever it is, as a journalist who has promised to protect a source, you must resist pressure to name them. Protecting a source can be a matter of life and death, as we have seen with Dr David Kelly who, it is believed, committed suicide once he was identified as the source of Andrew Gilligan's story that the Government 'sexed-up' its dossier on Iraq. Further, if too many journalists buckle under the pressure and name confidential sources, in future no one will speak to them.

> Protection of the sources from which journalists derive information is an essential means of enabling the press to perform its important function of 'public watchdog' in a democratic society.[14]

The above quote by the European Commission was made during the case of Bill Goodwin, a trainee reporter on *The Engineer* magazine. He was ordered by an English judge in 1989 to reveal the source of information he had received that an engineering company was in financial difficulties. When he refused, he was fined £5,000 for contempt of court (see Chapter 10 for more on contempt of court). He appealed to the Court of Appeal and the House of Lords, who also held that he should name his source. Backed by the National Union of Journalists, he took the case to the European Court of Human Rights, which ruled that protection of journalistic sources was one of the basic conditions for press freedom.

But the Goodwin case hasn't ended the matter. There have been many high-profile cases since, including those involved with the Bloody Sunday Inquiry, the tribunal set up to find out how 13 civilians were killed following a civil rights march in Northern Ireland in January 1974.

In 2000, *Daily Telegraph* journalist Toby Harnden was 'placed in contempt' of the Bloody Sunday Inquiry. He had refused to comply with an order to identify two soldiers he had interviewed.

In 2002 two other journalists, former Channel 4 news producer Lena Ferguson and Alex Thomson, the station's chief news reporter, also refused to identify soldiers they had interviewed. They too were declared to be in contempt of the tribunal. They had interviewed the soldiers for a series of reports on *Channel 4 News* in 1997 and 1998.

These reports challenged the verdict of the original inquiry by Lord Widgery into the deaths on Bloody Sunday and helped persuade prime minister Tony Blair to set up a new inquiry. But without the guarantees of anonymity to the soldiers, the journalists argued, they would not have spoken to them and the reports could not have been compiled. Thomson spoke to ITN on 2 May 2002 outside the tribunal after he and Ferguson appeared before it and refused to reveal the identities of the soldiers:

> The principle that you do not betray sources is fundamental to everybody's journalism. It cannot be compromised. If it means serving a prison sentence that's what I shall do.

In February 2004 the Bloody Sunday Inquiry decided to take no further action against Lena Ferguson and Alex Thomson. It also dropped proceedings against Toby Harnden. The tribunal's chairman, Lord Saville, said it was not appropriate to take any further action in these cases as it was unlikely any new information of value would be forthcoming. Lena Ferguson, now the BBC's head of political programmes in Northern Ireland, said:

> After five years of co-operating with the BSI [Bloody Sunday Inquiry], I'm delighted our position has been vindicated. This is a boost not only for journalists but also for whistleblowers. We were never treating the BSI with contempt but upholding a principled promise made to the people who had helped us get our story on air. This was the only fair decision Lord Saville could have made.

Without whistleblowers some of the most important stories ever reported may never have come to light. The most famous whistleblower is 'Deep Throat', whose anonymous tip-offs led *Washington Post* journalists, Woodward and Bernstein, to Watergate. Their investigations revealed President Richard Nixon's role in and cover-up of a plethora of illegal activities including burglary, phone-tapping and slush funds.

The radio interviewer

Chris Legard of BBC Radio 4's *World at One* is on the day reporter shift. He explains his approach to interviews.

To prepare, I would read a couple of pieces from the reputable news agencies such as PA or Reuters. I always look at where the information I'm getting comes from. If it's from an agency I've never heard of, I would look to back up the information, and ask the desk here if anyone knows them. I use the internet: Government websites, the UN and EU sites etc. With anyone you've heard of such as Oxfam, you know their angle so you take that into account.

I think it's useful to work out two or three things you want to get out of the person you are interviewing. Write two or three headings and focus on those. Be prepared to ask the same question – phrased differently – a few times to get the answer. If you fail to get an answer at first, you can come back to the question later.

If you are challenging someone, think more carefully about how you phrase your questions. Also be aware of your phrasing if you are going to use your question in the final package, particularly if it is challenging the interviewee.

Always go for quality if you can. Gauge how prepared they are to travel for you. If you're only going to use the person for 20 seconds and it will take them two hours to get to you, let them know and ask if they are still prepared to travel.

On a day shift you are trying to balance – is it worth it for you to travel and get quality? Have you the time?

Before you start the interview tell people who you are and where you're from. Give them as much idea of what you want as you can. If you run through the main points before turning on the tape it saves time when you get back: there aren't a lot of irrelevant questions to listen back to.

Sometimes you get very nervous people and they need two or three questions before you get to the point. It's about relaxing people.

We interview a lot of politicians. They are so wise now, so with politicians it's in the preparation: knowing what you are talking about. Politicians are often very short of time, so after 3 or 4 minutes they will start to shorten their answers and shuffle, so go in knowing exactly what you want and be prepared to ask the same question – keep drawing them back to the question until you get an answer.

Today I interviewed an Afghani refugee. He's been here off and on for 10 years. He was reluctant to talk. You have to understand why they are reluctant. This man represented a small but close-knit community in London. He knew he would say something that would put him against the flow. So I can understand why he was reluctant but he was very intelligent, so I appealed to his intelligence – a bit of flattery often works. Discuss with them and appear to be reasonable. When I got there he'd changed his mind and he was willing to talk and be named.

He said everything I wanted him to. His point is that people are reluctant to go back to Afghanistan as it is comfortable here and there is no law and no security in Kabul. But Afghanis must go and create a law and help the Government rebuild. Without intelligent, educated people returning to Afghanistan it can't be rebuilt.

Summing up

A friendly but persistent nature, a smart appearance and a polite and trustworthy manner will help you to get your foot in the door.

Once you are in the interview, start in an unthreatening way to relax your interviewee. David Randall has a list of ice-breaker questions which include: What didn't you learn at school? What was your worst job? What do you do when you are nervous? Do you like Christmas?[15]

Make sure you get answers to all the important questions while staying polite. Check any salient facts before you leave the interview and make sure you get contact numbers in case you need to speak to the interviewee again. Try to write up an interview as soon as you can, while everything is still fresh in your mind.

REVIEW QUESTIONS

1 Explain the difference between closed and open questions and when you should use each.

2 Why is it important to be prepared for an interview and what sort of groundwork should you do if you have the time?

3 How do you ensure you make a good first impression?

4 What are the various approaches to questioning and when should they be used?

EXERCISES

1 Watch and listen to a variety of news programmes and find one example each of the informational, expositional and interpretative interview styles. Note the name of the interviewer, the name of the interviewee and which organisation they represent. Summarise one question and answer from the interview to illustrate why you put the interview in the category you did.

2 Choose one of the issues below and, using secondary sources such as the internet and your local library, carry out enough research to prepare three or four questions. Conduct a vox pop of seven or eight people in the local high street. See how effectively you approach people and notice whether you manage to put them at ease enough to give you interesting answers.

   (i)   Smacking children is harmful to their longer-term development.

   (ii) Smoke alarms save lives but not enough people have them fitted.

   (iii) The way crime is reported in the media makes people more afraid than they should be.

3 Interview someone you don't know very well, without any preparation. People love talking about themselves so it shouldn't be too difficult to find someone willing to be your subject.

(i)   Question them for five minutes and then summarise what you discovered.

(ii) Ask your interviewee how you came across. Did they feel comfortable with you? How did the interview flow? Did they feel you listened carefully and responded to what they said?

FURTHER READING

Adams, S., *Interviewing for Journalists*, London: Routledge, 2001.
Humphrys, J., *Devil's Advocate*, London: Hutchinson, 1999.
Keeble, R., *The Newspapers Handbook*, London: Routledge, 1998.
Mencher, M., *News Reporting and Writing*, Singapore: McGraw-Hill, 2000.
Welsh, T. and Greenwood, W., *McNae's Essential Law for Journalists*, London: Butterworths, 2003.
Randall, D., *The Universal Journalist*, London: Pluto Press, 1996.
Sergeant, J., *Give Me Ten Seconds*, London: Macmillan, 2001.

Notes

1 *Press Gazette*, 15 March 2001.

2 *Panorama*, 20 November 1995.

3 Melvin Mencher, *News Reporting and Writing*, Singapore: McGraw Hill, 2000, p. 360.

4 David Randall, *The Universal Journalist*, London: Pluto Press, 1996, p. 43.

5 John Sergeant, *Give Me Ten Seconds*, London: Macmillan, 2001, pp. 97–8.

6 David Triesman, quoted in *The Times* online edition, 10 April 2002.

7 Rod Liddle, *Ibid*.

8 John Humphrys, *Devil's Advocate*, London: Hutchinson, 1999, pp. 224–5.

9 Sally Adams, *Interviewing for Journalists*, London: Routledge 2001, quoted in *Press Gazette*, 3 August 2001.

10 *Press Gazette*, 22 August 2003.

11 Tom Welsh and Walter Greenwood, *McNae's Essential Law for Journalists*, London: Butterworths, 2003, p. 277.

12 *Ibid.*, p. 253.

13 A trainee journalist on a weekly newspaper writing under the pseudonym of Samuel Pecke, *Press Gazette*, 11 June 2004.

14 The European Commission, 1994, in the Bill Goodwin case, quoted in Welsh and Greenwood, *op. cit.*, p. 333.

15 Randall, *op. cit.*, pp. 56–7.

8

FINDING THE NEWS

Good journalists know how to dig out information. They don't wait to be given stories; they go looking for them. They

- have excellent contacts
- will not accept information in press releases, leaks or tip-offs at face value, but will always seek to verify it
- know where to find and how to use reference books, records and reports
- can interpret and analyse figures.

Sources of news

News organisations rely on their journalists to bring in stories and ideas and to follow up leads with a terrier-like persistence. Some are better at it than others, but any aspiring reporter wants to be known as a good newshound. So where do journalists go for information and inspiration?

There are two types of sources – primary and secondary. These will be discussed later in the chapter, but a journalist who understands and can use these sources quickly and effectively will unearth more and better stories than one who doesn't. Your sources will provide you with the information you need to research and develop articles. If you cultivate your personal contacts and use physical sources such as reports, records and references intelligently, you will produce original, accurate and thorough copy.

Interestingly, many of the best stories do not need a lot of investigative elbow grease to uncover them. They happen unexpectedly and are picked up quickly by the media. The events of 11 September 2001 came out of a clear blue sky. The bloody hostage-taking at school Number 1 in Beslan, Russia, on 3 September 2004, in which hundreds of children died, was another bolt from the blue. These stories, along with more run-of-the-mill accidents, fires, weather stories and robberies, come to journalists very often through check calls (regular calls made by journalists to the emergency services) or from a tip-off phone call to the newsroom or from the wires.

There are other strong news stories that, unlike those above, are expected but, in common with them, do not require much journalistic digging to bring them to public notice. These include wars, famines, epidemics or the devastation caused by a hurricane. All have a lead-in time when various governments, aid agencies or weather centres warn of the potential for catastrophe.

Diary stories

At the mundane end of the range of expected stories are diary stories, so called because they are noted down in the newsroom diary and a reporter is assigned to cover them. Diary stories include press conferences, council meetings, agricultural shows, court cases, openings of buildings/fetes etc, turning on of Christmas lights, announcements, elections, speeches, releasing of reports, royal visits and ministerial photo opportunities.

Off-diary stories

Then there are the stories that were not handed to the reporter in a press release, from the wires, from other newspapers or at a stage-managed event. Good off-diary stories come from original thinking, a refusal to take what you have been told at face value and a willingness to go digging for information. Reporters who regularly bring in off-diary stories are always valued members of the newsroom.

Primary and secondary sources

Reporters writing up news routinely combine both primary sources, which include interviews and things they have seen for themselves, with secondary sources such as statistics from a report, excerpts from a letter or information from a press release.

Primary sources

Contacts

A journalist's personal contacts are as important as their ability to turn a good phrase and hacks jealously guard their best sources from being poached by others. Some journalists have secured jobs on the strength of their contacts and their ability to cultivate people in positions of power.

It is good practice to keep a duplicate or back-up of your contacts book in a safe place. One journalist, who should have known better, didn't make a duplicate of his book and lost 28 years' worth of phone numbers on a train. He said it was like losing his right arm.[1] He didn't even have his own name and contact details in it. Luckily for him, an art student who found the book traced him via his old workplace, the *Sun*. He repaid the student by buying one of his paintings.

You'll build up your contacts book as you go about your job. Note down everyone you come across – you never know when they may come in handy. Keep a particular note of people you recognise as likely to be useful. It could be a headteacher heavily involved in their inner city community, or a GP with strong opinions about preventative health, or the leader of the local Sikh community you found approachable. You can cross-reference to make it easier to locate people. For example, Dr Baker can be under D for doctor, H for health and B for Baker. A good contacts book is invaluable when a news story breaks; if you have the right name and number you can get information or a quote without having to chase around.

Local calls

All news organisations have a system of regular calls. These are made hourly or daily to some sources, weekly to others and are an essential source of information. The most regular calls are to the emergency services: police, fire, ambulance and coastguard to see if they have been involved in any notable incidents. Other useful calls are to council officials, councillors, MPs, religious leaders, voluntary groups, undertakers and health authorities.

A lot of these calls, especially the ones made hourly, will be made over the telephone, but it is more fruitful if a journalist can make regular visits – daily or weekly – to the emergency services in their patch.

Tip-offs and leaks

It's a given that a newsroom has its lunatics and paranoids along with Mr and Mrs Angry, who contact them with a steady supply of conspiracy theories and libellous accusations against the authorities. Needless to say, these people should be listened to and politely but firmly rebuffed. All other tip-offs and leaks should be checked out as some will prove very useful indeed.

The *Sun*'s heavyweight political editor, Trevor Kavanagh, received details of the Hutton Report into the death of the weapons expert, Dr David Kelly, the day before it was published – a real journalistic coup. A furious Lord Hutton ordered an inquiry into the leak, but the source has not been found.

If you hold on to leaked documents, make sure you keep them somewhere safe, as the authorities are not above searching your home or office. But a word of caution: tip-offs and members of the public bearing gifts (in news terms) need to be handled carefully. Their information may be inaccurate or a hoax. You need to ask yourself what is the person's motivation for contacting you? It is unlikely to be out of the goodness of their heart.

They may want to advance their own cause, damage another person or business, or exact revenge. You need to check whether they are qualified or in a position where they could know what they are claiming to know. You should also ask what the other side of the story might be. This does not mean the tip-off is not valid, it just means you have to be careful. Double-check everything. Try and find a second source who will back up what your source says and insist on documents if any are likely to be available.

Being observant

Get out of the office as much as you can, as seeing things first-hand is always preferable to hearing a second-hand account. Keep your wits about you. Try and notice things around you and be aware of the mannerisms and mood of the people you meet.

With documents, the devil is in the detail and the best stories are buried in the hope a lazy journalist will miss them. Don't be that lazy journalist. Your powers of observation and willingness to graft will yield additional detail in your stories, fresh angles on old chestnuts and some great tales.

Courts and tribunals

The courts are a very productive source of stories and court reporting an essential part of a journalist's job. You may be sent to check if there is anything going on at the magistrates' court or to cover a big case at crown court or you may attend an industrial tribunal or hear a case at the coroner's court. See Chapter 10 for more on reporting the courts.

Local government

The press and public are entitled to attend council meetings. Young reporters complain at having to cover them, but a glance at any local paper shows the importance of decisions made there. We look in detail at reporting local government in Chapter 9.

Politicians

They can be among the best contacts a reporter will have. If you cultivate them carefully, they will give you stories and put you in touch with people who can help you. Local or regional journalists should build a good working relationship with the MPs, party secretaries and officials in their area. If a local MP is also a Government minister or an active and forthright backbencher, then you will rarely be without stories. The speeches they make, duties they perform, how they vote and what they get up to in their private life are all of interest to the journalist.

When dealing with politicians, remember that they want to protect their position and promote their beliefs and policies. Journalists should help publicise the opinions of those in power but also hold them accountable for the way they use their power. As well as mainstream political opinions, the public should also be informed about a wide range of alternative views.

When it comes to Government, journalists can be too ready to accept official explanations. It is the Government's job to try to put themselves in a positive light, but journalists should not go along with the propaganda. There has been some heart-searching in the media over their vulnerability to manipulation by Government in the so-called 'War on Terror'.

The story of the 'saving of Private Jessica Lynch' during the war in Iraq in 2003 was perhaps the most blatant piece of news management. Private Lynch had been captured during an ambush near Nasiriya. Nine of her company were killed and Lynch taken to hospital with, it was said, stab and bullet wounds. At the hospital it was alleged she was beaten and interrogated. Eight days after she was captured, US special forces stormed the hospital in a dramatic rescue, which they filmed on a night camera. The footage was released to the world's media, which reported it enthusiastically and uncritically along with a statement by US Government spokesman General Vincent Brooks. The statement said, 'Some brave souls put their lives on the line to make this happen, loyal to a creed that they know that they'll never leave a fallen comrade.'

Fine words, but an investigation by the BBC's *Correspondent* programme uncovered the probability that this rescue was stage-managed from start to finish and that no lives were put on the line in defence of a creed or anything else. The programme showed it was unlikely that there had been Iraqi soldiers guarding the hospital when US troops stormed it or that Private Lynch had been injured or interrogated there. Iraqi doctors claimed she'd been given the best treatment available and her injuries were in line with someone who'd been in a car accident.

Experts

Every day in universities and research institutes men and women carry out research that would make great stories if only you knew about them. For example, sending sexually explicit text messages, or 'text sex', is as damaging to your relationship as having a real affair, according to research by the British Psychological Society. And scientists at Stanford University have identified that fruit flies make insulin and have a chemical to control it. The discovery may be important to research into diabetes in humans. Besides providing stories, experts can lend authority to existing stories.

Before you turn to an expert for information or a quote, make sure you have the right expert. They can only provide information about their own research or area of speciality. Don't ring a university department and expect everyone who picks up the phone to be able to answer your questions. And don't expect them to talk about the results of their research or that of others until it has been published or presented at a conference. That is unethical. As with every other source of information, maintain a healthy scepticism. Media commentator Roy Greenslade has pointed to some of the barmier news stories based on 'that catch-all source known as "research"'.

So the *Daily Express* could not resist treating its readers last week to the findings of a 'senior academic' who claimed to have discovered that Cockney ducks quack in a different accent from Cornish ducks. A properly sceptical sub-editor obliged with the headline: 'Study is quackers'.

A couple of weeks ago the *Express* reported that 'Sunday is officially Britain's sauciest day of the week'. This study had evidently discovered that more couples have sex on that day than on any other.

The 'officially' was somewhat suspect, given that the research had been carried out by a lingerie retailer.[2]

Interest groups, self-help groups, trades unions and charities

These exist to promote a particular cause and range from the welfare of the elderly to the protection of trees. They include groups as diverse as those in favour of hunting to those trying to raise awareness of cot deaths. All these thousands of groups are producing reports, carrying out research and are desperate for publicity. They are an excellent source of stories but a journalist must be careful not to turn into an unpaid public relations officer for a group. Views and information given must be tested and not accepted at face value.

News conferences

Another occasion when you could, if you are not careful, turn into a PR officer is when covering news conferences. Organisations that want to promote a message or a product will organise a news conference and invite journalists along to cover it. The police, when launching a crackdown on speeding by using unmarked police cars and more speed cameras, will arrange a news conference. A cosmetics company launching a new perfume will hold one. A children's charity publicising new research saying record numbers of children are addicted to drugs will hold one. The Government when introducing a new policy will hold one.

In all these cases the reporter has to be careful not to rely too much on the promotional information given out by the organisation. You must remember these are staged events, they are not news in themselves.

When you arrive at a news conference you will be given a media information pack. Then the organisation will present the information or make their announcement and afterwards take questions. See Chapter 7 for more on covering news conferences.

News conferences can be mutually beneficial. The organisation can get a lot of reporters together, which ensures plenty of publicity. They can also make their announcements more dramatic and media friendly than they could in a press release. For the media it is a quick and relatively cheap way of newsgathering.

As ever, a word of warning – this time from a public relations professional: too many journalists accept pre-written copy without challenge and take the easy option by not checking the facts given to them or finding opposing voices.

What we are witnessing in many ways is what is called the PR-isation of the media. The independence of journalists can be called into question as they become more dependent on partisan sources, without this being made clear to readers. This dependence means that their ability to question and analyse is being challenged by public relations practitioners who wield real power. (Professor Anne Gregory, president-elect of the Institute of Public Relations)[3]

Secondary sources

The wires

These are the news service provided by newsgathering agencies such as the Press Association, Reuters, Associated Press, Agence France Presse and the dozens of local news agencies. Many news organisations rely on the wires for international stories, coverage of court cases and tip-offs on good local stories. They will also check with news agencies if they need a photo of someone in the news.

On the whole the well-known news agencies are very reliable, but if you are not familiar with an agency always try to get another source to back up the story.

Other news organisations

No news organisation likes to admit it, but they all use each other as a source of news. Broadcasters trawl the newspapers for good yarns, and newspapers listen to the hourly bulletins on radio and the main television bulletins for stories they've missed, and all access internet news sites regularly. They are fertile ground for material. Sometimes a journalist can find a new angle or development on a story lifted from another outlet. What is a passing reference by one news organisation can be an important story to another. Also remember national news can often yield a local angle. However, if you use another news organisation as the only source, you should credit it, otherwise you could be accused of taking another's work and passing it off as your own – plagiarism. On the other hand, there is no copyright on ideas, so you can borrow the ideas of others.

When lifting stories, make sure the original was correct. A story picked up by almost every news outlet from CNN to the tabloid press of a study from the World Health Organisation saying natural blondes would be extinct within the next 200 years was, it appears, too good to check. The reports said, because too few people are carrying the gene to continue reproducing it, natural blondes would die out. The World Health Organisation says there was no such study but that most journalists did not bother to check with them. They traced the story to an account on a German wire service, which in turn was based on a two-year-old article in a German women's magazine.

Classified ads are a good source of stories. A journalist spotted an advert offering £5 for friends to play with an autistic boy. A call to the mother discovered her 5-year-old son had no friends because the local children his age all refused to play with him.

Academic, specialist and trade magazines are also a rich vein to tap. Magazines such as *Computer Weekly*, the *Lancet*, and *Nature* are always worth a look.

Press or news releases

These are publicity handouts or stories given to the media for publication, and dozens of them arrive in newsrooms every day. Public relations companies or other organisations generate news releases as propaganda, not to help the poor, overworked hacks. But, because of the pressure to fill news pages with fewer staff, journalists are relying on press or news releases more and more, adding to the PR-isation of the media mentioned above.

Non-controversial releases, such as those giving information on an upcoming school speech day, do not usually need more than a rewrite in news English and a note in the newsroom diary. To turn a press release into a piece of proper journalism you need to work harder.

Even seemingly non-controversial press releases should not be accepted at face value. A weekly newspaper in Wales decided to do some checking when they received a press release claiming comedy character Ali G would open their local carnival. The press release said that Sacha Baron Cohen's creation, Ali G, would also attend a music event to be held by a promotions company. Tickets would cost £8.

Other news outlets published the press release word for word, but the staff at the *Milford and West Wales Mercury* didn't believe it. They doubted a man who was one of Britain's most famous people at the time would come to open a small town carnival. So they contacted Cohen's agents, who said he was not booked to open the carnival and would anyway be out of the country. Armed with this rebuttal, the paper contacted the man who, on the news release, claimed to be behind the booking. He insisted the booking was legitimate and had been made without involving the agents. The man even brought a contract confirming the booking into the *Mercury's* offices. The reporters were still not convinced and their article cast doubt on the booking. Trading standards officers became involved and the man was eventually convicted of fraud. In court it emerged that he had tried to pass off an Ali G lookalike as the man himself.

Letters

Letters to the editor often lead to good stories. A letter complaining about dust from a local landfill site and noise from the birds attracted to it would be worth following up, as would a letter claiming a family's brand new house has developed cracks in ceilings and walls and is letting in water in several places. Maybe other houses in the development are also experiencing problems; maybe the developer is at fault. Correspondence from a group of children saying a local landowner has suddenly closed the access to a wood they've always played in could also make good copy.

Before using a letter as the basis of a news story you have to get permission from the writer. All the points in the letter should be checked for accuracy and libel (see Chapter 11) and all sides of the argument, if there is one, contacted and represented.

Surveys

When a journalist receives the results of a survey, there are a few questions they must ask to test whether they can take it seriously and whether it would be ethical to use it as the basis of a news story. Who produced the survey? How big was the sample size? How representative was it? What were the questions?

Surveys carried out by businesses need to be handled with particular care. You know the sort: 'Eight out of ten cats actually preferred Catty Cat Bites to other cat food'. You need to ask how many cats were involved? If there were only ten cats then it isn't a large enough sample to prove much. Who were these cats? Where did they come from? If they are the pets of employees of the company and have been fed on that brand of cat food since they were kittens, then it isn't a representative sample. And you'd wonder why all ten cats didn't prefer Catty Cat Bites. What was so brilliant about the choice that made a cat weaned on one cat food switch? Talking of choices, what was the brand up against? Was it Catty Cat Bites versus all other leading cat foods, or was it Catty Cat Bites versus just one other at the cheaper end of the market in the most unpopular flavour?

If you take a small enough sample you can make the results sound significant. If a faith healer has three clients and two say that they believe their symptoms have eased since seeing the healer, then that healer can claim a 66 per cent success rate. With four clients and three claiming their symptoms have eased, the healer can boast a 75 per cent success rate.

When writing up a story based on a survey, always say who carried out the research and how many people they questioned. A piece in one evening paper claimed a third of men in their forties say they have resorted to plastic surgery or Botox. The reader was not told which organisation carried out the research or what questions they had asked. Did they distinguish between plastic surgery for cosmetic reasons and that following injuries such as burns? No information was given about how many men were questioned or whether they all lived in London and had jobs in the entertainment or modelling industry.

Government surveys and those carried out by polling organisations such as Mori or Gallup are usually reliable. They use large samples and their selection procedures are usually appropriate. Just as important, they are open about how many people they have questioned, how these people were chosen and what questions they asked.

Follow-ups

Following up stories they have already covered (as opposed to those from other news outlets) to note developments, or the lack of them, is something journalists do too infrequently. Yet revisiting a story can prove of huge interest to the audience. What happened to the church damaged by fire last month? How is that child who had to change schools because of bullying? What about the quads born six months ago, how is the family coping?

Anniversaries

An obvious follow-up is the anniversary of some event that you have covered. A year since the floods which had half the county submerged – how are the people doing? Other anniversaries which could give you good stories include major historic events, the invention of well-known goods, births and deaths.

The internet

The internet has revolutionised how journalists research stories, since it allows them to find and check facts much more quickly. It has also put them in touch with sources all over the world. At the click of a mouse you can, using a search engine such as Google, find what stories have been written on an issue or a person. You can check out news groups and find groups devoted to a phenomenal range of subjects and contributed to by people expert in the field. And of course many organisations have their own websites that you can use to carry out basic research and get contact details.

Some great stories have been hatched using the internet. A journalist with the *People* newspaper bought a police warrant card over the internet, exposing a legal loophole which allowed the cards to be hawked online. In another case, a trainee on a free weekly newspaper used the internet to get a false identity, which he then used to obtain a passport. His investigation led to a tightening up of Government procedures. (See Chapter 6 for more on using the internet for research.)

Archives/cuttings files

Most newspapers have their own cuttings library and many now have an online archive that can be searched. As a reporter, you will also build up your own files on stories or areas you cover regularly. However, it is advisable to check all archive material as journalists can get things wrong. If the original story had errors, you can end up repeating them. You could also fall foul of changes since the report was written, such as a guilty verdict being overturned on appeal.

Reference texts

Although you may use the computer for carrying out research, remember reference books can also be of use as a quick way to find information, if you know where to look. Some news organisations keep important reference books available, many are online and of course you can find them in your local library. Among the most important are: the telephone book, for getting addresses and phone numbers; *Whitaker's Almanac, Dod's Parliamentary Companion* and *Vacher's Parliamentary Companion*, for MPs' details; Hansard (verbatim account of Parliamentary speeches); *The Encyclopaedia Britannica*; the *Guinness Book of Records*; *Who's Who*; *Who's Who in the Theatre*; *International Who's Who in Popular and Classical Music*; *Oxford Companion to English Literature*; *Oxford Dictionary of Quotations*; *Crockford's Clerical Directory*; a world gazetteer; an atlas of the British Isles; Jane's *All the World's Aircraft*; *Lloyd's Register of Yachts*; *Stock Exchange Official Year Book* (has details of publicly quoted companies); *Navy List, Army List* and *Air Force List*, giving details of officers.

Gathering the facts ▰▰▰▰▰▰▰▰▰▰▰▰▰▰

Using one or more of the sources listed above, you have found a lead that you think is worth following. How do you go about hunting down the facts? What facts do you need? The newsgathering process should start as soon as a reporter is given an assignment. At that moment you should start thinking of the shape of your story and what information you will need to explain events to your audience, to tell them how it affects them and why it is significant.

You will collect your information in several ways. You may start with a press release, an official report, a survey or a letter; these are all secondary sources. Your task is to verify the facts, balance the arguments and flesh out the main points, and so you interview people involved in the story and perhaps use the internet to check some facts or find other sources. You also send an email with some questions to a source. You may go out to the scene of the incident or to a meeting where you can use your keen eye to add some observational details.

With every news story it helps if you identify the main idea early on. Then you can begin to concentrate on developing it. It is easier to do this with some stories you have to cover than with others. Let's look at the sort of events you are likely to be assigned to and the material you should be gathering to cover them properly.

Traffic accidents and fires

Accidents and fires kill and injure many people each year and so you are likely to have to cover these incidents routinely. If you are not careful they can settle into a familiar pattern. You've got to look for the unique in each incident. It could be the incident itself: where it happened (York Minster, Downing Street), how it happened (man was reading a brief for a business meeting and didn't see the cars in front had stopped; a car swerved to avoid a llama). Or it could be the people: who it happened to (Princess Diana; a bus full of children); the bravery of passers-by, victims and rescuers (man fights through burning building to bring out an elderly neighbour; young boy survives on chocolate bar and carton of juice after car crashes down a ravine).

Traffic accidents

Information about accidents comes from several different sources. You go to the police for the particulars of the accident; the fire brigade if anyone needed cutting out of the vehicle; and the ambulance service for how many ambulances were sent to the scene and how many people were taken to hospital. The hospital can also give you the number of injured, their injuries and their current condition. By putting the information from all the services together, you should get a full picture. Then eyewitnesses can say what they saw and how they and others reacted. If you go to the scene, you can describe any damage to property, broken glass, whether any flowers have been laid.

Questions you should ask include:

- Is anyone dead or injured? If so you need to know who they are, their names and ages.
- What were the injuries?
- Who else was involved and what are their details?
- Were the injured taken to hospital and what is their condition?
- What time did the accident happen and where did it happen?
- What were the circumstances of the accident (speed of the vehicles, where they were headed)?
- What type of vehicles were involved?
- Do the police know the cause of the accident? (Be careful not to apportion blame to one of the drivers, as there may be a court case.)
- Weather conditions?
- Were there any heroic rescues?
- Funeral arrangements, if appropriate?
- Damage to the vehicles?
- Is there to be an investigation?

Fires

Who to ask what?

1 **The fire brigade**: how many engines (appliances) went to the fire; accounts of any rescues; severity of the fire; how they tackled it.
2 **The ambulance service**: how many ambulances they sent; how many injured were taken to hospital.
3 **The hospital**: number of injured received; details of injuries; treatment received and current condition.
4 **The police**: how fire started (if known); time it started and who discovered it; if there were any deaths or injuries and whether there will be an investigation into any suspicious circumstances.
5 **Eyewitnesses**: account of what they saw; how the fire spread and what happened to the building.

The owners of the building may be able to give you an estimate of the cost of repairing the damage and whether they are insured. If you are at the scene you can describe the site and the reactions of the people around.

Theft, burglary and robbery

Crime interests almost everyone and so crimes on your patch are likely to be written up, even if only briefly. As with accidents and fires, you are looking for the uniqueness of each crime. The first thing to note is that the terms 'theft', 'burglary' and 'robbery' are not interchangeable. Theft is the taking of someone else's property with the intention of permanently depriving them of it; burglary is unauthorised entry or breaking and entering and stealing or attempting to steal; robbery is theft by force or by the threat of force. When covering crime you must be aware of when arrests are made or are likely to be made, as this affects what you can write. These restrictions are outlined in Chapter 11. Who to ask? Police for the details, victims and eyewitnesses, but you must be sensitive (see Chapter 7 on how to question victims).

Questions to ask:

- Who is the victim/s?
- What was taken? What is its value?
- Date and time of the crime and where was it committed?
- How was the crime carried out? How did they gain entry to the property? What weapon was used?
- Description of the perpetrator/s?
- Anything unusual about this incident?

A MAN armed with a hammer stole cash from Tim's Food and Wine store in Wellington Road, Hampton, on Monday, April 5.

He entered the shop at 10.30 p.m. and selected a magazine before threatening the 53-year-old shopkeeper with a hammer.

The victim feared for his safety and allowed the robber to take £200 in cash from the till. He then left the store and headed towards Fulwell Bus Garage.

The suspect is described as a 35-year-old white male, 5 ft 11 ins, of medium build. Anybody with information please contact DC Mary James at Twickenham CID. (*Richmond & Twickenham Times*, 16 April 2004)

This brief story was written from details given by the police. What the reporter has rightly decided is what makes this robbery different is the weapon used. Nobody was injured and the amount taken was not significant.

Handling a news release

Faced with a huge pile of handouts – often with unappealing titles and unwieldy opening sentences – the journalist can be overcome by an urge to tip them in the bin. Stop. Scan each release before binning it. It may have a hidden treasure. Take this press release from the United Road Transport Union (URTU):

Lorry Drivers' Union Call to End Slavery

The General Secretary of the United Road Transport Union, David Higginbottom, will recognise the irony of speaking from the birthplace of William Wilberforce when he calls this weekend for an end to the wage slavery of Britain's lorry drivers.

URTU is holding its Biennial Delegates Meeting this coming Sunday and Monday at the Forte Crest Hotel, The Marina, Hull, right at the water's edge where ships used to ply their evil trade in slaves.

Now David Higginbottom is calling for an end to the low pay and poor working conditions of our professional drivers which, he claims, amounts to wage slavery existing nearly 190 years after Wilberforce achieved the abolition of slavery in this country.

'The skills of professional drivers are not fully recognised,' says David Higginbottom. 'They are expected to work up to 15 hours a day, driving in all kinds of weather on our congested roads and with wholly inadequate roadside facilities simply in order to earn what most of us would hardly consider a living wage.'

In a recent survey conducted by the Union, more than half the drivers reported that they felt under pressure to exceed speed limits in order to meet delivery deadlines and almost one-third felt that they were expected to exceed the load capacity of their vehicle. Even more worrying, more than one third reported that they were expected to use vehicles with known defects that would affect their safety and put both the driver and the travelling public at risk.

Many fully qualified professional drivers earn up to £1 an hour less than their wives and daughters working in supermarkets, and the roadside facilities provided for them fall far short of the standards offered to the private motorist.

The beginning of this press release is very unpromising. But just when you think you've read enough, the fifth paragraph delivers a sensational story of Britain's lorry drivers being forced to break the law to carry out their work.

Obviously you need to check the survey in the way mentioned earlier in the chapter and put a call into the Health and Safety Executive (the HSE have a work-related road safety task group) and ask for their reaction. On the HSE website you can find a list of employers' responsibilities. It says employers should do all that is necessary to ensure the safety of their employees when on the road and not impose unrealistic delivery schedules or fail to maintain vehicles properly. There may be recent cases of prosecutions the HSE can tell you about. You should also speak to the union about being put in touch with workers (or former workers) who would be willing to talk about the pressures they are under to break the law.

The lesson is that there are people writing press releases who are not professional journalists and they may have a different idea of what the story is.

How to handle a news release

In the above case the story was not deliberately buried. Sometimes it is. So when BBC transport reporter, Tom Symonds, receives a press release he thinks of it purely as an interesting starting point.

> The organisation is not writing press releases to tell the press what is going on. They are making a public declaration of the process of managing their organisation. And they are paid to manage smoothly.
>
> I'm finding that as I get more experienced, when I make follow-up calls on the release, my questions are getting dumber and dumber. If I don't understand something, I say I don't understand. I make them explain it to me. If they can't, I tell them to go away and come back when they can explain it.
>
> Press officers rarely know. They're there to field journalists. If you ever hear the phrase: 'as far as I am aware', you make them find out. Find out what they are really up to.

He received this news release from what was then the Strategic Rail Authority (SRA), the organisation that manages the railways:

Bowker Initiates Debate on Fares Policy for Britain's Railways

The SRA has today begun the process of consulting passengers, train operators and other key stakeholders on fares policy by inviting comment and suggestions on issues that would both help deliver the growth targets set for rail by government and be affordable for taxpayers.

'Future Fares Policy – Seeking Your Views' published today, is a discussion document, not a policy paper. No decisions have yet been made.

The three-month consultation marks the first major review of fares regulation conducted since privatisation in 1996. The outcome will inform the Authority's thinking on a wide range of fares related issues and should lead to policy changes being implemented from 2004.

Announcing today's consultation SRA Chairman, Richard Bowker, commented:

'The time is right for a thorough investigation of rail fares. The original policy achieved many of its objectives and has helped to bring growth of a third in rail passenger volume.

'The debate starts here. Today's consultation will help us create a policy that will strike the right balance between the needs and aspirations of passengers, taxpayers and train companies. Fares play a part in funding investment in the rail industry. In devising a fares policy for the future, we will need to align decisions with the revitalised 21st century railway we are creating through our Strategic Plan.'

Key issues to be addressed include whether more, or fewer, tickets should be regulated; whether regulated fare levels should continue to decline in real terms; the link between fares changes and performance; scope for simplification of fares structures and types.

As Tom reads the release he is looking for the key words 'first' and 'new' and asking himself a few questions: What are they actually trying to tell us? What's being discussed? Why are they doing it now?

In this case one line stands out: 'Today's consultation will help us create a policy that will strike the right balance between the needs and aspirations of passengers, taxpayers and train companies. Fares play a part in funding investment in the rail industry.' It is clear it's about money.

A further hint to the real story was what Tom already knew. He had been to the regular monthly briefing by the Strategic Rail Authority that was given to reporters the day before the press release was issued. In answer to a question, the authority's spokesperson said the cost of running the railways was rising while fares were falling. That's how the SRA sees it, but as a reporter you don't have to go along with that.

Press releases are written from the perspective of the organisation. You have to have a clear mind when you read one. I try to see it from the perspective of the user – say a passenger sitting on the train. What do I know? What are my impressions of the service? First, it's expensive. Second, it's a bad service.

Then add what you have found out. So if people are paying a lot for a bad service, then clearly they are not going to be pleased if they have to pay more. A lot of people when they start out write what the organisation wants and then balance it rather than starting off with what most people know. (Tom Symonds, BBC transport reporter)

Here is how Tom wrote up the story for BBC Radio 4's morning bulletin and then BBC television's *Ten O'Clock News*. First it's the radio version:

A major review of rail fares is suggesting some passengers may have to pay more – particularly those using the most overcrowded routes.

The Strategic Rail Authority said the cost of running the railways had risen significantly since privatisation – and lower fares on busy commuter routes were 'unlikely to be sustainable much longer' because of overcrowding. A consultation document has been published this morning – but no decisions have yet been made. Here's our transport reporter Tom Symonds …

This will be the biggest review of how we pay for our train travel since privatisation. The Strategic Rail Authority's doing it because the cost of running rail services, and improving them for the future has risen. But there's a problem.

Ministers want to get more people onto trains, while at the same time reducing overcrowding – especially on the busy services into London.

For the last six years many commuters have benefited from a cap on the amount their fares can rise – it's kept prices one per cent below inflation. But the SRA's view is that the lower fares might have led to more overcrowding.

One option for the future could raise fares on the busiest lines at the busiest times to pay for a better service. Another could see price cuts for off-peak tickets to encourage passengers to travel when it's quiet.

The authority says tough decisions are needed – though changes won't come in until 2004.

'With radio,' Tom says, 'I'm writing. But in television you can't say something unless you've got the pictures.' He also emphasises that it's important not to put too much information in, although you need a good interview and strong pictures with actuality (sound). 'To get the pictures for this story, we got on a train from Oxford in the rush hour. It was bedlam.'

Here is the working copy of Tom's television script. For how to lay out radio and televisions scripts formally, please see Chapter 5.

Getting home on the London to Oxford line can be as tough as a day at work.

When the railways were privatised, struggling commuters were promised their fares would stay low – with price caps to keep them down. One promise that was kept.

But privatisation's also increased the cost of running the trains. Now it may be time to squeeze the passengers for extra money.

It's simple market forces – trains are getting overcrowded, the Government's rail authority is considering higher fares – to persuade people to travel when there's more space.

But in the country's more crowded carriages – it's not going to be popular.

[Vox pops with passengers (they are against rises)]

No big decisions have been made yet – there could also be even lower fares for avoiding the rush hour and fewer restrictions on popular cut-price saver tickets. But train companies insist they will still need more money.

[Quote from spokesman for train companies:]

'I don't want to pay any more for anything, nor does anybody else. But I think what we need to say is, well if you do pay more, then actually that money will be used to improve services, to invest. Then people may take a different view, that if they are paying more then they're going to get more for their money in the future.'

But if you spend thousands a year on rail travel – like long distance commuter Andy Whitman – the promise of a better service may not be enough …

[Andy Whitman quote:]

'We're a developing world as far as rail travel is concerned. When we've got a fast, efficient, safe, reliable service, then ask us to pay more money.'

And if passengers can't be convinced – they may give up train travel altogether – something the Government is desperate to avoid. (Tom Symonds, BBC News.)

Tom says when he did the story again for the 1800 bulletin on Radio 4, he had to have a new top line for the cue. So he went to the statutory watchdog, the Rail Passenger's Council. 'This is the oldest trick in the book for freshening up a story. I'm almost embarrassed to admit it,' he said. This was the intro to the story:

The watchdog representing rail passengers has said it would be wrong to make them pay in advance for an improved service.

The government's rail authority is suggesting fares may have to rise – because the cost of running trains is going up. The authority also said fares had fallen in real terms for many commuters, and that might be making over-crowding worse.

A consultation paper has been published – but no firm decisions have yet been made. Here's our transport reporter Tom Symonds …

Human interest stories

People are fascinated with other people and that is why, in news, human interest stories and the human interest angles to stories in all genres are popular. In human interest stories we look for the basic human emotions of love, hate, anger, joy, tragedy, greed and lust. The events are the dramatic, tragic or extraordinary that have affected ordinary people.

There are certain themes that make good human interest stories:

- triumph over adversity
- bravery
- generosity
- pets
- the quaint and the outlandish
- victims.

We have the woman suffering from terminal cancer who runs the marathon, despite great pain, to raise money for cancer charities. There's the heiress who gives millions to the arts; the pensioner who collects clocks; the wife who keeps a life-size cardboard cut-out of a football star (and talks to it); the vet who removed cataracts from a gorilla; the 10-year-old boy who saved his sister from drowning; the dog who found his owner's new home 40 miles away. All human life is here.

Journalism by numbers

Let's be honest, your average journalist breaks out in a sweat when faced with numbers. I know because I'm one of them. But dismissing it as 'all Greek to me', or blithely stating, 'I'm dyslexic when it comes to numbers' isn't good enough. To carry out the job effectively and in order to protect the public from all sorts of shady goings-on, you have to get to grips with the basics. These include knowing how to work out often-used tools of deception: averages, percentages and rates. Anyone who is blinded by numbers should take a deep breath and tackle their weaknesses head-on. There are some very good books on the market giving easy-to-understand explanations. I've referred to a couple at the end of the chapter, but a quick search on amazon.co.uk will show you how many there are to choose from.

In his job as transport reporter, Tom Symonds has to deal with a lot of statistics. When he received a press release from the airline regulator along with some figures, he needed to be able to match what the press release said to the figures and then decide whether he agreed with their story.

PRESS NOTICE
AIR TRANSPORT USERS COUNCIL (AUC)

Air Transport Users Council warns on internet bookings

In its Annual Report for 2001/2002, published today, the Air Transport Users Council (AUC) reports a slight increase in complaints and enquiries compared with 2000/2001. AUC chairman Ian Hamer said that the Council was concerned to note the continuing high numbers of complaints about mishandled baggage. But another problem area giving the Council increasing cause for concern was in the category of 'ticketing problems'. Mr Hamer said:

> 'We are handling increasing numbers of telephone enquiries about reservations errors, most of which appear to have arisen from direct bookings with airlines either over the telephone or via the internet. More and more of us are choosing to make our reservations direct with the airlines. We should always be very careful to make sure the details are correct. Putting mistakes right can be very costly.'
>
> For internet bookings, it is a good idea to print off the page before the final 'send' or 'confirm', as well as printing off the confirmation. That way you have proof if the confirmation details are not as you expected.'

Elsewhere in the report, the Council publishes, for the first time, numbers of written complaints received against individual airlines. Mr Hamer said:

> 'We received written complaints against over 120 airlines. The table in the report gives the top twenty. It complements the breakdown by category that we have always published in past reports.'

Tables of complaints by category and by airline are attached.

We are just going to look at the top part of the table showing the number of complaints against airlines to illustrate how Tom came to understand the figures.

Top Twenty Airlines by number of complaints to AUC 1 April 2001–31 March 2002

Position	Airline	Total	Total last year
1	British Airways + subsidiaries	117	124
2	Air France	110	81
3	Ryanair	77	138

What the press release announced as the news line is not very exciting – that complaints have increased a little bit. But further down the handout we see that it's the first time the watchdog has published the number of complaints received against individual airlines. This is much more interesting – naming and shaming poorly performing airlines.

Turning to the figures, on the face of it, it looked as if British Airways had the worst record. But Tom realised that if a company had more passengers it was likely to get more complaints. What was a fairer figure was the rate of complaints. He worked it out that the AUC received twice as many complaints against Ryanair (1 in every 143,000 passengers) as they did against British Airways (1 in every 300,000). He checked his findings with the watchdog and they confirmed Ryanair's record. They also said that the fall in complaints about Ryanair this year is owing to the airline's refusal to deal with complaints sent to the AUC, not that they have improved their service. This means passengers have to take complaints to the airline, bypassing the AUC. Tom asked user groups if they could put him in touch with someone who had had a bad experience with Ryanair and was able to write up his story for the BBC's morning radio bulletins on Radio 4 and breakfast television bulletins.

> The watchdog representing the country's air passengers has criticised the standard of service provided by some airlines – especially when baggage gets lost.
>
> The Air Transport Users Council is particularly concerned about the budget airline, Ryanair – which it says often displays a poor attitude towards its passengers.
>
> The council dealt with thousands of phone calls from angry passengers last year – damaged and delayed bags were top of the list of grievances. Here's our transport reporter Tom Symonds …
>
> The Air Transport Users Council only gets a fraction of complaints about airlines – most go to the airlines themselves.
>
> In the past Ryanair attracted more grievances than bigger operators like British Airways which carries three times more passengers – the number has only fallen this year because the airline is refusing to accept complaints from the UK's airline watchdog.
>
> The Council says passengers are often confronted with a take it or leave it attitude when they complain to Ryanair staff – Ryanair points out that it carried an extra four million people last year – proving passengers like the service.
>
> According to today's report all airlines need to improve the way they deal with lost or damaged baggage – which along with flight delays attracted the most passenger criticism.
>
> Phone and internet reservations have also caused problems – partly because passengers make mistakes themselves when booking their tickets.

The television story started with the human interest angle of a disgruntled Ryanair passenger looking through her holiday snaps.

Janina Coghlan had a great holiday in Sardinia – her twin baby daughters loved it too and husband David – at least until they got back to Stansted airport –

[picture of grumpy husband]

Where this picture was taken – during a five-hour wait to find out Ryanair had sent all their luggage to . . . Cornwall.

[Clip with Janina Coghlan saying she found out from another airline where the bags were.]

In recent years it's been Ryanair that's attracted the most complaints to the Air Transport Users Council – British Airways has three times more passengers. The Council's only now dealing with fewer grievances because Ryanair refuses to reply to its letters.

The council says too often passengers are left wondering when their suitcases will turn up – in several cases whole planeloads of baggage have gone missing. The watchdog wants airlines to make more of an effort and obey a new Code of Conduct designed to protect passengers.

[Janina Coghlan: 'I've never been to Newquay but the bags have.']

As for Janina, well her tersely worded letter to Ryanair is written and ready to send. (Tom Symonds, BBC News)

Case Study　　　　**A radio reporter tracks down a story**

Gillian Hargreaves reports how a personal life-event uncovered a lead for a much bigger story:

My mother was treated in a mixed sex ward for a fracture. I thought the Government had got rid of mixed sex wards. I remembered Frank Dobson the then health minister had said in 1997 that the public don't like them and that they would get rid of them. So I asked a researcher to do a search with Hansard and sure enough he [Dobson] had said this. But the date was put back and back and the latest Government announcement said they'd be got rid of by 2002.

I rang the hospital my mother had been in and asked them about mixed sex wards. They denied having them. I said yes they do as I knew someone who'd been treated in one. All my instincts were saying there is something funny going on. So I spoke to my editor, he said why don't we pay for a survey to survey health trusts? In the end we surveyed every health authority in England. We asked: 'Will you meet the Government's target to get rid of mixed sex accommodation by 2002?' The survey took two to three days. We rang 90 health authorities and got 74 replies. In the survey we asked if they'd be willing to speak to [be interviewed by] us; a few said they would. I had gone to the editor with the hunch that the trusts would be nowhere close to meeting the Government's targets to get rid of mixed sex wards. This survey was nailing the lie. It was the first thing Frank Dobson said needed doing in the NHS and it hadn't been done.

I've never had so many comments about a story. People don't like being misled. (Gillian Hargreaves, BBC Radio 4)

This example illustrates how important it is to have a good general knowledge. If Gillian had not known that Frank Dobson had made a pledge about abolishing mixed sex wards, then she would have missed the story. It also shows that you have to be willing to follow your instincts and chase down the truth. Truth checking can be time-consuming and unglamorous: it took Gillian and her small team four weeks to research this story.

Summing up

Good exclusive stories do not usually land in your lap. You need a network of first-class contacts who trust you; you also need the knowledge and the tenacity to hunt down information. Lazy reporters rely on news releases and rarely check the claims made in them. Don't be that kind of reporter; instead use news releases as an interesting starting point to the real story or better angle. And never be afraid to question authority; you don't have to listen to the Pied Piper's tune. In fact the louder it plays, the more you should doubt it.

REVIEW QUESTIONS

1 If a relatively unknown contact gives you a tip-off, what precautions should you take before publishing the information?

2 List six reference texts that you would want in your office.

3 Write out a checklist of questions you need to ask if covering a road traffic accident.

1 Buy a contacts book and write in your name, address and phone number. Decide how you are going to organise it and how you will lay out a contact's details.

2 By using a phone book and the telephone, or personal visits, find the name of the person who deals with media enquiries in your local police and fire services and at your nearest hospital. Enter them, with their contact details, into your contacts book.

3 Using secondary sources (the internet, reference library, etc.) research and answer the following questions:

    i   Who is Lady Davina Windsor?

    ii   What are the symptoms of meningitis?

    iii Who is the MP for Sheffield Brightside?

FURTHER READING

Best, J., *Damned Lies and Statistics*, Berkeley: University of California Press, 2001.

Best J., *More Damned Lies and Statistics*, Berkeley: University of California Press, 2004.

Frost, C., *Reporting for Journalists*, London: Routledge, 2002.

Harris, G. and Spark, D., *Practical Newspaper Reporting*, Oxford: Focal Press, 1997.

Keeble, R., *The Newspapers Handbook*, London: Routledge, 1998.

Mencher, M., *News Reporting and Writing*, Singapore: McGraw-Hill, 2000.

Peak, S. and Fisher, P. (eds) *The Guardian Media Guide*, London: Bath Press (annually).

Randall, D., *The Universal Journalist*, London: Pluto Press, 1996.

Rudin, R. and Ibbotson, T., *An Introduction to Journalism*, Oxford: Focal Press, 2002.

Notes

1 Mike Ridley interview with *Press Gazette*, 19 September 2003.

2 *Guardian*, 7 June 2004.

3 Professor Anne Gregory, from her essay 'The press, public relations and the implications for democracy' quoted in the *Observer*, 6 July 2003.

9

LOCAL GOVERNMENT REPORTING

Local government can be complex and boring, but good journalists realise its importance to our lives. They

- are familiar with the structure of local government
- know where to go and who to approach for information
- understand and are willing to defend their right to attend meetings
- can identify important or interesting stories and write them up in plain English.

Mention local government and people groan. It's not sexy and it's not glamorous. To most, local government begins with refuse collection and ends with street lighting and public parks. If you think this way, prepare to have your mind changed – for journalists local government is a valuable source of news.

Why local government is important

Nothing has a greater effect on the lives of readers, listeners and viewers than local government; yet it can be a turnoff for both the media and the public.

In this statement Bob Satchwell, executive director of the Society of Editors, puts his finger on the paradoxical relationship between local government and the people in this quote. It plays a vital part in our lives and yet it appears remote and irrelevant and its language and workings can be incomprehensible. It is the journalist's job to break through the barriers and explain it to the public. But why bother?

Because local government is not about a small group of people sitting around deciding how to spend a few quid on some new swings in the children's playground. It is much more than that. A few statistics will show you what I mean.

Local government in England and Wales involves more than 400 authorities employing around 2 million staff. They spend in excess of £70 billion a year – that's a quarter of all public spending – on providing services for 50 million people. It is democratically account-able to the people through more than 21,000 elected councillors serving on district, county and unitary authorities.[1]

The range of services provided places some local authorities alongside multi-national corporations in terms of the staff they employ and the revenues they generate from their activities – Kent County Council outstrips both Beechams and Burmah Oil in this regard.[2]

The services provided by councils, either directly or on their behalf by private companies that are awarded contracts, include some of the most significant in the everyday lives of many people. They are:

- **Education**. More than 8 million children are taught in nearly 26,000 Local Education Authority schools by 360,000 teachers. Other services include adult education and under-fives' teaching and learning. Education accounts for 43 per cent of all local authority spending.
- **Social services**. They are responsible for caring for the most vulnerable in society. They administer children's homes, arrange care for the elderly, run adoption and fostering services and disability services along with many other services for those needing help.
- **Planning**. Councils have extensive powers to control development in their area and, depending on the type of authority, can give the nay or the yea to developments from a small extension on the side of a house to the location of a new shopping centre. They also protect listed buildings.
- **Libraries**. This is one of the most heavily used services. Every year millions of people borrow books from their local library or read newspapers there, consult historical col-lections, even surf the internet. There are more than 3,000 libraries in England and Wales and 24 million adults are members of their public library.
- **Waste disposal and collection**. Local authorities collect the equivalent of half a tonne of waste per adult per year from households in England and Wales. Just over 10 per cent of waste is recycled.
- **Fire and rescue**. The fire service has 1,500 fire stations across the country and employs 33,000 firefighters. Besides fighting fires, they deal with road traffic accidents, floods, chemical spills and carry out fire safety inspections.
- **Trading standards**. Officers ensure that trading standards legislation is being complied with. They can prosecute those who flout the law.
- **Disaster planning**. The emergency planning service coordinates the response of the emergency services to disasters such as floods and terrorist attacks. Local authorities are also responsible for civil defence.
- **Roads, highways and transportation**. Local authorities provide, manage and maintain 96 per cent of roads in England and Wales, as well as maintaining large parts of the motorway and trunk (main) road network for the Department of Transport, a service which costs almost 1 billion pounds a year.

- **Housing**. Councils provide around 3.5 million homes in England and Wales.
- **Environmental health**. The environmental health service is one of the oldest services in local government and its responsibilities include food safety, housing standards, pollution control, animal health, noise control, pest control and dog wardens.

The size of local government and the range of its services make it tempting for central government to try to assert some control. Over the years governments have subjected local authorities to reforms and reorganisations. The latest is the Local Government Act, which received Royal Assent in 2000. It had a significant effect on the internal organisation of local authorities and the way they carry out their functions.

Local government structure

The structure of local government is a mishmash of different arrangements in different parts of England and different again in Scotland, Wales and Northern Ireland. The type of local authority dictates the services it delivers.

There are 468 local authorities in the United Kingdom. In Scotland, Wales and urban areas of England, single-tier unitary authorities provide all local services, whereas the remainder of England is served by a two-tier system split between district councils (sometimes called boroughs) and county councils. Under the two-tier system a county council provides most of the main services, such as education and social services, with a number of districts or borough councils below them. Despite being a lower tier, these have important functions such as responsibility for issuing and collecting council tax.

Many areas of England, particularly rural areas, also have parish or town councils (community council in Wales). There are around 10,000 of these made up of nearly 100,000 councillors. These fulfil a more localised role, where they exist, in planning, promoting tourism, licensing, providing community halls and street lighting.

London

London is different again. There are 32 borough councils and the Corporation of the City of London in addition to the strategic citywide government, the Greater London Authority (the GLA).

The boroughs have responsibility for local services within their areas, including education and social services. The Corporation of London provides services for the square mile – the financial heart of the capital. It is the oldest authority in the country and has some unique traditions: for example, no candidate stands as a representative of a political party. It is governed by the Lord Mayor (not to be confused with the elected mayor of the GLA), aldermen and members of the Court of Common Council. In addition to services such as housing, refuse collection, education, social services, environmental health and planning, the Corporation runs its own police force and the Central Criminal Court, the Old Bailey.[3]

Over these councils is the Greater London Authority, which makes strategic decisions to provide services for the whole of London. It consists of a directly elected mayor and an assembly and is responsible for transport, planning (the overall planning framework for London but not individual planning decisions), health (health improvement but not running the health service), culture (tourism, arts and sports), police, fire, emergency planning and the environment (air quality, waste and noise).

The mayor is head of the GLA and is elected for a four-year term. He manages a budget of approximately £5 billion and develops strategies to improve the city.[4]

How councils work

The Local Government Act 2000 introduced the biggest changes in the political structure of councils for more than a century with the intention of boosting leadership and decision-making in councils.

All councils with a population of more than 85,000 were required to consult their electorate on a new style of local governance. The changes would revolutionise the way councils do business, scrapping the traditional committee system and replacing it with a streamlined cabinet of executive councillors. Backbench councillors were given an overview and scrutiny role, akin to the parliamentary style of government.

The Government put forward four options:

1 **A directly elected mayor with a cabinet**. The mayor is elected by the whole electorate in mayoral elections. Once elected, he or she selects a cabinet from among the councillors and each member is allocated a portfolio (area of responsibility) for which they take executive decisions. The cabinet members can be drawn from a single party or a coalition. The office of directly elected mayor is separate from the traditional ceremonial mayor.

2 **Mayor and council manager**. The mayor is directly elected to give a political lead to an officer or 'council manager' who makes the strategic and day-to-day decisions. The council manager is a paid appointee of the council. In this model the mayor's role is primarily one of influence, guidance and leadership. Again this office is separate from that of the traditional ceremonial mayor.

3 **Leader and cabinet**. Under this option a leader is elected by the council, and the cabinet is made up of councillors, either appointed by the leader or elected by the council. The leader provides political leadership, makes executive decisions and proposes the council's budget. The model looks like that of the mayor and cabinet system, except that the leader has no mandate from the electorate and relies on the support of members of the council. If he or she loses that support, they can be replaced by the council.

4 **Alternative arrangements**. For smaller councils with a population under 85,000 or those that have had a referendum for a mayor and it has been rejected by the local electorate, there is a fourth option of adapting and streamlining the old committee system. As with the other options, alternative arrangements must involve effective overview and scrutiny of all council decisions.

Standing orders

These regulate how business is to be transacted at council meetings – how questions and petitions can be submitted and how any debate is to be conducted. It is a boring task to read them, but worth it for a journalist so that they understand council procedures.

Scrutiny committees

To ensure the mayor and the executive are answerable for their decisions these are examined through scrutiny committees. Councillors who are not members of the executive or cabinet – backbench councillors – sit on the scrutiny committees in numbers that reflect the political balance of the council. They are able to question and check the work of the council and review proposals from the cabinet as well as explore new policy ideas.

The full council

The meeting of the full council is the sovereign body of the local authority and all councillors should attend. The full council agrees the budget and sets the policy framework of the authority within which the executive councillors have to work. It also appoints chief officers and makes constitutional decisions.

Standards committees

The Local Government Act 2000 introduced a strengthened ethical code for councillors and standards committees to deal with complaints.

Standards committees must be set up by every local authority except parish councils and include elected members as well as independent or lay members. Serious complaints and accusations of misconduct by local councillors will be referred to the Standards Board for England. In Wales the job will be done by the Commission for Local Administration in Wales.

Central to the ethical framework is a code of conduct for councillors that states when they should not take part in council business. This includes instructions on when a councillor should make a declaration of personal interest and when they should record in the public registers their financial or other interests along with gifts or hospitality they receive. The definition of a personal interest has been widened to include interests of relatives and close friends. A councillor declaring a personal interest may still take part in, and make decisions on, council business in much the same way as before, when such an interest is classified as non-pecuniary. If a councillor has an interest which is both prejudicial and personal, they will not be able to take part in council business or decision-making.

Every councillor will have to record his or her interests in a register. They will also have to record any gifts or hospitality valued at more than £25. Reporters have a right to inspect the register and use it as the basis for stories.

Best value

Best Value replaced the Conservative Government's controversial policy of Compulsory Competitive Tendering (CCT). It meant putting services out to competitive tender to out-side companies in order to get the best price for work such as refuse collection and school cleaning. The Conservatives argued that it brought competition into complacent and ineffi-cient services; those against the policy believed it was all about cheapest not best.

When Labour came to power in 1997 it was clear it had to replace CCT and so it came up with Best Value. An important difference from CCT is that local authorities are no longer obliged to put their services out to competitive tender, but must demonstrate that they are obtaining Best Value for local people.

They do this by producing a performance plan, which reviews the provision of services by examining the past and present performance and identifying future plans and targets for improvement. This is done under the auspices of the Audit Commission's inspection service. Councils must use the following criteria in their reviews: challenge, compare, consultation and competition.

In addition to Best Value, the government has introduced Beacon Council status for those authorities it considers are performing exceptionally well.

Taxing and spending

At present councils are funded through a combination of locally raised tax and central government grants. Only about 25 per cent of the total cost of local government services is raised locally through council tax, the other 75 per cent is from central government grants which include business rates.[5]

The council tax is a tax on both the person and the property they live in. The tax is levied and collected either by the unitary authority or the district/borough council in two-tier councils. The tax assumes there are two or more adults living in the property. As the individual side of the tax accounts for 50 per cent of the charge, there is a 25 per cent reduction for single-person households. The property side of the tax depends on the value of the property which is set in bands (A for the lowest value properties and H for the highest value properties).

There are two types of local government spending:

- **Revenue spending.** Money that councils use to pay for day-to-day activities such as salaries, electricity and road maintenance.
- **Capital spending.** Used to buy items such as land, building and machinery.

The role of the councillor

There are around 20,000 councillors (as of January 2005) serving on principal authorities (unitary, county and district councils) in England and Wales. They are elected to represent an area – a constituency or ward seat – in the council and thus may be approached by a constituent who has a problem and asked to look into an issue. These can be anything from a plea for more home help, to neighbours in council flats complaining about an infestation of cockroaches, to a tenant who has six children and is unhappy at being placed in a three-bedroom house, or traders in the town centre who believe their businesses will be ruined if an application to build an out-of-town shopping mall is agreed. All may go to their councillor for help.

The majority of councillors represent one of the main political parties and they organise themselves into party groups with a leader, deputy leader, etc. Each of these groups will hold group meetings to decide their stance on particular issues. In many councils there will be one party with a majority of seats and therefore the decisions at the group meetings of the majority party are crucial. While these meetings are held in private, it is often possible for journalists to receive 'leaked' information.

Many councillors sit on at least one committee of the council, and some will be chosen to act as chairmen or vice chairmen of these committees. Councillors also elect a council leader; in a council dominated by one party this will be the leader of the majority group.

In addition, they must elect a council chairman or mayor whose job it is to act as an impartial chairman of the council (not to be confused with an elected mayor). Mayors or chairmen preside at full council meetings and have ceremonial and public duties to perform and, as a result, often appear in local newspapers opening galas or meeting local schoolchildren.

Since the Local Government Act 2000, there is now a division between executive councillors, who are leaders or part of the cabinet and have the legal powers to make certain decisions without the approval of a committee or the council, and non-executive councillors, who are not able to make decisions by themselves. Non-executive or back-bench councillors have a role in scrutinising the effectiveness of the council's work through the scrutiny committees. They are also expected to spend more time being 'front-line councillors' and community champions by virtue of the reduction in hours they are required to put in at the council.

Yet the new governance arrangements seem to have done little to change the profile of councillors from overwhelmingly white older or retired males. The rate of female councillors has increased by only 1 per cent over five years (to 26 per cent), and few councillors are aged under 35 or from black and ethnic minorities. Only a third of councillors have full-time jobs outside local government.[6]

Officers

Local government officers are not politicians. They are employees of the council and work for the whole council not on behalf of the majority political party. The role of senior local government officers is to manage staff and resources, and to support and advise elected members. They are full-time and often specialists in areas such as planning or the environment while councillors are not usually specialists. Therefore the job of drawing up strategies for the local authority falls upon officers, who provide advice and guidance and write up committee reports and agenda items, with the councillors' role being to listen to the advice and analysis and make political decisions based on what they are told.

Sometimes this relationship can lead to tension, as councillors complain that officers are not accountable for their advice. Officers would counter that if their advice is faulty they can be fired. Officers are useful for background information but cannot comment on political issues.

Reporting local government

When the Government introduced the Local Government Act 2000, it heralded the changes as ushering in a new era of local democracy. At the time the deputy prime minister, John Prescott, said: 'Opaque and unclear decision-taking weakens the link between local people and their democratically elected representatives'.[7] The reforms, he said, would bring greater openness and accountability to local government decision-making.

According to many journalists, this is not what has happened. When editors and local government reporters were asked in an online survey what they felt about the reforms, most gave them the thumbs down. Rather than ushering in a new era of openness, they said cabinet-style government had been bad for local democracy and had led to more secrecy in decision-making. Eighty per cent of those who responded thought more decisions were now being made behind closed doors. In fact, one said, 'The doors aren't just closed – they are locked.' Another commented that cabinet-style government 'has provided a wealth of stories about secrecy and undemocratic decision-making. And the council leaks like a sieve.'[8]

One of these stories involved a reporter from the *Hereford Times* who was turned away from a council meeting despite being invited by a councillor to attend. The meeting was about flooding problems, which the newspaper had been writing about for two years, but when reporter Ian Morris turned up he was told it was a training session and he couldn't go in. Morris's editor, Liz Griffith, was not impressed:

> The council has pledged its commitment to open government. There are mighty issues facing this county at the moment and our readers, as council tax-payers and electors, are entitled to know how decisions are made and on what they are based.[9]

Even the press officers who responded believe the reforms haven't made the process easier for the public to understand and there was a call to cut the jargon. 'We're wrestling with incommunicable names. I mean, how do you introduce someone as Chair of the Community Information and Support Services Overview and Scrutiny Committee!'

Both press officers and journalists agree that the reforms have resulted in journalists attending council meetings less often than in the past. So while they agree that the new system has led to faster decision-making, there has been a price to pay.

The Local Government Act and council meetings

Whereas previously decisions were made at meetings open to the press and public, the provisions of the Local Government Act 2000 allow more decisions to be made in private by the cabinet. This worries many journalists.

The press and public are allowed to attend any council meeting and cabinet meetings where 'key' decisions are made. The definition of 'key', however, is broad enough to allow different interpretations. The Act defines a 'key' decision as:

1 One likely to result in the local authority incurring expenditure or making savings that will significantly affect the budget for the service or function to which the decision relates.
2 One likely to be significant in terms of its effects on communities living or working in an area comprising two or more wards or electoral divisions in the area of the local authority.

According to the Act, cabinets must meet in public when they are discussing or voting on key decisions, unless the item is deemed to be 'confidential' or 'exempt' or would disclose the advice of a political adviser. In this case a resolution must be proposed and passed before the press can be legally excluded.

- **Confidential items**: a matter initiated by central government that forbids its public disclosure, or information that cannot be publicly disclosed by Court Order.
- **Exempt items:** a person's civil rights or obligations. This may concern an employee, council tenant or client, or if there is commercially sensitive information.

A written record of all key decisions and other executive decisions (including those made at private cabinet meetings) must be made available 'as soon as is practicable' after the meeting. A record of decisions made by an individual must similarly be made available. These can make good stories, such as the decision by officers at Bradford Council to approve initial plans for a supermarket and 610 parking spaces without councillors voting on it. It was made clear that a more detailed application would be needed to be approved by the council before any building could begin. But such a large development being approved behind closed doors, even in outline only, caused fury among local residents and backbench councillors and made a strong story.

To alert the press and public to future key decisions, every council must publish a forward plan containing details of the key decisions it is likely to make over the coming four months.

Meetings of backbench scrutiny committees are open to the media and the public, with advance agendas and papers available beforehand.

The agenda

Q: How does a journalist know what is coming up at a particular meeting?
A: By reading the agenda.

The agenda is a list of things that will happen during the meeting in the order they will happen. Copies of reports from the officers that will be considered at the meeting are attached to the agenda. Journalists can pick up copies from the council offices and increasingly they are being posted onto council websites. A news organisation that wants agendas sent through the post can arrange this, although there may be a charge. Agendas should be available at least five days before the meeting, and there should be sufficient copies available at the meetings themselves.

A journalist should read the agenda and attached reports before going to a meeting. Much of it will be in dull, legal language that can hide a really good story. Resist the temptation to skim or skip passages if there is any hint of news value in them – you may miss something important.

What happens at the meeting?

When you arrive at the meeting you should sit on the seats set aside for the media. The Local Government (Access to Information) Act 1985 says councils must afford reasonable facilities for reporters to take their report.

The chairman or mayor will open the meeting and ask for any apologies for absence. The meeting then agrees the minutes of the last meeting. If a minute is debated, make sure you listen for the page number and item number so you know what is being discussed. Councillors are asked to declare any interests they may have in any items on the agenda. This is followed by the main business of the meeting which is set out in the agenda.

To reach a decision on any matter being discussed, the members have to vote on a proposition (to do something), which has to be proposed and seconded before the debate begins. A majority of those present has to vote in favour for it to be passed.

From your reading of the agenda you should have a reasonable idea which items will be of interest. However, that doesn't mean some innocuous item cannot suddenly turn into a fascinating and heated debate. For example, a small item in an agenda applying for permission to convert an old church and graveyard made a very good story for a reporter when he attended a planning meeting at Denholme Town Council in West Yorkshire.

Michael Taylor from the *Keighley News* found emotions running very high when an item to convert St Paul's Anglican Church in Denholme into a house and part of its graveyard into a garden came up. His article was full of colourful quotes from the debate. Here are a few paragraphs from the middle of the story:

> At Denholme Town Council planning meeting Councillor Graham Astell-Burt said: 'I think it's disgusting. I found out last week and was gobsmacked – the place is full of history. I think it's sacred ground. There's so much history in the gravestones ...'
>
> He added: 'They have been burying people up there since the church closed too. It makes me not want to get buried.' ...

Speaking as churchwarden of St Paul's, Mayor Anne Jay added: 'They are actually wanting to move some of the gravestones to one side. Human remains will stay as they are … untouched.'

'Although we are sad we are not in the building, we realised that we had to move on because a church is not just a building, it's its people.'[10]

Getting quotes down accurately and capturing the mood as the reporter in this example has done is essential to making your reports vivid and readable. Good shorthand helps, as does an instinct for when someone is about to say something interesting.

One difficulty for reporters, especially in large authorities, is knowing who everyone is. Some councils give seating plans but councillors have a habit of changing seats. Sometimes you are lucky and a councillor is referred to by their name – but that doesn't always help with spellings. If you aren't given a clue, write down some characteristics – colour of hair or shirt, whether they are wearing glasses – and ask a member or officer after the meeting for the name. Of course, you can check the council website for mug-shots as many now carry them.

If there are items that need to be discussed in private session, the meeting is able to vote to exclude the public from the meeting. These items are usually at the end of the agenda. The reasons for excluding the public and press are laid down in law and must be given.

Records of meetings

The record of what goes on in meetings is called the minutes. These are written up shortly after the meeting and, when their contents are agreed, they can be read at most council offices and public libraries as well as on council websites. As the first business at the next meeting, the minutes have to be approved as a correct record, or have inaccuracies corrected, before being agreed. In this way a permanent record is kept of all the business dealt with by councils. They can be referred to by journalists as an accurate record when researching stories.

Writing your report

It is not a good idea to take too many notes. Some council meetings can go on for several hours and you could end up with pages and pages of notes. Experience will help you to be selective and take down only the important points to illustrate the items you are interested in. You will find each council meeting will usually yield two or three stories, a main one and a couple of smaller stories.

Remember to bring back the agenda and any reports as well as documents issued during the meeting. You will need these for information.

When writing your report you must translate all officialese and council-speak into plain English. That means having a clear idea of what it all means and the effect of any decisions on local people. If there is anything you don't understand, don't be afraid to ring the relevant council officer or speak to one of the councillors involved.

Some items may be worth following up with a phone call or interview. For example, a family failing to get retrospective planning permission (planning permission after the structure has been built) for a three-bedroom bungalow they built on the site of a dog kennels were told by the council that they had to demolish the bungalow. A news organisation would want to get the family's reaction and be there when the house was demolished – particularly television news for pictures and radio for the sound of the demolition.

Stories to look for

The importance of the decisions made by local councils in our everyday lives means there are potentially many worthwhile stories for reporters. The challenge is identifying them and writing them up in plain English.

Sources to keep in mind are:

- **the agendas**, which can be very thick and a difficult read.
- **councillors**, who are in touch with their constituents and may have been contacted by someone with a complaint about a service or a planning application or the state of a council house.
- **council officers**, who can explain council policy and give background information.
- **council press officers**, whom most councils now employ and who can act as a first point of contact.

Some national stories have local implications that are worth following up, such as reports of more money for pre-school education or shortages of social workers.

Case Study

Unearthing news stories from council planning agendas

At 2BR, the local independent radio station in Burnley, reporter Stuart Clarkson finds council planning agendas a rich vein of stories. He is poring over a planning agenda when he spots a name he recognises – Stan Ternant, the manager of Burnley Football Club. A few phone calls later and the copy-only story is leading the bulletin.

Council planners have approved proposals for a conservatory at Burnley manager Stan Ternant's home, despite recommendations to refuse permission.

The Clarets' boss turned up to last night's meeting to object to the plans to refuse the application.

The project has now been given the green light, even though objections were raised about the size of the proposed conservatory and whether it was in keeping with surrounding buildings at his home in Worsthorne.

The head of planning at Burnley Borough Council has refused to comment, but wished to point out that the application was dealt with as any other case would be.

Days later Stuart spots another good story in another planning agenda. This time it's an application from a housing association to build flats for single people. The planning agenda reads:

APPLICATION RECOMMENDED FOR APPROVAL

Whittlefield with Ightenhill Ward

Application for Full Planning Permission
12 no. flats with ancillary accommodation
Corner of, Spa Street, Junction Street,
Pendle Way, Burnley.

Objections have been received.

The applicant is West Pennine Housing Association. A description of the proposal explains that the scheme provides self-contained accommodation for 12 single young persons with housing needs. Three staff will assist residents in building independent living skills and support when the residents move on. It does not provide emergency homeless accommodation; all applicants are thoroughly assessed before they are given a tenancy.

The project is controlled by a Manager and two Resettlement Workers on duty during working hours. At other times there will be a Security Officer on duty in the communal building. CCTV is planned to deter disruption by residents or outside persons. The organisation manages another similar project in Burnley, which has assisted a significant number of residents to establish their own homes. There has been no reported crime at this scheme or by residents elsewhere. Neighbour complaints have been minimal and have been dealt with promptly and brought to a satisfactory conclusion.

Later in the application (it runs to five pages) Stuart sees there have been letters from 32 residents objecting to the proposal and a petition with 321 signatures opposing the flats has been handed in to the council.

He reads through the application and, when he comes to a paragraph outlining objections from a couple of ward councillors, he goes onto the council website and gets their phone numbers. Within half an hour he has written a voice piece for the next bulletin (see Chapter 5 for more about voice pieces).

> Plans to build 12 flats in Burnley could be given the go-ahead later today,
> despite strong opposition from local residents.

> For 2BR News Stuart Clarkson reports:

West Pennine Housing Association wants to build accommodation for 12 single youngsters at the corner of Spa Street and Junction Street in the Whittlefield area of town.

They say the development will help residents learn to live on their own.

There's significant opposition in the area, with a petition of 321 names handed over to council planners.

Local people say they're worried about who will live there and the impact on house prices in the area.

Planning chiefs are recommending the plans go ahead, and a decision is due to be made by councillors tonight.

Council accounts: an untapped mine of stories

An under-used area for stories is that of a council's accounts. The Audit Commission Act 1998 gave journalists and 'any persons interested' the right to inspect a local authority's accounts and 'all books, deeds, contracts, bills, vouchers and receipts related thereto' and make copies for 20 days before a date appointed by the auditor. The date should be advertised in at least one newspaper 14 days before the date the documents become available, but *McNae's Essential Law for Journalists* advises you to ask the authority directly. Since 1995 a local authority has been required to send information showing the amounts paid to councillors in the previous financial year to the local media.

ITV West tried to use the Audit Commission Act to gain access to the public accounts of Bristol City Council, who denied it, using the Data Protection Act. The broadcaster was looking into council payments to a Bristol landlord housing 'vulnerable members of the community' who was also a former council officer who had been sacked for gross misconduct. They took the case in May 2004 to the high court. The judge ruled that media organisations did not automatically qualify as 'persons interested' but in ITV West's case they did because the broadcaster was based within the city of Bristol and paid non-domestic rates there. This means that, to use the law as a journalist, you need to live in the area you wish to investigate.

Freedom of information

The Government and editors hope the introduction of the Freedom of Information (FoI) Act will help create a culture of openness. (See Chapter 11 for more on FoI.) The Act means that the press and public have a right to access documents and information with some exceptions, for example the personal details of someone in the care of social services. Councils must publish which of their documents is accessible under the Act and how to get copies. This information is likely to be found on a council's website or by ringing the press office.

The nations and regions

Scotland

Scotland has 32 unitary authorities with a budget of about £6.5 billion. Legislation for local government has now been devolved to the Scottish Parliament.

Wales

There are over 1,200 councillors serving on Wales's 22 unitary local authorities. They are responsible for £4 billion of public expenditure, which is over one third of the total Welsh budget.

Northern Ireland

Ireland has 26 unitary district councils with nearly 600 councillors and a budget of around £10 billion.

Summing up

It is hoped that this chapter whets the appetite of every young journalist for the local government beat, so that when asked to cover a council meeting, their response is not of having drawn the short straw but of keen anticipation. And when a council agenda thuds (and they do as they are so thick) onto the journalist's desk, their eyes will light up knowing good stories are within.

Councils are involved in the everyday lives of most people and their decisions affect us all. Do not let the swollen and often pompous language of local authorities put you off. It is your job to cut through all that and hold these officials accountable. Keep a close eye on all key decisions and cultivate good relations with the councillors on your patch. When writing up your stories remember your audience, report the effect of decisions on them and use everyday language.

REVIEW QUESTIONS

1 What are the four options that the Government gave councils in the Local Government Act 2000?

2 What is the difference between a directly elected mayor and a ceremonial mayor?

3 Councillors can be either executive or non-executive. Explain the difference.

EXERCISES

1 Find out what type of council there is in your area.
2 What are the names of your local councillors?
3 Look through your local paper, and answer the following:

(i) How well does it cover the meetings and decisions of the council?
(ii) Do the reports you read come from press releases, agendas or other information from the council, or has the reporter attended the meetings?

FURTHER READING AND RESOURCES

Byrne, T. *Local Government in Britain*, 7th edn, London: Penguin, 2000.
Fenney, R., *Essential Local Government*, London: LGC/National Council for the Training of Journalists, 2002.
Stevens, A., *Politico's Guide to Local Government*, London: Politico's, 2003.
Welsh, T. and Greenwood, W., *McNae's Essential Law for Journalists*, 17th edn, London: Butterworths, 2003.

1 **www.lga.gov.uk**., the Local Government Association website.
Journalists' Guide to Local Government (2004), a guide produced by the Local Government Association and the *Guardian* can be read or downloaded from www.lgib.gov.uk/lg-alliance/documents/journalists_guide.pdf.
2 **www.odpm.gov.uk/localvision**, the 'local vision' area of the website of the office of the deputy prime minister contains research findings about the effects of the Local Government Act 2000 on councils.

Notes

1 For more information visit the website of the Local Government Association www.lga.gov.uk.
2 Andrew Stevens, *Politico's Guide to Local Government*, London: Politico's, p. 80.
3 For more information see www.cityoflondon.gov.uk.
4 See www.london.gov.uk.
5 Figures are from the report of the joint central-local government Balance of Funding review, which concluded that a shift towards local government would give it more flexibility. In response the Government set up an inquiry which should give recommendations by December 2005. See the website of the office of the deputy prime minister: http://www.local.odpm.gov.uk/finance/balance/report.pdf.
6 Francesca Gains, Stephen Greasley, Gerry Stoker (the Evaluating Local Government research team at the University of Manchester), *A Summary of Research Evidence on New Council Constitutions*

in Local Government, p. 17, on www.odpm.gov.uk/localvision. The research was carried out for the office of the deputy prime minister in July 2004.

7 *Press Gazette*, 2 May 2003.

8 The survey was conducted by Carol Grant, of Grant Riches Communications, on behalf of LG Communications, the organisation which represents council press officers, with the help of the Society of Editors. They received 110 responses, half from journalists and half from local council press officers. See www. lgcomms.org.uk.

9 *Press Gazette*, 27 May 2004.

10 *Keighley News*, 23 April 2004. See www.thisisbradford.co.uk.

COURT REPORTING

Good journalists support the system of fair and open justice. They

- cultivate sources who will tell them when important cases will be heard
- keep a full and correct note of proceedings
- know what they can and cannot report from a case
- are fair and accurate in their reporting
- challenge unjustified restrictions imposed by the court.

The criminal courts in the UK process around 2 million cases a year and 100,000 men and women are convicted and sentenced to immediate imprisonment. In the civil courts approximately 2.5 million civil actions are begun, of which about 26,000 go to trial.[1]

Every one of these people has a right to a fair hearing. In Britain we believe this is ensured by our system of open justice – justice being done and being seen to be done. This means with a few exceptions, particularly concerning the family courts, that the press and public are allowed into the courts and that all evidence given in court can usually be reported. The European Court endorsed this view when it declared that 'by rendering the administration of justice transparent, publicity contributes to the achievement of a fair trial'.[2]

As editor of the *Richmond and Twickenham Times*, Malcolm Richards tried for 27 years to cover every case coming to the courts on his patch from TV licence-dodgers to drink-drivers. On his retirement he acknowledged that nowadays this is not the practice of most newspapers:

> Very superficially they'll pick a case that's interesting or they think is newsworthy. It's very hard to defend in a community, because why should Mrs Jones's shoplifting case be publicised when another case wasn't, just because one is slightly more newsy?[3]

As Richards points out, truly open justice would, of course, mean every one of the cases coming before a court would be reported. But in reality there aren't enough reporters to cover all the courts, let alone all the cases heard in them. A good reporter will get around this problem by using their knowledge of the law, network of contacts and news sense to pick up on and follow the most significant and newsworthy cases and they will wish to report these cases in as much detail and as vigorously as possible. A thorough knowledge of the law will give them the confidence to report everything they legally can. But how much law is it necessary for a journalist to know?

News organisations, while not requiring their journalists to be legal authorities, do want them to know enough not to get themselves or their employer into legal hot water. Shelley Bradley, a solicitor with the BBC's Programme Legal Advice Department, says reporters should know when they need to ask for advice:

> We don't expect journalists to be experts on the law – that would put us out of work! But we do expect some basic knowledge and the ability to recognise when something may be a legal problem, i.e. to know when alarm bells should ring. People should not shy away from seeking advice even if they think they should know the answer.

This chapter is a first step: an introduction to the court system and court reporting in the UK. For books that build on this introduction, see the suggested further reading at the end of the chapter.

The structure of the court service

The service is broadly divided into those courts dealing with criminal cases and those dealing with civil cases.

Criminal cases

Those arrested and charged by the police end up in the criminal courts, unless they are younger than 18, and then (with some exceptions) they go to the youth court. A person who is charged with a criminal offence is called a defendant. In most cases, the prosecution of that defendant is handled by the Crown Prosecution Service (CPS), which takes the case over from the police. The CPS reviews the evidence gathered by the police and then decides whether to proceed with a prosecution.

Serious/indictable cases

If the offence is serious (an indictable offence) the defendant will be tried on the basis of a document called the indictment, in which are listed the charges. The first stage of the prosecution is called the sending for trial and is dealt with in the magistrates' court on the basis of written evidence provided by the prosecutor. If the case proceeds, it is heard at crown court before a judge and jury. The judge presides over the trial process by attempting to ensure clarity and fairness. The judge also considers and decides on legal issues (whether a piece of evidence should be presented to the jury, etc.) and explains the relevant law to the jury. It is the 12 men and women of the jury who reach a verdict on the guilt or innocence of the defendant. They decide who to believe and what are the facts; they then apply the law to the facts and come to their verdict. (Note that court names differ in Scotland and they have 15 on a jury).

In criminal cases, it is not the defendant who must prove he or she is innocent but the prosecution who must prove the defendant is guilty, i.e. it is the prosecution who has the burden of proof. What they must prove is not just that the defendant is possibly or probably guilty, but that they are guilty beyond reasonable doubt.

Less serious cases

Less serious criminal cases (around 90 per cent of all cases) are sent for summary trial in the magistrates' court. A summary trial means there is no jury. The trial is before a bench of, in most cases, three magistrates (justices of the peace). These are 'lay' people, which means they are not professional judges or lawyers but respected people from the community. They are advised on the law by a legal adviser or justices' clerk. There are, however, in some large cities district judges who are legally qualified as barristers or solicitors and may sit alone and decide cases.

Either-way offences

A third type of offence is one triable either-way. This means it could be tried either at crown court or at the magistrates' court. Offences that fall into this bracket include theft and indecent assault. When a defendant appears at the magistrates' court charged with an either-way offence, they will be asked whether they intend to plead guilty or not guilty, If they say they will plead guilty, they will be tried summarily by the magistrates. But if they indicate they intend to plead not guilty, the magistrates must decide whether the case is appropriate for them to try summarily or should be committed to the crown court to be tried there. Even if they believe it should be tried summarily, the accused may still elect to be tried by a jury at the crown court. If they wish, or the magistrates decide, for trial by jury at crown court, the hearing will usually be adjourned for formal committal for trial proceedings.

Magistrates usually commit the defendant for trial on the basis of written statements without consideration of the contents of the documents, unless the defence submit there is insufficient evidence to put the accused on trial or if one of the accused is not legally represented.

Appeals

If a defendant is dissatisfied with a verdict they may appeal:

- from the magistrates' courts to the crown court against conviction or sentence
- from the crown court, against convictions and sentences to the criminal division of the Court of Appeal on matters of fact or law and from there to the final appeal court in the UK, which is the House of Lords
- from both the magistrates' court and the crown court, if there are certain legal disputes, to the Divisional Court of the High Court
- from the Divisional Court to the House of Lords, on points of law of general public importance.

Civil cases

In the civil courts a claimant (a private person or organisation) brings cases against a defendant. The cases are often about contracts, land disputes and civil wrongs (called torts) such as negligence, nuisance or defamation (see Chapter 11). Smaller claims start in the county court, which also deals with divorce and bankruptcy. Claims under £5,000 can be dealt with by a small claims procedure. Other claims are assigned by a judge to either a fast-track procedure (claims worth between £5,000 and £15,000) or a multi-track procedure (£15,000 and above).

The High Court is organised according to case type into divisions. The Family Division deals with divorce and child welfare. The Chancery Division's work is varied, but much of it involves land disputes, wills, companies and insolvency and the Queen's Bench Division deals with, among other things, disputes about contracts or torts including negligence, personal injury or defamation. It also has some specialist divisions including a Commercial Court, dealing with large and complex business disputes, and an Admiralty Court, which deals with shipping matters.

Civil proceedings are commenced by the issue of a claim form (which used to be called a writ). It sets out the claim and what remedy the claimant wants from the court, which may be an injunction, declaration of ownership of land or an order to make payment. If it is a monetary claim, the remedy sought will be the amount claimed or damages to be decided by the court.

A civil trial is usually heard by a judge sitting alone, but a few cases, particularly defamation ones, may be heard by a jury too. Many cases started in the civil courts are settled out of court before they come to trial.

Appeals

- From the county court or the High Court there is an appeal to the Civil Division of the Court of Appeal.
- From the Court of Appeal there can be an appeal to the House of Lords on fact or law, but usually appeals are only allowed on matters of public significance.

Tribunals

Tribunals exist to determine disputes and are considered cheaper, quicker and less formal than traditional courts. They deal with a wide range of cases including employment disputes, immigration, tax and pensions. There is a right of appeal to the Divisional Court or the Court of Appeal.

European Court of Justice

The European Court of Justice is part of the European Union and it makes judgments on the law of the Union. It sits in Luxembourg and consists of judges appointed by member states of the European Union, and so there is a British judge. This court is the highest authority on points of EU law. UK courts have a legal duty to comply with EU law.

European Court of Human Rights

The European Court of Human Rights is part of the Council of Europe. It sits in Strasbourg and investigates breaches of the European Convention on Human Rights. British courts must take account of decisions made by the Court although they are not necessarily bound by them.

Inquests

These are held to inquire into violent, unnatural or sudden deaths. They are presided over by a coroner who must be a barrister, solicitor or doctor of at least five years' standing. Some inquests have juries too. Reports of inquests must include the cause of death and the verdict. They are subject to the law of contempt, so be careful not to report that a death was a suicide unless the coroner records a verdict of suicide.

Covering the criminal courts

What happens?

For a journalist, covering the courts can be an intimidating experience at first. They are often housed in large, impersonal buildings and are full of people in gowns and wigs. The language of the court is archaic and the rules strict. But once you have a handle on the way things are done, court reporting is not much different to other forms of reporting and there is one big advantage: terrific tales unfold in front of you.

Your dress for court should be smart, which means a jacket for men and no sleeveless tops for women. You may not be made welcome if you are inappropriately dressed. Cameras and tape recorders are not allowed and your mobile phone must be switched off.

It is a good idea to arrive early and get a copy of the court list. In magistrates' courts and crown courts this is usually on display. The list should contain:

- the names of the people appearing in court that day
- their ages

- their addresses
- a summary of the offences they are alleged to have committed.[4]

Go to the courtroom a few minutes before the court session or case is due to start, and familiarise yourself with the set-up. The court ushers, in plain black gowns and no wigs, are usually helpful at telling you what's going on. It is their job to make sure that those involved in a court case are present. At the magistrates' court the legal adviser, formerly known as the court clerk, is someone to note. They keep track of the cases and advise the magistrates on the law and usually sit at a big desk in front of the magistrates. Opposite them are the defence lawyers, representing the accused, and the Crown Prosecution Service. You will normally find any and all of these people willing to talk to you about the cases they are handling. If you have any questions or need to double-check facts, go and speak to them.

Court cases start with the defendant being asked to confirm their name and address and the charges being read out. (Check them against the court list to make sure you have them down correctly). The defendant will then be asked if they plead guilty or not guilty. If the accused pleads guilty, then it is a case of the prosecution outlining the evidence and the accused and their lawyer saying why the punishment should not be too harsh. If the accused pleads not guilty, then, at the magistrates' court, the case will usually be put off to another day for a trial.

At the trial the prosecution will put its case and probably call witnesses. At crown court this will be before a jury. Once the prosecution has set out its case, it is the turn of the defence. They will challenge the prosecution's account of events with the defendant's own account and may also call witnesses. At the end, in the magistrates' court, the magistrates consider and announce their verdict. If an accused has pleaded guilty or been found guilty, they impose a sentence. In the crown court the judge sums up for the jury, who retire to consider their verdict. When they return they give their verdict and, if it is guilty, sentence is passed. At this point the judge's comments are worth noting, because they may be newsworthy.

Being fair

Accuracy is crucial when covering court cases as decisions are being made about a person's liberty. Make sure you have the correct names and the part played by that person in the trial. Never mix up a defendant and a witness. A young journalist I knew did just that. She was covering a trial for the first time and confused the names of the defendant and witness in a sexual abuse case. It was a hugely embarrassing and damaging mix-up and she lost her job over it.

If you are unsure of any of the facts of the case, check them with the legal adviser, clerk, prosecution or defence lawyer or another reporter. And write your story up as soon as you can after the case while the facts are still fresh in your mind. In some magistrates' courts the acoustics can be very bad and you may have trouble hearing, so do not be afraid to double-check anything.

It is a good idea, if a case is ongoing, to say, 'the case continues' at the end of a report, especially if your report has had to concentrate exclusively on only one side of the story. Remember that balanced reporting is an important part of fair reporting. To be fair, if you have reported one side, say, the prosecution, you should report the other side, the defence, in a subsequent story.

Checklist for court reporting

Make sure you include:

- defendant's name, address and age
- charges and what the plea is
- summary of the crime
- the title of the judge in the crown court, (e.g. Judge Jane Brown or Mrs Justice Brown, depending on whether she is a circuit or High Court judge)
- prosecution's opening statements and what they want to happen
- case for the defence
- key witness statements
- judge's summing-up (in crown court cases)
- how long the jury took
- verdict
- statements by the magistrates or the judge (in crown court cases)
- sentence – fines, community service, imprisonment.

Restrictions on reporting

As we have seen, almost all criminal cases begin in the magistrates' courts. In summary cases, where the case is to be heard in its entirety in this court, the journalists can normally report everything that is said in front of the magistrates.

For cases where the defendant is being remanded or during preliminary proceedings before committal to or sending for trial to crown court, reports are restricted to the following ten points. This is to ensure that when the case comes to the crown court and before a jury, no jury member has read anything or heard anything that may influence them.

1 the name of the court and the magistrates
2 the names, addresses, ages and occupations of those charged and any witnesses
3 a description of the offence or offences with which the defendant is charged
4 the names of the solicitors and barristers
5 the decision taken by the court as to whether to send for trial
6 the charges on which the defendant is to be committed for trial and the name of the court to which he is committed
7 if proceedings are adjourned, the date and location of the adjournment

8 bail arrangements – but not the reasons why bail was opposed or refused. So if bail is refused you can report this, but not give the reasons why it was refused. These could be because the police believe a defendant may escape or commit another crime. A future jury could be influenced by this knowledge

9 whether legal aid is granted

10 any decision of the court to lift or not lift reporting restrictions. These can be lifted if the defendant asks for them to be, or if the court decides not to commit for trial or deals with one or more of the defendants.

These restrictions for pre-trial hearings are in place to protect the legal process. Contravening them brings you into conflict with the laws of contempt of court. On the other hand, these rules are broken almost every day by newspapers and broadcasters in their attempts to add colour to their stories and background details about the defendant or the crime. Details of the accused's dress, their demeanour and so on are technically not permitted but in practice are often used to spice up a report. Be careful about mentioning increased security around the court or a defendant being handcuffed to police officers as these, it is sometimes argued, could indicate a person's guilt.

If a report goes too far the results can be serious. The news organisation risks the court imposing a heavy fine or imprisoning the editor and journalists for contempt. The punishments are potentially severe for good reason: if a report prejudices a trial so that it has to be stopped, the costs of a retrial are large. And if trials have to be abandoned altogether, guilty people go unpunished and innocent ones are unable to clear their names.

Contempt of court

The laws of contempt of court try to strike a balance between the principle of open justice and the defendant's right to a fair trial. They seek to ensure UK media reports are fair and accurate and report only what is said in open court. This in turn prevents juries and witnesses having access to information that might influence them, other than that which is presented in open court.

What is contempt of court?

You will be in contempt if you publish anything that creates a substantial risk of serious prejudice or impediment to particular proceedings while the proceedings are active. The law on contempt of court forbids disrupting a court's work or bringing it into contempt. For journalists the biggest danger is in prejudicing a trial. This could involve publishing a defendant's past convictions or reporting statements made to the court when the jury is not there. You can also be in contempt if you behave in a way that could prejudice a fair trial, such as refusing to give evidence (see later in the chapter) or attempting to bribe the jury.

The judge in the trial of Harold Shipman, the GP accused of the murder of 15 of his patients, had to haul into court several employees of a radio station in Preston, Lancashire.

The judge was angered by comments made on air between a DJ and a traffic girl from Rock FM, which could have resulted in the trial being halted. Only because none of the jury had heard the conversation, which made clear both believed Shipman to be guilty, did the judge not abandon the trial at a potential cost to the taxpayer of hundreds of thousands of pounds. The broadcasters were lucky to escape contempt charges.

The conversation included these comments by the DJ:

> Harold Shipman's trial is going into its umpteenth month . . . Innocent until proven guilty, of course, because that's the way it works in this land. It's innocent until proven guilty as sin.

The traffic girl is heard in the background saying: 'guilty'. The judge, Mr Justice Forbes, said it was 'about as irresponsible a piece of broadcasting as I have ever heard'.[5]

Harold Shipman was found guilty in January 2000 and given 15 life sentences. An official report later concluded that he had killed between 215 and 260 people over a 23-year period in Greater Manchester and West Yorkshire. He was found dead in his cell in Wakefield prison in January 2004.

While the trial of Harold Shipman was allowed to continue, contempt by the *Sunday Mirror* caused the collapse of another high-profile trial, this time involving well-known footballers. Two players for Leeds United, Jonathan Woodgate and Lee Bowyer, were on trial for assaulting an Asian student in April 2001 when the *Sunday Mirror* published an interview with the father of the victim, who said his son's attackers must have had a racial motive. Because the prosecution had dropped the charge that the attack was racist, to print this assertion by the victim's father was very damaging. The day after the story was published the judge halted the trial. The *Sunday Mirror* was fined £75,000 plus £54,000 costs for the contempt and several of the paper's senior people, including the editor and deputy editor, left the paper. The cost of the retrial was said to be about £10 million.

In the second trial Lee Bowyer was acquitted of causing grievous bodily harm and affray and Jonathan Woodgate was found guilty of affray and sentenced to 100 hours' community service.

Since the collapse of the Bowyer/Woodgate trial, the courts have received new powers enabling them to make third parties pay the costs of an aborted criminal trial. Now if the court thinks there has been serious misconduct such as prejudicial reporting, it can order the media or whoever it thinks is at fault to pay some or all the costs of abandoning the trial. This law came into effect in October 2004 and reinforces how much care is needed when reporting the courts.

At what stage do the contempt laws start to apply?

It is not just when a defendant has come to court that the contempt laws apply. A journalist is in danger of committing contempt of court as soon as proceedings are active, which is before the defendant appears in court – it can even be before they are charged. Proceedings become active when

- an arrest has been made
- a warrant for an arrest has been issued
- a summons has been issued
- an indictment or other document specifying the charge has been served
- a person has been charged orally with a crime.

In other words, proceedings become active when formal steps have been taken to identify a person with a crime.

Contempt of court is one of those laws, along with libel, that gets journalists all in a lather, not least because it is a strict-liability offence. That means the courts do not have to prove that the journalist intended to commit contempt. It is the journalist's responsibility to establish if and when a case becomes active.

Contempt of court is also very confusing. There are many grey areas and journalists see it as an inconsistent law because some news organisations get away with coverage that appears to be obviously breaching the law while others are punished.

More reporting restrictions

Youths

Offences committed by young people who are under 18 when the offence is committed are usually dealt with in youth courts. These courts are closed to the public, but open to journalists. They have very strict rules about what can be reported. You may not name or identify in any way any child or young person under 18, except on rare occasions when restrictions are lifted. This means naming a young offender's school or their friends and relatives, if that would lead to identification, is banned. The restrictions also apply to witnesses taking part in the proceedings who are under 18.

When a child appears as a defendant or witness in an adult court, there is no automatic ban on naming them, but the judge may impose a Section 39 (of the Contempt of Court Act 1981) order, which effectively prevents naming or identifying the child in reports.

If the child or young person is then found guilty of the crime, the ban on identifying them may be lifted, especially if it is very serious. This happened with Robert Thompson and Jon Venables, two young boys found guilty of killing the toddler Jamie Bulger in 1994. But other young people continue to have their identity protected even after being found guilty of a crime.

A child's name should not automatically be withheld if they are appearing in an adult court. Orders should only be placed if the reasons to do so outweigh the legitimate interests of the public to be told of events, and the names and addresses of people concerned. A dead child cannot be the subject of Section 39 restrictions.

If a child or young person is appearing in an adult court, it is always best to check the status of any orders as they can change at any time. The *South Wales Evening Post*'s crown court reporter was lucky to spot an order banning identification of a 17-year-old defendant in a case he was covering. It had been pinned to a noticeboard in the press room after the case had finished and was made by a judge not involved in the case. When the young man had first appeared on charges of drug dealing, his defence barrister did not apply for a Section 39 order and the judge in the case did not make one. The paper named the defendant on that occasion.

Three weeks later when the young man and his 18-year-old accomplice appeared for sentencing before a different judge, again no Section 39 order was applied for or made. The 17-year-old was jailed for three-and-a-half years and his accomplice for 18 months. When the reporter returned to the pressroom to file his story later that day, he found the Section 39 order pinned to the noticeboard. There was no chance to challenge it for several days as it was made on the Thursday afternoon before the Easter holidays. The *Post* ran the story but did not name the defendant and when the courts reopened the following week, the paper challenged the order successfully. In lifting the order the judge said that there was legitimate public interest in knowing the outcome of the proceedings.[6]

Sexual offences

Victims of rape or other sexual attacks have a right in law to remain anonymous. Once an allegation of rape or any other sex offence has been made, nothing can be reported that could identify the victim in his or her lifetime. There is no anonymity for the defendant, except where naming them would lead to identification of the victim.

A victim can, if they decide to, waive their right to anonymity. If you are writing a story with such a person you should get their consent in writing. It is normal editorial practice to assume that a victim under 16 cannot waive consent nor can a parent waive it on their behalf but there is no legal ruling on this.

Anonymity for adult witnesses

Section 11 orders (of the Contempt of Court Act 1981) give the court the power to prohibit the publication of the name of a person involved in a court case. The power is intended to protect blackmail victims or people involved in national security from being identified.

A court can also grant lifelong anonymity to a fearful or distressed adult witness in any criminal proceedings, thanks to the Youth Justice and Criminal Evidence Act 1999 (this part came into force in October 2004). If the court feels that the quality of a witness's evidence or their level of co-operation is likely to suffer if they are identified as a witness in a case, it can make an order preventing the media from publishing anything that could identify them as a witness. Before deciding whether or not to make such a reporting direction, the court has to consider whether it would be in the interests of justice to make the order.

Orders, such as the Section 11 order, are sometimes made in cases where it is inappropriate and journalists should challenge them. When magistrates in Huddersfield in West Yorkshire made a Section 11 order forbidding the press from giving the name or address of a man charged in connection with a fire in which eight people including five children died, a journalist from the Press Association (PA) felt it was wrong. When the man appeared at Leeds Crown Court, the PA challenged the order. The defence lawyer argued that the benefits to justice of keeping his client anonymous outweighed that of 'simply publishing his name and address and the benefit of that to the press'. The judge disagreed, saying: 'The ability of the press to report matters of public interest is critical. Once the important cases cannot be reported then the public and the press have a real grievance.'

PA news copy editor Mike Dodd said he was becoming increasingly concerned at the willingness of magistrates' courts to make orders forbidding the press from reporting the names and addresses of defendants in criminal cases. There is even guidance given in a booklet *Reporting Restrictions in the Magistrates' Court*, which states that orders should only be made if it would impede or frustrate the administration of justice not to. However, 'the courts seem not to have heard of the booklet. They also seem to be increasingly willing to overrule or ignore the principle of open justice.'[7]

Postponing orders

A judge may make an order postponing the reporting of evidence; for example if a defendant is to be tried later on other charges.

Other ways of falling foul of contempt

While the greatest risk to a journalist of committing contempt of court is when reporting a crime or a court case, there are other ways, for example refusing to disclose confidential sources.

The Contempt of Court Act 1981 recognised there is a public interest in allowing journalists to protect their sources. Section 10 says:

> No court may require a person to disclose, nor is any person guilty of contempt of court for refusing to disclose, the source of information contained in a publication for which he is responsible, unless it is established to the satisfaction of the court that disclosure is necessary in the interests of justice or national security, or for the prevention of disorder or crime.[8]

This is a bold statement, but it does not give as much protection as might first appear. In a number of cases the courts have ordered journalists to disclose their sources, as we saw in Chapter 7. The journalists placed in contempt of the Bloody Sunday Inquiry had the proceedings against them dropped, but only after several years of facing the prospect of heavy fines and jail.

The verdict

Once the jury has delivered a verdict, most news organisations believe it is legally safe to publish background reports, using all interviews and other material. Now a defendant's past convictions and other details, which could have influenced the jury, can be published. In theory the case is still active until sentence is passed. Yet the jury and witnesses have had their say and the judge is not likely to be influenced by the media.

A criminal case ceases to be active when

- the arrested person is released without charge or bail
- the defendant is found unfit to be tried
- the case is formally discontinued or an order is made for the charge to 'lie on file'
- no arrest has been made 12 months after the issue of a warrant
- the defendant is acquitted or sentenced.

Reporter's rights in court reporting

The media's duty in reporting crime and the courts is to be the eyes and ears of the public. In this chapter we have spent some time noting all the restrictions on what can be reported by those ears and eyes in order not to prejudice the justice system. Now we shall look at some special protections enjoyed by the journalist when reporting court cases.

If you report court proceedings fairly and accurately, you and your news organisation cannot be sued for libel (see Chapter 11 for more on libel) for anything said in the report. This protection is called privilege and it covers what is said or read out during the proceedings by people involved in them. So a witness can make offensive allegations against a defendant and, as long as they were said in open court in front of the magistrates or a judge and jury, a journalist can report them in a fair and accurate report. Such a report would be protected against a libel action.

Privilege does not cover material said while the jury is absent or anything said after the proceedings, and it may not include outbursts during the proceedings by people in the public seats – though these can be reported if they are not defamatory. It also does not cover anything said outside court. Note that Parliament is also covered by privilege, as are fair and accurate reports of tribunals, inquiries, commissions, council meetings and public meetings including press conferences. (See the defamation section in Chapter 11 for full details of this defence.)

Ethical issues

No payments to witnesses

Following several high-profile cases, several years of debate and the threat of legislation, the Press Complaints Commission finally introduced a clause into its Code of Practice in March 2003 to ban payments to witnesses in criminal trials once proceedings have become active.

Payments to people who may become witnesses are permitted before the case becomes active, but only if the information obtained is in the public interest and payment is the only way to get it. Under no circumstances must witnesses be offered more money in the event of a conviction.

In 2002, the Lord Chancellor threatened to legislate to ban payments after the case of Amy Gehring, the teacher accused of having under-age sex with some of her pupils. The trial collapsed after it became known some of the boys had sold their stories.

Gehring's was not the first case to have witnesses who had been paid for their stories. In the trial of Rosemary West in 1995, her lawyers complained about her conviction on the grounds that around 19 witnesses in the case were thought to have been paid by the media. After the West trial, there were calls for the Government to legislate, and the Press Complaints Commission tightened its Code.

It was felt that witnesses may feel obliged to stick to the story they had originally told the journalist while under cross examination in court, even if they wanted to change it, because they feared they might not get the money promised to them. They might also exaggerate the evidence to make it more newsworthy or because, if they secured a conviction, their stories would be worth more. They could even withhold relevant evidence from the court in order to give newspapers exclusive coverage later on. And once they knew a witness had been paid, juries may wonder if their evidence has been affected by the contract.

The issue came up again when the rock singer Gary Glitter was acquitted in 1999 of indecent assault after what the judge called a 'highly reprehensible' payment of £10,000 by the *News of the World* to one witness, with a promise of £25,000 more on conviction. The jury did find him guilty of 54 offences of downloading child pornography from the internet and he was jailed for 4 months.

Even interviewing witnesses without paying them while a case is active is an ethical issue. They may still feel they have to stick to the story they told the journalist or have exaggerated their involvement or what happened to them. Yet finding people who are involved in a case, interviewing them and preparing 'backgrounders' for publication immediately after the trial is part of the journalist's role.

The BBC's *Producers' Guidelines* give some direction on interviewing witnesses or potential witnesses in a forthcoming trial. They say that nothing should be done that interferes with the course of justice and that once the trial is under way no interviews should normally be held with witnesses about any aspect of their evidence. Any journalist wishing to interview a witness before the end of a trial should seek advice from their legal department and editorial policy first.

Whom you cannot interview

It is contempt of court to attempt to interview the jury about their deliberations. The *Mail on Sunday* was found guilty of contempt of court in 1994 after it published interviews with jurors and told of their deliberations in the jury room. The paper, the editor and a journalist were fined a total of £60,000.

The courts also frown on journalists conducting interviews (for example for use in after-trial backgrounders) with people before they have given evidence in an upcoming criminal trial.

Possibility of filming court cases

The Government was, as this book went to press, consulting on the possibility of bringing cameras into court. The argument was made that it would help the principle of open justice by allowing people, through television, to see what happens in court.

While it may be good for journalists, especially television journalists – no more need for those court sketches and GVs (general views/wide shots) of the outside of the courthouse – the ethical issue is, would such a move be good for the justice system? Would witnesses be affected, perhaps by being more self-conscious or refusing to appear at all? Would it be justice being seen to be done or would 'Court TV' become just another form of entertainment?

At present the only filming or recording that is allowed for television reporters (except in Scotland) is outside the 'precincts of the court'. What constitutes the 'precincts' may be interpreted differently from one court to the next and you should ask the ushers or the police at the gate exactly what area is included.

Contempt in civil proceedings

This is generally perceived to be less of a problem as lay people such as juries are not used very often in civil cases. However, seek legal advice before publishing something prejudicial about an active civil case and obviously you need to take extra care with a jury case. Civil proceedings become active for contempt purposes when a date is fixed for a case to be heard. Liability lasts until the case has been heard or it has been abandoned, discontinued or withdrawn.

Examples of crime reporting

We're going to look at some real articles and discuss how they came to be published. The first is an article that appeared in a tabloid newspaper. The names and some of the details have been changed, but the article is essentially what was printed.

> A drink-driver killed a 7-year-old girl when he lost control at 70mph and crashed into a group of children.
>
> Chloe Summers was playing with her brother Daniel, 6, and two pals after spending the day with her family at a barbecue. Then Sean Kemp, 26, careered down the road in a high-powered Fiat and smashed through railings hitting the little girl. She died instantly from horrific injuries beside a bench.

Chloe's mum saw the tragedy after shouting a warning to the youngsters when she heard the roar of the approaching car. Daniel and the other children managed to scatter as she called out and they were unhurt.

Kemp tried to run from the scene but was grabbed by a dozen men and women who dashed from the barbecue on the other side of the street.

He was beaten up by the crowd then saved by police who arrived within minutes. A second man who fled from the car was soon caught by cops.

Locals said Kemp and his passenger had just left a pub 100 yards away. They failed a breath test.

A regular at The Frog and Crow, in Margate, said: 'He roared off down the street clipping the kerb as he went. We all knew something terrible would happen. He might as well have had a loaded gun in his hand. He had been drinking and he knew it.'

And Susan Bowler, 42, who witnessed the crash said:

> 'He was driving like a maniac and you could tell he was not in a fit state. It was obvious both men had been drinking. People had seen the car outside the pub. The engine was roaring like mad and it was going at least 70mph when he clipped the kerb – and then he came flying across the road and smashed into the railings. Even then he tried to run away. You could smell the alcohol on his breath.
>
> The girl's mum was being comforted by her partner but she was hysterical. I went to her aid with a doctor who lives next door. The little girl had no chance. One leg looked twisted and broken and the other was snapped in several places.
>
> There was a lot of blood coming out of her mouth. The paramedics were doing their best but you could see she was dead. It was awful.'

Kemp and his passenger were still being held by police in Margate last night.

A spokesman said: 'Two men aged 28 and 29, are in custody on suspicion of drink-driving after failing a breath test.'

Questions we have to ask are:

- Is the case active?
- Is anything published likely to influence a jury in a subsequent court case?

It would appear that the case is active as the men have been arrested and are in custody, having failed a breath test. Sometimes it is not clear if someone has been arrested or charged but one way to try to find out is to ask police if they are free to leave. If the answer is no, the case is very likely to be active.

Once a case is active then, as we know, we cannot publish anything that creates a substantial risk of serious prejudice or impediment to particular proceedings. The details written up here point very clearly to Kemp being guilty of the crime. The story puts him behind the wheel, driving dangerously having been drinking, careering into the little girl and then trying to run from the scene. On the face of it, this is a clear case of contempt. Would it influence a jury?

There are a few points on the side of the press in publishing stories like this one. To qualify as a contempt of court, the risk of prejudice must be substantial and judges have said risks of prejudice which are other than substantial are the price we pay for an open press. You might try to argue that there is a less than substantial risk owing to the lapse of time there will be before these men come to trial. It could be eight or nine months. Judges take such time lapses into account. But in this particular case the seriously prejudicial nature of comments that leave no doubt as to the lack of sobriety and guilt of the driver puts the reporter at serious risk of prosecution.

A safer way of writing the story would be to avoid naming Kemp as the perpetrator but include the reports from eye witnesses of how they saw the car being driven. Kemp could then be referred to at the end of the piece as having been arrested, although it is not usually the case that the media name people on arrest (as opposed to charge), save where they are particularly of interest, for example if they are a celebrity.

This next article was accompanied by a still taken from CCTV footage.

> Detectives want to speak to the man pictured in connection with a series of armed robberies.
>
> Cops believe he has struck at a minimum of nine betting shops in the past nine months, threatening staff with a gun.
>
> He is believed to have robbed a branch of Ladbrokes in London Road, Tooting, on Thursday, March 25.
>
> He is also suspected of carrying out at least eight other raids across South London and Surrey since July last year. (*South London Press*, 20 April 2004)

You will find stories like this one in newspapers and on radio and television bulletins regularly. They are appeals from the police for help in tracing a criminal. Occasionally there is a warrant for the person's arrest and the police need to find him or her; and by publicising details, they will perhaps receive valuable information from the public. Technically the media publishing a police appeal linking a wanted person to a crime is a contempt of court, but the media have a defence. In 1981 the attorney-general said in the House of Commons debate on the Contempt of Court Bill that it was right that the police should be able to warn the public about a dangerous criminal or ask for help in finding a wanted man either using a photograph or other details. He said: 'The press has nothing whatever to fear from publishing in reasoned terms anything which may assist in the apprehension of a wanted man and I hope that it will continue to perform this public service.'[9]

Summing up

The language of courts can be archaic and complicated. As a reporter you have to understand it, but remember not to fall into using it when you are writing up the story. It is your job to explain the proceedings in layman's terms.

Nothing should be reported whilst the case is active unless it is said in open court and, in criminal cases, in front of the jury. If the journalist knows something more than the jury, they should keep it to themselves. Often during a trial the jury is sent out while 'legal arguments' are carried on, for example the admissibility of evidence. None of this can be reported until the case is over.

Before writing up any story make sure you know what, if any, orders have been made by the court. Don't assume, for example, that in a case involving a child the order was a Section 39. Check the exact statute and section number. You can also ask what reasons, if any, were given for an order being made. Then if you wish to challenge the order you know what you will have to rebut.

Reporters should always be willing to challenge any orders they feel are unjustified and be willing to defend their rights to information. Sometimes a journalist will know more than lawyers or magistrates. In September 2004 a freelance journalist forced a magistrate to give his name after he refused to do so during a case involving a child truant. The case, at Sevenoaks Magistrates' Court, concerned a mother convicted of failing to ensure her daughter attended school. The case was adjourned because the mother had failed to turn up and the magistrate criticised her for jeopardising her daughter's GCSE prospects. The reporter asked the clerk afterwards for the name of the magistrate but was told they 'did not see why it was necessary'. The journalist went away and came back with a copy of the 1987 Queen's Bench Divisional Court ruling by Lord Justice Watkins, which stated that magistrates should not be anonymous. The clerk gave him the name.

REVIEW QUESTIONS

1 When is a news article in contempt of court according to the 1981 Contempt of Court Act?

2 What does the strict liability rule mean for journalists?

3 When does the risk of contempt for a journalist begin in criminal proceedings and when does the risk end?

4 What are the ten points you can report in a preliminary hearing?

EXERCISES

1 Visit your local magistrates' court and take one of the seats allocated for the public. Spend a morning listening to the cases and see if you can identify a couple of stories, bearing in mind the reporting restrictions outlined in this chapter.

2 Write up your stories when you get home. Did you write full enough notes? Did you check the names (first and surname), addresses and ages of the defendants? Do you think you noted the charges accurately?

3 Look through two or three newspapers for any crime or court stories and see if there are any that may be in contempt of court. Why do you believe the newspaper has decided to print the story?

FURTHER READING AND RESOURCES

BBC Producers' Guidelines, London: BBC.

Crone, T., *Law and the Media*, 4th edn, Oxford: Focal Press, 2002.

Press Complaints Commission, *Code of Practice*. Available at www.pcc.org.uk. This site also lists PCC adjudications.

Welsh, T. and Greenwood, W., *McNae's Essential Law for Journalists*, 17th edn, London: Butterworths, 2003.

www.ukeditors.com. The site for the Society of Editors is useful for updates on legal issues, court cases and press freedom.

Notes

1 Figures are for 2000 for the number of criminal cases, 1995 for the number of civil cases, and 2002 for prison sentences. See www.homeoffice.gov.uk and UK Law Online.

2 In the case of *Gautrin v. France*, 1999. Cited in T. Welsh and W. Greenwood, *McNae's Essential Law for Journalists*, London: Butterworths, 2003, p. 107.

3 Malcolm Richards, on his retirement as editor of the *Richmond and Twickenham Times*, interviewed in the *Guardian*, 17 March 2003.

4 In 1989 a Home Office circular said that as a minimum the lists should contain the name, age and address of the accused and their occupation if known, *Guardian*, 17 March 2003.

5 *Press Gazette*, 4 February 2000.

6 *Press Gazette*, 2 May 2003.

7 *Press Gazette*, 7 June 2002.

8 Welsh and Greenwood, *op.cit.*, p. 335.

9 *Ibid.*, p. 190.

11

◼ REPORTERS AND THE LAW

Good journalists understand the law as it applies to them. They

- are familiar with the rules of libel
- keep full and accurate notes of conversations
- are careful to report only what is accurate and can be proved
- keep abreast of changes to the law
- challenge unjustified refusals to release information.

Law and the media

One of the first responsibilities of a young journalist is to make sure you are familiar with the law as it affects the media. It's not easy – almost every year there is more law that a journalist needs to be aware of. But not knowing where the legal pitfalls are makes it more likely that you will fall straight into them. The consequences of this can be serious for both the journalist and the news organisation. Smaller operations can be shut down by such mistakes. The magazine *LM* (*Living Marxism*) went into liquidation after it lost a defamation case against ITN and two of its reporters. *LM* had run a story in 1997 attacking an ITN report under the headline 'the picture that fooled the world'. It accused the reporters of sensationalising the image of an emaciated Muslim pictured with other men through barbed wire at a Serb-run detention camp in Bosnia. *LM* claimed it was the reporters who were behind the barbed wire not the Muslim men. ITN sued and won. The jury awarded £375,000 damages against *LM*.[1]

What the law tries to do

It's a given that falling foul of the law is dangerous for journalists. But the legal system does recognise that it is important for journalists in a liberal democracy to act as watch-dogs, exposing crime, corruption and hypocrisy. However, this does not mean that jour-nalists can go around poking their noses in wherever they wish and accusing whoever they wish of whatever they wish. This is because the law also recognises that a person's repu-tation and what others think of them is important. This means unsubstantiated and unjustified attacks on the reputation of people or unfair intrusions into their private lives cannot be tolerated.

The attempt to balance the right of free speech and to expose wrongdoing with the right of individuals not to have their reputation damaged is enshrined in several laws which journalists need to be aware of. This chapter outlines the most significant, although it is only a basic introduction. Further reading is encouraged and a reading list included at the end of the chapter. Chapter 12 looks at the regulators whose job it also is to keep the competing rights in balance.

Defamation

This is possibly the area of the law that you are most likely to encounter and can pose one of the greatest hazards for reporters. Its role is to protect the reputation of people or companies from wrongful attack.

What is defamation?

The law of defamation covers slander and libel. Slander is defamation by the spoken word, that is in a transient form. Libel is defamation by the written or printed word, that is in a permanent form. Television, film, radio, print and the internet all count as perma-nent. Any defamatory words published by these media are considered as libel not slander. So although journalists need to be mindful of the slander law, when making telephone calls for example, it is the law of libel that they are more likely to have to consider when filing their stories.

Defamation cases are civil claims and are usually heard in the High Court, with a jury or a judge sitting alone. A person who believes they have been defamed can sue for damages and, if successful, the court will award an amount of money by way of compensation. In a libel trial the judge decides whether the words used are capable of a defamatory meaning. If there is a jury, it will decide whether or not the claimant has been defamed, whether damages should be awarded and, if so, how much. The judge is likely to rule a statement about a person or organisation is defamatory if it tends to do any of the following:

- expose them to hatred, ridicule or contempt
- cause them to be shunned or avoided

- lower them in the estimation of right-thinking members of society
- disparage them in their office, business, trade or profession.

Many libel cases are settled out of court and never come to trial. News organisations are reluctant to fight defamation actions and may even consider settling out of court even if they have a reasonably strong case. That's because libel trials are risky. The outcome of any case is uncertain and the damages awarded by juries can be considerable. More importantly, on top of damages the loser has to pay their own legal fees and those of the other side.

Given these concerns, you'd think there would be very few occasions when journalists fell foul of the libel rules. Not so. Tom Crone, News International's legal manager gives three reasons why he and his kind will never be unemployed as newspaper libel lawyers:

1 Sometimes journalists deliberately mislead people.
2 Sometimes journalists get it plain wrong.
3 Sometimes people lie, and keep on lying for financial or image reasons. Jeffrey Archer and Jonathan Aitken have been caught lying. Others have got away with it.[2]

Crone's list is quoted by the seasoned defender of libel actions, Kelvin MacKenzie, editor of the *Sun* from 1981 to 1994, writing about some of the libel actions the *Sun* faced. Two of his examples fall into the first two of Crone's categories – you decide which.

The pop star Sting sued over a story in the paper's Bizarre column headlined 'Sting: Why I Have Taken Drugs'. His solicitors wrote to the paper saying the story was untrue and demanded an apology and a large sum in damages. Clearly, saying someone has taken illegal drugs lowers them in the eyes of right-thinking members of society. MacKenzie stood his ground. He'd checked with the reporter who claimed the evidence was all on tape. They were issued with a libel writ. When MacKenzie, the legal team and the reporter met to prepare their defence to the action, they played the tape of the interview with Sting.

> [There was] a lot of boring dribble about what great songs he sings, why he sings them and then, finally, the crunch. The Bizarre reporter says: 'Tell me Sting, have you ever taken drugs?' Sting pauses and then replies firmly: 'No.'
>
> A quiet descends on the legal conference. We turn on the reporter. In unison we say: 'But you said he admitted taking drugs'. The reporter nods and says: 'But it was the *way* he said no'. Sting pocketed £75,000 in damages.[3]

Another pop star to win substantial damages for stories in MacKenzie's *Sun* was Elton John. He received £1 million after the paper wrongly claimed that he had had sex with under-age rent boys and £250,000 more when it accused him of another equally – in some people's eyes – sinful act.

> One of the *Sun's* finest had come up with an absolute belter; the story was that Elton was having difficulty sleeping at night because of the barking from guard dogs that patrolled the perimeter of his mansion outside London.

> So he had decided to have the voiceboxes of the dogs removed so that, although their jaws would move as though they were barking, no sound came out ...
>
> I later learned that the news editor of the day sent a reporter down to the mansion who was surprised to hear the barking of guard dogs. He told the news editor: 'I don't think those dogs have had their barks removed, listen to this,' and shoved a mobile phone through the impressive gates. The dogs duly barked down the phone. The news editor refused to accept this evidence saying: 'You must have the wrong dogs.'[4]

The amounts paid out in damages or settlements in those days were quite generous. As MacKenzie said about Sting's £75,000: 'you'd have to lose both arms in a car crash to receive the same payout from an insurance company.'

Perhaps the hardest cases to fight are those involving a claimant who is prepared to lie. This is because a libel claimant has to prove nothing other than the defamatory statement referred to them and that it was published. The law presumes the defamatory words are false and that the claimant is of good character. It is the publisher who has to prove the truth of what has been alleged. Therefore, unless the news organisation can show the allegations are true, it comes down to whom the jury believes. That or the news organisation settles out of court.

In 1987 Jeffrey Archer, the deputy chairman of the Conservative Party and successful novelist, launched libel actions against the *News of the World* and the *Daily Star* for a story that accused him of paying money to a prostitute.

The *News of the World* first ran a story 'Tory boss Archer pays off vice girl' after it secretly photographed Archer's aid, Michael Stacpoole, giving £2,000 in a brown envelope to the woman at Victoria train station in London. As a result of the story, Archer resigned his post.

Archer admitted he had given the woman, Monica Coghlan, the money, but denied he had ever met her. He said the article implied he'd had a sexual relationship with her. The paper said it had not intended to suggest this, but it had to pay Archer £50,000 damages in an agreed settlement.

The *Daily Star* published a follow-up story to that of the *News of the World* saying Archer had paid Miss Coghlan £70 for sex. His wife Mary, a Cambridge academic, told the jury the idea of her husband having sex with a hooker was 'preposterous'. Archer also had alibis for both of the nights mentioned by the paper as dates he met Miss Coghlan. It was the word of a tabloid newspaper and a prostitute against a Cambridge academic, noted politician and friends. In his summary, the judge, Mr Justice Caulfield, asked the jury:

> Remember Mary Archer in the witness box. Has she elegance? Has she fragrance? Is he in need of cold, unloving, rubber-insulated sex in a seedy hotel round about quarter to one on a Tuesday morning?[5]

The jury thought not and awarded Archer £500,000 in damages and the *Star*'s owners Express Newspapers also had to pay Archer's reported £750,000 legal bill. It didn't help the paper's case that none of the journalists had kept an adequate note during their investigations.

It was not until 13 years later, in 1999, that it was discovered that Jeffrey Archer had lied in the witness box. His friend and one of his alibis, Ted Francis, admitted his story was a fabrication. In 2001 Archer was found guilty of perjury and perverting the course of justice in the libel action and jailed for four years. He repaid the damages to the two papers, and their costs.

These cases are hard to fight and often complex. The *Guardian* had its work cut out to defend a case brought against it by Conservative cabinet minister Jonathan Aitken. The paper had accused him, among other things, of allowing a weekend stay at the Ritz Hotel in Paris in 1993 to be paid by an Arab businessman, in breach of ministerial rules. Aitken sued. He denied meeting any businessmen or that his bill had been paid for him. In the speech launching his action in April 1995, he called the journalists 'malignant cells who are prepared to abuse media power to destroy honourable individuals'.

> If it falls to me to start a fight to cut out the cancer of bent and twisted journalism in our country with the simple sword of truth and the trusty shield of British fair play so be it. I am ready for the fight. The fight against falsehood and those who peddle it.[6]

In its defence the *Guardian* went to enormous lengths to unravel the complexities of the affairs of Jonathan Aitken. It had to prove what it had said about him was true. During the trial at the High Court, Aitken claimed that his wife had paid the bill. He also filed a signed witness statement from his daughter, Victoria, in which the 14-year-old told how she had travelled to Paris that weekend by ferry and train. This backed up her father's story.

But the *Guardian* produced evidence of British Airways flight coupons and Budget car hire documents, which showed Aitken's wife and daughter had flown directly to Geneva and had never visited Paris as he had told the High Court. His wife had flown back from Geneva, while his daughter went on to boarding school. Aitken's action collapsed. He faced costs of £1.8million, which the *Guardian* would have had to pay, in addition to damages, if it had lost. Aitken was later jailed for perjury.

The lesson is this: if you are going to write something about someone that is defamatory, then make sure you get it right and you can prove it. Otherwise make sure you are covered by one of the defences to defamation highlighted below. The most common cause of libel actions against newspapers is the journalist's failure to be accurate and fair.[7] But knowing what is defamatory can be tricky.

Defamatory language

What would lower you in the estimation of right-thinking members of society has changed over time and will continue to change as society and what is acceptable to it change. During the First World War, saying someone was German could be defamatory. In the past it was also defamatory to call someone a homosexual, whereas nowadays it is not so clear cut.

The difficulty in deciding whether something is defamatory lies in there being no single definition of defamatory language. That aside, in many cases it is obvious what is defamatory. To call somebody a liar, a cheat, a thief, a hypocrite or a murderer is defamation, as it is to say they are incompetent or unqualified for their job.

In July 2004 the *News of the World* was forced to apologise and pay damages to the singer of Primal Scream, Bobby Gillespie, after it wrongly said he had had an affair with model Kate Moss. The article was headlined 'It Moss Be Love' and claimed the model was comforting Gillespie after a supposed split with his fiancée, Katie England. Actually, as the paper later accepted, the couple were happily engaged and living together. A photograph accompanying the article appeared to show Gillespie and Moss alone and holding hands. In fact England was the one holding hands with Gillespie, but she was obscured by Moss who was walking in front of the pair.[8]

So it is not just words but photographs and pictures that can lead to libel actions. Broadcast journalists have to be particularly careful: the pictures must illustrate the story. Do not talk about thieves targeting corner shops over pictures of ordinary shoppers. This implies the innocent shoppers are thieves. Beware too of using shots of genuine criminal behaviour such as football hooligans and assuming everyone in the pictures is a hooligan. There may be innocent bystanders in the shots: the script should reflect this or the people should not be identifiable.

Innuendo

There are seemingly innocent statements that have a defamatory meaning to those with special knowledge. These are called innuendo and can be used as a basis for a libel action.

For example, if a report says someone doesn't like supermarkets and never shops at them, this in itself is not defamatory. But if the readers or viewers know this person appears in adverts for a well-known supermarket and is shown shopping there and using the products to cook with, then the report implies the person is a liar. It is likely the news organisation would be sued for libel. The claimant would have to prove that at least one person reading or hearing the report understood the innuendo and for its part the court must decide how an ordinary, reasonable person with the special knowledge that the person appeared in the adverts would understand the words.

Repetition of a libel

It is wrong to believe that it is safe to write defamatory things about someone just because you are quoting someone else – even if you properly attribute it. Saying, 'a school friend said Jones had been a thief since primary school' is likely to result in a writ for libel unless you can prove it to be true.

Repeating a libel in this way is one of the most common legal mistakes made by journalists, according to Shelley Bradley, a solicitor with the BBC's Programme Legal Advice Department.

> Thinking that because a contributor makes a defamatory remark the publisher, i.e. the BBC or newspaper, isn't liable is a mistake. As is thinking that a comment or story is safe because it has already been in the papers.

Even if no one sued the first time, you are in danger if you repeat a libel that has already been published. So far as the law is concerned, each publication of the defamation is a fresh publication and can give grounds for a new legal action.

The lesson is to be wary of publishing articles which adopt the allegations of someone else, unless you can prove the truth of those allegations and not merely that the allegations have been made, or unless one of the other defences we will learn about later applies.

Unintentional libel

What if you accidentally libel someone you didn't mean to libel? Tough luck. That you didn't mean to do so is no defence. Statements are either libellous or they are not – your intention is irrelevant.

The magazine *Dog World*, a leading weekly dog publication, came a cropper on this rule. It published an article about allegations of abuse by a dog trainer. It reported that he had traumatised and injured a small dog by yanking his choke chain and swinging him in the air. Unfortunately for *Dog World* there was another trainer with the same name who was well respected. He sued *Dog World* for libel. Although the paper had no intention of defaming him, lack of intention is no defence to a libel action. The test is whether the reasonable reader would understand the article to be referring to the complainant. The answer in this case was yes and the paper had to apologise and pay damages.

The only thing a journalist can do to lessen the times when an innocent third party may be defamed is to take care that the identification of their subject is as clear as possible. In the case above, the writers of *Dog World* should have been aware of the 'innocent trainer' and taken appropriate steps. Be as specific as you can, publish names, addresses and ages. This is especially important in court cases where people are being identified with crimes.

Damages and costs

It is difficult to assess what the damages might be in any given case. This is because it is usually juries who decide the amount of an award. In the 1980s when MacKenzie edited the *Sun*, as we have seen, juries in libel cases gave very high awards. Since then they have tended to be reined in because the judge can now point out to juries what awards would be given in personal injury cases so they can compare. The Court of Appeal and the House of Lords can substitute their own award when a jury's award is held to have been excessively generous or inadequate. In 2002 the House of Lords cut to £1 a jury award of £85,000 to Bruce Grobbelaar, the former Liverpool goalkeeper, for a *Sun* story claiming he took bribes for match fixing.

But having to pay damages is not the only financial penalty facing a defendant losing a libel case: the loser usually also has to pay the entire costs of the case, including those of the other party. And in defamation cases the costs can be far more than the damages. In Jeffrey Archer's action against the *Daily Star*, the damages were £500,000 but the costs were reported to be £750,000. In fact, costs can now be so high that they can act as a deterrent to fighting cases for some poorly funded defendants.

What the claimant has to prove

To proceed with a defamation claim a person must prove:

- that the material is defamatory
- that the defamatory statement refers to them – at least as far as the reasonable person is concerned
- that the statement has been published, which is clearly the case if it's been broadcast or printed
- that the claimant is alive (you cannot defame the dead).

Statement refers to them

The claimant has to prove that people acquainted with them believe the statement refers to them. Whether the journalist intended the statement to refer to the person is irrelevant as we saw in the examples of unintentional libel.

Vagueness is no excuse

Do not think that by not naming someone you will escape a libel action. In fact not being specific can open you up to even greater trouble. If you say something about a group of people: for example 'all teachers are sadists', it is unlikely that any one teacher or school could say it referred to them. But if you narrowed it down enough and said 'all primary school teachers in Noplace are sadists', then each one could say they'd been defamed. The test of whether the statement identifies the person is whether it reasonably leads people who know them to believe it refers to them. It is difficult to come up with a 'safe' number but it is generally accepted that if there are over 15 people who could come into the category referred to, they are unlikely to be able to prove that they have been identified as the subject of the libel.

When the *News of the World* in 1986 reported a claim by a man that policemen at Banbury CID had raped and beaten his wife, each of the ten men working at Banbury CID sued. The story did not name any individual officers, but all claimed they had been tainted by the allegations (which were completely false) and all were awarded damages.

Defences

It's probable you are thinking that you will never be able to report anything, but a glance at any newspaper will have you scratching your head. How can all these unflattering

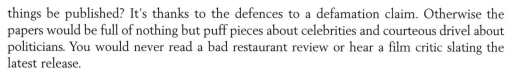

things be published? It's thanks to the defences to a defamation claim. Otherwise the papers would be full of nothing but puff pieces about celebrities and courteous drivel about politicians. You would never read a bad restaurant review or hear a film critic slating the latest release.

The main defences are:

- justification
- fair comment on a matter of public interest
- privilege
- offer to make amends
- accord and satisfaction
- innocent dissemination.

Justification

The material is true in substance and in fact. This defence protects the freedom to tell the truth no matter how stongly the person written about objects to your story – as long as you can prove it is substantially true. Lawyers will want records of conversations, tape recordings, letters, memos, photos, etc. as evidence, together with witnesses prepared to testify.

Fair comment on a matter of public interest

This applies only to statements of comment not the publication of defamatory facts, although the comment must be based upon true facts that are stated accurately in the story.

This is the defence that allows reviewers to be harsh in their criticism of a new book or the food at a newly opened restaurant or political journalists to be highly critical about an MP. If sued for a comment piece, a publisher does not have to prove the truth of the comments, but they do have to prove the truth of the facts upon which the comments are based and that the person making them was expressing an honest opinion. It is important to note that this defence can be defeated by malice, i.e. where the person making the comment has a deliberate intention to injure the defamed person. Examples can be sacked salesmen wanting to get back at their former employer or spurned lovers.

Privilege

The law says that there are times when freedom of speech is needed without the risk of libel actions. These occasions are privileged. Privilege comes in two forms: absolute and qualified.

- **Absolute privilege.** This is a complete defence to an action for defamation no matter how false and defamatory the statement complained of. Absolute privilege applies in the following cases:

— statements made in, or as part of, the course of parliamentary proceedings
— statements made in the course of judicial proceedings
— fair, accurate and contemporaneous reports of judicial proceedings in open court.

Note that while statements made in Parliament enjoy absolute privilege, reports of what is said enjoy qualified privilege. If an MP repeats the defamatory statements outside Parliament, they are not covered by privilege and may be sued – as indeed may be the news organisation if it reports the comments at that time.

- **Qualified privilege**. Offers just as much protection to a journalist as absolute privilege as long as they are not motivated by malice. If a defendant is shown to bear ill-will towards the claimant then, unlike with absolute privilege, the defence will fail. In practice it is almost unheard of for a journalist to be shown to have been motivated by malice when reporting on an occasion that is covered by privilege. Qualified privilege covers a huge variety of statements and occasions. These are all listed in *McNae's Essential Law for Journalists*, but in general qualified privilege covers 'circumstances where it is considered important that the facts should be freely known in the public interest'.[9] These include council meetings, official police statements, general meetings of public companies in the UK, public meetings and press conferences.

In recent years a category of qualified privilege has grown up out of the area which covers defamatory statements made in the course of performing a legal, moral or social duty, for example, statements made when giving job references or reporting suspected crimes to the police, etc. It is now being applied to the media where allegations are published which ultimately turn out to be untrue but where the matter was published responsibly.

This new category is known as the Reynolds Defence after the libel action by former Irish Prime Minister, Albert Reynolds, against the *Sunday Times*. It is still being developed but it gives news organisations protection from libel suits if they can prove they acted responsibly in publishing the defamatory allegations and that they were published in the public interest. For the defence to succeed, the court has to decide that the duty and interest tests have been met.

The duty test is that the journalist and news organisation have behaved responsibly in informing the public and the interest test is that of the public and a free press in a modern democracy engaging in discussion on matters of public interest. The defence fails if the publishers were reckless or did not believe the story was true or, most importantly, if they did not give the person about whom the comments were made a full opportunity to know what was going to be said and a proper opportunity to respond.

In cases where a defendant pleads the Reynolds Defence, judges go through ten points to determine whether the article concerned was published responsibly. These include the nature of the allegations, the urgency of publication, the reliability of the source, the steps taken to verify the material, the tone of the article, and whether the victim was given a chance to puts his or her side of the story.[10]

Following the Reynolds decision, the case of Loutchansky in 2001, in which an international businessman sued *The Times*, recognised the new development in the defence of qualified privilege. Grigori Loutchansky sued for defamation over articles published by *The Times* accusing him of involvement in a Russian criminal organisation, money-laundering and smuggling nuclear weapons. *The Times* argued it had a duty to publish the allegations in the public interest. The court agreed but added that the publisher must act responsibly if a defence of qualified privilege is to arise. This could mean a journalist's methods are on trial more than the defamation claim itself.

The paper failed to win the libel case because it failed to prove it had acted responsibly.

> the allegations made were vague, the sources were unreliable, sufficient steps had not been taken to verify the information, and no comment had been obtained from Loutchansky before publication.
>
> The judge said 'such steps as were taken' by the reporter in his unsuccessful attempts to contact either Loutchansky or his company Nordex or their lawyers were far less diligent than was required by the standards of responsible journalism.[11]

The reporter also failed to produce the notes he had made when interviewing an important source; he said he must have made them on a scrap of paper which he later threw away.

The Reynolds Defence proved useful for the *Leeds Weekly News* being sued over an article headlined 'Give' 'em the chop', which was critical of a company selling karate lessons door to door. In 2000, following a trial in front of a judge and jury, the newspaper won. The claimants had accused the reporter of falling far short of the standards of responsible journalism and that she had not made enough effort to contact them with the accusations. She had phoned the firm and left a message with its paging service, but did not speak to them before publication. She also relied heavily on information from an administrator in the governing body of karate.

The judge Mr Justice Popplewell disagreed with the claimants. He said he found the reporter to be an honest, sensible and responsible person who based her article on what she honestly believed was reliable evidence. He endorsed the comments of Lord Nicholls in the Reynolds case that the press discharged vital functions as a bloodhound as well as a watchdog.

The key to the defence is that the media must be careful in reporting even the matters that are clearly in the public interest. Only if they can show they have behaved responsibly will the defence succeed.

Offer to make amends

This defence provides for the publisher that has made a mistake and in invoking it the organisation is accepting that the story is not correct. It is intended to encourage sensible compromises in defamation claims and affords some protection to the media when they are prepared to own up to a mistake.

It comprises an offer in writing to publish a suitable correction and apology together with appropriate compensation and costs. The amount may be agreed later and fixed by the court if it is not agreed between the parties. If the claimant accepts the offer to make amends, the defamation action comes to an end. If it is rejected, the news organisation may rely upon the terms of the offer as a defence but cannot use any other defence. Therefore, one cannot make an offer of amends but later claim the article was true and switch to justification.

Accord and satisfaction

This arises when the news organisation says it has already dealt with the complaint by publishing a correction and apology, which has been accepted by the complainant.

Innocent dissemination

A libel complainant can sue the original publisher of the material and anyone who publishes after that. But those secondary publishers such as distributors of the magazine, online publishers of bulletin boards or chat rooms, or broadcasters during a live broadcast such as a phone-in, have a defence of innocent dissemination. To succeed with the defence, the court must be persuaded that:

- they were not the author, editor or publisher (as defined by the Defamation Act 1996) of the statement complained of
- they took reasonable care in relation to the publication of the statement (to prevent it or could not be expected to have prevented it)
- they did not know or had no reason to believe that what they did caused or contributed to the publication of a defamatory statement.

Dealing with complaints

How you deal with complaints can have a bearing on your defence in court. The worst thing you can do as a young, inexperienced reporter is to avoid facing up to the mistake. If you receive a letter or phone call from someone pointing out an error, do not try and sweep it under the carpet or bury a correction in a follow-up story. This could anger the person concerned and provoke them to more formal steps such as consulting a solicitor or approaching the Press Complaints Commission. You should inform your editor so that he or she is involved with the handling of the matter.

If you take a call from someone with a complaint, you should take a note of the nature of the complaint, thank them for calling, and tell them that the matter is being referred to someone senior. At this point you should not admit to a mistake but make sure the complaint is acted upon and keep your notes of the conversation.

Advice from an old hand

The late Peter Carter-Ruck, the influential libel lawyer, once told a young reporter:

It matters not what you know or believe to be true or feel certain must be true or is obviously true or must – as a matter of logic – be true. What matters is what you can actually show to be true.

He advised the reporter that whenever he was unsure, to imagine himself in the witness box in a case potentially involving many thousands of pounds in damages, under cross-examination by a very sharp and very hostile barrister, who barks: 'What proof do you have personally that you can actually show us, to substantiate that allegation?'[12]

Libel and the internet

Many users of the internet assume that it is a place of uninhibited free expression, not subject to law or regulation. They are wrong. International organisations are taking steps to try to regulate the internet and domestic courts are also beginning to set precedents in relation to activity on the net. Rulings in lawsuits involving internet libel have shown that web publishers should work within the law and avoid publishing anything libellous. These cases also illustrate the willingness of courts to allow publishers to be sued anywhere in the world.

There are an ever increasing number of ways to publish content using the internet, and journalists should be aware that all could give rise to an action for defamation. Whether it goes via email or directly onto a website or via an RSS feed or a new method of internet delivery that allows others to be party to that information, you are in effect publishing for the purposes of defamation. Some of the main areas to be considered are:[13]

1 websites
2 archives
3 newsgroups
4 email
5 blogs
6 bulletin boards, notice boards and chat rooms.

If someone publishes something on the internet, it is accepted that it is published to a third party. If the material is defamatory, the author is responsible and can be sued whether they publish it on their own website or someone else's. Moreover, the publisher, including online newspapers and magazines, can also be sued, although they should be able to use the innocent dissemination defence (see above) if they took the posting down when they received the complaint. A disturbing trend recently has shown that courts look at where the material is accessed as well as where it originates.

Websites

A case in 2002 pointed to any publication accessible online being held accountable for violating the laws of any country where it is downloaded, no matter where the publication is based. An Australian court allowed a libel suit against US-based Barron's, part of the Dow Jones publishing company, to proceed in an Australian court. The case brought by mining boss Joe Gutnick claimed that an article published in *Barron's Magazine* and on the website of the *Wall Street Journal* (also part of Dow Jones) in October 2000 portrayed him as a schemer and a fraud. He sued and argued that the case should be heard in Australia where he had lived for many years. Dow Jones argued the case should be heard in the United States, where libel rulings are seen as more favourable to publishers, because the article was originally published there. The High Court of Australia ruled the case could be heard in Gutnick's home state of Victoria because people there had read the article online. It was settled out of court in November 2004 with Barron's paying damages and costs.

The case has been followed by several other cases that serve as a warning to internet publishers. A British court ruled in February 2004 and was upheld on appeal in October 2004 that the boxing promoter Don King could sue boxer Lennox Lewis and his lawyer in a British court for allegedly defamatory remarks on two California-based websites, boxingtalk.com and fightnews.com.

The ruling highlights the dangers of making statements that will be published on the internet, as the case involves one US citizen suing over statements made in America by another US citizen. The statements, strongly denied by King, suggested he was anti-semitic. Despite being based in the US, the sites are apparently read by boxing fans in the UK. The court ruled that King had a substantial reputation in Britain where he had promoted British boxers, including of course Lennox Lewis, and therefore King could sue for defamation in the UK.

A ruling in Ontario, Canada, in February 2004 allowed the *Washington Post* to be sued in Canada for articles published online about a United Nations official called Cheickh Bangoura while he was working in Kenya. What alarmed the media about this case is that at the time the articles were published, Bangoura was living in Africa and had no connection with Canada and so the paper could not have been expected to take into account the laws of Canada. In addition, although Bangoura was aware of the articles when they were first published in 1997, he did not sue until 2003. A judge allowed the action because the newspaper was circulated in hard copy (although in a limited way) in the province as well as on the internet (although for only 14 days before it was available to subscribers only). The decision was overturned on appeal. The court found that Bangoura had no 'real and substantial connection' to Ontario – being a resident was not sufficient. After being available for 14 days on a free-of-charge website, the article was then transferred to a paid-for archive. The only person who had accessed the article was in fact Mr Bangoura's lawyer.

However, it is still possible for internet publishers to find themselves being sued abroad for publishing pictures or comments that are perfectly legal in their own country, says John Morris, a lawyer with the American Center for Democracy and Technology.

> The spectre of 200 countries around the world imposing potential liability for speech that is lawful in the United States is worrisome . . .

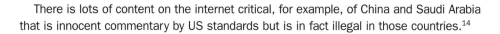

There is lots of content on the internet critical, for example, of China and Saudi Arabia that is innocent commentary by US standards but is in fact illegal in those countries.[14]

Archives

These are also anxious times for internet publishers such as newspapers and broadcasters, which maintain an online archive, because of the potential for claims for defamation.

The Loutchansky case mentioned above highlighted the danger of online archives for the publisher. Loutchansky sued over articles published in the original paper and copies posted on *The Times* website. The second action over the website articles was started a year after the first and more than a year after the articles had first been posted on the internet.[15] Yet libel claims must be brought within a year of publication of the defamatory statement, so how could this case be brought?

It could because in UK libel law publication is a technical term meaning communication of the defamatory statement by the defendant to at least one person other than the claimant. Therefore, each time an online article is accessed, it is a publication with its own limitation period. In the Loutchansky case, *The Times* argued that English courts should follow the United States and adopt a 'single publication' rule, which means that publication of defamatory material gives rise to only one action with a time limit beginning with the original publication. The court rejected that argument and recommended that where it is known that archive material is or may be defamatory, an appropriate warning notice to users against treating it as the truth should be attached.

Newsgroups

These are internet groups where people discuss and post comments about a chosen subject, and there are newsgroups for almost every topic you can think of. As soon as a message is posted, it is published to a third party as anyone can read a message posted on a newsgroup board.

Interestingly, the first court ruling in England on the issue of internet defamation involved a posting on a newsgroup.[16] In *Godfrey v. Demon Internet Ltd* (2001) Laurence Godfrey sued internet service provider Demon after it refused to remove defamatory statements posted on a newsgroup that it hosted. Demon claimed it was not responsible for material posted by its users. The court accepted that internet service providers such as Demon are not authors, editors or publishers as defined by the Defamation Act 1996. This meant Demon could plead innocent dissemination under section 1 of the Act. However, Demon was unable to claim it was unaware of the defamatory statements because it had been told by Godfrey and this seriously undermined the defence. It could not say it had taken reasonable care in relation to the publication or that it had no reason to believe that the part it had in the publication caused or contributed to the publication of a defamatory statement. It settled out of court in 2000 with Demon paying Godfrey damages and costs.

The result of the Demon case is that internet service providers began to remove defamatory statements from their service as soon as they became aware of them. This has led to at least one website being forced to move abroad because no British internet company would host it.

Email

Emails spread quickly and often those involved believe they are nothing more than innocent gossip or chit-chat. But email defamation is treated as libel as it is in a permanent form, rather than slander which relates to spoken words. Therefore sending a defamatory email to anyone other than the person it is about will amount to publication under English law.

Blog

A blog is a website log or journal, personal in style and frequently updated. It is a publication to a third party and therefore subject to the laws of defamation.

Bloggers though may not enjoy the same privileges as traditional journalists, for example the defence of qualified privilege. If a journalist publishes a story that is defamatory but its publication was in the public interest and they employed responsible journalism in terms of checking facts and putting the allegations to the victim, then they may employ the defence of qualified privilege. But the courts have required a very high standard from journalists before allowing the defence to succeed and it seems unlikely that a court would see most web bloggers as exacting enough for the defence to apply.

Bulletin boards, notice boards, chat rooms

Bulletin boards are electronic forums that host messages and articles related to a common subject.

Notice boards are usually specific to and part of a website, often enabling a short comment or feedback to be posted onto the web page concerned.

Chat rooms enable a virtual meeting to be held online where people may log on and type messages which are visible immediately to the other members in that chat room. Each message is identified by the person's log-on name.

Each of the above satisfies the requirement of a publication to a third party.

Data Protection Act 1998

This is a complex law which aims to protect the individual from the misuse of information or 'personal data' about him or her. Personal data – medical records, information in paper or computer files, personal photographs, etc. – must be obtained and used fairly and lawfully. For media organisations, this means the data subject (the person in the records, photograph, etc.) should have given their consent; or that the collection and use of the data are necessary for the purposes of legitimate interests pursued by the news organisation. The data should be relevant, not excessive, and be kept no longer than necessary. They should also be accurate. Processing or using the data is allowed if there is substantial public interest and for journalists there is an exception where there has been unlawful activity, dishonesty, malpractice or other improper conduct or incompetence.

The Act has also affected journalists because in some cases they now find it more difficult to obtain information from authorities who are or believe they are prevented from releasing information. The police in particular have been accused of 'hiding behind' the Data Protection Act to avoid giving out names and addresses of murder victims, accident victims and other routine crime information to the press. The *Basildon Yellow Advertiser* reported that Kent Police cited the Data Protection Act when they refused to release the address of a man who was found dead in the river Medway with a gunshot wound. In fact, information about dead people is not subject to the Data Protection Act.

> When my reporter asked which part of the Act protected the victim's personal details, he was told that it was up to us to say which part of the Act entitled us to the information we wanted. (Graeme Allen, editor, *Basildon Yellow Advertiser*)[17]

It has become such a frustration that the Society of Editors' executive director, Bob Satchell, has claimed the Act is being used for 'operational or administrative convenience' by the police to stop information reaching the press.[18]

McNae's Essential Law for Journalists gives some useful advice to journalists who come into conflict with public bodies that are reluctant to release information. It suggests that the journalists should remind them that the Human Rights Act (HRA) 1998 requires public authorities to act in a way consistent with the European Convention on Human Rights, which contains a guarantee of freedom of expression, including the right to receive and impart information.[19] In fact guidelines circulated by the Association of Chief Police Officers in 2000 remind chief constables that the HRA requires that each police officer and member of the civilian support staff act in a way that is consistent with the Convention.

Human Rights Act 1998

The Act came into force in 2000 and guarantees basic human rights such as the right to life, liberty and freedom of expression. For working journalists it is the right to freedom of expression (article 10) and the right to respect for private life (article 8) which are of particular importance. These are set out in the European Convention on Human Rights, which the Human Rights Act (HRA) incorporated into British law.

Article 10 section 1 sets out the right to freedom of expression. This is the right to hold opinions and to receive and impart information and ideas without interference by public authority. Section 12 requires the courts, when considering granting an injunction, to have 'particular regard' to the importance of freedom of expression, guaranteed by article 10.

Section 2 puts some limitations on these rights, but only what is necessary in a democratic society.

Lord Justice Hoffman called this right 'the trump card' in a case in 1994. He said that outside the established exceptions 'there is no question of balancing freedom of speech against other interests. It is a trump card which always wins.' Despite this statement, two other important rights have had an impact on article 10 and freedom of expression:

- **Article 6**: the right to a fair and public trial by an independent and impartial judiciary.
- **Article 8**: the right to respect for private and family life. It states that there shall be no interference by a public authority with the exercise of this right except where it is necessary in a democratic society.

Article 8 is the first time the law of England has recognised the right to privacy. But as yet there is no stand-alone privacy law in the UK. The case that tested this involved film stars Catherine Zeta-Jones and Michael Douglas. The media watched the case carefully because if the couple were to win, a legal right to privacy – separate from the law of confidence – would have been asserted for the first time.

The Douglases claimed that the Human Rights Act afforded them a right to privacy during their wedding and the reception at the Plaza Hotel in New York in November 2000. This is despite their having sold the rights to approved pictures for £1million to *OK* magazine. Therefore when *Hello* magazine published unauthorised, if poor, snapshots smuggled out of the event, the pair sued for damages of £500,000. *OK* also sued, claiming £1.75million.

At the High Court, counsel for the Douglases argued that there existed in English law a right to privacy separate from the law of confidence. In the end the judge found in favour of the Douglases, but the judgment was not based on a law of privacy or the Human Rights Act, but relied on the established principles of the law of confidence. In being able to grant rights to publish pictures, the Douglases had a commodity, the value of which depended, in part at least, upon it being kept secret and then made public in a controlled way. The event was private and elaborate steps had been taken to exclude the uninvited. Any unauthorised publication of photographs would be a breach of commercial confidence. Put simply, all photographs of the wedding were deemed to be confidential information. The illicit photographs of the wedding were a disclosure of information that was protected by confidence and the publication by *Hello* of those photographs was a breach of confidence.

In coming to his decision, the judge said he had struck a balance between freedom of expression and confidentiality, and in doing this had taken into account the Press Complaints Commission's Editors' Code of Practice (see Appendix). The Code said that everyone is entitled to respect for his or her private and family life and there should be no intrusion into individuals' private lives without consent. The PCC's code was broken and *Hello* must have known that.

The judge avoided creating a law of privacy, as he felt that the arguments for the existence of a free-standing right of privacy had not been made. But in giving his reasons, Lord

Justice Lindsay did say that a privacy law is a matter for Parliament: 'That Parliament has failed so far to grasp the nettle does not prove that it will not have to be grasped in the future.' He added:

> That inadequacy will have to be made good and if Parliament does not step in then the Courts will be obliged to. Further development by the Courts may merely be awaiting the first post-Human Rights Act case where neither the law of confidence nor any other domestic law protects an individual who deserves protection. A glance at a crystal ball of, so to speak, only a low wattage suggests that if Parliament does not act soon, the less satisfactory course, of the Courts creating the law bit by bit at the expense of lit-igants and with inevitable delays and uncertainty, will be thrust upon the judiciary.[20]

The couple were awarded £14,600 for breach of confidence and £3million in costs against *Hello*. *OK* won £1,033,156. *Hello* appealed in December 2004. The court over-turned the decision to award damages to *OK* on the basis that the right to privacy could be commercialised but not traded.

The willingness of celebrities to claim invasion of privacy to control their image wor-ries Bob Satchwell, executive director of the Society of Editors. A year after the Human Rights Act became law, he asked editors to monitor the instances in which people quote the legislation to challenge publication of stories about them. It was not what the Convention was originally about, he said.

> The European Convention on Human Rights was designed to protect people from totali-tarian governments. Yet it could be misused in a free and democratic society like ours where surely the public's right to know must hold sway over people's individual privacy?[21]

Law of breach of confidence

As we have seen, there is still no stand-alone privacy law in the UK. Litigants and the judi-ciary have tended to rely on the law of breach of confidence to protect information which they view as secret. The law is intended to prevent a person who has acquired informa-tion in confidence from taking unfair advantage of it.[22]

The use of breach of confidence to protect privacy has advanced since the introduction of the Human Rights Act. In the past, judges took a strict view of where an obligation of confidence existed, i.e. only where a recognised relationship existed between the parties such as a doctor and patient, employer and employee, or husband and wife.[23] But since the case of Douglas above, the courts have broadened the definition.

In 2001 a judge used the law of breach of confidence while taking into account the requirements of the Human Rights Act to impose an unprecedented injunction banning all media from identifying the two killers of the child James Bulger. The two were expected to be given new identities on their release from custody and, it was argued, they were entitled to protection under the Human Rights Act, where the evidence showed that publication of the material, and thus identification of the claimants, would result in a real risk of their being harmed by those who wished to avenge the murder of the toddler. The judge, Dame Elizabeth Butler-Sloss, accepted that the law of confidentiality, in light of the direction of the human rights legislation, could cover the unique circumstances of the claimants and that the court had jurisdiction to grant an injunction. Under the European Convention their right to life, to privacy and to protection from torture outweighed the freedom of expression of those who might want to unmask them. The ban is to last for their lifetimes.

In granting the injunction, the judge, Dame Elizabeth Butler-Sloss said:

> In my judgment, the court does have the jurisdiction, in exceptional cases, to extend the protection of confidentiality of information, even to impose restrictions on the press, where not to do so would be likely to lead to serious physical injury, or to death, of the person seeking that confidentiality, and there is no other way to protect the applicants other than by seeking relief from the court.

Note that the same judge used the Human Rights Act to forbid disclosure of the current identities and whereabouts of the child killer Mary Bell and her daughter two years later in May 2003. As only the second lifelong injunction ever made, it guarantees them life-long anonymity to protect their right to private and family life under article 8 of the European Convention on Human Rights. Bell was convicted in 1968 of the manslaughter of Martin Brown, aged 4, and Brian Howe, aged 3. She was 11 years old at the time.

Because judges will use the granting of injunctions to prevent breaches of confidentiality, this presents a problem for a journalist who wishes to check out a story with the subject or get a comment from them. If the journalist has received information about an organisation from a source that is in a confidential relationship, for example an employee, and the journalist contacts the organisation to put the information or allegations to them, they can be served with an injunction. Sometimes these injunctions are last-minute, 'eleventh hour' injunctions – obtained late at night after the paper has been printed or the broadcast recorded and/or publicised. No matter how late, once an injunction has been served it is contempt to disobey it, and therefore papers have to be pulped and broadcasts scrapped unless or until the injunction is lifted. This can be very expensive for news organisations.

Bill Goodwin was a young journalist from the *Engineer* magazine in 1989 when he received details, from an unidentified source, of the business plan of a company, Tetra Ltd, that was in financial difficulties. A copy of the plan had gone missing from the company's offices the day before. When Goodwin rang the company to check the story, they obtained an injunction to prevent him using details from the plan. Later they tried to force Goodwin to hand over notes that would lead them to the source of the leak. He refused and was fined £5,000. He took the case to the European Court of Human Rights which ruled that his rights to freedom of expression under article 10 of the convention had been violated.

Note that confidence proceedings can be defended if the publisher can show that publication is in the public interest.

Injunctions

Although injunctions are most commonly used by people claiming that a story breaches confidentiality, they can be used in other situations. An injunction can be granted banning the publication of libellous material if it is believed that the material is so defamatory that the damage arising from publication could not be put right afterwards and if the publisher cannot demonstrate that they would have a full defence to a libel action if the case came to a full hearing. In rare cases an injunction can be issued to stop a threatened contempt of court, such as banning the interviewing of witnesses in a court case before they have given evidence.

Injunctions stopping or delaying publication (known as 'prior restraint') severely compromise the concept of free media and have led to bitter complaints by journalists and editors. They occur less often these days as courts are loathe to restrict freedom of speech and prefer any complaint to be acted on after publication.

The Government has used the Official Secrets Acts to obtain injunctions against publication of disclosures by former members of the SAS. In 2001 the Defence Secretary obtained an injunction against News Group Newspapers and *Sun* editor David Yelland, banning the paper from publishing or disclosing the identity of wounded members of the SAS and giving the MoD access to all the documents and files held by the paper referring, either directly or indirectly, to their identities. The *Sun* claimed the injunction was unnecessary as it had given assurances at the highest level that they would not publish anything that would lead to individuals being identified.

Official Secrets Acts 1911 and 1989

These Acts are intended to protect national security by preventing anything being published or broadcast that would imperil the security and peace of the population. The Acts cover a wide range of categories of information, including intelligence, defence and international relations. Under the Official Secrets Act 1911, it is an offence to obtain, collect, receive or communicate any information that might be or is intended to be useful to an enemy. Breaking this law carries a penalty of up to 14 years in prison.

The 1989 Act relates to six broad classes of information: security and intelligence, defence, international relations, crime, interception of communications, and sensitive information disclosed to other states or international organisations. The Act's main intention is to prevent the disclosure of information by civil servants that might be damaging to national security. However, journalists might be liable under section 5, if they disclose information knowing, or having cause to believe, that it is covered by the Act. But in cases involving security and intelligence, defence and international relations, a prosecution can only take place if the disclosure causes damage to the security and intelligence services. It is not enough that the revelations are undesirable, a betrayal of trust or an embarrassment to the Government. In cases of information concerning crime and Government interception of communications, however, damage is assumed. Breaking this law can result in up to two years in prison. It should be noted that there is no defence of disclosure in the public interest.

Prosecutions of journalists under the Official Secrets Acts are rare. In fact, so far, there have been no successful prosecutions under the 1989 Act. However, this does not mean that the security and intelligence services do not act to prevent publication of material they object to.

In recent years, journalists have been charged or threatened with prosecution under the Acts but no case has been carried through to trial. In 1998, Tony Geraghty, a former defence correspondent on the *Sunday Times*, was charged over disclosures in his book, *The Irish War*, regarding computerised intelligence surveillance in Northern Ireland.

A year later, Liam Clarke, the Northern Ireland editor of the *Sunday Times*, was also threatened with prosecution under the Act for revelations about secret agents in the province. No case was brought.

Clarke was again in trouble in 2003 following publication of the paperback edition of a biography of Sinn Fein MP Martin McGuinness and the publication of extracts in *The Times*. The book, *From Guns to Government*, included material that was alleged to be secret, including conversations between Martin McGuinness and Government members. Clarke and his wife Kathryn Johnston were searched. Police battered down the door of their home in Co. Antrim (Northern Ireland) at 2 a.m. and 21 bagfuls of contact books, computers and documents were taken away.

In a statement, the editor of *The Times*, Robert Thomson, said publishing the extracts in his paper was in the public interest: 'While the disclosures will no doubt cause awkwardness within Government, the Official Secrets Act is not the Official Embarrassments Act, and is hardly designed to keep such important information from public view.'[24]

While it is rare for journalists to be prosecuted under the Official Secrets Act, journalists' sources have been. A number of civil servants, police officers and military personnel have been convicted and have received sentences of up to one year in prison.

One reason for this is, as mentioned earlier, the Act does not include a defence of public interest. When former MI5 agent David Shayler was prosecuted for providing details of the agency's operations to newspapers, he sought to argue that his revelations were in the public interest and, in particular, that his conviction would be contrary to his right to freedom of expression under the European Convention on Human Rights.

The House of Lords confirmed that there was no public interest defence under the Act and held that his prosecution would not infringe his rights under the Convention. The court said where a potential whistleblower had information the release of which was in the public interest, the proper course was for him to seek consent for its disclosure from the appropriate authority. If that authority decided to refuse consent, the whistleblower could, in theory, seek judicial review of the decision in the courts.

David Shayler was sentenced to six months in jail in November 2002 for breaking the Official Secrets Act by disclosing secret information and documents from telephone taps. He had copied 28 files on topics including Libyan links with the IRA and Soviet funding of the Communist Party of Great Britain. He was released early after seven weeks in prison.

A journalist about to publish an article which reveals official secrets would be prudent to consider destroying all material that would lead to the identity of a source.

To help journalists navigate this complex law, there is the 'D' notice committee, its full title being the Defence Press and Broadcasting Advisory Committee. It is chaired by a civil servant, namely the permanent under-secretary of state for defence. The committee's role is to counsel editors about to publish things that are a potential security risk. However, it is advisory and voluntary and editors do not have to seek advice, nor do they have to take any advice that is offered. There are five standing or permanent Defence Advisory (DA) Notices, which you can find on www.dnotice.org.uk.

Freedom of Information Act 2000

The Act came into force on 1 January 2005 and gives people a general right of access to information held by public authorities. It is intended to create openness and accountability amongst public sector bodies. In Lord Falconer, the Lord Chancellor's words, 'In short, the need to know culture is gone. There is now a statutory right to know.'[25]

Under the Act people have the right to make a request for information held by a public authority and the authority will have to comply with the Act in responding. That means they should be told whether the authority holds the information and must be supplied with the information unless an exemption applies. If an exemption does apply, in most cases the authority will then have to consider whether the information must be released in the public interest.

The law applies to all recorded information held by English, Welsh and Northern Irish public authorities. What are public authorities? There are around 100,000 of them in the UK and they exercise public functions, such as central government departments, local government, the police, health service and education service. But there are also more obscure bodies such as the Poisons Board, National Gallery and Parole Board.

A journalist wishing to make a request should apply in writing or by fax or email to the authority concerned, describing the information they want. The authority must reply to a request promptly, usually within 20 working days. This can be extended for a 'reasonable' period where decisions are taken under the Act's public interest test. Extensions are also allowed for requests received by schools during vacations, for closed files held by the National Archives, or for information held overseas or which has to be obtained from military personnel on active service.

The test being put on the Act by journalists is how the Freedom of Information Act will affect the disease endemic in just about every British public authority – chronic secrecy. The Lord Chancellor, who is also secretary of state for constitutional affairs, insists the legislation will make government more open: 'Good government is open government and good government is effective government.'

No matter how good the intentions, it's unlikely that the Act will be of use for stories that need to be written quickly – on-the-day stories – as you will still probably have to wait days or weeks rather than hours for information. But for journalists working on documentaries or longer-running investigations it should be very useful.

The FOI Act does contain exemptions. Information is exempt if its disclosure would be likely to prejudice (or in Scotland 'prejudice substantially') interests such as defence, international relations, law enforcement, commercial interests, the economy, the frankness of internal discussions or the effective conduct of public affairs. However, most exempt information will have to be released if the public interest in disclosure is greater than the public interest in confidentiality. The benefits of disclosure, in protecting public safety, exposing wrongdoing, preventing the public from being misled, accounting for public spending or ensuring informed debate, may swing decisions in favour of openness.

Some exemptions have no prejudice test and disclosure depends solely on whether its release is deemed to be in the public interest. These include information obtained during investigations by the police or prosecuting authorities and information relating to the formulation of government policy. There will be no access to information whose disclosure is prohibited by other laws; for example personal information about others will not be released if disclosure would breach the Data Protection Act.

If you are refused information, the authority should tell you under which exemption and why it thinks disclosure is not in the public interest. Maurice Frankel, the director of the Campaign for Freedom of Information, explains how you should go about challenging a decision.

> The first step should be to complain under the authority's own complaints procedure, when a more senior official with greater authority to release information is likely to be involved. Strictly speaking, it's the authority's job to show why information should not be disclosed, not yours to prove that it can. But if you feel the authority may have an exaggerated view of the likely harm from disclosure or has failed to recognise the public interest in openness, you should point that out. If you're still unhappy after the authority's review, you're free to complain to the UK or Scottish Information Commissioner, who have the power to compel disclosure.[26]

But Frankel adds that in the last analysis there is – and it's the legislation's most contentious feature – a ministerial veto, allowing cabinet ministers to override the Commissioner if he orders a government department to release information on public interest grounds. Frankel suspects ministers will not be able to resist its use where politically damaging information is at stake.

Trademarks

If whenever you vacuum a room you 'Hoover' it, or if whenever you photocopy a document you 'Xerox' it, or if whenever you put a sticking plaster on a child you use a 'Band-aid', there is the possibility that you could get yourself into hot water legally with the owners of those trademarks. Trademarks are valuable commodities that companies spend millions of pounds marketing in order to distinguish them from other similar products. If they do not protect them, they argue their names soon pass into everyday use. Companies such as Outward Bound and Jacuzzi fight very hard to avoid their names being used as generic names. It is, anyway, preferable to use the generic term to the trade name to avoid giving free advertising. To check whether a word is protected by a trademark you can use the Patent Office website, www.patent.co.uk.

Summing up

All working hacks have to get to grips with the nitty-gritty of the laws that affect the media. In fact it is positively dangerous for a news organisation to use reporters who do not have a fair amount of legal knowledge. And knowing the law and being confident in how far you can push it helps you to write your stories in more detail and with more colour. It also means you know when you can challenge a public body such as the court, the police or a school, when you believe they are not giving you the information to which you are entitled.

But the amount and complexity of the laws that affect journalists may have another, more subtle effect in the stories that don't get written. As one commentator said after Jeffrey Archer was jailed for perjury, it really wasn't a case for celebrating as it took all in all 15 years finally to settle the case, even though journalists knew what was going on. Many were too afraid of litigation to publish what they knew.

Even when they know the law, there will be a time in the career of most journalists when they will make a mistake and have to deal with a complaint. A few will have made the kind of mistake that makes headlines and ends careers but most complaints will, if handled properly, result in an apology and a correction.

Face up to the mistake and talk to your editor. If you receive a call or an email, make a note, thank them for calling and refer the matter to someone senior. Always ensure you deal with complaints courteously and promptly.

And if you want to stay out of court, you would do well to remember the advice of Peter Carter-Ruck never to make allegations that you cannot defend. What matters is not what you think you know, what matters is what you can actually show to be true or fair comment or able to be defended by one of the other defences available to you.

REVIEW QUESTIONS

1 A statement is defamatory if it does what? Name the four categories of defamatory statements.

2 Typically, how is the law of confidentiality enforced and how does it affect news organisations?

3 What defence would you use if you were sued for saying that visiting an exhibition by a local artist was 'like going to hell and back – and a badly drawn hell at that. Rarely has so little talent been on show to so many.'

4 Name the six classes of information that are covered by the Official Secrets Act 1989.

EXERCISES

1 Read through several newspapers and note how many reports are potentially libellous. Decide how many you believe may be covered by the main defences justification, fair comment and privilege.

2 Use the internet to research and read up on model Naomi Campbell's case against the *Daily Mirror*.

    (i)   What were the claimant's (Naomi Campbell) and defendant's (the *Mirror*) main arguments?

    (ii) with whom do you sympathise and why?

    (iii) Do you believe Britain needs a privacy law? If so, why?

3 Visit the Patent Office website, www.patent.co.uk, and look at the list of trademarks. See how many you can spot that are frequently used in ordinary conversations and news reports when a generic term should be used.

FURTHER READING AND RESOURCES

Crone, T., *Law and the Media*, 4th edn, Oxford: Focal Press, 2002.

Welsh, T. and Greenwood, W., *McNae's Essential Law for Journalists*, 17th edn, London: Butterworths, 2003.

www.cfoi.org.uk. Website of the Campaign for Freedom of Information. Provides some excellent articles explaining the Act and how it can be used by journalists.

www.dca.gov.uk/foi. Website of the Department for Constitutional Affairs, the government department responsible for implementing the Freedom of Information Act.

www.dnotice.org.uk. Website of the Defence Advisory Notice system.
www.foia.blogspot.com. UK Freedom of Information Act blog, maintained by Steve Wood, lecturer at John Moores University, Liverpool.
www.opsi.gov.uk. is the website of the Office of Public Sector Information where you can find the full texts of the Data Protection Act 1998, the Human Rights Act 1998 and the Freedom of Information Act 2000 as well as other useful information. For example the office is to merge with the National Archives.
www. patent.co.uk. Patent Office website.

Notes

1 Some journalists and academics accused ITN of an attack on freedom of speech. They said a large and powerful media group such as ITN should not use the libel laws to silence a small, radical magazine.
2 Tom Crone quoted in the *Guardian*, 11 March 2002.
3 *Ibid.*
4 *Ibid.*
5 Mr Justice Caulfield quoted in the *Daily Star*, 27 September 2000.
6 'The Simple Sword of Truth', www.guardianunlimited.co.uk. 10 April 1995.
7 T. Welsh and W. Greenwood, *McNae's Essential Law for Journalists*, London: Butterworths, 2003, p. 214.
8 The Press Complaints Commission code bans newspapers from publishing 'inaccurate, misleading or distorted material, including pictures'. See Chapter 12 for more on the PCC.
9 Welsh and Greenwood, *op. cit.*, p. 263.
10 For a full list see Welsh and Greenwood, *op. cit.*, p. 274.
11 Welsh and Greenwood, *op. cit.*, pp. 276–7.
12 Matthew Lewin, former editor of the *Hampstead and Highgate Express*, was the young reporter. He was quoted in *Press Gazette*, 1 September 2004.
13 These have been identified by Tom Crone, *Law and the Media*, 4th edn, Oxford: Focal Press, 2002, p. 66. I have made some additions to the list.
14 Quoted in Mark Thompson, 'Lawyers alarmed by international libel lawsuit trend', *USC Annenberg Online Journalism Review* at www.ojr.org, 2 November 2004.
15 A discussion of the effect of the case on online archives is carried on www.tjg.co.uk, the website of law firm Taylor Wessing. The information here is taken in large part from this source.
16 Tom Crone, *op. cit.*, p. 66.
17 *Press Gazette*, 14 May 2004.
18 *Press Gazette*, 9 January 2004.
19 Welsh and Greenwood, *op. cit.*, pp. 484–5.
20 Mr Justice Lindsey in *Douglas & Ors v. Hello Ltd & Ors*, 2003, paragraph 229 iii of the full judgment, which can be found on www.bailii.org.
21 *Press Gazette*, 2 March 2001.

22 Welsh and Greenwood, *op. cit.*, p. 305.

23 *Ibid.*, p. 309.

24 PR Newswire on behalf of *The Times*, 1 May 2003.

25 Lord Falconer, 'Freedom of Information', news.bbc.co.uk, 1 January 2005.

26 Maurice Frankel, director, Campaign for Freedom of Information, 'Freedom of information for journalists', www.cfoi.org.uk.

THE MORAL MAZE

Good journalists work ethically and listen to their consciences. They

- know their code of practice
- approach people with tact and sensitivity
- deal with people in an honest and straightforward manner
- express their concerns if they disagree with an assignment.

An ethical job

To see ourselves as others see us is more painful for journalists than it is for most workers. In fact many refuse to accept the image the public has of us. The most responsible of us see ourselves as society's messengers, bringing the important stories of the day to the public as quickly and accurately as possible, holding those with power to account and defending our democratic freedoms. Others of us would struggle to describe our role, but may rather enjoy being labelled a troublemaker or maverick. This is closer to the way the public sees us but still a little on the positive side. The common view of journalists is as Uriah Heep characters, posing as honest acquaintances while gathering what damaging or embarrassing titbits we can get our grubby hands on. From this perspective there are no depths to which we wouldn't go for a good scoop. Survey after survey confirms this. Journalists, along with politicians, come at the bottom of the list of trustworthy occupations.

The reason for this low ranking? Some journalists would put it down to 'shooting the messenger' or society not liking having a mirror put up to it. Perhaps this explains some of the antipathy. But if journalists are honest with themselves, it is the public's perception that we are not always straight dealers, that we are ruthlessly ambitious as well as lazy and arrogant that is doing the damage. The public are also of the opinion that the media are more interested in passing on tittle-tattle about the latest C-list celebrity to walk into their spotlight than in enlightening people about truly important stories.

Despite the unpopularity of journalists, the news media in Britain have enormous power because of their ability to reach the population. As John Wilson in *Understanding Journalism* points out, news is seen as a grubby necessity.[1] On average people spend more time consuming all forms of media than doing anything else except work, and it is through the media that we learn about the outside world. The media point out the goodies and the baddies, tell us what to believe and what to view with suspicion, explain what is important, worrying and exciting. They mould our view of the world. Yet this power to influence public opinion is one many journalists are reluctant to accept and as a result are often unwilling to take responsibility for what they write.

John Lloyd, in his polemic, *What the Media Are Doing to Our Politics* (2004), says news organisations have to recognise the effects of their reporting. For example, he argues that the assumption that all politicians are corrupt and debased is damaging our democratic institutions. Unless they can think of a better system, journalists should seek to understand and explain the complex truth of public life, moving away from the dramatic splits, personal setbacks and betrayals, which are bite-sized, fast-food news, towards explaining the central issues of politics and public affairs.

> Media are at the centre of our public life. They define what that life is. If the definition they give of it is chronically, structurally wrong, then it's a serious matter, more serious than many of the things with which the media concern themselves. Media claim to have a central role to play in the construction and preservation of democratic life, liberty and the pursuit of happiness. Diverse views find expression through them – indeed, beyond a purely local existence, can do so only through them. Yet, outside the United States, media reflect relatively little on how they fulfil the central democratic purpose.[2]

We have to take our responsibilities seriously because what journalists report feeds into and influences the way society views itself and others. How honest, accurate and balanced those reports are will have an effect on how full and comprehensive is that picture. The quality of news will also affect the levels of trust society has in its media. It is crucial that journalists earn and maintain the confidence of the public and they can only do this by behaving honestly and ethically.

> If you start treating politics as a game or people's lives as soap opera or crime as some sort of peep show, it degrades society and can have appalling repercussions. Journalists have to live in the wider society. You may make short-term gains but reap the whirlwind in the long term. (Jo-Anne Pugh, home news desk editor, BBC News)

At a Society of Editors' conference, speakers struggled with the question of how to improve the public's image of the media. It was agreed it would help if journalists showed more sensitivity and courtesy in the way they dealt with people. For example, don't promise more than we can deliver; say sorry more often when we make mistakes; try to curb our nasty streak; stop revelling in our readers' misfortunes; think carefully about the impact that stories and campaigns will have on the community and tone down our self-importance.[3]

We need to remember that we meet and talk to people either at the best (lottery win, miraculous survival, sport's triumph), worst (floods, fires, bereavement) or most stressful or controversial (corruption scandal, adulterous affair) times of their lives. When we interview them, they confide in us, trust us to tell their story fairly and accurately. The least we can do is our very best.

This chapter looks at the ethical dilemmas facing journalists and what checks are in place to help them.

Grey areas

One problem for journalists is the number of grey or disputed areas where the trade itself is unsure of what is acceptable. The pressures of the job do not lend themselves to spending time agonising about the ethics of a situation. Tight deadlines, stiff competition and demands for exclusive stories all conspire against a journalist giving a lot of thought to ethical questions. They may even push them into some questionable or plainly unethical practices.

A colleague told me of a woman who had precious photographs of her dead son stolen from her mantlepiece and coffee tables by journalists while they were in her house interviewing her. The pictures later appeared in several national newspapers. This is clearly unacceptable, but perhaps the reporters thought it was better to take the photographs than risk being yelled at by their editor or perhaps even fired for not 'having what it takes'.

For most journalists ethics is not a common subject for discussion. A recently graduated journalism student said, 'When at university we write essays on ethics and objectivity but once you get out there no one is really interested. There are good people working in journalism and that's what makes it all right.'

Journalists may not talk much about ethics but if you ask them whether they believe they are ethical in their work, the majority will tell you that they are, or they try to be. Mike McCarthy, bureau chief of Sky News in Manchester, explains: 'To be honest I don't follow any textbook advice on ethics. It's an instinctive thing. You know what's right and you know what's wrong.'

But do we? Do most journalists have a clear idea of what they think is acceptable practice and a line over which they will not cross? Or could they be pushed into actions they do not feel comfortable with in pursuit of a story? And do journalists realise how important it is for the media to behave with integrity? Responsible, honest and ethical journalism is what gives it its authority. If no one can believe what they hear or read, then journalism loses its role as a source of information. Throughout this book ethical questions have been addressed from the importance of protecting sources (Chapter 10) to never promising an interviewee what you cannot deliver (Chapter 7), because whether or not it is talked about, ethics infuses everything we do.

One of the thorniest ethical issues is objectivity. How objective should our reporting be? We touched on this in Chapters 1 and 2 and at impartiality in Chapter 5. I don't intend to rehearse the points set out there but to move the argument on.

Objectivity/impartiality

> In an ideal world, the BBC strives to give a balanced report as a reasonable responsible member of society would see it. That doesn't mean present arguments for and against because some things are objectively wrong, for example child abuse. However, even when dealing with a man accused of child abuse, one should be fair in dealing with the case. (Jo-Anne Pugh, home news desk editor, BBC News)

Broadcasters are required by law to be impartial while newspapers are not. Broadcast journalists have to report the facts; they may provide professional judgments but never promote their personal opinions. The press, on the other hand, plays a different role. They may give a view or take a stand on an issue. Two different newspapers will take identical facts and use them to build conflicting arguments.

That said, being objective in news reporting is traditionally one of the most important journalistic ethics, yet it is now the subject of fierce debate. Those in favour of objectivity in news argue that if the public do not believe they are getting a fair and accurate representation of events, then they will not trust reporting by the media. In that case there is very little justification for having news media.

Sceptics argue that being impartial or objective is not possible or even necessarily desirable. All journalists write out of their experiences. All wear their own spectacles of bias, which distort the world according to their education, cultural background, political leanings, religion, etc.

> It's absurd to think that people working in the media don't have opinions. Do people think that when I go home, or to the pub, or whatever, that I am a neutral observer? What an absurd idea. (Rod Liddle, then editor of BBC Radio 4's *Today* programme)[4]

What stories we cover and how we cover them are also affected by how much time we have available to investigate the story, how much space or time we have been given to tell the story, and a myriad other influences discussed in Chapter 2.

If we take it as given that all people are biased to a degree then, so the argument goes, those news organisations that try to be objective are being dishonest. They can lead people wrongly to believe they are more truthful than other news organisations when in fact they are just as partial as the more blatantly biased.[5] Supporters of objectivity would counter that, far from being less truthful, organisations attempting to be objective are aiding a journalism that is honest and fair. They are endeavouring to set out the facts rather than opinion, trying to present many sides of an issue, being dispassionate and even-handed – all these militate against bias. They argue that there is no excuse for allowing journalism to become one-sided or simply a pedlar of propaganda. As Edward Murrow, the respected CBS reporter puts it: 'Everyone is a prisoner of his own experiences. No one can eliminate prejudices – just recognise them.' By suggesting that it is not a person's bias but how they choose to work around it that is important, Murrow speaks for many of those who support an objective approach to news.

Tom Rosenstiel, director of the Project for Excellence in Journalism affiliated to Columbia University, New York, holds a similar view. He argues objectivity doesn't preclude a person having opinions:

> It doesn't mean that you are without personal bias, and it doesn't mean neutrality. It means that the journalist's working method is objective – that you're independent, disinterested, and you're not going to let your interests determine the outcome of your journalism. The notion that objectivity is a myth because everybody has opinions . . . that's a misunderstanding of the concept.[6]

Rosenstiel was commenting on Fox News, the news channel based in the United States and owned by Rupert Murdoch. Its opinionated and highly charged news is very popular with the US public, attracting an audience bigger than CNN. The channel was openly supportive of the Iraq War and pro President Bush and has been described as a 'rabidly rightwing 24-hour news channel' and 'nakedly right-wing'[7]. However, far from admitting or publicly recognising its bias, it claims it is objective in its coverage. Fox's own mottos are 'We report, you decide' and 'Fair and balanced'.

Even when Fox's chairman, Roger Ailes, was revealed as having acted as an adviser to President Bush in the days after the September 11 attacks on New York and Washington, he insisted his actions were not at all partisan. Ailes said he was acting as a concerned citizen.

Rosenstiel argues these working methods are not objective, that at the very least Fox should have admitted that the chairman of the network had consulted with the president. 'The reason they didn't is because if people knew, they would trust Fox less,' he said.[8]

Fox appears to be part of a trend towards partisan news in the United States, perhaps aided by the crisis of confidence which seems to have affected mainstream news organisations. Several well-respected organisations have faced scandals and criticism about the honesty and quality of their reporting; these have in some notable cases led to painful reflection and soul-searching.

At the *New York Times* a young reporter, Jayson Blair, was found in May 2003 to have plagiarised numerous stories. Then in early 2004 *USA Today*'s top foreign reporter, Jack Kelly, was discovered to have fabricated stories from around the world during 21 years with the paper. Both these papers wrote extensive corrections once they discovered the deceits. The *New York Times* published more than 7,000 words across four pages and *USA Today* carried two broadsheet pages of examples of Kelly's fabrications.

The failure to find any weapons of mass destruction in Iraq has plunged other news organisations into a time of judicious self-reflection. The *Washington Post* on its front page of 12 August 2004 admitted that articles questioning the threat from Iraq's weapons of mass destruction often didn't make the front page whereas articles stressing what the administration were saying against Iraq did.

This willingness of the American news organisations to self-flagellation has surprised some in Britain though not the media commentator, Roy Greenslade. He said the failure by US media to question their masters is not new: 'America's journalistic community has long failed to question the ruthless self-interest of their country's foreign policy, and that has become infinitely worse since September 11.'[9]

Sections of the American public are also doubtful their media are giving them the full picture. Such people have turned away from the mainstream media to look elsewhere for information. Online blogs (personal journal-style websites easily allowing contribution or update by the owner and also allowing others easily to contribute) and alternative news websites (indymedia) have become more and more important as initiators of news and debates on current issues.

Some say the internet has become a fifth estate as the fourth estate has lost confidence and trust.[10] It's led by the likes of Matt Drudge of www.drudgereport.com, who broke the story of former President Bill Clinton's affair with White House intern Monica Lewinski. Since then bloggers have used the internet to gather information and put pressure on those with whom they disagree.[11]

The American public's hunger for news from other sources is also shown in the numbers seeking information from overseas sources. The *Guardian* reports that almost 45 per cent of the 9.6 million users accessing its website originate in the US.[12] The BBC's international television news service, BBC World, is another to benefit. It saw a significant rise in viewing figures during the war in Iraq in 2003 – particularly in the United States.[13]

Greg Dyke, while he was BBC director general, spoke about differences showing up, since September 11, in the definition of impartiality on either side of the Atlantic. At a speech during a symposium on journalism at Goldsmith's College in London, he expressed shock at how unquestioning the broadcast news media in America were during the Iraq War. He singled out Fox News for its bias towards President Bush and its 'gung-ho patriotism'. If the BBC followed suit, he said, it would undermine the trust of the audience. He dismissed accusations that the BBC had been soft on Saddam Hussein, saying its commitment to independence and impartiality was 'absolute'.[14]

> If Iraq proved anything, it was that the BBC cannot afford to mix patriotism and journalism. This is happening in the United States and if it continues will undermine the credibility of the US electronic news media.[15]

Regulation in the industry

> 'Western civilisation needs good flows of information like it needs good flows of air to breathe.'[16]

There are an estimated 1,523 newspapers, 1,764 magazines, 761 radio stations and 484 television stations on offer to the British public.[17] But few people realise that they are owned by a limited number of media organisations and therefore the bulk of our news comes from only a few companies.

It is the task of the regulators to check that individual companies do not have too much control of the market and that the journalists in those companies are delivering news that meets certain agreed standards. These standards are stated in the regulations that govern the industry. They delineate what is expected of companies and individual journalists and set standards of behaviour that are acceptable to the industry and the public. The regulations attempt to reconcile the journalists' right to report freely with other people's rights to privacy.

In Britain there is a split between the regulation of the broadcasting industry and the regulation of the newspaper industry. The first is set down in legislation and the second is voluntary self-regulation. Whether legally enforceable or voluntary, the regulations are administered by the regulators, the biggest of which is Ofcom.

Regulating the broadcasters

Ofcom

The Office of Communications (Ofcom) was created in 2003 by the Communications Act of that year. It was immediately dubbed a 'super regulator' because it replaced five regulators covering radio, television and programme standards: the Independent Television Commission, the Radio Authority, Broadcasting Standards Commission, Radio Communications Agency and Oftel (the telecommunications watchdog). Their roles were merged into Ofcom, which became the most powerful regulator in British broadcasting history.

Duties

Ofcom handles everything from telephones to television and radio. It licenses and regulates independent television companies (non-BBC companies) such as ITV plc, Channel 4, Channel Five and a range of cable and satellite services. It also awards licences to broadcast to independent radio companies.

Ofcom's duties include:

- maintaining a range of television and radio services of high quality and wide appeal
- making sure there is competition in order to promote 'plurality', which means consumers have access to different sources of information
- ensuring that a variety of electronic services, such as broadband, is available throughout the country
- overseeing the switchover proposed to take place between 2007 to 2012 from analogue to digital broadcasting
- ensuring the best management of spectrum (airwaves).

Ofcom is also responsible for maintaining standards in the content of programmes. It has to ensure that programmes on television and radio do not cause harm or offence to people and that television programme makers treat people fairly and do not infringe on their privacy.

To guide broadcasters on standards in programmes, Ofcom is required by the Communications Act 2003 and also by the Broadcasting Act 1996 to draw up a Code of Practice for broadcasters, setting out what is expected of them.

On news, Ofcom's draft code states it is committed to impartiality, accuracy and representing a range of views in news coverage.

5.1 News, in whatever form, must be reported with due accuracy and presented with due impartiality.

5.2 An appropriate range of views should be fairly and dispassionately reported and presented over an appropriate time-scale when covering controversial political and industrial events and issues and matters of current public policy.

5.3 Significant mistakes should be acknowledged as quickly as possible and corrected on air with due weight.

5.4 No active politician should be used as a newsreader, interviewer or reporter in any news programmes. Where, in exceptional circumstances this may be editorially justified, the political allegiance must be made clear to the audience.

5.5 Simulated news bulletins in other programmes (dramas, current affairs) must be produced in such a way that there is no reasonable possibility of listeners or viewers being misled into believing they are listening to or watching an actual news bulletin.

It states what it means by 'due impartiality':

Impartiality requires fairness, accuracy and an appropriate level of objectivity and even-handedness of approach to a subject. 'Due' is an important word in the context of impartiality. 'Due impartiality' does not mean an equal division of time has to be given to every view, or that every argument and every facet of every argument has to be represented. It means adequate or appropriate to the subject and nature of the subject, the type of programme and channel, the likely expectation of the audience as to content, and the extent to which the content and approach is signalled to the audience.

Ofcom has the authority to punish broadcasters if they break the rules on what they should broadcast. The powers come from the Communications Act 2003 and the Broadcasting Acts 1996 and 1990 covering all licensees and the BBC and S4C.

If it deems it necessary – if a broadcaster has repeatedly, deliberately or seriously breached the terms of its licence conditions or Ofcom's statutory codes – Ofcom may:

- issue a Direction not to repeat a programme
- issue a Direction to broadcast a correction or a statement of Ofcom's finding
- impose a financial penalty (including a maximum fine of £250,000 on the BBC and S4C)
- shorten a licence (not applicable to the BBC, S4C and Channel 4) or
- revoke a licence (not applicable to the BBC, S4C and Channel 4). (www.ofcom.org.uk)

Ofcom handles complaints over broadcasting standards through its Content Board. So far it has upheld complaints against companies including the BBC, ITV, Sky and several local radio stations. Some of these cases have resulted in fines or apologies, but in at least two cases Ofcom has revoked the licence of the broadcaster.

Ofcom does not, in the main, regulate the BBC except on issues of taste and decency, privacy, fairness and programme standards. It can consider complaints from members of the public about BBC programme standards, and monitors the BBC's adherence to around 60 individual targets and quotas each year – including levels of independent and regional production and volume of news, current affairs and original programmes on BBC channels.

BBC Governors

Its Board of Governors has traditionally regulated the BBC. Since its beginnings in 1927 the Corporation has been overseen by a board of 12 governors appointed by the Queen on the advice of the Government. They regulated and represented the BBC and acted as trustees of the public interest in ensuring that the BBC was accountable to listeners, viewers and Parliament.

This arrangement, as well as the way the BBC is financed, is laid down in the Royal Charter, which is renewed every ten years. The Government has said the licence fee will be kept for at least the next ten years, but has announced a change in the management structure of the BBC.

The Board of Governors is being replaced in 2007 by two bodies: the BBC Trust and the Executive Board.

The BBC Trust

The BBC Trust, whose members will be appointed by the Queen on the advice of the Government, will take the place of the governors and be the public's voice within the Corporation. It will be responsible for how the licence fee is spent and for making sure that the Corporation fulfils its public service obligations. It will be the Trust's job to uphold standards of accuracy and impartiality. It will also appoint an Executive Board.

The Executive Board

The Executive Board will be chaired by the BBC's director-general. It will be responsible for the day-to-day management of the BBC and for delivering the BBC's services under a framework set by the Trust. The Board will include a minority of non-executive directors appointed from outside the BBC to act as 'critical friends'.

As we have already seen, Ofcom regulates the BBC on issues of taste and decency, privacy, fairness and programme standards. It also considers complaints from members of the public about BBC programme standards.

On a day-to-day basis, individual journalists can refer to the BBC's *Producers' Guidelines* for advice on good practice. These are circulated to all editorial staff in the Corporation, who are expected to familiarise themselves with them early in their employment. Among many other things, the Guidelines state that reporting should be dispassionate and well informed. A reporter can offer journalistic judgment on an issue but not a personal opinion.

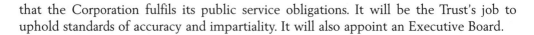

Regulating the press

Broadcasters can and have been fined by the broadcasting regulator Ofcom when they have been found to have misled viewers. But what happened to the *Sun* newspaper when it misled its readers?

The paper ran a front-page story in which it claimed it had a signed confession from footballer Stan Collymore that he was a 'lying scumbag' who had 'wasted his talent'. Headlined 'I Lied', the story on 3 November 2004 said that the player admitted beating up women, having public sex ('dogging') in car parks, and inventing stories to publicise his autobiography. The *Sun* also claimed that Collymore had admitted to starting a fight with six Bath rugby players at a nightclub in Dublin two days earlier.

It was only in the fifth paragraph of the story printed on an inside page that the paper revealed it had tricked Collymore into signing the confession at a book signing.

> Knowing he would never sign the confession willingly, we got *Sun* girl Michelle Dickie, 19, to hand it to him at a book-signing session at a WH Smith branch in Newcastle. Collymore thought he was giving a fan an autograph and signed the piece of paper with 'best wishes' – not realising the confession was on the other side. (*Sun*, 3 November 2004)

Collymore complained to the press watchdog, the Press Complaints Commission (PCC), and his complaint was upheld. The *Sun* was found guilty by the PCC of a 'serious' breach of the Code of Practice because it had not taken sufficient care to highlight the way the confession had been obtained. The PCC added that the story was 'entirely misleading' and that the paper had not made it clear enough to readers that the confession was bogus. The ruling further criticised the *Sun* for not having a public interest reason for using subterfuge in this way.

Pretty serious stuff. So how much did the paper have to pay?

Nothing actually.

They must have had to print an apology on the front page?

No, they didn't. They did print the Commission's adjudication. But, while the original story appeared on the front page, the adjudication was reported in a 94-word story on the bottom right-hand side of page two, under the headline 'Colly Rap'. The full adjudication was printed on page 32. No danger of anyone noticing it then. Not surprisingly, Collymore's lawyers complained again, saying the headline was misleading and that the adjudication had not been given the due prominence required by the PCC's Code of Practice.

Why is it that a broadcaster receives fines and can have their licence to broadcast revoked, but a newspaper that prints inaccurate or misleading stories is punished only with an order to print an apology and/or a correction and the adjudication? The answer lies in the way that the broadcast and print media are regulated. As we've seen, the broadcast media are regulated by a body (Ofcom) set up by legislation and required, by law, to enforce its rules. A purely voluntary body, the Press Complaints Commission, covers the print media.

The Press Complaints Commission

The Press Complaints Commission (PCC) is an independent self-regulatory organisation, which deals with complaints from members of the public about the editorial content of newspapers and magazines. Most of the complaints they receive are about accuracy, as with the Collymore case, or invasions of privacy.

There are 17 members of the Commission and the majority should have no connection with the press, thus attempting to ensure its independence from the newspaper industry. The newspapers and magazines, however, pay for the PCC. This support, the PCC claims, is its strength. Its website says that 'self-regulation works because the newspaper and magazine industry is committed to it'. Its power comes from it being set up by the industry and newspapers and magazines volunteering to be overseen by it. The rules the industry must adhere to are written down in the Editors' Code of Practice (see Appendix). It is the PCC's job to ensure these rules are complied with.

What the PCC claims is its strength, detractors see as its Achilles' heel, namely that its close relationship with the industry is just too cosy, especially with the tabloids. Because of this perception of being in the pocket of the editors, particularly tabloid editors, the PCC has faced calls for the end of self-regulation and criticism of the manner in which it handles complaints. Examples such as the Collymore case, where editors appear not to take the adjudications of the PCC seriously enough and it appears the punishments do not fit the transgression, have resulted in calls for the reform of the PCC.

So far the PCC has seen off these criticisms, and defenders say that it is not the job of the PCC to punish newspapers. It does not sit in judgment of wrongdoers and then hand down sentences. The PCC's role is as an arbitrator, attempting to resolve disputes in as amicable a way as possible. It claims that while it does not award damages or costs or fine newspapers, an upheld complaint represents in the eyes of many a significant criticism of the newspaper.

In 2003, when Sir Christopher Meyer took up the position of chairman of the PCC, he attempted to address some of the concerns. He proposed improving the workings of the PCC by opening it up to scrutiny and bringing it to the attention of more people. His changes included the appointment of an extra person to the Commission unconnected with the press, an annual audit of the Commission's customer service (a report on how well it is doing), an obligation for newspapers to publish adjudications clearly and prominently, and regular reviews of the Code of Practice. He also set up a 24-hour advice line, intended to provide an emergency response to complaints of harassment.

Sir Christopher presided over a toughening-up of the Code of Practice in the first major review of the code for six years. The last comprehensive revision had been in 1997 following the death of Diana, Princess of Wales and public concern that she had been hounded by the paparazzi.

The 2004 Review saw the PCC outlaw the interception of private and mobile telephone calls and text messages – a reaction to the *News of the World* exposé about footballer David Beckham's affair with Rebecca Loos, which centred on the publication of text messages between the pair. The Review amended the Code to prevent all photography of people in private places and toughened the restrictions on payments to criminals by stopping newspapers from paying them for material that 'exploits, glorifies or glamorises crime'.

The Editors' Code of Practice

The Code provides the rules by which the Press Complaints Commission polices the newspaper industry and is drawn up by a committee of editors. It prescribes what constitutes acceptable and unacceptable journalism (see full text in the Appendix).

Besides the Code, some organisations give their own guidelines to reporters, the *Guardian* being one of them.

Some practical issues and how to handle them

Criticisms of how journalists cover minority groups and sensitive issues focus on their uncaring attitude, and the way they pander to prejudices and stereotypes. In some cases the criticisms are unfair, in many others they are spot on. It can be as simple as the facts that are useful to the journalist's story giving only a partial picture, which leads to a misleading image of the person or issue.

John Wilson says this about the newsgathering process:

People who appear in stories are partially portrayed because only part of them is relevant. . . If a person in a wheelchair is involved, say as a victim of a robbery at home, the fact of the wheelchair nearly always matters more to the story than the full-time job the person does. The wheelchair will be prominent because it adds interest, the full-time job at best referred to in passing because it is not relevant and, in the context, not interesting.[18]

He adds that journalists dislike being told what they can and cannot or should and shouldn't use in their stories, especially when it is said for ulterior, non-journalistic reasons either to appease a political or commercial pressure or to concede a point to a well-intentioned lobby group or 'image-improver'. Understandably, journalists resist such pressure.

I hope the issues I refer to here and the advice this section offers will be an aid to good, responsible and accurate journalism and are not about pandering to image-improvers.

Reporting suicide

Responsible reporting of suicide can save lives by informing readers and viewers about the likely causes of suicide, its warning signs and new treatments for mental illness. On the other hand, careless and irresponsible reporting can lead to copy-cat suicides, encouraging vulnerable individuals to imitate the reported suicides. Research has found that in the days following media coverage of a suicide there is an increase in suicides using a similar method.

To help journalists cover suicides sensitively, a group in the United States involving the National Institute of Mental Health, the Office of the Surgeon General, the American Foundation for Suicide Prevention and the Annenberg Public Policy Center has issued guidelines. These are reproduced on the website of the American Foundation for Suicide Prevention (AFSP) at www.afsp.org. The site also gives examples of the good and the problematic coverage that has appeared in the press. This article from the *New York Daily News*, 15 May 2002, highlights some of the problems:

DESPERATE COUPLE FACE SPEEDING TRAIN . . . A KISS BEFORE DYING

Loving couple chose death on the tracks

They kissed one last time. Then the young couple took out their wallets and carefully placed them next to each other on the train platform.

Theresa LaMarca, 22, and Damien Conners, 26, pushed open a gate and walked hand-in-hand down the seven steps leading to the tracks at the station in North Elizabeth, NJ.

The two lovers clutched one another as they stood for a moment under the concrete walkway that spans the tracks. At exactly 4:15 p.m,. they plunged in front of a New York bound train and killed themselves.

The AFSP describes this article as presenting both a sensationalised and romanticised view of suicide from the headline to the end quote and expresses concern that it could encourage other vulnerable people to copy it.

The couple's drug addiction is played down, while the suicide is portrayed as the ultimate romantic act. The reporter does not inform the reader that drug abuse is a problem in half of the young people who go on to commit suicide. Instead the couple are described as being 'very much in love'. The superintendent of their former residence says their financial situation was so desperate that they were going to be forced to move home with their parents and attributes the potential separation as the catalyst for their suicide. The story finishes with a quote from the superintendent who describes the suicide as a 'Romeo and Juliet thing . . . they wouldn't allow anyone to keep them apart and they kept their word. When the train hit them they became one.'

This romanticising of the suicide encourages others to identify with the couple and may lead to imitation. The AFSP says compounding the risk is the very detailed description of the suicide given in the article, where the reader is walked through the couple's final moments.

Here are some facts the AFSP believes we should bear in mind when reporting suicide:

- More than 90 per cent of suicide victims have a significant psychiatric illness at the time of their death.
- When mood disorders and substance abuse are present, the risk of suicide is much greater.
- Presenting suicide as the inexplicable act of an otherwise healthy or high-achieving person may encourage identification with the victim.
- Research suggests that portraying suicide as a heroic or romantic act may encourage others to identify with the victim.
- Exposure to the suicide method through media reports can encourage vulnerable individuals to imitate it.

The AFSP encourages reporters to stress that effective treatments for many mental disorders are available. The language used in the report can help the message. The AFSP asks reporters to avoid using the word 'suicide' in a headline.

MediaWise, the media ethics group, has also published an excellent leaflet on reporting suicide. It can be downloaded at www.mediawise.org.uk.

Mental health

Related to reporting suicide is the reporting of mental health issues because, as we have seen, 90 per cent of suicide victims have a mental health problem. Their friends often express surprise at the suicide; they didn't know the person suffered from depression or mental illness. It's not surprising when you think of the stigma attached to mental health.

Among the articles highlighted by the AFSP on its website is one that appeared in the *New York Times* under the headline: 'Grim Reminder on Mental Illness':

> DETROIT, July 20 – It was the kind of event that Heinz Prechter, chairman of ASC Inc., would have enjoyed, darting about to greet friends in his German-accented English, shaking hands and patting shoulders. Instead, the throng of 700 had gathered for Mr Prechter's funeral, held five days after he committed suicide on July 6 at age 59.
>
> The news was a jolt to Detroit's business community, which knew Mr Prechter as an ebullient German immigrant who arrived in the United States with $11 in his pocket and made a fortune in the auto business. Even more shocking was the cause. For years, Mr Prechter has been under treatment for severe depression. (New York Times, 21 July 2001)

The article later mentions that Mr Prechter's depression was a secret to everyone other than his family and a few close friends. He wouldn't have wanted them to know, considering the embarrassment and disgrace associated with mental health problems. Indeed this situation was highlighted by the reporter, who had consulted an expert on depression before writing the article. It goes into detail about the stigma of mental illness and how depression is still widely misunderstood, stating that 'as many as 10 per cent of senior executives have at least some symptoms of depression', yet nine out of ten sufferers go undiagnosed and untreated.

Unsurprisingly, this article is lauded as being an excellent example of how to report mental illness and suicide. The writer includes important data on clinical depression and emphasises the need for better resources and effective treatment programmes than are currently available. Yet much reporting of mental health in the media is nowhere near as illuminating and thorough. Research by the mental health charity Mind carried out in 2000 found that negative and unbalanced media coverage actually increases mental health problems.[19]

So how do we feel about the *Sun*'s coverage of former boxer Frank Bruno's mental illness? Its headline in early editions of the paper on 23 September 2003 read 'Bonkers Bruno locked up' and referred to him as a 'nut'. Many readers were angry at the coverage and rang the paper or spoke on radio phone-ins. Some also complained to the Press Complaints Commission. The *Sun* responded by changing the front page in later editions of the paper to 'Sad Bruno in mental home' and joining with mental health charities to launch a support fund for people with mental health problems.

But would people have been so sympathetic if the person in the story had not been one of Britain's most popular sports stars?

Covering grief and trauma

Covering grief is one of the hardest parts of the work of a journalist, especially if it comes in the form of a 'death-knock', where you go to the house of someone involved in a tragedy (see Chapter 7). But like it or not, accidents, violent crimes, terrorist attacks and natural disasters are important stories. At some point in your career you will have to cover one of these events, either by going to the scene or interviewing people involved or affected. You may be welcomed by the bereaved, anxious to talk about their loved one. Often though you will not be appreciated.

For journalists, questioning the bereaved and covering traumatic events is a necessary part of the job. When editors gave evidence to the House of Commons Culture, Media and Sport Committee in February 2003 they defended the right to approach the bereaved. Their reasons included the fact that it allowed people to honour the life that had been lost and that talking to the close family was the only way to ensure that details were accurate. They also asserted that many people welcomed reporters who made enquiries sensitively.

Efforts have been made to balance the needs on the one hand of the news media, for whom grief is an inevitable part of such incidents and where not to cover it would be to misrepresent events and, on the other, the sensibilities of those (including MPs) who believe that the grief-stricken should never be approached. The Editors' Code of Practice, while accepting the media will approach people, says: 'In cases involving personal grief or shock, enquiries must be carried out and approaches made with sympathy and discretion.'

If you fail to approach people with sensitivity and tact, you are unlikely to secure an interview or get a comment. Pragmatism aside, the bereaved or shocked should be treated with respect, no matter how close to deadline you are or how much you want to beat the opposition. For example, never harass the bereaved; if they tell you to go away, then do so. Calling back several times just to make sure can cause distress. Close-up shots of grieving people can be prurient; use long and wide shots to be less intrusive. Television reporters should ensure the camera does not linger too long on shots of people in distress.

Handling interviews with the bereaved or the traumatised means not only being tactful and sensitive but also being responsible. At these times, people are not always able to think through the consequences of what they say. What if someone agrees to talk to you and in their grief opens their heart, telling you things that could lead them to be ostracised in their communities? While working on a local newspaper, I interviewed a young woman who had been sexually abused by her grandfather and had discovered he'd since abused her 4-year-old niece. She spoke in great detail about the things that had happened to her and said she wanted to be identified in the story. After speaking to my editor, we counselled her against identification and we left out many of the details she had given. We felt this was an angry, vulnerable woman who did not realise the impact that publicising her experiences could have on her life.

The presentation of stories involving trauma or grief can be tricky but getting the tone right is important. A rule of thumb should be to write in a way that minimises distress to the audience but maximises understanding. Covered well, these stories can inform and educate the audience, cajole authorities into action and provoke charitable acts. Covered badly, they oversimplify issues, are too sentimental and ghoulishly voyeuristic. They can also cause unnecessary anxiety – for example, if the coverage of a violent crime mentions other similar crimes and neglects to mention how rare such crimes are. Careless reporting of unsubstantiated rumour or exaggerated casualty figures can also cause distress.

Alex Gerlis, leader of the BBC's Journalism Centre for Excellence argues that

> Thinking more carefully about how we deliver such stories gives us a better appreciation of their emotional dimension. That means a more respectful and accurate representation of the experience of those we are reporting and a more meaningful connection with the audience. The result is better journalism.

The key, he adds, is to keep those most directly affected by the story at its centre.

> If a news report begins, 'It was the night that hell visited this small Yorkshire town', then that raises the emotional level of a story which may be traumatic enough anyway. It is a powerful image, but clichéd. Far more effective would be, 'One eyewitness described it as the night that hell visited their small town'. It is still a strong image, but this time it is telling the story through someone involved in it.[20]

We should always try to see these stories through the eyes of those who were there. We should stick to facts and avoid clichés.

There is no more traumatic story than a war. Do the same rules apply? Should we edit footage and soften descriptions of distressing scenes to avoid upsetting the audience? For some journalists this is unacceptable because it sanitises and can even romanticise war. Martin Bell believes what he calls 'the good taste brigade' have got it wrong:

> What you show are almost heroic figures in uniform blazing away with their Kalashnikovs or whatever they have got, and there are big artillery and it's all very spectacular. What you don't really see is what happens at the other end. You don't see the maiming of civilians, you don't see the killing of civilians, you don't even see the wounding and the killing of soldiers very much.[21]

Robert Fisk of the *Independent* believes that there is a journalistic duty to show the effect of war on television as well as write about it honestly in newspapers. He believes the reasons for not showing pictures of the dead, dying or badly wounded are political rather than about taste and decency and certainly aren't about respecting the dead:

> We don't want to respect the dead, we kill them. What we want to do is to stop people seeing these images because if they saw them, they would never ever again support war. And we want a population that will, when we want, support wars.[22]

The images he's talking about include those he saw during the 1991 Gulf War on the road to Basra, Iraqi soldiers massacred by Allied troops. There were skeletons with what he said were 'mortal juices' still dripping from their bones, sitting in army trucks and the smell of faeces and rotting flesh.

> On the right-hand side of the road were a group of Iraqi soldiers, dead, and wild dogs had come in across the sand, over the desert and were tearing them to pieces for food. Running off with someone's arm between their teeth. You know, the fingers dragging through the sand. Ripping out stomachs to eat. Verminous dogs.[23]

Those out in the field can feel differently to those back at the office – that the sanitised version of what's happened which is shown to the public fails to reflect the reality on the ground. A BBC training tape that addresses the question of how much violence can be shown on the news suggests the answer lies in what we are reporting on and what is our duty by it.

When reporting famine, viewers accept distressing images are needed to portray the full horror of the situation, but when it comes to extreme violence of one human against another, more care is needed. We need to show enough for viewers to judge the true consequences.

> The dilemma for editors, reporters and producers is this: show too much and we stray into voyeurism and intrusion. We may also saturate the viewers so such scenes lose their power, or we may alienate them so they switch off. We can warn viewers in advance or show them after children are in bed. But our overwhelming duty must be to the truth, to report the world as it is.[24]

The proliferation of images through the internet has complicated the debate. Some would ask what is the point of carefully editing footage to avoid upsetting or alienating the audience when they can access the unexpurgated version on the internet?

Point of death

We've talked about the bereaved and about showing the dead. What about showing the point of death, where someone is being killed? Is that ever justified? The Ofcom code states that broadcasters should only show the point of death in exceptional circumstances, but for the press the guidance is less clear. The Editors' Code of Practice only says newspapers should not intrude into personal grief or shock.

Pictures of the accident at the Burghley Horse trials in which the international eventer Caroline Pratt was killed when her horse fell on her clearly show the moment when the rider died. Among those papers that illustrated the incident was the *Daily Telegraph*. It used the headline: 'The horrific moment that a horse crushes its rider in the water jump at Burghley' and showed a sequence of three photographs of the fall with the caption: 'The jump that lead [*sic*] to Primitive Streak landing on top of Caroline Pratt, killing her'.[25]

Every story like this is a balancing act between the public's right to know what has happened against the pain of the bereaved, who may not want to see or be reminded of the point of death. In this case it perhaps tilted too far towards the public's right to know.

Decisions like this have to be made every day, often quickly and under great pressure. Most journalists will make ethical mistakes at one time or another during their career. Many do things as young reporters that they wish they hadn't. Others too are pressured either directly by their editor or indirectly by the fear of what will happen if they don't secure the interview or get the pictures.

Organisations such as MediaWise have argued for a 'conscience clause' to allow reporters to refuse an assignment if they oppose it on ethical grounds. So far this has been rejected.

Racism

Journalists on the *Daily Express* who complained they were being forced to write stories that claimed thousands of gypsies and travellers were about to 'invade' Britain and live off the state if they failed to get jobs – 'If there's no job I'll get benefits' – would have welcomed a conscience clause. In its absence they wrote to the Press Complaints Commission reminding it of 'the need to protect journalists unwilling to write racist articles which are contrary to the NUJ's Code of Conduct.' In October 2003 the PCC issued a guidance note to editors warning of 'the danger that inaccurate, misleading or distorted reporting may generate an atmosphere of fear and hostility that is not borne out by the facts'.

The gypsy and traveller communities are used to receiving coverage in the national and local press that represents them as scroungers who steal from the settled community, live in filthy conditions and leave a trail of litter behind them. This kind of journalism dehumanises people and has led to assaults and abuse, according to MediaWise. In response and to highlight the issues, it has produced a leaflet on reporting asylum and refugee issues. In it, it says that asylum seekers and refugees who have already fled conflict and persecution, and the communities identified with them, have suffered attacks and these have been encouraged and legitimised by misleading reports in the media.

Following the events of September 11, refugees from Afghanistan, rather than being seen as fleeing the Taliban regime, were labelled its supporters:

> Taliban henchmen have sneaked into the UK posing as refugees, it was revealed last night. The disclosure comes less than a month after the *Daily Express* warned that Osama Bin Laden's foot soldiers were heading for Britain. (*Daily Express*, 7 December 2001)

Would anyone reading this have welcomed a refugee from Afghanistan into their neighbourhood?

What about giving space or airtime to racists, for example the far right British National Party (BNP)? Those in favour argue that, rather than gagging the likes of the BNP, journalists should challenge them and show them up for what they are. They would also say free speech is not only for our friends. We may not agree with the BNP's views but we should defend their right to express them. Those against say that it is too dangerous to allow the arguments of racists to be heard, that their message of hate is seductive to poor whites and creates fear in the black and Asian communities.

Cheque-book journalism

The Press Complaints Commission has banned payments or offers of payment to witnesses or potential witnesses in criminal trials, and it rules out payments that are conditional on the outcome of a trial in any circumstances. It has also banned payments to convicted criminals for stories, pictures or information, which seek to exploit a particular crime or to glorify or glamorise crime, unless there is a demonstrable public interest argument for doing so. Similar restrictions are included in the BBC *Producers' Guidelines* and the Ofcom Code of Practice for broadcasters.

The ban on payments to witnesses follows several high-profile cases, including that in 2002 of Canadian supply teacher Amy Gehring, who was on trial for having sex with someone who was under-age. The press bought up all three of the main prosecution witnesses. The barrister who defended Ms Gehring admitted he was able to cast doubt over the credibility of the witnesses that accepted large deals:

> 'One day one witness was telling the court how traumatic his sexual encounter had been, and then 24 hours later they were selling their stories for £10,000 for millions of people to read about in the *Sunday Mirror*.'[26]

Gehring was cleared of indecently assaulting two schoolboys.

Also in 2002 was the case of Damilola Taylor, the 10-year-old boy who died after bleeding to death from a thigh wound caused by a broken bottle. In that case the evidence of a 14-year-old witness, Bromley, was demolished in court because of financial rewards offered by police and also a £50,000 reward offered by the *Daily Mail*. The defence barrister in that case, Courtenay Griffiths QC, said: 'It [paying witnesses] simply encourages people to come forward who know nothing about the case in the hope that they can get some money.'[27]

With regard to payment for other stories, readers should be informed when money has been paid for revelations, and to whom. But the practice has meant that now people expect to be rewarded financially for speaking to the media. Even those with very ordinary tales to tell will demand a few quid. It is the national tabloid newspapers that are the biggest payers and regularly pay thousands of pounds for exclusive rights to a story.

David Randall argues that the practice of signing people up to ensure they only tell their story to one newspaper restricts the free flow of information and the media's ability to get to the truth. It also has another damaging side effect: the temptation to exaggerate.

> They know the stronger the story, the more you will pay; so they elaborate, embroider and flesh out a few facts with their fertile imaginations. This is especially the danger with stories about politicians and celebrities.[28]

Randall reminds us that the story the *Sun* paid a male prostitute to give them about an affair with Elton John (see Chapter 11) had come straight from the young man's imagination. It ended up costing them £1 million in libel damages and a front-page apology.

Freebies

From payments *by* journalists to payments *to* journalists, which usually come in the form of free trips, restaurant meals and tickets to the theatre. These are normally given to encourage a good review, and the journalist may feel obliged to be kind in the report. *Don't* – be honest both in the review and with the reader, listener or viewer and include mention somewhere in the piece that the ticket, trip or meal was provided for free.

In its editorial guidelines, the *Guardian* warns its staff that they must not use their position for private benefit and that no payment, gift or other advantage should undermine accuracy, fairness or independence. Any 'freebies' can only be accepted on the understanding that the journalist will report the assignment as he or she sees fit.

Tricking people into giving information

Three scenarios are given below. All are based on real investigations/interviews by journalists. Each has its ethical questions and each was, or would be, defended by the news organisations that carried the story.

1   You are going to interview an MP about the case of a constituent, but your editor wants you to throw in a question about the MP being stopped by police and questioned while walking a dog late at night in a park frequented by gay men.
2   Teachers' unions are complaining that there is a serious shortage of teachers in your area. You want to find out the effect of the shortage in the classroom and intend to write a hard-hitting report. You ring a local school and claim to be a young man interested in becoming a teacher and are offered three days' supervised work experience. During your three days you are taken into the confidence of the teachers, who explain that they don't have enough staff to deal with disruptive children and tell you of a child they believe may be suffering sexual abuse at home. You are also popular with the children, who interact with you freely.
3   You hear that a local trainer of horses is willing to fix races for a fee. You know he will never admit this to a journalist, and so you pose as an antiques dealer who is a serious gambler and secretly film your meeting with him.

These scenarios throw up two important ethical dilemmas: When, if ever, is it right to hide or change your identity? Is it fair to pretend you want to talk about one story when really you are interested in another?

Journalists often try to talk to people about things they do not want to discuss, especially not with the media. We develop roundabout ways of approaching these people. Perhaps we don't own up to who we are to their switchboard operator or private secretary so as to have a sporting chance of talking to them on the phone. Maybe then we avoid admitting we are reporters for the first minute or so. Perhaps we pretend to an interviewee that we are interested in one of their causes or passions when actually we want to talk about a controversy they were or are involved in. Many of us have behaved in this way, not being quite straight all the time. Where do we draw the line?

The danger is that by not being straight with people, we are trusted even less and our reputation is further damaged. If people have a basic distrust of all journalists, it makes it even harder for us to do our job. When we ask to interview people, we should be clear to them about the purpose of the interview.

Another equally serious concern is about the reliability of information given by people during what they believe is an informal chat. If people do not realise they are talking to a reporter they are less guarded, more likely to be careless with the facts, embellish the story to make it better in the telling, not realising they may have to defend its truth.

In the first scenario above involving the MP, if we had learned about the walk in the park the night before or the morning of the interview, after it was already scheduled, then it is fair to ask a question; the MP would expect it. Otherwise if you must ask it, then do so at the end so an indignant refusal does not ruin the rest of the interview. When asking, be as polite as possible.

At almost all times, reporters should be honest about who they are to people they are approaching. It is only in special circumstances, such as going undercover, that you should consider hiding your identity. These should be well-planned operations, approved by a senior person in your organisation and only considered if there is no other way of obtaining a story/interview/pictures.

Scenario two at the school appears to have no justification. The reporter is on a fishing trip to discover if there are any problems with teacher shortages. No one has tipped him off that this school is in dire straits, in fact it has a good teaching record. It appears as if the reporter does not believe he can get at the truth of the teacher shortages by asking schools or the unions directly. He hasn't even tried that tactic. The report he writes is in the form of a diary and he changes names and details such as nationalities in an attempt to disguise the children. But once the story is published there is a clue that could lead to the identity of the sexual abuse victim. Parents and teachers from the school complain to the newspaper and the Press Complaints Commission pointing out three breaches in the Editors' Code: (i) obtaining information by misrepresentation, (ii) interviewing school children without permission and (iii) identifying a child victim of sexual assault. The Press Complaints Commission upholds all three complaints.

The final scenario is a case of an investigation into corruption. The reporter has received a tip-off that this is occurring but knows that in order to discover the truth, he will have to use subterfuge. He poses as an antiques dealer; the danger with this is that he is involving himself in the story. In these cases, including investigations into any illegal trade where you are posing as a buyer or a seller, there is the possibility of changing the circumstances or the market. You need to have plenty of evidence of what is going on before you get involved.

Summing up

It is generally accepted that some parts of the industry need to clean up their act. The National Union of Journalists has advocated a system of registration similar to those for accountants or lawyers. Having a professional register, it argues, would help to raise standards and increase public esteem. At the moment, it says, journalism is open to charlatans, miscreants and the literary equivalent of snake-oil salesmen.

Many others vehemently reject the idea of a register. Journalism, they say, benefits from being accessible to all. People come into it from many different avenues and, far from being a negative influence, this eclectic mix is a good thing. For the time being, at least, journalism stays open and it is up to the individual to work within acceptable boundaries.

Throughout this chapter I have attempted to show the benefits of working ethically. No one is saying this is easy, but if you always do your best to report the verifiable facts, quote people accurately and deal with them in an honest, straightforward and sensitive way, then you will be well on the way to being a credit to the practice of journalism. In the end it is up to you, the individual journalist, to exercise your personal conscience. During your career you may be subjected to pressures to write positive stories about businesses associated with your news organisation. You may be bullied by politicians, or ordered by your editor to approach people you believe should be left alone; you may even be tempted to make up quotes. It is at those times that you need your still, small voice of integrity to help determine what you do.

Whenever you feel under pressure, remember these thoughts from David Randall:

> Our aim is to devise a way of working which enables us to justify our actions with a clear conscience. That way we will keep our reputations intact; for, in the end, the only thing that determines our worth as journalists is our reputation. You can let an editor take away your social life or your proper allocation of sleep, but never your reputation.[29]

REVIEW QUESTIONS

1 What does the Editors' Code of Practice say about paying witnesses in criminal trials?

2 Why is it a problem to describe the way a person has killed him or herself?

3 What was the Society of Editors' advice for raising the esteem in which journalists are held?

4 Explain the main duties of the Office of Communications.

EXERCISES

1 Consider the following scenario and decide how you would tackle it. This is an important story and your editor wants photographs. What would you do?

An aeroplane is missing, relatives and friends are at the airport to pick up passengers when the news is relayed that the plane has gone down. Do you take pictures of the reaction? One mother collapses, wailing with grief. Do you take close-up pictures of her or is that too intrusive?

2 Read the Editors' Code of Practice in the Appendix to this book and then have a look through a couple of national newspapers and see if you can spot any breaches.

3 Write down your own ethical code. Try to decide where the line is over which you wouldn't cross and what you would do if you were ever asked to behave in a manner you believe to be unethical.

FURTHER READING AND RESOURCES

Bibliography

BBC Producers' Guidelines, London: BBC.
Keeble, R., *Ethics for Journalists*, London: Routledge, 2001.
Kovach, B. and Rosenstiel, T., *The Elements of Journalism*, London: Atlantic Books, 2003.
Lloyd, J., *What the Media are Doing to Our Politics*, London: Constable, 2004.
Randall, D., *The Universal Journalist*, London: Pluto Press, 1996.
Wilson, J., *Understanding Journalism*, London: Routledge, 1996.

www.afsp.org   Website of the American Foundation for Suicide Prevention.
www.bbc.co.uk   Website of the British Broadcosting Corporation.
www.bbccharterreview.org.uk   Website of the Department of Culture, Media and Sport on the review of the BBC's Charter.
www.billroggio.com/easongate   The blog that was created after Eason Jordan, CNN's chief news executive, made statements at the World Economic Forum in Davos, interpreted by some as an accusation that American servicemen had intentionally killed journalists in Iraq. This shows how blogs can be used to oppose organisations and individuals. Eason Jordan resigned on 11 February 2005.
www.ethicalspace.org   Website of the International Journal of Communication Ethics.
www.drudgereport.com   Internet gossip supremo and the breaker of former US President Bill Clinton's affair with Monica Lewinski.

www.mediamatters.org   A liberal site dedicated to 'monitoring, analysing and correcting conservative misinformation in the US media.'

www.mediawise.org.uk   Website of the UK media ethics body.

www.mediauk.com   An independent media directory for the UK.

www.newshounds.us   Blog set up to monitor Fox News and counter what they believe is bias.

www.ofcom.org.uk   Website of the Office of Communications, the UK regulator for the broadcasters.

www.pcc.org.uk   Website of the Press Complaints Commission, the regulator for the press.

www.undercurrents.org   Alternative news service.

www.spiked-online.com   An independent news website based in London.

www.schnews.org.vk   Alternative news service advocating direct action.

Notes

1 John Wilson, *Understanding Journalism*, London: Routledge, 1996, p. 25.

2 John Lloyd, *What the Media are Doing to Our Politics*, London: Constable, 2004, p. 141.

3 *Press Gazette*, 17 October 2003.

4 *Daily Telegraph*, 28 September 2002.

5 Wilson, *op. cit.*, p. 46.

6 *Media Guardian*, 25 November 2002. See also Kovach and Rosenstiel, *The Elements of Journalism*, London: Atlantic Books 2001, pp. 72–75.

7 David Tether, *Guardian*, 23 August 2004 and Paul Harris, *Observer*, 20 February 2005.

8 *Media Guardian*, 25 November 2002.

9 *Media Guardian*, 20 June 2003.

10 Paul Harris, *Observer*, 20 February 2005.

11 The phenomenon of blogging is not confined to America. In the UK, alternative news sources – grassroots news organisations known as indymedia and video activists, many taking advantage of cheap digital technology – have become increasingly popular.

12 *Guardian*, 23 August 2004.

13 *Press Gazette*, 2 May 2003.

14 Greg Dyke in the *Guardian*, 25 April 2003.

15 Greg Dyke, cited in the *Press Gazette*, 2 May 2003.

16 Wilson, *op. cit.*, p. 29.

17 www.mediauk.com The site constantly updates the number of media outlets in the UK.

18 Wilson, *op.cit.*, pp. 58–9.

19 *Guardian*, 25 September 2003.

20 *Press Gazette*, 2 April 2004.

21 *Press Gazette*, 14 November 2003.

22 Fisk quoted in *Press Gazette*, 14 November 2003.

23 *Ibid*.

24 Peter Sissons, 'Violence in the News', BBC training video, 14 July 1993.

25 *Daily Telegraph*, 5 September 2004. See www.telegraph.co.uk.

26 *Press Gazette*, 2 May 2003.

27 *Ibid*.

28 David Randall, *The Universal Journalist*, London: Pluto Press, 1996, p. 72.

29 *Ibid.*, p. 93.

APPENDIX: THE EDITORS'
CODE OF PRACTICE

The Press Complaints Commission is charged with enforcing the following Code of Practice which was framed by the newspaper and periodical industry and was ratified by the PCC on 13 June 2005.

All members of the press have a duty to maintain the highest professional standards. This Code sets the benchmark for those ethical standards, protecting both the rights of the individual and the public's right to know. It is the cornerstone of the system of self-regulation to which the industry has made a binding commitment.

It is essential that an agreed code be honoured not only to the letter but in the full spirit. It should not be interpreted so narrowly as to compromise its commitment to respect the rights of the individual, nor so broadly that it constitutes an unnecessary interference with freedom of expression or prevents publication in the public interest.

It is the responsibility of editors and publishers to implement the Code and they should take care to ensure it is observed rigorously by all editorial staff and external contributors, including non-journalists, in printed and online versions of publications.

Editors should co-operate swiftly with the PCC in the resolution of complaints. Any publication judged to have breached the Code must print the adjudication in full and with due prominence, including headline reference to the PCC.

1 Accuracy

   (i)   The Press must take care not to publish inaccurate, misleading or distorted information, including pictures.

   (ii)   A significant inaccuracy, misleading statement or distortion once recognised must be corrected, promptly and with due prominence, and – where appropriate – an apology published.

   (iii)   The Press, whilst free to be partisan, must distinguish clearly between comment, conjecture and fact.

   (iv)   A publication must report fairly and accurately the outcome of an action for defamation to which it has been a party, unless an agreed statement states otherwise, or an agreed statement is published.

2 Opportunity to reply

A fair opportunity for reply to inaccuracies must be given when reasonably called for.

3 *Privacy

(i) Everyone is entitled to respect for his or her private and family life, home, health and correspondence, including digital communications. Editors will be expected to justify intrusions into any individual's private life without consent.

(ii) It is unacceptable to photograph individuals in private places without their consent. Note – Private places are public or private property where there is a reasonable expectation of privacy.

4 *Harassment

(i) Journalists must not engage in intimidation, harassment or persistent pursuit.

(ii) They must not persist in questioning, telephoning, pursuing or photographing individuals once asked to desist; nor remain on their property when asked to leave and must not follow them.

(iii) Editors must ensure these principles are observed by those working for them and take care not to use non-compliant material from other sources.

5 Intrusion into grief or shock

In cases involving personal grief or shock, enquiries and approaches must be made with sympathy and discretion and publication handled sensitively. This should not restrict the right to report legal proceedings, such as inquests.

6 *Children

(i) Young people should be free to complete their time at school without unnecessary intrusion.

(ii) A child under 16 must not be interviewed or photographed on issues involving their own or another child's welfare unless a custodial parent or similarly responsible adult consents.

(iii) Pupils must not be approached or photographed at school without the permission of the school authorities.

(iv) Minors must not be paid for material involving children's welfare, nor parents or guardians for material about their children or wards, unless it is clearly in the child's interest.

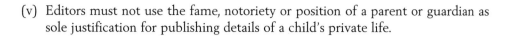

(v) Editors must not use the fame, notoriety or position of a parent or guardian as sole justification for publishing details of a child's private life.

7 *Children in sex cases

(i) The press must not, even if legally free to do so, identify children under 16 who are victims or witnesses in cases involving sex offences.

(ii) In any press report of a case involving a sexual offence against a child:

    (a) The child must not be identified.

    (b) The adult may be identified.

    (c) The word 'incest' must not be used where a child victim might be identified.

    (d) Care must be taken that nothing in the report implies the relationship between the accused and the child.

8 *Hospitals

(i) Journalists must identify themselves and obtain permission from a responsible executive before entering non-public areas of hospitals or similar institutions to pursue enquiries.

(ii) The restrictions on intruding into privacy are particularly relevant to enquiries about individuals in hospitals or similar institutions.

9 *Reporting of crime

(i) Relatives or friends of persons convicted or accused of crime should not generally be identified without their consent, unless they are genuinely relevant to the story.

(ii) Particular regard should be paid to the potentially vulnerable position of children who witness, or are victims of, crime. This should not restrict the right to report legal proceedings.

10 *Clandestine devices and subterfuge

(i) The press must not seek to obtain or publish material acquired by using hidden cameras or clandestine listening devices; or by intercepting private or mobile telephone calls, messages or emails; or by the unauthorised removal of documents or photographs.

(ii) Engaging in misrepresentation or subterfuge can generally be justified only in the public interest and then only when the material cannot be obtained by other means.

11   Victims of sexual assault

The press must not identify victims of sexual assault or publish material likely to contribute to such identification unless there is adequate justification and they are legally free to do so.

12   Discrimination

(i)   The Press must avoid prejudicial or pejorative reference to an individual's race, colour, religion, sex, sexual orientation or to any physical or mental illness or disability.

(ii)   Details of an individual's race, colour, religion, sexual orientation, physical or mental illness or disability must be avoided unless genuinely relevant to the story.

13   Financial journalism

(i)   Even where the law does not prohibit it, journalists must not use for their own profit financial information they receive in advance of its general publication, nor should they pass such information to others.

(ii)   They must not write about shares or securities in whose performance they know that they or their close families have a significant financial interest without disclosing the interest to the editor or financial editor.

(iii)   They must not buy or sell, either directly or through nominees or agents, shares or securities about which they have written recently or about which they intend to write in the near future.

14   Confidential sources

Journalists have a moral obligation to protect confidential sources of information.

15   Witness payments in criminal trials

(i)   No payment or offer of payment to a witness – or any person who may reasonably be expected to be called as a witness – should be made in any case once proceedings are active as defined by the Contempt of Court Act 1981.

This prohibition lasts until the suspect has been freed unconditionally by police without charge or bail or the proceedings are otherwise discontinued; or has entered a guilty plea to the court; or, in the event of a not guilty plea, the court has announced its verdict.

*(ii)   Where proceedings are not yet active but are likely and foreseeable, editors must not make or offer payment to any person who may reasonably be

expected to be called as a witness, unless the information concerned ought demonstrably to be published in the public interest and there is an overriding need to make or promise payment for this to be done; and all reasonable steps have been taken to ensure no financial dealings influence the evidence those witnesses give. In no circumstances should such payment be conditional on the outcome of a trial.

*(iii)   Any payment or offer of payment made to a person later cited to give evidence in proceedings must be disclosed to the prosecution and defence. The witness must be advised of this requirement.

16   *Payment to criminals

(i)   Payment or offers of payment for stories, pictures or information, which seek to exploit a particular crime or to glorify or glamorise crime in general, must not be made directly or via agents to convicted or confessed criminals or to their associates – who may include family, friends and colleagues.

(ii)   Editors invoking the public interest to justify payment or offers would need to demonstrate that there was good reason to believe the public interest would be served. If, despite payment, no public interest emerged, then the material should not be published.

The public interest

There may be exceptions to the clauses marked * where they can be demonstrated to be in the public interest.

1   The public interest includes, but is not confined to:

   (i)   Detecting or exposing crime or serious impropriety.
   (ii)   Protecting public health and safety.
   (iii)   Preventing the public from being misled by an action or statement of an individual or organisation.

2   There is a public interest in freedom of expression itself.

3   Whenever the public interest is invoked, the PCC will require editors to demonstrate fully how the public interest was served.

4   The PCC will consider the extent to which material is already in the public domain, or will become so.

5   In cases involving children under 16, editors must demonstrate an exceptional public interest to override the normally paramount interest of the child.

GLOSSARY

Actuality/Natsof (natural sound)   Interviews or sounds recorded on location such as chanting, children playing, fire engines etc.

Angle   The approach the journalist has taken to the story, i.e. which elements are stressed.

Archive   1. Files where background material, clippings and previously broadcast stories are kept. 2. Archive/library material is material pulled out of the archive.

Arrest   When a person is detained or deprived of their liberty for a legally determined length of time.

As live   A pre-recorded 2-way between a reporter and a presenter or reporter and guest/s or presenter and guest/s and set up as if it were live.

Aston/name super   Aston is the machine which generates the words which go onto the screen, but the term now means words which go on the screen such as 'Denise Wallace reporting' or 'library pictures'. Also used to give the name and job title of interviewees.

Backgrounder   Feature looking at the issues involved in or story behind the main news story.

Backpack/multimedia journalist   A journalist who can work across different media. They can write a print story, a television or radio script, operate a video camera, compile a photo gallery, edit an audio clip and make a web page. They can also put together multimedia stories that include video and audio clips, still photos as well as text.

Bail   The sum put up by the accused or another person to ensure the accused's appearance at their trial. It allows them to be free until the trial.

Barristers   Known, singly or collectively, as 'counsel', these are lawyers who represent their clients in court. They wear a wig and gown in the higher courts, the crown courts and in the county courts but not in the magistrates' courts. They are instructed by solicitors and should not be confused with them.

Best value   New Labour policy which replaced compulsory competitive tendering (CCT). Local councils must now demonstrate that they award the contracts for delivering local services to companies that provide 'economy, efficiency and effectiveness' rather than to those that are simply the cheapest.

Big close-up (BCU)   Shot used to show intense emotion; an angry or shouting or singing face. It is a very close shot. When filming one person, the whole screen is filled with the features of the face.

Blog   Personal journal-style website allowing updates to be made easily by the owner and allowing others to contribute comment.

Breach of confidence   The law which protects an individual from the misuse of information about him or herself.

Break   When a news story becomes known. Also the point of interruption in a story.

Breaking news/spot news   A story that is happening or unfolding right now.

Brief   Instructions given to a reporter or camera person about covering a story.

Broadsheet   Large-size newspaper such as the *Daily Telegraph* or the *Financial Times* as opposed to tabloid. Also implies quality, although a number of former broadsheets have now become 'compacts' (e.g. the *Independent)* which means they are smaller in size.

Browser   Software needed to interpret and display web pages which allows you to navigate the internet.

Bulletin board   Electronic forums that host messages and articles related to a common subject.

By-line   Gives the name or names of the journalist(s) who wrote the story.

Catchiine   Word or words identifying the story placed at the top of the article.

Check calls   Regular calls by journalists to the emergency services and hospitals to find out if any news is breaking.

Circuit judge   Judge appointed to sit at the crown court or county court within a circuit (one of the administrative regions of England and Wales).

Civil defence   The organising of civilians to deal with enemy attacks.

Claimant   Previously known as the plaintiff. The person who takes action in the civil court. *See also* defendant.

Cliché   A phrase or word which is so overused it means little – dumb blonde, innocent bystander.

Clips/cuts/insert   Audio which has been pre-recorded from an interview and one answer or part of an answer has been edited to form a news clip or 'sound bite'.

Closed question   Question that demands a yes or no answer.

Close-up (CU)   Shot showing the head only.

Committal for trial   Where a case is committed from the magistrates' court to be tried at crown court before a jury.

Compact   A broadsheet newspaper printed in a tabloid-size format. *See also* Broadsheet.

Contact   Someone who provides the journalist with information.

Contempt of court   The laws that try to strike a balance between the principle of open justice and the defendant's right to a fair trial. They seek to ensure UK media reports are fair and accurate and report only what is said in open court; this in turn prevents juries and witnesses having access to information which could influence them, other than that which is presented in open court.

Copy   The text of the story.

Copy-only story   News story with no audio or visuals.

Councillor   People who are nominated by at least ten electors in the area can stand for election to the local council. They must also be at least 21 years old and must live or work in the council areas. Once elected they represent the people of their ward.

Crown Prosecution Service (CPS) The official agency that decides on and carries out prosecutions in the criminal courts. The Director of Public Prosecutions heads the CPS.

Cue 1. Introduction to a broadcast report. 2. Instruction to a presenter or reporter to start and stop speaking.

Cutaway Shot used as a bridge in editing, often in interviews. If you want to edit two answers together, you may use a shot of the interviewees' hands as a cutaway.

Cuttings file Collection or portfolio of stories you, as a journalist, have written. They should usually have your by-line (e.g. by Jo-Anne Wallace) attached.

Cuttings library Files of material from newspapers cut out and stored in a library by subject. Large organisations file material from all newspapers; local or regional papers may just keep articles published in their own papers and these could be stored in a filing cabinet. Increasingly, large organisations are storing them electronically.

DA Notice Defence Advisory Notice. These notices offer guidance on national security to the media. There are five standing DA Notices.

Damages The monetary sum ordered by the court to be paid by the defendant to the claimant in civil actions. Damages usually represent compensation for loss, but they may also be used as a form of punishment.

Deadline The time by which the journalist must complete the story and submit it.

Death-knock Visiting the home of the recently bereaved in pursuit of a story.

Defamation Covers slander and libel. Slander is defamation by the spoken word, i.e in a transient form; whereas libel is defamation by the written or printed word, i.e. in a permanent form.

Defendant A person appearing in a criminal court charged with a criminal offence or a person appearing in a civil court having been issued with a claim form (in a civil hearing defendants must not be said to be charged or prosecuted).

District judge Legally qualified person, either solicitor or barrister of seven years' standing, who hears cases sitting alone in magistrates' and county court.

Doorstepping Involves a journalist going uninvited to someone's house or waiting outside a restaurant, cinema or court in the hope of getting a few comments for a story.

Down-the line interview An interview with a presenter or journalist asking the questions from another studio so the interviewer and interviewee cannot *see* each other. In these interviews, the interviewee looks straight at the camera and listens to the questions through an ear piece.

Drop intro or delayed intro Approach to a news story which delays the important facts for effect.

Edit 1. To select the pictures and cut them together into the final package for TV broadcast.
2. To select interviews clips and put together with recorded links for a radio report.
3. To select and formulate copy for written media.

Either-way offence An offence which could be tried either at crown court or at the magistrates' court. Offences that fall into this bracket include theft and indecent assault.

End item/And finally Story that runs at the end of the television or radio news programme. It can be a lighter item or a quirky story.

European Court of Justice (ECJ) Highest authority on points of EU law.

Exclusive   Story carried by just one newspaper, internet site, television or radio station.

Executive and non-executive councillors   Since the Local Government Act 2000, there is now a division between executive councillors, who are leaders or part of the cabinet and have the legal powers to make certain decisions without the approval of a committee or the council, and non-executive councillors, who are not able to make decisions by themselves.

Face-to-face interview   Interview where the journalist meets the interviewee in person.

Features   These are longer than straight news articles and concentrate on the human or entertaining aspects of the story. They usually include more background, description and colour.

Fifth estate   The fourth estate is the press and journalism, while the internet has been called by some the fifth estate. The estates refer to Estates of the Realm. The other three refer either to the priesthood, the aristocracy and the common people or the powers of the executive, legislature and judiciary.

File   To submit or send the story to the office, usually by computer or over the telephone, or to put the news on the wires.

Flash   Software used to develop interactive graphics.

Follow-up   Where a journalist does a follow-up or update on a story they covered at an earlier time. Or a follow-up can be a story covered by one news organisation that is used as the basis for a story by another news organisation.

Footage   Raw, unedited material as recorded on camera. *See also* Rushes.

Fourth estate   The fourth estate is the press and journalism. The estates refer to Estates of the Realm. The other three refer either to the priesthood, the aristocracy and the common people or the powers of the executive, legislature and judiciary. *See also* Fifth estate.

GIF/JPEG/TIF   Are files used by computers to digitally represent images.

Graphics/captions   Still photographs, maps, charts, courtroom sketches, written statements etc. These can make a short report for a bulletin or form part of a package.

GVs   General views. A wide view of the scene, often buildings, shots of crowds, etc.

Hack   Slang term for journalist, sometimes considered abusive, but used by journalists themselves.

Hard news   Stories of current events focusing on the factual detail of what has happened or what has been said. *See* Soft news.

Headlines/summary   Short roundup of the main news events, each story is summed up in one or two sentences.

Homophone   A word that is pronounced the same as another word, but has a different spelling and meaning (e.g. weight and wait).

HTML   Format or protocol that allows information to be distributed on the internet so that a page downloaded from the internet looks the same on all computers. Without it no page would be formatted, and so there would be no punctuation, only a succession of words without breaks.

Hyperlinks/Links   Highlighted piece of text or a graphic that takes the user to another part of the web – it could be a different place on the same web page, a different page on the same website or a page on a different website altogether. Links allow the user to follow different threads in the story.

In quality interview   Radio term meaning that a source was interviewed in person, not simply recorded on a telephone line.

Indictable offence   One that may be tried on indictment at crown court before a judge and jury.

Indictment   Document containing the charges that are read out to the accused/defendant when they stand trial at crown court.

Indymedia   Network of independent and alternative media activists offering non-commercial coverage of social and political issues.

Injunction   Court order instructing a person to do or refrain from doing something, such as to ban the publication of material identified by the court. It may be for a short period of time or permanent. Breaching an order is contempt of court.

Inquest   Hearing held to inquire into violent, unnatural or sudden deaths.

Internet   Infrastructure that allows computers to talk to each other.

Interview   Presenter interviews someone involved with a news story. This can be a politician, an expert, a celebrity or a member of the public. *See also* Vox pop.

Intro   First paragraph in a news story. In a hard news or direct or straight intro the main facts are summarised. In a delayed or drop intro they are held back for effect.

ISP   Internet Service Provider. It hooks into the system and provides users with a storage area. Most offer a web access and email service.

Leak   Unauthorised supply of information to a journalist.

Libel   Defamation by the written or printed word, i.e. in a permanent form. *See also* Slander; Defamation.

Link or bridge   Linking or transitional words and phrases, e.g. 'after', 'following' 'however,' 'although'. In broadcasting the 'bridges' or 'links' can be pieces to camera (PTCs).

Long shot (LS)   Often used for establishing shots or general views (GVs) to show the location or all the action. Can also use a very long shot (VLS). A long shot of a demonstration outside a council chamber would show the whole group and much of the building. If filming a person it takes in the whole person from head to feet.

Magistrates   Representatives of the local community who decide matters of guilt and what action to take against defendants. There will usually be three magistrates in the court.

Mayor   A ceremonial mayor or chairman of the council presides at full council meetings and has ceremonial and public duties to perform, such as opening galas or greeting foreign dignitaries. An elected mayor is the political leader for the community with a wide range of decision-making powers.

Medium close-up (MCU)   The standard TV interview shot, showing head and shoulders. We can see facial detail, but it is not too intrusive.

Medium long shot (MLS)   When filming one person it would show from their head to just below the knees.

Metaphor and simile   A metaphor describes one thing in terms of another (e.g. the president is a lame duck). A simile makes a comparison using the words as or like (e.g. he is as big as a barn).

Mid-shot or medium shot (MS)   Frames from the head to the hips.

Minutes The record of what goes on in meetings, written up shortly after the meeting. When their contents are agreed, they can be read at most council offices and public libraries as well as on council websites.

Moral panic Mass response to a group, a person or an attitude that becomes defined (often mistakenly) as a threat to society.

Multimedia journalist *See* Backpack journalist.

Multi-skilling Where journalists are skilled in more than one area. A print journalist who can take pictures and record audio clips is multi-skilled, as is a television journalist who can write scripts and film and edit pictures.

News agency News service provided by newsgathering agencies such as the Press Association, Reuters, Associated Press, Agence France Presse and the dozens of local news agencies. Many news organisations rely on these for international stories, coverage of court cases and tip-offs on good local stories.

News bulletin Usually on the hour, this is a synopsis of the main news stories. It will consist of about half a dozen stories, some containing audio (clips, voicers, etc.).

News clip Interview or speech extract from an interview with a source. Also known as a sound bite.

News 'peg' Sometimes you need a peg to get into a story. For example, a report on the number of teenage heroin addicts could be the news peg for a story on drug taking by young people. A celebrity divorce could be the news peg for a story on the number of failed marriages.

News programme This is longer than a news bulletin, usually 15 or 30 minutes or an hour and broadcast at breakfast, lunchtime, early evening or even late evening. It includes extended reports, packages and interviews.

News release Also called a handout. A story given to the media by a public relations company or organisation that wishes the story to be published.

Newsroom diary A diary in which is noted all the known events and stories that are taking place that day.

Noddies *See* Reverse shots.

Ofcom The Office of Communications (Ofcom) was created in 2003 and replaced five regulators covering radio, television and programme standards.

Off the record Information offered in confidence. The material should not be able to be traced back to the source and should only be used as background.

Oftel The Office of Telecommunications, the telecommunications watchdog, which was replaced by Ofcom.

On-diary/off-diary A reporter working on-diary is covering a story known to the newsroom, hence it's been written 'in the diary'. The reporter working off-diary is working on a story they have originated themselves.

Online When you access the internet you are online.

On the record When what is said can be reported and interviewees quoted.

OOV Out of Vision. This is a reporter/presenter voicing a script over pictures.

Open question One that needs a full answer giving details and explanation, as opposed to a closed question.

Opt-in and opt-out The process of switching between local and network transmissions or different networks, such as BBC1 and BBC World. Opting-in occurs when one station or network joins another and opting-out occurs when that station or network returns to its own programmes.

Out of court settlement Refers to civil cases and mean the parties agree on how they should resolve the case and therefore it never comes to trial.

Package Report containing interview clips, music, graphics and reporter script.

Page 2 Details of the first and last words of a television report as well as aston times and overall duration. Page 1 has the cue on it.

Pan The camera moves from left to right or right to left in the horizontal plane. Must start and end on strong frames. A pan can follow a person, car or bird.

Paparazzi Photographers who follow the rich and famous to get photographs of them.

Participles Part of a verb. Present participle – coming, going etc., the past participle – fallen, parted etc. A hanging or dangling participle is where the participle has no subject, e.g. 'Having been chopped down 10 years ago, I missed seeing the tree I used to climb.'

PDA Personal digital assistant.

Piece to camera (PTC) or stand-upper Script delivered by a reporter straight to the camera often in front of the event or at the scene.

Plaintiff Now known as the claimant. The person who takes action in the civil court.

Portal Entry point onto the web providing a window onto many services including email, news and search facilities. Yahoo is a well-known portal.

PPC Press Complaints Commission, which is an independent self-regulatory organisation dealing with complaints from members of the public about the editorial content of newspapers and magazines.

Press conference or news conference An organised gathering to which the media are invited.

Press release Also called a news release or handout. A story given to the media by a public relations company or organisation that wishes the story to be published.

Q&A See 2-way.

Real Player/Windows Media Player For playing audio and video files. Most computers have them already installed when they are sold. To create the files you need Real Producer.

Reverse shots/noddies Shows interviewer listening to the interviewee, often nodding. Can help the editor piece together the interview.

Round table discussion/DISCO This includes several participants with contrasting views on a subject and is chaired by a journalist.

Running order Order of transmission of items in a programme.

Running story Event that develops and is covered over a period of time.

Rushes Pictures shot by the journalist or camera operator which have not been edited.

Search engine Search engines scan web pages looking for documents that match the keyword or words you have requested. One of the most popular is Google.

Set-up shot Introduces the players and can show the geography of the location. Also known as the establishing shot.

Slander   Defamation by the spoken word, i.e. in a transient form. *See also* Libel; Defamation.

SMS   Short Messaging Service to mobile phones. Generally messages should be between 140 and 160 characters in length.

Snap on the wires   Short news release of something that has just happened.

Snapper   Photographer.

Soft news   Lighter, more colourful than hard news, and is often more about entertaining the audience than informing them.

Solicitors   Lawyers who deal directly with clients. They advise them and prepare the client's case. They can represent the client in court, but in the past have usually only done so in the magistrates' courts and the county courts. More recently some solicitors, who have gained a higher courts qualification, have been allowed to appear in the higher courts, where they compete with barristers in representing clients. Otherwise they instruct a barrister to conduct the case.

Sound bite   Interview or speech extract from an interview with a source. Also known as a news clip.

Source   Individual, publication, document or event that supplies the information for a story.

Spike   Literally a metal spike on which journalists traditionally used to put press releases, documents, copy etc, that they had decided were not newsworthy.

Splash   Also called on some papers the 'front page lead'. This is a newspaper's main story of the day and will be given the prime spot on the front page. In broadcasting the main story is often referred to as the 'top' story because it is placed top of the bulletin.

Story   This does not refer to a piece of fiction, but is what journalists often call a news item.

Summary trials   Cases tried by magistrates.

Tabloid   Smaller size newspaper used to describe the 'popular' or 'down-market' press (e.g. the *Sun). See also* Broadsheet; Compact.

Talking head   Any interviewee. It can be used pejoratively if a story has too many talking heads in it.

Tautology   Saying the same thing more than once: a fatal accident in which people were killed.

Tilt   Camera movement up or down in the vertical plane. This can be from the face of a child to the jigsaw they are completing or from the front step of a house to the top window where someone is leaning out.

Tip-off   Information given to a journalist by a member of the public or a contact about a story.

Tort   Civil wrong such as negligence, nuisance or defamation.

Tracking shot   This is where the camera films while moving. Typical tracking shots are filming from a moving car, walking through a house, or down an alleyway, moving through the woods.

Two-shot   Shows back of interviewer's head and interviewee's face listening.

2-way/Q&A (Questions and Answer)   A presenter interviews a reporter on air about a story he or she is covering.

TX   Transmission.

Usher   Manages cases between courts, checks that everyone involved is present and offers assistance to those attending court. In the magistrates' courts, ushers are the only people who wear black gowns.

Video-journalist (VJ)   Reporter who shoots and edits their own pieces.

Voice piece, voice report, voicer   Details and explanation of a story by a reporter. Tells more than a copy story. Permits a change of voice from a newsreader.

Voice track   The reporter's voice recording of the script.

Vox pop   Latin '*vox populi*' which means 'voice of the people'. Refers to short (usually one or two question) interviews with people selected at random to get a flavour of public opinion on a specific subject.

'War on Terror'   Phrase used to describe the campaign by the United States and its allies to stop terrorism around the world, following the attack on the World Trade Center in New York in September 2001. Most often used in connection with trying to destroy the group al-Qaeda and its leader Osama Bin Laden, believed to be behind the attacks.

Web   Interface that allows people to exchange information including text, pictures and sound.

Wild track   Real sound recorded on location which is related to the picture.

Wire services or the wires   Press agencies to which news organisations subscribe and are sent copy. They include the Press Association, Reuters, Associated Press, Agence France-Presse, as well as dozens of local agencies.

Wrap   Voice report that contains clips.

Zoom   Varies the focus length of a shot, taking it in or pulling it out. Inexperienced camera operators tend to use too many zooms. Only zoom when necessary otherwise your audience gets dizzy.

INDEX